CATALOGUE OF SOURCES FOR A LINGUISTIC ATLAS OF EARLY MEDIEVAL ENGLISH

This *Catalogue* is a state-of-knowledge list of the English written between ca. 1150 and 1300, whether later versions of Old English texts or original early Middle English. With over 500 entries to manuscripts containing writing in English, it describes in detail literary material, both prose and verse, documentary texts, and glosses. The *Catalogue* conveniently draws together an extensive body of information only available up to now in widely scattered sources. As well as being listed by their repositories the manuscripts are also separately indexed by text. Information is provided on dates, hands, manuscript associations and language. Also given are copious references to editions and secondary literature.

The *Catalogue* is the first stage in the creation of *A Linguistic Atlas of Early Medieval English* which seeks to provide a wide range of new knowledge about the spatial distribution of forms in texts of the period. But the relevance of the *Catalogue* goes far beyond the concerns of the philologist and dialectologist. It is an invaluable reference book to any student of the English language and to medievalists of many different disciplines — demographers, social historians, palaeographers, codicologists and historical geographers.

Margaret Laing is a Research Fellow in the Institute for Historical Dialectology, School of Scottish Studies, University of Edinburgh. As well as assisting with the production of *A Linguistic Atlas of Late Mediaeval English* (Aberdeen, 1986), she has also edited *Middle English Dialectology: essays on some principles and problems* by Angus McIntosh, M.L. Samuels and Margaret Laing (Aberdeen, 1989).

CATALOGUE OF SOURCES FOR A LINGUISTIC ATLAS OF EARLY MEDIEVAL ENGLISH

MARGARET LAING

D. S. BREWER

© Margaret Laing 1993

All Rights Reserved. Except as permitted under current legislation
no part of this work may be photocopied, stored in a retrieval system,
published, performed in public, adapted, broadcast,
transmitted, recorded or reproduced in any form or by any means,
without the prior permission of the copyright owner

First published 1993 by D. S. Brewer, Cambridge

D. S. Brewer is an imprint of Boydell & Brewer Ltd
PO Box 9, Woodbridge, Suffolk IP12 3DF, UK
and of Boydell & Brewer Inc.
PO Box 41026, Rochester, NY 14604, USA

ISBN 0 85991 384 8

British Library Cataloguing-in-Publication Data

A catalogue record for this book is available
from the British Library

Library of Congress Cataloging-in-Publication Data applied for

The paper used in this publication meets the minimum requirements
of American National Standard for Information Sciences –
Permanence of Paper for Printed Library Materials, ANSI Z39.48-1984

Printed in Great Britain by
St Edmundsbury Press Ltd, Bury St Edmunds, Suffolk

CONTENTS

Preface by Angus McIntosh	vii
Acknowledgements	ix
Introduction	1
Bibliographical Abbreviations	11
Abbreviations	17
Catalogue of Sources	19
Index of Middle English Texts	
A: Titles	158
B: Incipits	165
Index of Old English Texts	180
Index of Texts in Latin	182
Index of Texts in French	186

This volume is dedicated to the memory of my father
George Bradford Caird (1917–1984)
and to my mother
Mollie Caird
in love and gratitude

PREFACE

A comprehensive inventory of the source material available for the study of Early Middle English has long been needed by all those seeking to add to what is known about the language of that period. The present work modestly claims only to be the necessary precursor of just one kind of enquiry bearing on the language of that time, namely the detailed investigation of its dialectal manifestations. In fact it supplies information about a large amount of source material vital to a whole range of further studies relating to the English language in the early medieval period and in turn to yet others that are far beyond being 'merely' linguistic.

The core period on which the *Catalogue* concentrates falls between 1150 and 1300. The main purpose is to list and to provide information about the various kinds of consecutive English, whether original or copied, surviving from within or near this period. By so doing, it facilitates the serious pursuit of every kind of analytical work on the characteristics of English, and on the changes it undergoes, at a revolutionary stage in its history. During that time a great deal happened that affected the language in every area where it was spoken and written. In consequence, *all* forms of English current in 1300 are very different from *any* form of English current in the eleventh century. And though those current in 1300 vary considerably between one area and another, they nevertheless all manifest certain basic similarities such that all are structurally more similar to each other than any one of them to its 'ancestral' late Old English form. In other words, they had all deviated from their ancestral forms in the same general direction. The result is that by the beginning of the fourteenth century these new varieties are and — despite their differences — are all felt to be, members of a single larger entity called English. Throughout this period, strong centripetal forces must have been at work to prevent the language in different places, not by any means from changing or 'evolving' at all, but from diverging beyond a certain relatively small degree. The details of what went on are of great interest.

Every bit of vernacular material surviving from the period with which this *Catalogue* deals is therefore relevant, far beyond dialectology, to all serious students of medieval English. Indeed, the relevance extends beyond them to all those for whom information about the language, and derivable from the language, is highly important. Dialectologists themselves have not always shown sufficient awareness of the relevance of their own subject to such others as these, and this has impeded progress both within their own discipline and beyond it.

This is not the place to elaborate this last point but one example might be given. Among the most grossly neglected subjects, bearing both on medieval English itself and its entire cultural background, is the serious and systematic study of the history of orthography in the three centuries or so after the Norman Conquest. It so happens that material available for this is quite scarce and regionally very patchy right up till the later years of the fourteenth century. What there is is scattered in many different repositories and such transcriptions as exist are in many cases inadequate for linguistic analysis. The result is that the history of English *sounds* over that period is based on information far more flimsy than is in principle obtainable. As for the history of English *letters*, and the highly complex evolution of their forms and functions in this same period, even some elementary aspects of it await adequate and sytematic treatment.

Perhaps more important than this is that no co-ordinated effort has ever been made to analyse individually and then to compare, as written *systems*, the output of different scribes during this time. What is now needed is an investigation of the attempts made by scribes, first to 'convert' their own (or somebody else's) spoken

English to an acceptable written equivalent and secondly to convert something already written in one dialect of English into its equivalent in another. It is part of the merit of this *Catalogue* that it provides references not only to such material but also to conversions of that other type where scribes have felt the need to modernise some earlier text, often an Old English one, and have at least in some cases been fully equal to the task. Besides, where they have not been entirely successful in any of these activities, there is something to be learnt from their efforts.

I began by saying that this volume offers more than it modestly claims and that it provides information (much of it not at all easily accessible elsewhere) about source material relevant to various aspects of early medieval English other than its dialectology. The main late nineteenth-century motivation for studies of earlier periods of the English language fostered from the start an often excessive preoccupation with what we might call genetic and evolutionary relationships and with just those phenomena which best illustrate these. So strong is this even now that it might lead some to assume that a linguistic atlas of Early Middle English will necessarily manifest such a preoccupation. It is of course true that the Atlas will seek to add substantially to information about the relationship between varieties of Old English and varieties of earlier and later Middle English. Thus it will doubtless placate the insatiable comparativist craving to have the language of the *Ormulum* or the *Ancrene Wisse* linked ever more securely, via Primitive Germanic, to Proto-Indo-European. But the source material cited in this book, while it may have relevance to this kind of objective, has probably a greater value in facilitating access to material vital to studies of other, very different kinds. Some of these, as I have tried to indicate, bear directly on questions which are not primarily linguistic at all.

So this volume is not only for dialectologists. It is not only for students of the language. I should count among its merits that its *enabling* properties are more extensive than that and I believe that medievalists of many persuasions will find it useful. It is no disservice to it to say that those who draw most from it will be the persons best fitted to ensure that successive editions of it reflect the further discoveries and results that its existence will, I hope, make possible.

Angus McIntosh
Edinburgh
November 1992

ACKNOWLEDGEMENTS

This *Catalogue* owes its origin to preliminary work on Early Middle English done by Professors Angus McIntosh and Michael Samuels in relation to the later Middle English dialect survey. These investigations resulted in an incidental collection of reference slips to manuscripts containing dialectal English but of too early a date to appear in *A Linguistic Atlas of Late Mediaeval English*. This collection was enlarged by Dr Patrick Stiles, who was a member of the then Gayre Institute, 1985–87. Dr Stiles was responsible for putting the preliminary manuscript list on to computer. It was of enormous help to me to inherit the results of this early search work and I am very grateful for the freedom with which it was made available to me. During the time that he was working on the manuscript list, Dr Stiles was given help and supplied with information by Dr Malcolm Parkes and Dr Alex Rumble; I here also acknowledge with gratitude their vicarious assistance.

It will be apparent from the references in the *Catalogue* that I have drawn heavily on the published works of others. I have tried in all cases to acknowledge published sources and I apologise for any omissions of accreditation. Dr David Pelteret, Dr Kathryn Lowe, Mr Richard Hamer and Dr Oliver Pickering have been very generous in allowing me access to their work before publication. I have also received valuable information, comments on early drafts and advice from Dr Ian Doyle, Dr Richard Beadle and Professor Michael Benskin. I remain, however, entirely responsible for any errors in the *Catalogue* as it stands.

Much of the detail on texts, hands and language provided in the *Catalogue* has depended on the acquisition of photographic reproductions of the relevant portions of the manuscripts. The beginning of a collection for the Institute of microfilms and photographic enlargements was made possible by a grant from the Moray Fund of the University of Edinburgh.

The librarians and archivists from whom I have sought assistance and information have shown great courtesy and patience. I wish to thank the following: Professor R.I. Page, The Parker Library, Corpus Christi College, Cambridge; Frank Stubbings, Hon. Keeper of Rare Books, Emmanuel College, Cambridge: Mrs. Alison Sproston, Assistant Librarian, Gonville and Caius College, Cambridge; Amanda Saville, Librarian, St John's College, Cambridge; the Librarian of King's College, the staff of Trinity College Library and the photographic department of the University Library, Cambridge; the staff of the Cumbria Record Office, Carlisle; Jill Ivy, Dean and Chapter Library, the College, Durham; from the Edinburgh University Library: Mr J.V. Howard, Mrs J. Currie and the staff of Special Collections, Mr N. Hanna of the photographic department, Miss J. Evans and the staff of inter-library loans; the staff of the National Library of Scotland; A.M. Wherry and the staff of the Record Services, Hereford and Worcester County Council; the photographic department of the British Library, London; the Archivist, Corporation of London Records Office; E.G.W. Bill, Librarian, Lambeth Palace Library, London; Guy Holborn, Librarian, Lincoln's Inn Library, London; the photographic and search departments of the Public Record Office, London; Dr. Penelope Bulloch, Librarian, Balliol College, Oxford; Kathleen Firkin and the photographic department of the Bodleian Library, Oxford; Christine Butler, Assistant Archivist, Corpus Christi College, Oxford; John Burgass, Librarian, Merton College, Oxford; the Librarians of Jesus College and New College, Oxford; the staff of Oxford City Archives; Lord Vestey, Stowell Park, Gloucestershire; Patricia Gill, County Archivist, West Sussex Record Office; Ronald Stratton, Assistant Librarian, Worcester Cathedral Library.

I am grateful for the help and enthusiasm of my collaborator on the Early Middle English survey, Dr Jeremy Smith. I am greatly indebted to my colleague Dr Keith Williamson for his constant support and advice and for the numerous occasions when he has taken time from his other commitments to come to my aid at the computer. I thank my husband Dr Ian Laing and my children Alexander and Catriona for keeping me laughing. I especially thank Professor Angus McIntosh who has been unstinting both with moral support and practical assistance; above all I am grateful for the inspiration derived from his unwavering conviction of the importance of the work in which we are engaged.

Institute for Historical Dialectology
School of Scottish Studies
University of Edinburgh
November 1992

INTRODUCTION

The compilation of this *Catalogue of Sources* was a necessary first step towards the creation of *A Linguistic Atlas of Early Medieval English* (*LAEME*).[1] It aims to list all the potential sources for *LAEME*; that is any surviving text written down in English between *ca*. 1150 and 1300. It does not attempt full codicological descriptions of the manuscripts containing the listed texts, which for the most part are available elsewhere; but it does provide a great deal of information about the English writings themselves. The *Catalogue* should therefore be a useful reference book for any study of English at this period, whether its primary concerns be linguistic, textual, literary or historical. It is for this reason that I have chosen to publish the *Catalogue* in advance of the production of *LAEME* itself. The task of analysing the listed texts is likely to be long and slow and it will certainly be some years before *LAEME* can be completed.[2] It would be a pity if other scholars were prevented meantime from making use of such information as is already available. It follows from this that the *Catalogue* is a beginning only; the information in it, especially where it describes hands and language, is as yet partial and provisional. All texts written in English within the period that have come to my attention have been listed as potential sources for dialectal study. It is evident from the outset that some of these texts will be much more useful witnesses for early medieval English than others. As the work of linguistic analysis progresses it will be possible to say more about the language of each text. Even if the language of a text turns out not to be precisely localisable, it is likely that something can be said about its dialectal character and if not, then this itself be may not be without interest.

1 *Scope of the* Catalogue

The period covered by this *Catalogue* is that commonly known as Early Middle English. The choice of fixed dates to delimit a period of language is problematic since linguistic evolution is a continuous process. Often manuscripts can be dated only from palaeographic evidence and this method is always approximate. Dates judged from

---

[1] This investigation is part of the work of the Institute for Historical Dialectology, School of Scottish Studies, University of Edinburgh. I am doing this project in collaboration with my colleagues in the (Edinburgh-Glasgow) Joint Programme in Historical Dialectology (JPHD), Dr Jeremy Smith and Dr Kathryn Lowe of the English Language Department, University of Glasgow, and in consultation with Professor Angus McIntosh, Professor Emeritus, University of Edinburgh. We hope in due course to produce a linguistic atlas for the early Middle English period, complementary to *A Linguistic Atlas of Late Mediaeval English* (*LALME*).
[2] The method of analysis we are adopting is very different from that used for the making of *LALME*. Instead of completing questionnaires consisting of a set of predetermined items, we are developing a new method based on modern techniques of information storage and retrieval. Entire texts are transcribed on to computer disk where they can be analysed linguistically using bespoke programs. Each word or morpheme is tagged lexico-grammatically and added to a corpus of tagged texts. A set of programs then allows information on particular 'items' (defined by one or more tags) to be abstracted from the corpus to determine the spatial or temporal distribution of the forms associated with the item. The programs are being developed by Dr Keith Williamson of the JPHD. The approach is based on similar techniques used successfully by Anthonij Dees and his team of the Free University of Amsterdam for the making of linguistic atlases of Old French and Middle Dutch. See A. Dees, P.Th. van Reenen and J.A. De Vries, *Atlas des formes et des constructions des chartes françaises du 13e siècle*. Beihefte zur Zeitschrift für Romanische Philologie 178 (Tübingen, 1980) and A. Dees, M. Dekker, O. Huber and K. van Reenen-Stein, *Atlas des formes linguistiques des textes littéraires de l'ancien français*. Beihefte zur Zeitschrift für Romanische Philologie 212 (Tübingen, 1987).

script and decoration are usually given as lying somewhere within a quarter-century period. It has not therefore proved practicable to impose strict time limits. Texts written from before 1150 already begin to display some of the grammatical and lexical features associated rather with Middle English than with Old English.[3] The study of linguistic variation in these 'transitional' texts must, however, be undertaken separately in relation to the changes already evident in late Old English. A time-span of 150 years is in any case long enough that diachronic changes in the language are likely to affect any pattern produced by synchronic regional variation. However, it seemed desirable to choose a terminal date for the survey sufficiently late to allow for overlap with the material presented in *LALME* and therefore some material from the first quarter of the fourteenth century is also included.

The period covered by *LALME* is roughly 1350–1450 in the Midlands and the North and 1325–1425 in the South. For the southern part of the country *LALME* also includes several texts from the late thirteenth and from the early fourteenth century, so overlap between the two surveys is here assured. Unfortunately very little Middle English survives from the North and North Midlands from this earlier period. Texts in early Middle Hiberno-English are also very scarce. Accordingly, I have included early fourteenth century texts if their language suggests northerly or Anglo-Irish origins. Some texts in manuscripts of a rather later date are also listed if they are linked with versions in other manuscripts known to have been written before 1300. Besides, the language in the later manuscripts themselves is sometimes conservative in character.[4] I have however included no literary texts from later than *ca.* 1340. The inclusion of late copies of documents is explained in **2.2.1** below. Apart from these exceptions, the criterion for inclusion has been the date at which the scribal text was actually written down rather than the date of composition, which in some cases was evidently much earlier than the date of the manuscript version listed. The dates given in the *Catalogue* always apply to the date of the manuscript or the portion of the manuscript containing text in Early Middle English. These datings will not necessarily match the date(s) of other parts of such a manuscript.

2 Types of text

2.1 The linguistic situation in England after 1066

Before the Norman Conquest in 1066 English was the language of both government and literature. Unlike other European nations (including Scotland) for whom Latin was the administrative language, the Anglo-Saxons used the vernacular for drawing up legal documents. After the Conquest, following Continental practice, Latin began to replace English as the standard language of government and of literature. The French-speaking invaders also introduced their own vernacular literature and during the first half of the thirteenth century French had become a literary language of high social status, the second language of culture alongside Latin. By the mid-thirteenth century French was also being used as the official language of the law courts. Much has been written about English, French (in both their written and spoken forms) and Latin, and their changing

---

[3] For studies of some of these changes see Samuel Moore, 'Loss of final *n* in inflectional syllables of Middle English', *Language* 3 (1927), 232–59; 'Earliest morphological changes in Middle English', *Language* 4 (1928) 238–66; and Kemp Malone, 'When did Middle English begin?', *Curme Volume of Linguistic Studies*, ed. J.T. Hatfield, Language Monographs published by the Linguistic Society of America 7 (Philadelphia, 1930), pp. 110-117.

[4] One important example is British Library, Harley 2253. This manuscript was probably written *ca.* 1340; see N.R. Ker's introduction to the facsimile edition in EETS OS 255 (1965 for 1964), pp. xxi–xxii. It shares material with Bodley, Digby 86 and with other manuscripts which are known to have been written before 1300. Harley also contains, however, some of the same texts as are to be found in other manuscripts from the first half of the fourteenth century: Edinburgh, Advocates 19.2.1 (Auchinleck), Cambridge University Library, Additional 4407 art. 19 and Gg.I.1.

relative status in the centuries following the Conquest.[5] For the purposes of the Early Middle English dialect survey, the most important effect of the disruption in the use of written English after 1066 is that there survives from our period much less in English than we would like. Much of what does remain is to be found in manuscripts containing mainly Latin or, less often, French texts and in these cases the English text is often very short or fragmentary.

However, writing in English did not cease completely after the Conquest. Old English texts continued to be copied and studied in religious centres for well over a hundred years. But there was apparently very little new composition in English in the century after the Conquest apart from a few late additions to the Anglo-Saxon Chronicle. It was only from the late twelfth century that new writings in English began to appear in any quantity.

From the period 1150–1300, therefore, there survive two very different sorts of written English: (a) versions of Old English texts and (b) new compositions in Early Middle English. The second type is clearly distinct from the first, indicating that in its spoken form English had continued to change throughout this time. Where a text listed in the *Catalogue* is derived from an Old English original I have placed an asterisk before the date of the manuscript copy.

As well as distinguishing texts in this way, according to whether they are copies of Old English texts or original Early Middle English compositions, it is convenient to divide them into three different types: documents, literary texts and glosses. The *Catalogue* entries for these three types are prefixed by [δ], [λ] and [γ] respectively; see **3.1** item 3 below.

2.2 *Documents*

The term 'document' here includes legal and administrative writings such as charters (a designation itself often used to cover a wide variety of texts),[6] writs, grants, wills, papal letters, diplomas, manumissions and laws. For *LALME* it was the documentary texts, of known date and local origins, that provided the dialectal matrix into which the linguistic profiles of scribes of unknown origins were 'fitted'. The situation for *LAEME* is very different. Although documents continued occasionally to be drawn up in English until as late as the reign of Henry II, very few original English documents

---

[5] See R. Berndt, 'The linguistic situation in England from the Norman Conquest to the loss of Normandy (1066–1204)', *Philologia Pragensia* 8 (1965), 145–63 (reprinted in *Approaches to English Historical Linguistics*, ed. R. Lass (New York, 1969), pp. 369–91); N.P. Brooks, ed., *Latin and the Vernacular Languages of Early Medieval Britain* (Leicester, 1982); M.T. Clanchy, *From Memory to Written Record: England 1066–1307* (London, 1979); idem, *England and its Rulers 1066–1272* (London, 1985); Cecily Clark, 'The myth of the Anglo-Norman scribe', in M. Rissanen *et al.* eds. *History of Englishes: New Methods and Interpretations in Historical Linguistics*. Topics in English Linguistics 10 (Mouton de Gruyter: Berlin and New York, 1992), pp. 117–29; R.H.C. Davis, *The Normans and their Myth* (London, 1976); Tony Hunt, *Teaching and Learning Latin in Thirteenth-Century England*, 3 vols. (Cambridge, 1991); Hans Käsmann, *Studien zum kirchlichen Wortschatz des Mittelenglischen 1100–1350* (Tübingen, 1961); M. Richter, *Sprache und Gesellschaft im Mittelalter. Untersuchungen zur mündlichen Kommunikation in England von der Mitte des elften bis zum Beginn des vierzehnten Jahrhunderts*, Monographien zur Geschichte des Mittelalters 18 (Stuttgart, 1979); W. Rothwell, 'The teaching of French in medieval England', *Modern Language Review* 63 (1968), 37–46; idem, 'The role of French in thirteenth-century England', *Bulletin of the John Rylands Library* 58 (1975–76), 445–66; idem, 'Language and government in medieval England', *Zeitschrift für französische Sprache und Literatur* 93 (1983), 258–70; P. van Dyke Shelley, *English and French in England 1066–1100* (Philadelphia, 1921); I. Short, 'On bilingualism in Anglo-Norman England', *Romance Philology* 33 (1980), 467–79; R.M. Wilson, 'English and French in England 1100–1300', *History* 23 (1943), 37–60; G.E. Woodbine, 'The language of English law', *Speculum* 18 (1943), 395–436.

[6] A useful introduction to the various types of Anglo-Saxon documents is to be found in F.E. Harmer, *Anglo-Saxon Writs*, 2nd edn. (Stamford, 1989), pp. 1–118.

were produced in the thirteenth and early fourteenth centuries.[7] A large majority of those written in English between 1150 and 1300 are cartulary copies of Old English charters. A cartulary is a collection of charters, writs and grants relating to the property rights and privileges of its possessor — very often a religious house. The original documents themselves are sometimes incorporated, but more usually they are copied into the volume in batches, presumably for convenience and ease of reference. The cartulary copy was not a substitute for the original charter, which alone would constitute proof of the grant. In spite of this, it is often only the cartulary copy that now survives.

2.2.1 *Copied Old English documents*

The use of post-Conquest copies of Old English documents as source material for a study of Early Middle English dialects naturally presents a variety of more or less intractable difficulties.[8] It is already apparent that these texts cannot be relied upon to provide a network of localised material comparable to the way that documents were available to do so— at least in the Midlands and the North Midlands — for *LALME*.

Preliminary investigation suggests that twelfth- and thirteenth-century copyists of Old English documents do not usually modify the text to a form of language similar to that which they themselves would write spontaneously. Instead they attempt, with varying degrees of success, straight transcription of the original Old English. Nevertheless, it is important that the language of all these twelfth- and thirteenth-century copies be examined in order to ascertain whether they afford, if only here and there and inadvertently, some glimpses of the (presumably) Early Middle English language of the copyists themselves. Moreover there is late thirteenth-century evidence, that at least one scribe from Bury St Edmunds did modify the language of his Old English exemplar in the direction of his own East Anglian usage.[9] It is to be hoped that more examples of linguistic modification of this kind will emerge and that their contributions will help with the localisation of Early Middle English literary texts. For this reason, I have also listed in the *Catalogue* some fourteenth- and fifteenth-century, and some even later, copies of earlier documents. It may be that these will be found to provide hints about only the later Middle English of their own period or, instead, that they are more or less direct reproductions of the original Old English documents. However, they have been included in the hope that some may themselves be linguistically interesting copies of some intervening version, itself probably no longer extant, from the twelfth or thirteenth century.[10]

---

[7] One notable example of such a document is the well-known proclamation of 1258 by Henry III. See the *Catalogue* entries for London, Public Record Office, C 66, Patent Rolls, 43 Henry III, m. 15.40 and Oxford City Archives, Town Hall, St Aldates, H 29.

[8] See Margaret Laing, 'Anchor texts and literary manuscripts in early Middle English', in F. Riddy, ed., *Regionalism in Late Medieval Manuscripts and Texts* (Cambridge, 1991), pp. 27–52 and Kathryn A. Lowe, '"As fre as thowt"?: Some medieval copies and translations of Old English wills', *English Manuscript Studies 1100–1700* 4 (1993), forthcoming.

[9] See the *Catalogue* entry for Cambridge University Library Ff.II.33 from Bury St Edmunds. On the Bury material see Angus McIntosh, 'The language of the extant versions of *Havelok the Dane*', *Medium Ævum* 45 (1976), 36–49 and Kathryn A. Lowe, 'Two thirteenth-century cartularies from Bury St Edmunds: a study in textual transmission', *Neuphilologische Mitteilungen* 94 (1993), 1–9.

[10] P.R. Kitson considers that, of the surviving OE charter material, about one eighth "is extant in contemporary manuscripts (mainly of the tenth century)", that half is "extant in cartularies, generally faithful, [i.e. accurately copied OE] of the late OE and transitional periods (to about 1250)" and that three eighths survives in "generally corrupting later cartularies". See P.R. Kitson, 'On the chronological and geographical spread of Old English combinative *u*-mutation', *Studia Neophilologica* 64 (1992), 3-23 (3). Kitson's work on the OE charter boundaries indicates that their linguistic forms are probably mostly of local origin and that they show some distinct regional variation. See P.R. Kitson, 'On Old English nouns of more than one gender', *English Studies* 71 (1990), 185–221 and op. cit. above where he refers also to forthcoming works on the subject.

In order to identify documentary texts copied between 1150 and 1300 I have drawn heavily on P.H. Sawyer's *Anglo-Saxon Charters*. This work lists all versions, early or late, of the pre-Conquest charters known to him and has the rare merit of stating whether or not a charter or its bounds are couched in English or in Latin. I have listed in the *Catalogue* all the documents surviving in copies of the relevant date which are said by Sawyer to be in English or to contain English. For many of those listed only the estate boundaries, usually appearing between the main part of the charter and the witness list, are in English.[11] The relevant documents are referred to by their numbers in Sawyer. Where printed versions exist from the manuscript listed in the *Catalogue* I have cited alongside the Sawyer number the relevant reference numbers from Birch's *Cartularium Saxonicum*, Kemble's *Codex Diplomaticus Ævi Saxonici*, Harmer's *Anglo-Saxon Writs*, Robertson's *Anglo-Saxon Charters*, Whitelock's *Anglo-Saxon Wills* and occasionally from elsewhere. For the most part, however, further references are to be sought in Sawyer.

2.2.2 *Post-Conquest documents*

For documents originating after 1066 I have depended on David A.E. Pelteret's *Catalogue of English Post-Conquest Vernacular Documents* which lists 148 documents in English produced between the years 1066 and 1189, the end of the reign of Henry II. Pelteret indicates that his cut-off date is not meant to imply that vernacular documents ceased to be produced thereafter, but in fact it appears that very few documents in English survive from the thirteenth century and perhaps not many were ever produced.

2.3 *Literary texts*

A number of categories of text may be termed 'literary' as opposed to documentary. They include (a) major works in prose such as homilies, rules (e.g. *Ancrene Riwle*), biblical translations and paraphrases, chronicles and grammars; (b) lengthy works in verse such as Laʒamon's *Brut*, the *South English Legendary, Havelok* and *The Owl and the Nightingale*; (c) large verse anthologies such as Cambridge, Trinity College 323 (B.14.39) and Oxford, Jesus College 29; (d) one or more short lyrics in manuscripts containing mainly works in Latin; (e) fragments of verse and prose such as proverbs, quotations, prayers and charms.

2.3.1 *Copied Old English literary texts*

Ker's *Catalogue of Manuscripts containing Anglo-Saxon* lists twenty-seven manuscripts written after *ca.* 1100.[12] I have included in this *Catalogue* all texts or parts of texts listed by Ker which are dated by him 's.xii med.' or later. I have not normally included texts labelled by Ker 's.xii' unless I have some reason for supposing that they belong to the second half of the century.

2.3.2 *Early Middle English literary texts*

Much work has already been done on the indexing of manuscripts containing literary works both from the early and late Middle English periods. The output of writings bearing on these early English texts is also large. This has been of great value in the task of compiling a corpus of texts for the Early Middle English survey. But the mass of relevant material that these sources provide is at present only obtainable by much

---

[11] I have not listed documents where only isolated words of English appear embedded in a text otherwise in Latin. Nor do I take note of place-names given in their English form. It is likely, however, that a systematic search for such citations throughout the corpus of Latin documents would yield a considerable quantity of phonological evidence.

[12] See N.R. Ker, *Catalogue of Manuscripts containing Anglo-Saxon* (Oxford, 1957), pp. xviii–xix.

searching in many places. I have therefore tried in this *Catalogue* to match manuscripts, texts and references in order to assist those searching the various indexes and other sources of information.[13] I have given references wherever possible to Wells's *A Manual of the Writings in Middle English* and its updated version edited by Severs and Hartung, to the *Index of Middle English Verse* and its supplement, to the *Index of Middle English Printed Prose* and to the available volumes of the *Index of Middle English Prose*. R.M. Wilson and more recently Siegfried Wenzel[14] have unearthed large numbers of short and fragmentary early English texts embedded in Latin works and for these I have drawn heavily on their work. Other bibliographical references include editions and, for the verse especially, anthologies such as Carleton Brown's *English Lyrics of the Thirteenth Century*. No attempt has been made to make the bibliographical references definitive; they are contributions only and the aim throughout has been to render information more accessible and to provide details about where further references may be found.

2.4 *Glosses*

It seemed sensible to categorise glosses separately from literary texts because, unlike even the most fragmentary examples of prose or verse, they cannot be described as connected writing; the exception to this distinction is the continuous gloss which might with some justice be termed a literary text. Alongside glosses I have therefore included any writing that might be called 'unconnected' or 'discontinuous', e.g. lists, notes and annotations. Non-continuous glosses are commonly of two kinds: (a) marginal or interlinear glosses to individual words in a (usually Latin) text; (b) glossaries which take the form of lists of Latin words and their vernacular equivalents.[15] Glosses to individual words are generally confined to rare words or those of restricted use and during the period covered by this *Catalogue* most of such glosses are in Latin. The next largest numbers are in French and only comparatively few are in English. The same is true of the glossary type. For this reason it is evident that glosses are of only limited value for the dialectal study of Early Middle English. Moreover, because the glossed words are predominantly those of restricted use it is rarely possible to compare them with their equivalents in any continuous Early Middle English text. Nevertheless, I have included Early Middle English glosses because it would clearly be wrong to discard them as valueless dialectally without first studying their forms in relation to the rest of the Early Middle English corpus.

For glosses by the famous tremulous scribe, who was working on Old English manuscripts in Worcester in the early thirteenth century, I have depended on Ker's *Catalogue* and latterly on the admirable work of Christine Franzen.[16] The majority of the tremulous scribe's glosses and annotations are in fact in Latin not in English. Unfortunately, Ker does not indicate which manuscripts listed by him as containing work by the tremulous hand have glosses only in Latin. Although the information in Franzen's book is much fuller on this score and it is usually possible to infer the language of the glosses from her descriptions of their types, she nowhere makes separate lists of manuscripts containing glosses in English and those containing only

---

[13] A great advance in this direction for verse texts is now provided by Richard Hamer, 'A manuscript index for the *Index of Middle English Verse*', *English Manuscript Studies 1100–1700* 4 (1993), forthcoming.

[14] See R.M. Wilson, 'English and French in England 1100–1300', *History* 28 (1943), 37–60; *ibid.*, *The Lost Literature of Medieval England*, 2nd edn. (London, 1970); Siegfried Wenzel, 'Unrecorded Middle English verses', *Anglia* 92 (1974), 55–78; *ibid.*, *Verses in Sermons: Fasciculus Morum and its Middle English Poems*, The Medieval Academy of America Publication 87 (Cambridge, Mass., 1978); *ibid.*, *Preachers, Poets, and the Early English Lyric* (Princeton, 1986).

[15] For the history of these and other kinds of glossing in Latin and in English and other vernaculars, including useful references, see the introduction to volume 1 of Tony Hunt, *Teaching and Learning Latin in Thirteenth-Century England*, 3 vols. (Cambridge, 1991).

[16] Christine Franzen, *The Tremulous Hand of Worcester: a Study of Old English in the Thirteenth Century* (Oxford, 1991).

Latin glosses. I have not myself yet made a detailed study of these glosses. I have therefore chosen to list here all the manuscripts known to have contributions in the tremulous hand and as far as possible I indicate from the information provided by Franzen whether they are in English or in Latin.

A large number of manuscripts of the thirteenth century, containing mainly grammatical works and other school texts written in Latin, have been glossed in both Latin and the vernacular. For these glosses I have drawn mainly on the work of Tony Hunt, much of which is now digested in his impressive three volume publication *Teaching and Learning Latin in Thirteenth-Century England*. I have listed in the *Catalogue* all the manuscripts of the relevant period mentioned by him whenever I have been able to find in his printed lists more than half a dozen or so vernacular glosses that are certainly English. Manuscripts with fewer than that number in English I have usually ignored and anyone interested in pursuing these further must have recourse to Hunt. If my cut-off point in this respect sounds a little arbitrary it is because it raises an interesting question with regard to some of these glosses which has implications for the whole study of English at this period. Many of the 'French' or 'Anglo-Norman' glosses are words which would eventually enter the language and become 'English' words. During the thirteenth and early fourteenth centuries they were in the process of doing so. Are they then French or English? This perhaps explains why Hunt himself refers consistently to 'vernacular' glosses and does not attempt even in his index volume completely to separate French from English, though he does include the label *Anglice* where it precedes a gloss in the manuscript. Help is sometimes provided in this way by the glossator himself, the glosses often being labelled *g.*, *gall.* or *gallice* for French versions, *a.*, *angl.* or *anglice* for English. Unfortunately however, it seems that the glossators found themselves in a quandary similar to ours and their perceptions about whether a word is French or English are sometimes surprising. This is particularly so in the glossed text of the *Graecismus* of Eberhard of Bethune found in Oxford, Corpus Christi College 62, fols. 1r–90v. Here the habit of the glossator(s) is to mark the French glosses *gallice* and to leave the English unmarked, though occasionally these are distinguished as *angl*. There are about 130 Latin lemmata to which Hunt prints vernacular glosses. Of these, eighteen glosses of certainly Old English origin have been labelled *gallice* by the glossator. Most of those which are of Old French origin have been correctly marked *gallice* but one has been left unmarked and another labelled *angl*.[17] The glossators of this manuscript are not unique in attributing to one language words originating in the other and these contemporary perceptions are themselves interesting to those studying the history of either English or Anglo-Norman.

3 *Organisation of the* Catalogue *entries*

The manuscripts containing the source texts are listed in alphabetical order by repository. The relevant writings in English are identified by folio number(s), and frequently also by title and/or incipit. The texts are indexed at the end of the volume in the two-part Index of Middle English Texts A: Titles and B: Incipits. Old English texts, including those that are cited as twelfth- and thirteenth-century copies of texts originally written in Old English, are listed in a separate Index of Old English Texts. Documentary texts, with very few exceptions, are not separately indexed here since Sawyer's and Pelteret's catalogues, which are always cited, are in any case arranged by text. For the purposes of *LAEME* I am concerned only with writings in English, and especially English written within the Early Middle English period. Texts in Latin and French are also sometimes listed incidentally to show the context within which the English contents survive. The Latin and French texts that are cited are also indexed at

---

[17] E.g. *syrenes* glossed 'mermen', *orphanus* glossed 'stepchil', *palus* glossed 'stake', *malus* glossed 'mast': all marked *gallice*; and *latomus* glossed '*angl.* massun'. For these and other examples see Tony Hunt, 'Vernacular glosses in medieval manuscripts', *Cultura Neo-Latina* 39 (1979), 9–37, esp. 22–27.

the end of the volume. I have not attempted to make any regular differentiation between Continental French and Anglo-Norman.

The categories of information provided for each manuscript are exemplified in the skeleton entry below. The categories listed there will appear in the *Catalogue* as bold numbers, followed by any information relevant in that category. Where information is as yet lacking for a particular manuscript entry, the category is omitted.

3.1 *Skeleton* Catalogue *entry*

1 *Manuscript* Designation of the manuscript by its repository, name and number.
The first word is usually the town or city in which the repository lies followed by the name of the repository and then the name of the manuscript, e.g. *London, British Library, Cotton Caligula A ix*. If the name of the institution is better known than the town where it is to be found, it is listed under the name of the institution. For instance, the manuscripts of the *Henry E. Huntington Library in San Marino, California* are listed under *Huntington*. Manuscripts in the possession of private owners are to be found under 'Private:' followed by the manuscript designation, e.g. *Private: Bath, Marquess of, Longleat 39*.

2 *Date* Date of the manuscript, or relevant portion of it, where known.
The date in this entry always refers to the Early Middle English text(s) noted in category **3** below. This will not necessarily match the date of the manuscript as a whole nor need the date apply to other texts or to other parts of the manuscript. A date preceded by * indicates that the relevant text in the manuscript derives, at one or more removes, from an Old English (pre-Conquest) original. Dates are given in the form C13 = 13th century; C13a = first half of 13th century, C13b = second half; C13a1 = first quarter of 13th century, C13b2 = last quarter, etc. To manuscripts referred to by other sources as e.g. 'mid-13th century' I have given the formula C13a2–b1 since such designations imply a considerable margin of error. If a date more precise than the one given is known it follows in brackets. For palaeographically based datings I have followed the generally accepted authorities. Where relevant, the source of the dating is also given, e.g. C13a2 (*ca.* 1230, Dobson, *Origins of Ancrene Wisse*, pp. 16, 121 n. 2). When I have found wider than usual disagreement about the dating of a MS, the views of the different authorities are also given.

3 *Text* Contents of the manuscript.
For the most part this entry is restricted to noting the relevant Early Middle English text(s) by folio or page numbers and title or description. Other contents are sometimes mentioned for the sake of clarity. Where this entry refers to literary text(s) it is preceded by [λ]. Entries for documentary texts are preceded by [δ] and those for glosses (including annotations, notes and lists of *synonyma*) are preceded by [γ]. A single manuscript will often contain more than one type of text. When more than one English text is cited from a manuscript the texts are numbered and listed, each on a separate line, in order of their appearance in the manuscript. This format ensures that, for manuscripts containing multiple texts, the reader may easily match a particular text with the relevant bibliographical references in category **4** below.

4 *References* Bibliographical information.
This category includes a variety of different kinds of reference and from one manuscript to another coverage is very uneven. This unevenness is inevitable and reflects partly the often very diverse types of text listed and partly the fact that consistency of annotation is not here seen as necessarily of any advantage to the reader. No attempt has been made to create in this section a definitive bibliography for each text. The information given is usually ordered as follows. First come references to indexes, e.g. CB Reg, *IMEV (Suppl)*, Wells, Ker, Davis; second, references to anthologies, e.g. CB13, Hall, D&W, BSD, *OBMEV*; third, references to further editions of relevant texts in the format, e.g. Edited: C. Horstmann, *Altenglische Legenden* Neue Folge (Paderborn, 1881), pp. 489–98; fourth,

references to other studies on the text(s) or manuscript; fifth, references to published facsimiles. When more than one text in English is listed in category **3** above, the references here which belong only to one particular text are similarly numbered. Each set of numbered references appears on a separate line so that the reader's eye may easily match the texts listed in **3** with the relevant references in **4**.

5 *Cross-references*
This category contains cross-references to other manuscripts, not necessarily listed in the *Catalogue*, and to the Index of Middle English Texts at the end of the volume. The most important of these references are those to other manuscripts containing versions of the same text(s). Texts surviving from the same period in more than one version are of great value for the study of dialectal variation. By comparing the language of different copies of a single text possible dialectal discriminants may be identified. Where one word has been substituted for another in a textually close version, a lexical choice may reflect a regional preference. The variants displayed in different copies of a single text confirm that translation from one dialect to another was beginning to occur even at this early period although less regularly and systematically than is apparent in the fourteenth and fifteenth centuries.[18]

6 *Associations* Extralinguistic associations with people and places.
It is not only documents for which the place of origin may be known. Literary texts themselves may sometimes serve as linguistic 'anchors' in the dialectal configuration. Manuscripts can often be associated confidently with particular religious houses, the connection being provided by early press marks, medieval library catalogues or an explicit record of ownership in the manuscript itself. When such extralinguistic associations are known I have listed them here, drawing mainly on Ker's *Medieval Libraries of Great Britain*. Manuscript associations with a particular place need not, however, imply that the language of the text or texts in the manuscript belongs in that place; it is a caveat frequently sounded that a scribe might have learnt his habits of writing in a place other than that in which he works. Moreover, for the Early Middle English period, more than in Late Middle English, it has already been noted that many scribes did not consistently 'translate' from the language of their exemplars into their own kind of language. The work of a single scribe, copying from different exemplars, may therefore attest linguistic features from more than one area. Linguistic placings based on manuscript associations must remain tentative unless or until they are confirmed by other local material.

7 *Hands*
For the purpose of linguistic study it is of the greatest importance that the output of different scribes should be assessed separately. It is therefore noted in this section whether or not the English writing cited in category **3** is in a single hand. If more than one hand is involved the hands are usually designated with the sigla A, B, etc. with folio references to their stint(s) and/or references to the text(s) they copy. Hands contributing material in languages other than English are not normally noted. Notes on script are also included in this category.

8 *Language* Geographical placing of the language of the text(s) cited.
In this category is given a provisional assessment of the area of origin of the variety or varieties of English in the manuscript. If an assessment is given with no further qualification it may be taken to represent a localisation based on preliminary analysis and comparison with the later material presented in *LALME*. In some cases the language of the texts in question has already been placed in *LALME*. These examples

---

[18] For a preliminary study of the language of the seven surviving versions of the early Middle English *Poema Morale* see Margaret Laing, 'A Linguistic Atlas of Early Middle English: the value of texts surviving in more than one version' in M. Rissanen *et al.* eds. *History of Englishes: New Methods and Interpretations in Historical Linguistics*. Topics in English Linguistics 10 (Mouton de Gruyter: Berlin and New York, 1992), pp. 566–81.

are given their *LALME* Linguistic Profile numbers and county designations. County names used here, as in *LALME*, are those of the English counties before the local government reforms of 1974. When localisation of the language of a text has not yet been attempted for *LAEME*, opinions from other published studies are sometimes offered; in these cases the source of the opinion is always acknowledged. A localisation given in this section is to be taken as indicating where the scribe of the manuscript learnt to write. This may or may not match the place of origin of the manuscript itself. A single manuscript may contain examples of English originating in different areas. Where a single *scribe* exemplifies more than one variety of English it suggests that he has, to some extent at least, perpetuated the language of his exemplar rather than his own usage. The results may represent discrete varieties of language which he has copied literatim or some admixture of his own usage and that of his exemplar; in these cases close analysis and comparison with other scribal outputs may reveal the linguistic status of the text.

4 Conclusion

The source material for Early Middle English is very variable in its type, length and likely yield of dialectal features. Although it is evident that some of the longer literary texts provide ample evidence for regional linguistic variation, the language of others as well as that of the documents and shorter texts may prove more difficult to assess.

The material available for study consists for the most part not of original writings but of copied texts whose exemplars may have been written in a different place or period. In the twelfth and thirteenth centuries there were probably few scribes engaged solely in the copying of English. The habits of the majority were formed in the writing of Anglo-Norman and especially of Latin. It is necessary for the preservation of meaning in Latin that texts should be copied as nearly as possible literatim. In a literate culture where writing was most often done in Latin, literatim copying also of English (and Anglo-Norman) texts was likely to be more common than linguistic modification. Indeed, it may not at this period have seemed necessary or even desirable to many copyists that English in its written form should reflect the regional variations of spoken English. It follows that a text copied in the Early Middle English period may differ very little from its exemplar. In these circumstances it may be that a scribe will manifest only small traces of his own usage. It might still be possible to associate these traces with linguistic features in other more richly dialectal texts of which the places of origin are known. In these cases our knowledge of the linguistic situation will not be greatly increased. However, what we do know of the dialectal configuration may enable us, using this 'forensic' approach, to say more about the movements of manuscripts, texts and scribes.

Work towards the creation of a linguistic atlas for the Early Middle English period is in progress. The atlas will be of a very different kind from *LALME*. The scarcity of surviving texts for this earlier period from the North and North Midlands is likely to render impossible any comparable linguistic maps for those parts of the country. However, it is apparent from the material listed in this *Catalogue* that, for the South and South Midlands at least, enough Early Middle English survives to make an atlas feasible. This achieved, comparison with the dialectal picture provided in *LALME* should greatly enhance our understanding of the progression, both spatial and temporal, of linguistic change between the two stages of English.

BIBLIOGRAPHICAL ABBREVIATIONS

The following books, articles and series are cited in abbreviated form in the Catalogue, as listed below. Titles have been abbreviated if they appear three or more times. Any other references are cited in full in the text. References are given in the Catalogue by page number, in the form e.g. (pp.) 3–26, except as indicated below.

SHORT TITLES OF JOURNALS AND PERIODICALS

Archiv	*Archiv für das Studium der neueren Sprachen und Literaturen*
EHR	*English Historical Review*
ES	*English Studies*
EStn	*Englische Studien*
E&S	*Essays and Studies*
JEGP	*Journal of English and Germanic Philology*
LSE	*Leeds Studies in English*
MÆ	*Medium Ævum*
MLN	*Modern Language Notes*
MLR	*Modern Language Review*
NM	*Neuphilologische Mitteilungen*
N&Q	*Notes & Queries*
PBA	*Proceedings of the British Academy*
PMLA	*Proceedings of the Modern Language Association of America*
RES	*Review of English Studies*
TCBS	*Transactions of the Cambridge Bibliographical Society*
TPS	*Transactions of the Philological Society of Great Britain*
TYDS	*Transactions of the Yorkshire Dialect Society*

BIBLIOGRAPHY

AM *Havelok*	Angus McIntosh, 'The language of the extant versions of *Havelok the Dane*', *Medium Ævum* 45 (1976), 36–49.
AM 'Wulfstan'	Angus McIntosh, 'Wulfstan's prose', Sir Israel Gollancz Memorial Lecture for 1948, *PBA* (1949), 109-42 (repr. *British Academy Papers on Anglo-Saxon England*, selected and introduced by E.G. Stanley (Oxford, 1989), pp. 111-44).
Arngart *P of A*	O.S. Anderson Arngart, *The Proverbs of Alfred*, 2 vols. (Lund, 1942, 1955)
B[irch]	W. de Gray Birch, *Cartularium Saxonicum*, 3 vols. and index (London, 1885–1899). Reference by number.
BM *Facs*	E.A. Bond, *Facsimiles of Ancient Charters in the British Museum*, 4 vols. (1873–78). Reference by volume and number.
Brook *HL*	G.L. Brook, *The Harley Lyrics* (Manchester, 2nd edn. 1956). Reference by number.

BSD	*Early Middle English Verse and Prose*, ed. J.A.W. Bennett and G.V. Smithers with a Glossary by N. Davis (Oxford, 1966, 2nd edn. 1968). Reference by number.
CB13	*English Lyrics of the XIIIth Century*, ed. C. Brown (Oxford, 1932). Reference by number except where page(s) specified.
CB14	*Religious Lyrics of the XIVth Century*, ed. C. Brown (Oxford, 1924, rev. G.V. Smithers, 1957). Reference by number except where page(s) specified.
CB Reg	C. Brown, *A Register of Middle English Religious and Didactic Verse*, 2 vols. (Oxford, 1916–20). Reference by volume number and page.
Crawford 1928	S.J. Crawford, 'The Worcester marks and glosses of the Old English manuscripts in the Bodleian', *Anglia* 52 (1928), 1–25.
Dahood *AW*	Roger Dahood, '*Ancrene Wisse*, the Katharine Group, and the *Wohunge* Group' in *Middle English Prose, A Critical Guide to Major Authors and Genres*, ed. A.S.G. Edwards (New Brunswick, 1984), pp. 1–33.
d'Ardenne *Iulienne*	S.R.T.O. d'Ardenne, *The Liflade ant te Passiun of Seint Iulienne*, EETS OS 248 (1961).
d'Ardenne & Dobson	S.R.T.O. d'Ardenne and E.J. Dobson, *Seinte Katerine*, EETS SS 7 (1981).
Davis	G.R.C. Davis, *Medieval Cartularies of Great Britain; a short catalogue* (London, 1958). Reference by number.
Dobbie 1937	E. van K. Dobbie, *The Manuscripts of Cædmon's Hymn and Bede's Death Song*, Columbia University Studies in English and Comparative Literature 128 (1937).
Dobson *AR*	E.J. Dobson, *The English Text of the Ancrene Riwle edited from B.M. Cotton MS. Cleopatra C VI*, EETS OS 267 (1972).
Dobson *Origins*	E.J. Dobson, *Origins of Ancrene Wisse* (Oxford, 1976).
D&H	E.J. Dobson and F.Ll. Harrison, *Medieval English Songs* (London, 1979).
D&W	*Early Middle English Texts*, ed. B. Dickens and R.M. Wilson (Cambridge, 1951). Reference by number.
Earle	J. Earle, *A Hand-book to the Land-Charters and other Saxonic Documents* (Oxford, 1888).
EETS	Early English Text Society: OS Original Series; ES Extra Series; SS Supplementary Series.
Finberg 1961	H.P.R. Finberg, *The Early Charters of the West Midlands* (Leicester, 1961).
Finberg 1964	H.P.R. Finberg, *The Early Charters of Wessex* (Leicester, 1964).
Franzen *Thesis*	Christine Franzen, 'A study of the Worcester "tremulous" hand with special reference to the glosses in Bodleian MSS Hatton 113, 114 and 116' Diss. D. Phil., University of Oxford (1986), unpubl.
Franzen 1991	Christine Franzen, *The Tremulous Hand of Worcester: A Study of Old English in the Thirteenth Century* (Oxford, 1991).
Görlach *SEL*	Manfred Görlach, *The Textual Tradition of the South English Legendary*, Leeds Texts and Monographs NS 6 (1974).
Hall	*Selections from Early Middle English 1130–1250*, 2 vols., ed. J. Hall (Oxford, 1920). References to volume i by number of piece, to volume ii by page(s).
Hamer 'MS index'	Richard Hamer, 'A manuscript index for the *Index of Middle English Verse*', *English Manuscript Studies 1100–1700* 4 (1993), forthcoming.

Har[mer]	F.E. Harmer, *Anglo-Saxon Writs* (Manchester, 1952; 2nd edn. Stamford, 1989). Reference by number.
Hartung	A.E. Hartung, *A Manual of the Writings in Middle English 1050–1500*, vols. 3–8 (The Connecticut Academy of Arts and Sciences, 1972–1989). Reference by volume, chapter and number. Cf. Wells.
Hill 1977	Betty Hill, 'The twelfth-century *Conduct of Life*, formerly the *Poema Morale* or *A Moral Ode*', *Leeds Studies in English* 9 (1977), 97–144.
Hunt *Plant Names*	Tony Hunt, *Plant Names of Medieval England* (Cambridge, 1989).
Hunt *Pop Med*	Tony Hunt, *Popular Medicine in the Thirteenth Century* (Cambridge, 1990).
Hunt *Teaching*	Tony Hunt, *Teaching and Learning Latin in Thirteenth-Century England*, 3 vols. (Cambridge, 1991).
IMEP	*Index of Middle English Prose*, General Editor A.S.G. Edwards (D.S. Brewer: Cambridge), *A Handlist of Manuscripts containing Middle English Prose in*:
	I *the Henry E. Huntington Library, San Marino*, ed. Ralph Hanna III (1984);
	II *the John Rylands University Library of Manchester and Chetham's Library, Manchester*, ed. G.A. Lester (1985);
	III *the Digby Collection, Bodleian Library, Oxford*, ed. Patrick J. Horner (1986);
	IV *the Douce Manuscripts in the Bodleian Library, Oxfor*d, ed. Laura Braswell (1987);
	V *the Additional Collection (10001–14000), British Library, London*, ed. Peter Brown and Elton D. Higgs (1988);
	VI *Yorkshire Libraries and Archives*, ed. O.S. Pickering and Susan Powell (1989);
	VII *Parisian Libraries*, ed. James Simpson (1989);
	VIII *Oxford College Libraries*, ed. S.J. Ogilvie-Thomson (1991).
IMEV	C. Brown and R.H. Robbins, *The Index of Middle English Verse* (New York, 1943). Reference by number.
IMEV Suppl	R.H. Robbins and J.L. Cutler, *Supplement to the Index of Middle English Verse* (Lexington, 1965). Reference by number.
IPMEP	R.E. Lewis, N.F. Blake and A.S.G. Edwards, *Index of Printed Middle English Prose* (New York & London, 1985). Reference by number.
James *Cat*	M.R. James, *Descriptive Catalogue of the Manuscripts in the Library of*:
	Corpus Christi College, Cambridge (1912);
	Emmanuel College, Cambridge (1904);
	Fitzwilliam Museum, Cambridge (1895);
	Gonville and Caius College, Cambridge (1908);
	Lambeth Palace (1932);
	Pembroke College, Cambridge (1905);
	Peterhouse, Cambridge (1899);
	St John's College, Cambridge (1913);
	Trinity College, Cambridge (1900–1904).
Joliffe *Checklist*	P.S. Joliffe, *Checklist of Middle English Prose Writings of Spiritual Guidance* (Toronto, 1974). Reference by number.

K[emble]	J.M. Kemble, *Codex Diplomaticus Aevi Saxonici*, 6 vols. (1839–48). Reference by number but when a volume number is specified (in roman numerals) it is followed by a page number.
Ker	N.R. Ker, *Catalogue of Manuscripts Containing Anglo-Saxon* (Oxford, 1957). Reference by number except where page(s) specified.
Ker 'Date'	N.R. Ker, 'The date of the "tremulous" Worcester hand', *Leeds Studies in English* 6 (1937), 28–29.
Ker *Facs*	*Facsimile of British Museum MS. Harley 2253*, with an introduction by N.R. Ker, EETS OS 255 (1965 for 1964). Reference by number.
Ker *Suppl*	N.R. Ker, 'A supplement to *Catalogue of Manuscripts Containing Anglo-Saxon*', *Anglo-Saxon England* 5 (1976), 121–31. Reference by number.
Ker *Med Lib*	N.R. Ker, *Medieval Libraries of Great Britain*, 2nd edn. (London, 1964). *Supplement*, ed. A.G. Watson (London, 1987).
Ker *Med MSS*	N.R. Ker, *Medieval Manuscripts in British Libraries* 3 vols. (Oxford, 1969, 1977, 1983).
Laing 'Anchor texts'	Margaret Laing, 'Anchor texts and literary manuscripts in early Middle English' in F. Riddy, ed., *Regionalism in Late Medieval Manuscripts and Texts* (Cambridge, 1991), pp. 27–52.
Laing *Thesis*	Margaret Laing, 'Studies in the dialect material of mediaeval Lincolnshire', 2 vols., Diss. Ph.D., University of Edinburgh (1978), unpubl.
Laing 'Versions'	Margaret Laing, 'A Linguistic Atlas of Early Middle English: the value of texts surviving in more than one version' in M. Rissanen *et al.* eds. *History of Englishes: New Methods and Interpretations in Historical Linguistics*. Topics in English Linguistics 10 (Mouton de Gruyter: Berlin and New York, 1992), pp. 566–81.
LALME	A. McIntosh, M.L.Samuels and M. Benskin, *A Linguistic Atlas of Late Mediaeval English*, 4 vols. (Aberdeen, 1986).
Lawrence *St Edmund*	C.H. Lawrence, *St Edmund of Abingdon* (Oxford, 1960).
Lowe 'Cartularies'	Kathryn A. Lowe, 'Two thirteenth-century cartularies from Bury St Edmunds: a study in textual transmission', *Neuphilologische Mitteilungen* 93 (1992), 293–301.
Lowe 'OE wills'	Kathryn A. Lowe, '"As fre as thowt"?: some medieval copies and translations of Old English wills', *English Manuscript Studies 1100–1700* 4 (1993), forthcoming.
Lowe *Thesis*	Kathryn A. Lowe, 'The Anglo-Saxon vernacular will: studies in texts and their transmision', Diss. Ph.D., University of Cambridge (1990), unpubl.
MED	*Middle English Dictionary*, ed. H. Kurath, S.M. Kuhn and J. Reidy (Ann Arbor, 1952–).
Plan & Bibl	*Plan and Bibliography. Plan*, ed. H. Kurath; *Bibliography*, ed. M.S. Ogden, C.E. Palmer and R.L. McKelvey (Ann Arbor, 1954).
Plan & Bibl Suppl	*Plan and Bibliography, Supplement I*, ed. Robert E. Lewis (Ann Arbor, 1984).
Millett *Hali Meiðhad*	Bella Millett, *Hali Meiðhad*, EETS OS 284 (1982).
Mon Angl	W. Dugdale, *Monasticon Anglicanum*, ed. B. Bandinel, J. Caley and H. Ellis, 6 vols. (1846). Reference by volume and page.

Morris *OEH*	R. Morris, *Old English Homilies of the 12th and 13th Centuries*, 2 vols. Vol. 1, EETS OS 29, 34 (1867–68; repr. as one vol. 1973). Vol. 2, EETS OS 53 (1873; repr. 1973).
Morris *OE Misc*	R. Morris, *An Old English Miscellany*, EETS OS 49 (1872; repr. 1973).
Murakami	Ryuta Murakami, 'A catalogue of early northern Middle English manuscripts chiefly written in the centuries between the 9th and the early 14th', *English Language and English Literature* 29 nos. 1 and 2 (Seinangakuin University Press, 1988), 61–123.
New Pal Soc	*The New Palaeographical Society Facsimilies of Ancient Manuscripts etc*, ed. E.M. Thompson, G.F. Warner, *et al.*, First Series, 2 vols. (London, 1903–1912); Second Series, 2 vols. (London, 1913–1930). Reference by volume and plate number.
OBMEV	*The Oxford Book of Medieval English Verse*, ed. C. and K. Sisam (Oxford, 1970). Reference by number.
OS Facs	W.B. Sanders, *Facsimiles of Anglo-Saxon Manuscripts*, 3 vols. (Ordnance Survey, Southampton, 1878–84). Reference by volume and number.
Pal Soc	*The Palaeographical Society Facsimiles of Manuscripts and Inscriptions*, ed. E.A. Bond and E.M Thompson, Parts i–viii (London, 1873–1878); Parts ix–xiii (London, 1879–1883). Reference by part and plate number. Second Series, 2 vols., ed. E.A. Bond, E.M. Thompson and G.F. Warner (London, 1884–1894).
Parkes *Orrm*	M.B. Parkes, 'On the presumed date and possible origin of the *Orrmulum*: Oxford, Bodleian Library, MS Junius 1', in *Five Hundred Years of Words and Sounds: a Festschrift for Eric Dobson*, ed. E.G. Stanley and Douglas Gray (Woodbridge, 1983), pp. 115–27.
Pelteret	D.A.E. Pelteret, *Catalogue of post-Conquest Vernacular Documents*, (Woodbridge, 1990). Reference by number.
Pope *Ælfric*	John C. Pope, *Homilies of Ælfric, A Supplementary Collection*, EETS OS 259 (1967).
Pope 'Ely Privilege'	John C. Pope, 'Ælfric and the Old English version of the Ely Privilege' in *England before the Conquest*, ed. P. Clemoes (London, 1971), 85–113.
Regesta	*Regesta Regum Anglo-Normannorum*, 4 vols., ed. H.W.C. Davis and H. Cronne (Oxford, 1913–69).
Rel Ant	T. Wright and J.O. Halliwell, *Reliquiae Antiquae*, 2 vols. (London, 1841). Reference by volume and page.
Richter 1979	Michael Richter, *Sprache und Gesellschaft in England im Mittelalter*, Monographien zur Geschichte des Mittelalters 18 (Stuttgart, 1979).
Robbins *HP*	*Historical Poems of the XIVth and XVth Centuries*, ed. R.H. Robbins (New York, 1959). Reference by number.
Rob[ertson]	A.J. Robertson, *Anglo-Saxon Charters*, 2nd edn. (Cambridge, 1956). Reference by number.
RS	Rolls Series.
S[awyer]	P.H. Sawyer, *Anglo-Saxon Charters an annotated list and Bibliography* (London, 1968). Reference by number.
SC	R.W. Hunt, F. Madan, H.H.E. Craster, N. Denholm-Young and P.D. Record, *A Summary Catalogue of Western Manuscripts in the Bodleian Library at Oxford which have not hitherto been catalogued in the Quarto Series with References to the Oriental and other Manuscripts*, 7 vols. in 8 (Oxford, 1895–1953). Reference by number.

Sec Lyr	*Secular Lyrics of the XIVth and XVth Centuries*, ed. R.H. Robbins (Oxford, 1952, 2nd edn. 1955). Reference by number.
Severs	J.B. Severs, *A Manual of the Writings in Middle English 1050–1500*, vols. 1–2 (Connecticut Academy of Arts and Sciences, 1967, 1970). Reference by volume, section and number. Cf. Wells.
Smith 'Tradition'	J.J. Smith, 'Tradition and innovation in South-West-Midland Middle English' in F. Riddy, ed., *Regionalism in Late Medieval Manuscripts and Texts* (Cambridge, 1991), pp. 53–65.
Stubbs *Hoveden*	William Stubbs, *Chronica Rogeri de Hoveden*, Rolls Series 51, 4 vols. (1868–1871).
Thomson *Archives*	Rodney M. Thomson, *The Archives of the Abbey of Bury St Edmunds*, Suffolk Record Society 21 (1980).
Thomson *Candet*	S. Harrison Thomson, 'The date of the early English translation of the *Candet Nudatum Pectus*', *Medium Ævum* 4 (1935), 100–105.
Thorpe	B. Thorpe, *Diplomatarium Anglicum Aevi Saxonici* (1865).
Vaughan 1953	R. Vaughan, 'The handwriting of Matthew Paris', *Transactions of the Cambridge Bibliographical Society* 1 (1953), 376–94.
Watson *BL*	A.G. Watson, *Catalogue of Dated and Datable Manuscripts c. 700–1600 in the Department of Manuscripts, the British Library* (London, 1979).
Watson *Ox Lib*	A.G. Watson, *Catalogue of Dated and Datable Manuscripts in Oxford Libraries*, 2 vols. (Oxford, 1984).
Wells	J.E. Wells, *A Manual of the Writings in Middle English 1050–1400* (New Haven, 1916), and *Supplements* 1–9 (1919–1951). Reference by chapter and number, e.g. Wells VII.6. Reference to the Supplements by supplement number and page followed by chapter and number in brackets, e.g. Wells *Suppl* 6, p. 1467 (XIII.183c). Cf. the updated version of this work under Severs (vols. 1–2) and Hartung (vols. 3–8).
Wenzel 1974	Siegfried Wenzel, 'Unrecorded Middle English verses', *Anglia* 92 (1974), 55–78. Reference by number.
Wenzel 1978	Siegfried Wenzel, *Verses in Sermons: Fasciculus Morum and its Middle English Poems*, The Medieval Academy of America Publication 87 (Cambridge, Mass., 1978).
Wenzel 1986	Siegfried Wenzel, *Preachers, Poets, and the Early English Lyric* (Princeton, 1986).
Whi[telock]	D. Whitelock, *Anglo-Saxon Wills* (Cambridge, 1930). Reference by number.
Wilson *Grimestone*	Edward Wilson, *A Descriptive Index of the English Lyrics in John of Grimestone's Preaching Book*, Medium Ævum Monographs NS 2 (Oxford, 1973).
Wilson 1943	R.M. Wilson, 'English and French in England 1100–1300', *History* 28 (1943), 37–60.
Wilson *Lost Lit*	R.M. Wilson, *The Lost Literature of Medieval England*, 2nd edn. (London, 1970).
Wright *Spec Lyr*	T. Wright, *Specimens of Lyric Poetry*, Percy Society 4 (1842). Reference by number.
Wright-Wülcker	T. Wright and R.P. Wülcker, *Anglo-Saxon and Old English Vocabularies*, 2nd edn. (London, 1884).
Zupitza 'Godric'	Julius Zupitza, 'Cantus Beati Godrici', *Englische Studien* 11 (1887), 401–32.

ABBREVIATIONS

abp.	archbishop	MLS	Michael Samuels
Add	Additional	MS(S)	manuscript(s)
AID	Ian Doyle	n.	note
AM	Angus McIntosh	N, NE, NW	north, north-east, north-west
app.	appendix		
art.	article	NME	Northern Middle English
A-S	Anglo-Saxon		
beg.	beginning	no(s).	number(s)
bibliog.	bibliography	NS	New Series
BL	London, British Library	ob.	date of death (*obit*)
Bodley	Oxford, Bodleian Library, (Bodley)	OE	Old English
		op. cit.	in the work cited (*opere citato*)
bp.	bishop		
BV	Blessed Virgin	opp.	opposite
ca.	about (*circa*)	p(p).	page(s)
Co.	County	pers. comm.	personal communication
col(s).	column(s)	q.v.	which see (*quod vide*)
CUL	Cambridge University Library	r	recto, as in fol. 33r
		ref(s).	reference(s)
Diss.	dissertation	repr.	reprinted
E	east	rev.	revised
ed.	edited by	S, SE, SW	south, south-east, south-west
edn.	edition		
eds.	editors	S., St	saint
EME	Early Middle English	seq.	following, and in what follows (*sequente*)
esp.	especially		
et al.	and others (*et alii*)	SS.	saints
fn.	footnote	s.v.	under the title (*sub voce*)
fol(s).	folio(s)	*temp.*	in the time of (*tempore*)
ibid.	in the same place (*ibidem*)	unpubl.	unpublished
		v	verso, as in fol. 33v
incl.	including	viz.	namely (*videlcet*)
intro.	introduction	vols.	volume
LP	Linguistic Profile	W	west
MB	Michael Benskin	W-S	West-Saxon
ME	Middle English	x	between the two years cited, as in 1066 x 1086
MHE	Middle Hiberno-English		

Abbreviations of County Names used in the *Catalogue*

Beds	Bedfordshire	Gloucs	Gloucestershire
Berks	Berkshire	Hants	Hampshire
Bucks	Buckinghamshire	Herefords	Herefordshire
Cambs	Cambridgeshire	Herts	Hertfordshire
ERY	East Riding of Yorkshire	Hunts	Huntingdonshire
		Lincs	Lincolnshire

Middx	Middlesex	Warwicks	Warwickshire
Monmouth	Monmouthshire	Wilts	Wiltshire
Northants	Northamptonshire	Worcs	Worcestershire
Notts	Nottinghamshire	WRY	West Riding of Yorkshire
Oxon	Oxfordshire		
Salop	Shropshire	Yorks	Yorkshire
Staffs	Staffordshire		

Old English Letters

æ	aesc	ȝ	yogh
ð	eth	ᵹ	insular g
þ	thorn	ƿ	wynn

CATALOGUE OF SOURCES

1 Aberystwyth, National Library of Wales 572.
2 C14a1.
3 [λ] Fols. 1r–4v binding fragments containing 1257 lines of *Guy of Warwick*, not all of them complete or legible.
4 Edited: Maldwyn Mills and Daniel Huws, *Fragments of an Early Fourteenth-Century Guy of Warwick*, Medium Ævum Monographs NS 4 (Oxford, 1974).
5 Once part of the same manuscript and in the same hand as similar binding fragments from BL Additional 14408, q.v.
7 One hand — the same as BL Add 14408.
8 NME.

1 Aberystwyth, National Library of Wales, Peniarth 390 C.
2 *C13a2–b1 (*ca.* 1240–1264, Sawyer, *Charters of Burton Abbey*, xiv).
3 [δ] Burton Cartulary containing 38 charters. English bounds (which are often omitted in this MS) appear on fols. 175r (p. 349) (only 5 words of English); 175r–v (pp. 349–50); 176v (p. 352); 179r–v (pp. 357–58). Fols. 179v–180v (pp. 358–60) contain a list of towns in English with some text. Fols. 180v–181v (pp. 360–62) contain the Will of Wulfric. Apparently no other English in this MS.
4 Davis 93. Sawyer as follows: S 545 (B 885); S 557 (B 890); S 602 (B 954); S 878; S 906; S 1536. See also P.H. Sawyer, *Charters of Burton Abbey*, Anglo–Saxon Charters 2 (Oxford, 1979) and S. Shaw, *The History and Antiquities of Staffordshire*, 2 vols. (1798–1801).
5 Eight of the charters in this MS exist in earlier (C10 and C11) versions on single sheets of parchment: Burton-upon-Trent Museum, Burton Muniments 1 and 2; Stafford, William Salt Library, 84/1/41 (probably the exemplar for fol. 176v), 84/2/41, 84/3/41 (exemplar for fol. 179), 84/4/41 (exemplar for fol. 179r–v), 84/5/41. Four charters are copied in the C13 Burton Cartulary, BL MS Loans 30 (Marquess of Anglesey), q.v. For King Æthelred's confirmation of privileges and lands to Burton Abbey, and for the Will of Wulfric (Sawyer 906 and 1536) the exemplar is the same as for BL Loans 30. (Cf. BL Cotton Vespasian E iii, fol. 4 an incomplete copy (C13) corresponding to fols. 179v–180v.)
6 Burton Abbey, Burton-upon-Trent, Staffs. Ker *Med Lib*, p. 15.
7 One main hand.
8 OE linguistic forms are not much modified.

1 Admont (Styria, Austria), Stiftsbibliothek 24.
2 *C13a.
3 [λ] A MS of *The Austrian Legendary* containing on fol. 145v Bede's Death Song in the text of Cuthbert's *Epistola de obitu Bedae*.
4 Murakami, pp. 101–102, no. 33. Edited: Dobbie 1937, p. 61.
5 For other MSS containing Bede's Death Song see the Index of Old English Texts.

1 Athelney Cartulary. Untraced: C18 transcript, formerly Phillipps 4810–11 was owned in 1957 by David Rogers, c/o Bodleian Library.
2 Date of MS not known.
3 [δ] Charters in Latin with English bounds.
4 Davis 15. Sawyer 343 (Oxford, Mr D. Rogers, pp. 34–38) and S 432 (Oxford, Mr D. Rogers, pp.116–19). Edited, probably from this manuscript, by Birch 546 and

715 via J. Collinson, *The History and Antiquities of the County of Somerset*, 3 vols. (Bath, 1791) 3, p. 197 and 1, part 2, p. 84 (bounds only). Also by Finberg 1964 nos. 415 and 436. Sawyer, p. 65 notes that Finberg prints all pre-Conquest texts not printed by Birch and Kemble. Cf. also Finberg nos. 398 and 483 (no English).
6 Athelney, Somerset.
8 Birch 715 and Finberg 1964 show the texts to be of considerable linguistic interest.

1 Auxerre, Bibl. et Musée, MS 123 (ancien 110).
2 C13a2–b1.
3 [λ] Fols. 1r–56v the Pontigny version of the *Liber Sancti Edmundi* said to contain the English words attributed to the dying Edmund.
4 See Lawrence *St Edmund*, p. 47. Cf. H.W.C. Davis, 'An unpublished life of Edmund Rich', *EHR* 22 (1907), 84–92 where this text is collated with that in Oxford, Balliol College 226, q.v. Edited: E. Martène and U. Durand, *Thesaurus Novus Anecdotorum* 3 (Paris, 1717), cols. 1775–1826. See also Dom Wilfrid Wallace, *St Edmund of Canterbury* (London, 1893) and F. de Paravacini, *St Edmund of Abingdon* (1898).
5 Other continental MSS of this version of the *Life of St Edmund* are listed in Lawrence *St Edmund*, pp. 47–48. Cf. two different versions written in England, one by Eustace of Faversham, the other known as the "Anonymous A" version, for which see refs. cited in the Index of Texts in Latin.
6 MS from Pontigny.

1 Bath, Marquess of. See **Private: Bath, Marquess of, Longleat.**

1 Berlin-Dahlem, Stiftung Preussischer Kulturbesitz, Staatsbibliothek, MS theol. lat. fol. 249.
2 C13b2 (*ca.* 1275, *OBMEV*).
3 [λ] Fols. 131r–v; 134r seven verse fragments.
4 *IMEV Suppl* 3167.3, 3897.5, 1631.3, 2794.6, 3900.5. See R.H. Robbins, 'Middle English lyrics: handlist of new texts', *Anglia* 83 (1965), 35–47 (46); *OBMEV* 267.
5 Cf. versions in Durham Cathedral B.I.18, fols. 56v, 117r and BL Harley 3823 fol. 182v for which see Wenzel 1974, nos. 53 and 80 (cf. also no. 81).

1 Blickling Hall. See **Private: Blickling Hall, Norfolk.**

1 Brugge, Stadsbibliotheek 546.
2 C13b.
3 [γ] A collection of works (in Latin) by John of Garland, with interlinear glosses and marginal annotations including some in the vernacular. Glosses in English appear in at least two of the texts: (1) fols. 2r–12r *Morale Scolarium* and (2) fols. 148v–174v; 145v *Parisiana Poetria*.
4 See Hunt *Teaching* 1, pp. 38 and 151. (2) Edited: Traugott Lawler, *The 'Parisiana Poetria' of John of Garland* (New Haven/London, 1974).

1 Cambridge, Corpus Christi College 8.
2 C13b2–C14a1 (*ca.* 1300, *OBMEV*).
3 [λ] English on flyleaf (p. 547): fragment of a song (part of the final line) and a complete song with musical notation beg. *Worldes blisce haue god day*. The flyleaf is four pages of a C13 music book with music on a five line stave. The pages are numbered 558, which contains music with Latin words; 547 containing the English texts; 548 which has a French song; and 557 which contains fragments of French and Latin. See James *Cat*.
4 CB Reg i 206. Wells *Suppl* 1, p. 975 (VII.20a). *IMEV* 4221 and *IMEV Suppl* *1500.5. CB13 58. *OBMEV* 40. D&H, p. 194.
5 Lines 9–16 of the above lyric are to be found also in Edinburgh, National Library of Scotland, Advocates' 18.7.21, John of Grimestone's Commonplace Book, fol. 124r. For a full catalogue of the English verses in the latter MS see Wilson *Grimestone*; the

extract from *Worldes blisce* is printed on p. 51, no. 200. For Advocates' 18.7.21, see also *LALME* 1, p. 88 and CB14 pp. xvi–xix. Note that a ten-line lyric in Worcester Cathedral, Dean and Chapter Library Q 46, fol. 288r has the same first line as this song but continues quite differently. This version concerns Christ's passion, the Worcester text deals with the vanity of worldly possessions.
7 English in one hand.

1 Cambridge, Corpus Christi College 12.
2 C13a2 (tremulous hand: see Ker 'Date').
3 [γ] Gregory's *Pastoral Care* in a hand of C10b but with glosses throughout in the Worcester tremulous hand. No English glosses noted by Ker or Franzen.
4 Ker 30. Franzen 1991, pp. 60–63. See also R.I. Page, 'Yet another note on Alfred's *Æstel*, *LSE* NS 18 (1987) and refs. there cited.
5 For other MSS containing glosses by the tremulous hand see Franzen 1991, Ker, p. lvii and the entry for Worcester Cathedral, Dean and Chapter Library F 174.
6 Franzen: "there is no conclusive evidence that [the MS] was in Worcester before the thirteenth century". Cf. Ker *Med Lib*, p. 206.
7 Latin glosses in the Worcester tremulous hand.

1 Cambridge, Corpus Christi College 26.
2 C13a (before 1259, D&H, p. 105).
3 [λ] Matthew Paris, *Chronica maiora*. P. 259 contains St Godric's Hymn A.
4 CB Reg i 206. Wells *Suppl* 1, p. 986 (XIII.27). *IMEV* 2988. Hall ii 241. D&H, p. 105: the date is established because the MS is corrected in many places by Matthew Paris himself. See also Vaughan 1953, p. 391 and Zupitza 'Godric'.
5 Matthew Paris was a St Albans chronicler. Two other MSS of his *Chronica maiora*, little later in date, contain St Godric's Hymn A, derived from the Corpus text. The first, BL Cotton Nero D v, (fol. 150v) was also corrected by Matthew Paris himself and is probably therefore a St Albans text too. The second is BL Harley 1620. For other MSS containing one or more of Godric's Hymns see the Index of Middle English Texts A: Titles.
6 St Albans, Herts. Ker *Med Lib*, p. 165.
7 English in one hand.
8 The spellings of the Corpus text are said by Dobson to "show the influence of a South-eastern dialect, probably that of St Albans itself".

1 Cambridge, Corpus Christi College 111, pp. 57–131.
2 *C12b.
3 [δ] Bath Cartulary. English, mostly bounds only, on pp. 57–58, 61–92 (including recto and verso of slip between 76 and 75*), 94–95.
4 Davis 23. Ker *Med Lib*, p. 7 fn. 7 indicates that pp. 7–8, 55–56 appear to have belonged to Cambridge, Corpus Christi College 140 (C11b) (Cf. Pelteret 70–78). Sawyer as follows: S 610 (B 927, K 452 and iii 444); S 414 (B 670, K 354 and iii 406–407); S 476 (B 767, K 388 and iii 416); S 508 (B 814, K 408 and iii 423–24); S 593 (B 957, K 457 and iii 446); S 664 (B 936); S 1555 (B 928, K iii 450–51, Rob 109); S 1426 (B 929, K 822, Rob 117); S 661 (B 1009, K 485 and iii 455–56); S 627 (B 973, K 440 and iii 436–37); S 643 (B 1001, K 463 and iii 451); S 265 (B 327, K 193 and iii 388); S 694 (B 1073, K 486 and iii 456); S 692 (B 1074, K 484 and iii 455); S 711 (B 1099, K 502 and iii 459–60); S 735 (B 1164, K 516); S 785 (B 1287, K 573); S 777 (B 1257, K 566); S 854 (K 643); S 1538 (K 694, Whi 21); S 1034 (K 811 and vi 244); S 1427 (Har 6, K 821). Pelteret 1, 30. Also edited in W. Hunt, *Two Chartularies of the Priory of St Peter at Bath* (Somerset Record Society, 1893).
6 Bath Cathedral Priory, Somerset. Ker *Med Lib*, p. 7.
7 Davis: "written in mid-12th cent. book hand (*temp.* Hen. II?)".

1 Cambridge, Corpus Christi College 145.
2 C14a1 (c1310–20, Görlach *SEL*, p. 78 and n. 28).

3 [λ] Fols. 1r–218 *South English Legendary*.
4 CB Reg i 206–210. Wells V.19 (p. 294) and cf. Wells v.44, 47, 50, 51, 52, 54, 59, 67 (p. 322), 78 (p. 331), 80. Severs 2 V.1 and cf. Severs 2, pp. 561–635. For individual entries in *IMEV* see Hamer 'MS index'. Görlach *SEL*, pp. 77–79. Ed. C. D'Evelyn and A.J. Mill, *The South English Legendary*, EETS OS 235, 236, 244 (1956 for 1951, 1956 for 1952, 1959 for 1957; repr. 1967 and 1969).
5 Cf. BL Egerton 2891 and the fragment in Leicester Museum 18 D 59 which, according to Görlach, are very similar to this MS textually and orthographically. For other early MSS containing parts of the *South English Legendary* see the Index of Middle English Texts A: Titles.
6 *Ex libris* inscription in a hand of early C15 indicates that the manuscript was owned by that date by Southwick Priory, Hants. Ker *Med Lib*, p. 181.
7 Hand A (the main hand): fols. 1r–210v.
Hand B (C14a2): 210v–213r.
Hand C (C14a2–b1): 214r–218 (end).
8 *LALME* has hand A as LP 6810 in W Berks and hand B as LP 5560 in Hants. Hand C has not yet been placed.

1 **Cambridge, Corpus Christi College 178 + 162, pp. 139–160** (originally parts of the same MS).
2 C13a2 (tremulous hand: see Ker 'Date').
3 [γ] A. Homilies; B. Bilingual (Latin/OE) *Rule of St Benedict* in hands of C11a; both parts contain glosses in the tremulous hand of Worcester. It is not clear either from Ker or Franzen whether any of the glosses are in English. According to Franzen, most of the glosses in the *Benedictine Rule* are culled directly from the Latin text. Most also are in the state of the tremulous hand labelled "B" by Franzen in which the glossator habitually used Latin; there are therefore probably few, if any, glosses in English.
4 Ker 41. Franzen 1991, pp. 49–51, 124–27. MS also described in Pope *Ælfric*, pp. 62–67.
5 For other MSS containing glosses in the tremulous hand see Franzen 1991, Ker, p. lvii and the entry for Worcester Cathedral, Dean and Chapter Library F 174.
6 It is not known where the MS was written but it was at Worcester in the mid eleventh century. Ker *Med Lib*, p. 206.
7 Glosses, probably only Latin, in the Worcester tremulous hand.

1 **Cambridge, Corpus Christi College 188.**
2 C13a1 (s. xiii in., Ker).
3 [λ] In a MS of C11a containing homilies by Ælfric, there appear on p. 408 in a later hand the words: *þine mot ihc gon mayde sweete lef wine mot hi*.
4 Ker 43 (p. 66).

1 **Cambridge, Corpus Christi College 198.**
2 C13a2 (tremulous hand: see Ker 'Date').
3 [γ] Homilies in several C11 hands are annotated throughout by the Worcester tremulous hand.
4 Ker 48. Franzen 1991, pp. 51–53. MS also described in Pope *Ælfric*, pp. 220–22. For glosses in English see William Schipper, 'Middle English glosses in CCCC MS 198', *Annual Reports, the Division of Languages, International Christian University* (Tokyo) 10 (1985), 95–110. For various opinions about a single gloss in this MS see William Schipper, 'OE *geflogen*, ME *ihuld*: the Worcester "tremulous" scribe nods', *Medieval English Studies Newsletter* (Tokyo) 13 (1985), 1–2; John C. Pope, 'OE *geflogen*, ME *ihuld*: a second look at the "tremulous" scribe's error', *Medieval English Studies Newsletter* (Tokyo) 14 (1986), 3–4; Shoko Ono 'A note on a note — a grammatical remark', ibid., 4–5; William Schipper, 'Response by W. Schipper', ibid., 5–6.
5 For other MSS containing glosses by the tremulous hand see Franzen 1991, Ker, p. lvii and the entry for Worcester Cathedral, Dean and Chapter Library F 174.

6 Pope (*Ælfric*, p. 22) considers that the MS may have originated in Kent, but it was in Worcester by the beginning of C13. Cf. Ker *Med Lib*, p. 206.
7 Glosses in the Worcester tremulous hand.

1 Cambridge, Corpus Christi College 302.
2 *C12b2–C13a1.
3 [λ] Homilies of C11–C12 but with additions including, on p. 189 in a hand of the turn of C13 (1300), the following: *Men ða leffostan us lareowhum gedafenað þa soðem lare ðe god silf gesette. ðurch vs halgan witegan. & þurch hine silfne. eowh gelome seggan to eowhres lifes richtinge. And Ge magon gehiran on ðare.* Alterations of C12 and C13 also on pp. 119, 157, 159 and 161.
4 Ker 56. MS also described in Pope *Ælfric*, pp. 51–52.
6 Ker gives no indication as to original provenance.

1 Cambridge, Corpus Christi College 303.
2 *C12a.
3 [λ] 73 Old English homilies, 61 of which are by Ælfric.
4 Ker 57. See also Pope *Ælfric*, pp. 18–20.
5 Some of the homilies were copied from Bodley 342 (Ker 309) which was itself altered by eleventh-century "correctors".
6 Bodley 342 is from Rochester, Kent and Ker considers Rochester to be the place of origin of this MS also.
7 Ker discerns three hands, the script being of the "prickly" kind found in Rochester (and Canterbury) in MSS of C12.
Hand A: pp. 1–50, 203–226/26, 231/29–251/9, 254/6–362.
Hand B: pp. 51–202.
Hand C ("a less good hand"): pp. 226/27–231/28, 251/10–254/5.
On p. 220 a hand of C13–C14 glosses *senne* to *leahter* and *prude* to *ofermodignysse*.
8 The language of Hand A is considered by Pope to be "markedly though inconsistently archaic". The scribe is "inclined to preserve the spellings of his exemplars. When he departs from it, he sometimes gives us the levelled endings we expect, sometimes sheer chaos". The language of Hand C is distinguished, according to Ker, by substitution of *e* or *a* for W-S *æ* and occasionally *u* for W-S *y*. Patrick Stiles considers (pers. comm.) that Hand C "basically writes ME".

1 Cambridge, Corpus Christi College 327.
2 C13–C14.
3 [λ] On fol. 228v are about fourteen three-line stanzas written in pencil and half obliterated. Other slightly later scribbles in English are on fol. 226r. The rest of the MS is in Latin of C15.
4 CB Reg i 211: "Perhaps relating to the Parable of the Labourers in the Vineyard". For the English on fol. 226r see *IMEV* 2194.

1 Cambridge, Corpus Christi College 367, part II.
2 *C12–C12b.
3 [λ] (1) Fols. 1, 2, 7–10 Ælfric's rendering of Bede's *De temporibus*. (2) Fols. 3–6, 11–29 Homilies — fragments of six quires muddled together.
4 (1) Ker 62. (2) Ker 63. See also B. Assmann, *Angelsächsische Homilien und Heiligenleben*, Grein: Bibliothek der angelsächsische Prosa 3 (1889), pp. 24–48.
6 Ker, p. 110: "Probably from Worcester".

1 Cambridge, Corpus Christi College 391.
2 C13a2 (tremulous hand: see Ker 'Date').
3 [λ] MS containing OE prayers and prognostics etc. in hands of C11 and C12. On p. 721 are four lines in the Worcester tremulous hand beg: *þreo dawes beoð on tweolf moneþ*. This is a later copy of an article on p. 718 noting three unlucky days for bloodletting. The MS has no tremulous glosses.

4 Ker 67. Franzen 1991, pp. 69–70. Edited: Max Förster, 'Die altenglische Traumlunare', *EStn* 60 (1925–26), p. 77.
5 For other MSS containing glosses by the tremulous hand see Franzen 1991, Ker, p. lvii and the entry for Worcester Cathedral, Dean and Chapter Library F 174.
6 Written at Worcester. Ker *Med Lib*, p. 206.
7 The Worcester tremulous hand.

1 Cambridge, Corpus Christi College 402.

2 C13a2 (*ca.* 1230, Dobson *Origins*, pp. 16, 121 fn. 2 and cf. E.J. Dobson, 'The date and composition of *Ancrene Wisse*', *PBA* 52 (1966), 181–208).
3 [λ] 4 flyleaves + 117 fols. *Ancrene Wisse* "MS A".
4 Wells VI.40. Severs 2 VI.1. Hall i IX, ii 354–407. BSD XVIII. D&W XVII. *IPMEP* 559. See also Dobson *Origins* and Dahood *AW*. Edited: J.R.R. Tolkien, *The English Text of the Ancrene Riwle: Ancrene Wisse*, with an introduction by N.R. Ker, EETS OS 249 (1962). For the six lines of verse introduced into the text on fol. 62r see CB Reg i 211, Wells *Suppl* 1, p. 975 (VII.15) and *IMEV* 3568.
5 For other EME texts of *Ancrene Riwle* see the Index of Middle English Texts A: Titles. Later ME versions are to be found in Cambridge, Magdalene College, Pepys 2498; BL Royal 8 C i; Bodley, Eng. poet. a. 1. the Vernon MS.
6 MS belonged to Wigmore Abbey, Herefords. Ker *Med Lib*, p. 198. Fol. 1r lower margin in a fourteenth century hand has "Liber ecclesiae *sancti* Jacobi de Wygemore: quem Joha*nn*es Purcel dedit eidem ecclesie ad instancia*m* fra*t*ris Wal*t*eri de Lodelowe senioris *t*unc precentoris". Dobson suggests (*Origins of Ancrene Wisse*, pp. 349–53) that the epithet *inoh meaðful ich am* on fol. 117v conceals the name of the original author of *Ancrene Wisse*, "Brian(us) of Lingen (Linthehum)". See also M. Benskin, 'The letters <þ> and <y> in later Middle English, and some related matters', *Journal of the Society of Archivists* 7 (1982), 13–30 (28–30). Lingen is about 3 miles SW of Wigmore.
7 One hand throughout.
8 Language of Wigmore, NW Herefords. This is in the 'AB language' common to this MS (A) and Bodley 34 (B). On AB language as a literary standard see J.R.R. Tolkien, '*Ancrene Wisse* and *Hali Meiðhad*', *E&S* 14 (1929), 104–26; J.R. Hulbert, 'A thirteenth-century English literary standard', *JEGP* 45 (1946), 411–14 (esp. p. 413); A.J. Bliss, 'A note on "Language AB"', *English and Germanic Studies* 5 (1952–53), 1–6; Millett *Hali Meiðhad*, pp. xiv–xvi and refs. there cited. For a more lengthy account see d'Ardenne *Iulienne*, pp. 177–250. Dobson considers that the author of *Ancrene Wisse* was also probably Scribe B of BL Cotton Cleopatra C vi. For a comparison of Scribe B's language with that of this MS see Dobson *AR*, pp. xciii–cxl (esp. cxxx–cxl). Cf. also Smith 'Tradition'.

1 Cambridge, Corpus Christi College 405.

2 C14a1.
3 [λ] In a composite MS containing mainly Anglo-Norman and Latin, on p. 22 English verses appear as follows.
   (1) Four English and three Latin lines on Fortune beg. *Of noman liche makeȝ hao in a stound many riche*.
   (2) Nine long lines with medial rhyme beg. *Heyl god ye schilde*.
   (3) Three long lines with medial rhyme beg. *All vnder sunne is wyt swynk her yvonne*.
4 (1) *IMEV* 2641.
   (2) CB Reg i 211, ii 655. Wells *Suppl* 6, p. 1467 (XIII.183c). *IMEV* 1047.
   (3) *IMEVSuppl* 228.8.
See also James *Cat* 2, pp. 277–88. Edited: H.A. Person, *Cambridge Middle English Lyrics* (Seattle, 1962), pp. 14 and 71. For a description of the MS and its contents, see K.V. Sinclair, 'Anglo-Norman at Waterford' in Ian Short, ed., *Medieval French Textual Studies in Memory of T.B.W. Reid*, Anglo-Norman Text Society Occasional Publication Series 1 (London, 1984), pp. 219–38.

6 James: "[MS] evidently belonged to the brethren of St John of Jerusalem at Waterford [Ireland]".

1 Cambridge, Corpus Christi College 438.
2 C13b.
3 [λ] Historical works in Latin by Gervase of Canterbury. In the text of the *Actus Pontificum Cantuarensium* is quoted the English sentence *Her lith Odo the gode*.
4 MS described William Stubbs, *The Historical Works of Gervase of Canterbury* 2, RS 73 (1880), pp. vii et seq. English printed p. 355. See also Wilson 1943, p. 47.
6 A Canterbury MS. Ker *Med Lib*, p. 31.

1 Cambridge, Corpus Christi College 444.
2 C14a1. (a1325, *MED Plan & Bibl*, p. 42; "cent. XIV (near 1300)", James *Cat* 2, p. 357).
3 [λ] Flyleaf + 81 fols. (verso of last fol. blank). *Genesis and Exodus*.
4 CB Reg i 211. Wells VIII.1. Severs 2 IV.1. *IMEV* 2072. Hall i XXII, ii 626–57. Edited: R. Morris, *The Story of Genesis and Exodus*, EETS OS 7 (1865, rev. 1873, repr. 1895); Olof Arngart, *The Middle English Genesis and Exodus*, Lund Studies in English 36 (Lund, 1968). For a commentary on the text see Philip G. Buehler, *The Middle English Genesis and Exodus* (The Hague, 1974). See also Kirsti Kivimaa, *þe and þat as Clause Connectives in Early Middle English with Especial Consideration of the Emergence of the Pleonastic þat*, Commentationes Humanarum Litterarum, Societas Scientiarum Fennica 39, 1 (Helsinki, 1966), pp. 22–23. Cf. AM *Havelok*, 41.
7 One hand.
8 Language of W Norfolk (cf. BL Arundel 292, *The Bestiary* and see AM *Havelok*, 40–41 fn. 11).

1 Cambridge, Corpus Christi College 557 and Kansas University Library Y 103.
2 C13a2 (tremulous hand: see Ker 'Date').
3 [γ] Two fragments of a C11 MS containing an OE version of *The Legend of the Cross*. Interlinear glosses by the Worcester tremulous hand are in Latin only.
4 Ker and Ker *Suppl* 73. Franzen 1991, p. 54. The Corpus fragment is edited and discussed by N.R. Ker, 'An eleventh-century Old English legend of the cross before Christ', *MÆ* 9 (1940), 84–85. For the Kansas folio see B. Colgrave and A. Hyde, 'Two recently discovered leaves from Old English manuscripts', *Speculum* 37 (1962), 60–78 (includes facsimile).
5 Colgrave and Hyde consider it possible that this text of *The Legend of the Cross* was the exemplar for the copy in Oxford, Bodley 343. For other MSS containing glosses by the tremulous hand see Franzen 1991, Ker, p. lvii and the entry for Worcester Cathedral, Dean and Chapter Library F 174.
6 Written at Worcester. Ker *Med Lib*, p. 206.
7 Latin glosses in the Worcester tremulous hand.

1 Cambridge, Emmanuel College 27 (I.2.6).
2 C14a1.
3 [λ] Miscellanea. Part II, fols. 13–194. Latin except for English on fols. 57v, 111v and 162r–163r.
  (1) Fol. 57v a proverb in English beg. *þe whyle þᵗ ich wore gold on mi gloue* .
  (2) Fol. 111v English verse on the *Ten Commandments* beg. *Ane god þov schalt wrschupe*.
  (3) Fol. 111v a couplet on the seven deadly sins: *Prute coueitise, slevþe, wreþe and Onde; / Glutonie, and, Lecherie, god bringe ut of londe*.
  (4) Fol. 162r *Pater Noster* beg. *Vre fader in heuene; yhalȝed bo þy name*.
  (5) Fol. 162r *Ave Maria* beg. *Heyl boe þov Marie; ful of godes grace*.

(6) Fol. 162r *Creed* in prose divided amongst the Apostles beg. *Petrus, Ih bi-leue in god, fader almiȝti.*

(7) Fol. 162r col. 2 *Confiteor* in prose beg. *Ih knovlechy to god and to vre / Leuedi seynte Marie.*

(8) Fol. 162r col. 2 *The Ten Commandments* beg. *No god ne haue þov; boten on.*

(9) Fol. 162r col. 2 a couplet on the seven deadly sins (cf. (3)): *Prute. ȝisscinge. slevþe. wrethe, and Onde; / Glotonie. and lecherie, God bringe hom vt of londe.*

(10) Fol. 162r col. 2 five rhyming lines on the elevation of the eucharist beg. *Wolcome louerd; in likninge of bred.*

(11) Fol. 162v *In Manus Tuas* beg. *In toe þine honden. louerd.*

(12) Fol. 162v couplet: *Me ydrechez þroe yfoon. mid þroe kunne rute / þe fond, and myn oȝe fleyhs, and þe world al abute.*

(13) Fol. 162v two couplets introducing *In nomine patris* beg. *Al fram [eh] vuele þinge / me schulde iesus þat may* (*eh* is for 'each' but has been crossed through in the MS).

(14) Fol. 162v four lines to put evil to flight beg. *Bi þis tokninge of þare rode.*

(15) Fol. 162v *Septem cogitanda* beg. *Myn oȝen deþ; and cristes.*

(16) Fol. 162v *The Seven Works of Mercy* beg. *Schrude and fede and drenche.*

(17) Fol. 162v a version of *Three Sorrowful Tidings* beg. *Boe war soe ih boe.*

(18) Fol. 162v for baptism: *Ih cristin þe, N, In þe name of þe fader, and þe sone, and of þe holi goste.*

(19) Fol. 163r three lines of verse beg. *Worldlih eȝte is ywonne.*

(20) Fol. 163r quatrain on St Swithin's Day: *In þe daye of seynte Svythone; vane ginneþ rinigge / Forti dawes mid ywone; ilestez sueh tiþinge.*

4 James *Cat*, pp. 22–27. CB Reg i 212. Wells *Suppl* 1, p. 967 (VI.11). Items (4), (5), (9)–(11), (13)–(16) are edited: H.A. Person, *Cambridge Middle English Lyrics* (Seattle, 1962), pp. 27–29.

(1) Wenzel 1974, no. 87 and cf. *IMEV Suppl* 4020.6.

(2) Hartung 7 XX.42. *IMEV* 2694. (N.B. *IMEV* 1129 seems to suggest that the version of *The Ten Commandments* beg. *Hawe on god in wrchipe* also appears on fol. 111v. In fact, it is only the version *Ane god þov schalt wrschupe*, but cf. a different version (8) on fol. 162r.)

(3) *IMEV* 2769.

(4) *IMEV* 2704.

(5) Hartung 7 XX.37. *IMEV* 1062.

(6) Hartung 7 XX.38.

(7) Apparently not in Hartung 7 XX.211.

(8) *IMEV* 2291. CB13 70B.

(9) *IMEV* 2769.

(10) Wells *Suppl* 6, p. 1455 (VI.24b). Hartung 7 XX.204. *IMEV* 3884.

(11) *IMEV* 1599.

(12) *IMEV* 2137.

(13) *IMEV* 177.

(14) *IMEV* 580.

(15) *IMEV* 2187.

(16) *IMEV* 3100.

(17) Wells *Suppl* 2, p. 1065 (VII.37). See also *IMEV* 695 and CB 13 p. 172.

(19) *IMEV* 4227.

(20) *IMEV* 1545. Edited (inaccurately): R.H. Robbins, 'English almanacks of the fifteenth century', *Philological Quarterly* 18 (1939), 321–31 (322 fn. 4) and in James *Cat*.

5 For similar ecclesiastical texts see Cambridge, Gonville and Caius College 52/29 and cf. further refs. in the Index of Middle English Texts A: Titles.

6 See M. Benskin, 'In reply to Dr Burton', *LSE* NS 22 (1991), 207–62, n. 50: "A possible connection of part II with Salisbury, whether city or diocese, appears in the text of fols. 172v–75r, 'statua dominorum episcoporum Sarum'. The front flyleaf is

an independent document and clearly of Salisbury origin: Dr Richard Beadle regards it as the kind of waste vellum commonly picked up locally and used to protect the outermost leaf of a manuscript proper. The text comprises two lists, (i) of the altars in Salisbury Cathedral, and (ii) 'nomina Regum in ecclesia Sarum', ending with Richard II. (For the text, see James, p. 23). A connection with Chichester is suggested by a dedication to Sompting Church, *anno* 1246, added to the Kalendar at the end of the volume (fols. 244–45); but this is in part III, and therefore no evidence for the origins of part II. Neither need it go against Salisbury as the place where parts I–III were bound together: as a verdict on the whole volume, James's 'Probably from Chichester' (p. 22) goes beyond the evidence. N.R. Ker rejected ascriptions both to Salisbury and Chichester [*Med Lib*, p. 339]; but he was concerned only with the holdings of named libraries and his strictures can preclude neither city as the manuscript's place of origin".
7 English in one hand except fol. 57v.
8 The language accords best with Salisbury, Wilts. *LALME* LP 5380.

1 Cambridge, Fitzwilliam Museum, McClean 123.
2 C13b2–C14a1 (*ca.* 1300).
3 [λ] *The Nuneaton Codex*, mostly French with some Latin. English on fol. 114v names of four English graphs; fols. 115r–120r *Poema Morale* beg. [þ]e holi gostes miȝte us all helpe & diȝte ... [I]ch am elder þane ich pas of pintre & of lore.
4 CB Reg i 156. Wells VII.25. *IMEV* 1272. Fol. 114v edited: Anna C. Paues, 'The name of the letter ȝ', *MLR* 6 (1911), 441–54 (442). *Poema Morale* edited: Anna C. Paues, 'A newly discovered manuscript of the *Poema Morale*', *Anglia* 30 (1907), 217–37. Cf. Hill 1977, and references therein.
5 *Poema Morale* survives in seven copies for which see the Index of Middle English Texts A: Titles, where MSS containing short quotations from the text are also listed.
6 Inscription of ownership of Nuneaton Priory, Warwicks. Ker *Med Lib*, p. 140. MS came into the possession of the Convent of Cistercian Nuns at Nuneaton in C14 (see Hill, p. 110 and fn. cited there).
7 *Poema Morale* in one hand.
8 MLS believes the language to be of Essex with some western admixture (Hill, p. 110). For a preliminary study of the language of the seven surviving copies of the *Poema Morale* see Laing 'Versions'.

1 Cambridge, Gonville and Caius College 52/29.
2 C13.
3 [λ] Latin tracts and sermons. On fol. 43r, *Creed, Pater Noster, Ave Maria, In Manus Tuas* in English.
4 Wells VI.11 and XIII.178 (Wells refers to this MS as "Caius College Cbg. 44"). *IPMEP* 171, 316. Edited (very inaccurately): *Rel Ant* i 282.
5 For similar ecclesiastical texts see Cambridge, Emmanuel College 27 and cf. further refs. in the Index of Middle English Texts A: Titles.
6 Apparently no indication as to provenance.
7 English in one hand. The scribe uses a single þ-like symbol for þ and y.
8 Language perhaps of Ely or Norfolk.

1 Cambridge, Gonville and Caius College 95/47.
2 C13b2 (not C15 as in James *Cat*).
3 [γ] A medical MS containing on pp 1–3 a short list of *synonyma* with English and French equivalents to Latin plant names. The first list is followed by another on pp. 3–6 which contains only two vernacular glosses.
4 See Hunt *Plant Names*, p. xxii and James *Cat* 1, pp. 94–96.

1 Cambridge, Gonville and Caius College 136/76.
2 C13b2.

3 [γ] MS containing grammatical works in Latin by Alexander Neckham (pp. 1–20), Adam of Petit Pont (pp. 21–30) and John of Garland (pp. 31–44 and 163–227). Also, pp. 45–52 *Distigium* or *Cornutus Antiquus*; pp. 52–55 *Merarium*; pp. 71–84, 125–30 the *Neutrale* and treatise on deponent verbs attributed to Adam Nutzard and pp. 131–162 *Liber Hymnorum*. The MS has a marginal commentary and interlinear glosses in Latin, French and English. Most of the vernacular glosses are French but some are English.
4 James *Cat* 1, pp. 147–49. MS also described P. Meyer, 'Les manuscrits français de Cambridge IV. Gonville et Caius College', *Romania* 36 (1907), 482–502 and Hunt *Teaching* 1, pp. 166, 178, 192, 299, 325, 349. Vernacular glosses edited: Hunt *Teaching* 1, pp. 41–42, 152–53, 159–60, and scattered through pp. 328–48 and 349–68 (Latin and Anglo-Norman only); *Teaching* 2, pp. 37–54, 65–81 and 82, 125–45 (Hunt's MS C).
6 Inscription of ownership indicates that the MS was a King's Lynn book. Ker *Med Lib*, p. 127.

1 Cambridge, Gonville and Caius College 221/236.
2 C13a2–b1.
3 [λ] Sermons in Latin. English appears as follows.
   (1) On the margin of fol. 18v is a scrap of verse *Wayloway so dere boht / þat it sal þus ben.*
   (2) Fol. 22r four irregular lines on the folly of the world beg. *Of is lif of foly & of synn þorw lawe.*
   (3) Fol. 47v, a verse in English, beg. *kyneriche wel idist.*
Richard Beadle reports on the lower margins of fols. 22r and 24r–v, almost illegible, some English rhymed divisions.
4 (1) *IMEV Suppl* 3899.6 and cf. R.H. Robbins, 'Middle English lyrics: handlist of new texts', *Anglia* 83 (1965), 35–47 (47)
   (2) *IMEV Suppl* 2627.5.
   (3) CB Reg i 205. Wells *Suppl* 1, p. 974 (VII.12). Hartung 5 XIII.12. *IMEV* 1824. Wenzel 1986, p. 85 fn. 75.
6 Richard Beadle (pers. comm.) thinks the MS likely to be East Anglian, judging from the names of certain friars which appear in the margins.
7 The hand of fol. 47v is different from the hand or hands of fols. 22r and 24r–v.

1 Cambridge, Gonville and Caius College 234/120.
2 C13b2.
3 [λ] Pp. 1–185 contain extracts from *Ancrene Riwle* ("MS G").
4 Wells VI.40. Severs 2 VI.1. Hall i IX, ii 355–88. *IPMEP* 559. See also Dahood *AW*. Edited: R.M. Wilson, *The English Text of the Ancrene Riwle*, with an introduction by N.R. Ker, EETS OS 229 (1954, for 1948, repr. 1957). Cf. Dobson *Origins*.
5 For other EME texts of *Ancrene Riwle* see the Index of Middle English Texts A: Titles. Later ME versions are to be found in Cambridge, Magdalene College, Pepys 2498; BL Royal 8 C i; Bodley, Eng. poet. a. 1, the Vernon MS.
7 One hand throughout.

1 Cambridge, Gonville and Caius College 351/568.
2 C13b2.
3 [λ] MS of sermons etc. in Latin containing English verse as follows.
   (1) Fol. 97r a couplet in an exemplar of a bishop of low birth reminding himself of his humble origins: *understond wel gris wat ȝou were and wat þu ert. and hou þou dru þi fader cart.*
   (2) Fol. 98r a couplet: *[W]ho þat wol nyde clippe and kisse aboute mydnyth / he scheld duelle in þe pyne of helle mid þat ys rith.*
   (3) Fol. 102v a six-line stanza from *The Proverbs of Hending* beg. *Meni man syngat / wan he hom bringat / A fayr yung wyf.*
   (4) Fol. 102v a warning to sinners beg. *Ho þat wol nyde hore be.*

4 James *Cat* 1, p. 398. CB Reg i 526.
   (1) Wilson 1943, p. 52. Cf. Wenzel 1974 no. 78.
   (2) Wenzel 1974 no. 90.
   (3) Wenzel 1974 no. 38. Cf. also Wenzel 1978, p. 95 and *IMEV* 2078.
   (4) Wells *Suppl* 6, p. 1457 (VII.13b). *IMEV* 4110.
5 For item (1) cf. similar lines in BL Cotton Claudius D vii. For MSS containing all or part of *The Proverbs of Hending* see the Index of Middle English Texts A: Titles.

1 Cambridge, Gonville and Caius College 365/728.
2 C13.
3 [λ] MS of late C12 containing Latin texts. Four flyleaves at each end are of C13 and contain part of Walter de Henley's *Hosbondria* (French). On the lower margin of fol. iii in the same hand is *þeys bet ȝe þre þat god for les / Holdman Gytles. Yongman recheles. Womman sameles.*
4 James *Cat* 2, pp. 414–15. *IMEV* 1820.

1 Cambridge, Gonville and Caius College 385/605.
2 C13b.
3 [γ] Collection of grammatical works in Latin, mostly by John of Garland, with interlinear and marginal glossing. Most of the vernacular glosses are French but some are English.
4 James *Cat* 2, pp. 441–46. MS also described M.B. Hackett, *The Original Statutes of Cambridge, The Text and its History* (Cambridge, 1970), pp. 166–67. Contents listed in Hunt *Teaching* 1, pp. 192 and 205. Vernacular glosses edited: Hunt *Teaching* 1, pp. 37, 137–38, 145–46, 150; and *Teaching* 2, pp. 81–82 and 125–46 (Hunt's MS C*).
6 The MS was given to the college by Roger Marchall. See A.B. Emden, *A Biographical Register of the University of Cambridge to 1500* (Cambridge, 1963), pp. 392–93 and C.E. Wright, *Fontes Harleiani* (London, 1972), p. 233. (Refs. from Hunt *Teaching* 1, p. 250 fn. 31.)
7 According to Hunt the glosses are in a number of different hands.

1 Cambridge, Gonville and Caius College 408/414.
2 C13.
3 [λ] Latin sermons in various hands. English couplets on fols. 135v beg. *teres tollet eyne bollet* and 150v beg. *Son [?] so he hauet coperun and te hod*. On fol. 258r is an English distich against the women's fashion of wearing horns: *pho haues hornes als ha ram. and ha neck als a swan And amidel als ha brock. ha tayl als ha pacoch*. James *Cat* 2, also mentions on fol. 127v seq. "a few English glosses in the margins" and that "on the margin of fol. 201 are some English words".
4 Hartung 5 XIII.136. *IMEV* 4093. For couplets see Wenzel 1974, nos. 55 and 62.
5 See the Index of Middle English Texts B: Incipits under *teres tollet*, etc. for other MSS containing these lines on the memory of Christ's passion.

1 Cambridge, Gonville and Caius College 512/543.
2 C13b2.
3 [λ] Fol. 260v contains 8 lines of verse on the love of Christ written as prose in a volume of Latin sermons belonging to John Rudham, an East Anglian friar. Begins *Lytel wotyt onyman hu derne loue was fnde*.
4 CB Reg i 206. Wells *Suppl* 1, p. 986 (XIII.46). *IMEV* 1922. (Cf. Wells XIII.203, *IMEV* 1923.) CB13, pp. 235–36 and James *Cat* 2, p. 853.
5 This appears to be a religious adaptation of an originally secular love lyric. Cf. a different attempt to adapt the lyric, this time in praise of the BV, in BL Egerton 613 item (4). See also the two versions, one religious, one secular, in BL Harley 2253 items (49) and (50).
6 For evidence linking the MS with East Anglia see James *Cat*, pp. 581–83. Fol. 252v has a piece (in Latin) by Rudham on the see of East Anglia ending with a list of the

bishops of Norwich. East and West Rudham are about 6.5 miles west of Fakenham in NW Norfolk.
7 The hand of Friar John Rudham.
8 AM considers the language to be certainly East Anglian and probably early Norfolk. There is however too little text to allow for a more precise placing.

1 Cambridge, Gonville and Caius College 593/453.
2 C13b2 (s. xiii ex., Hunt *Teaching* 1, p. 157).
3 [γ] A collection of grammatical treatises in Latin including, fols. 54r–106r, John of Garland's *Compendium Grammaticae* with some glosses in French and English. A set of lexical notes on fol. 130v also includes vernacular items.
4 See Hunt *Teaching* 1, pp. 49 and 157–58.
6 The MS is a Cambridge book, see Hunt who refers to M.B. Hackett, *The Original Statutes of Cambridge University. The Text and its History* (Cambridge, 1970), p. 12, no. 1 and p. 348.

1 Cambridge, King's College, Muniment Roll 2 W. 32 verso.
2 C14a (*ca.* 1325, Saltmarsh).
3 [λ] Poem (with music) on the back of an official copy of a papal bull. The bull is dated 1199. The hand of the poem is certainly much later. Begins *Bryd one brere brid brid one brere.*
4 Wells *Suppl* 6, p. 1485 (XIII.25c). *IMEV* 521. Edited: D&H, p. 183. The unemended text is printed on p. 185, as if prose, as in the roll itself. See also John Saltmarsh, 'Two medieval love-songs set to music', *The Antiquaries Journal* 15 (1935), 1–12 (includes facsimile).
6 The papal bull formed part of the muniments of the priory of St James by Exeter.
7 One hand.
8 The language of the poem itself does not seem to be south-western but has features suggesting an origin in the south part of the East Anglian area, at least south of Norfolk. Has *qu* for OE *hw*, *d* for ð (*greid, greyd*), *Hic* "I", *quan* "when", *quit* "white", *yhe* "she", *mikte* "might", *sorwe* "sorrow".

1 Cambridge, Pembroke College 32.
2 C14a1.
3 [λ] (1) On fol. 153r is a short passage in English: *þat ich et þat ich hadde. þat ich gaf þat ich habbe. þat ich ay held þat i nabbe.*
(2) On fol. 153v appears *Welawey swych wenet wel to lede god lyf and blis underfo. and te ded lyd him to stranglen wydinnen hyse scho.*
4 James *Cat*, p. 35. Wells *Suppl* 2, p. 1064 (VII.12).
   (1) *IMEV Suppl* 3272.5
   (2) *IMEV* 3900.
See also Max Förster, 'Kleinere mittelenglische Texte', *Anglia* 42 (1918), 147. (Note that there is some confusion with the entries in *IMEV*: 1267.5 belongs not in Pembroke 32 but in Pembroke 82, q.v.)
6 On fol. 1 is a pressmark of the Abbey of Bury St Edmunds. Ker *Med Lib*, p. 17.

1 Cambridge, Pembroke College 82.
2 *C12b2–C13a1.
3 [λ] Verses on the originally blank recto of the first leaf (fol. 1r) of a C12 MS containing a *Vita S. Alexis* (fols. 1v–4r), Bede's *Historia ecclesiastica*, etc.
   (1) *Ynguar. and Ubbe. Beorn wæs þe þridde. loþebrokes sunes. loþe weren criste.*
   (2) *In clench qu becche under ane þorne. liet kenelm kinebern heued bereued.*
4 Ker 75. Wells *Suppl* 2, pp. 1052–53 (IV.4a). Hartung 5 XIII.7. *IMEV Suppl* 1267.5 and 1477.5. But these texts are referred to erroneously in the latter two works as belonging to Pembroke College 281, fol. 1r and Pembroke College 32, fol. 141v. On Lothbrog, Hinguar and Hubba see Wilson *Lost Lit*, pp. 34–38; on Kenelm ibid. pp. 99–100. See also Murakami, p. 89, no. 21.

5 Ker (p. 124) notes that "a leaf used in a former binding and now kept separately contains a carol in northern English dialect, s. xiv." For other copies see *IMEV* 378.
6 Ker: "In the margin is added, s. xiii 'Versus do*mp*ni Iohannis primi abbatis de sancto albano [John de Cella, abbot 1195–1214] ...'". The MS almost certainly belonged to the cell of St Albans at Tynemouth (Ker, p. 124). See also Ker *Med Lib*, p. 191.

1 Cambridge, Pembroke College 100.
2 C13.
3 [λ] Distinctiones and Latin sermons. Two English couplets on fol. 114v:
   (1) *Quo sabet* [i.e. whoso haveth] *long ligge in sinne nu is tyme þat e blinne*.
   (2) *Zanne is to late Zanne the wlf etc*. [i.e. is at the gate].
4 Wells *Suppl* 2, p. 1064 (VII.12). Wenzel 1974, no. 92. Wenzel 1978, pp. 94–95. The second couplet is from *The Proverbs of Hending;* cf. *IMEV Suppl* 228.5.
6 *Ex libris* inscription indicates ownership by the Abbey of Bury St Edmunds (fol. 1 "Lib. monach S. Ed. S. 57."). Ker *Med Lib*, p. 19.

1 Cambridge, Pembroke College 101.
2 C13.
3 [γ] Fol. 83r contains a short list of Old English legal terms followed by definitions in French.
4 Hunt *Teaching* 1, p. 54.
6 MS from Bury St Edmunds. Ker *Med Lib*, p. 19.

1 Cambridge, Pembroke College 113.
2 C13.
3 [γ] In a C13 hand, a few vernacular glosses (including some in English) to a text of Juvenal on fols. 1r–35r.
4 Hunt *Teaching* 1, p. 62.
6 MS association with the Abbey of Bury St Edmunds rejected by Ker *Med Lib*, p. 22.

1 Cambridge, Pembroke College 169.
2 C13b2.
3 [γ] A copy of Gilbertus Anglicus, *Compendium medicinae* containing on the recto of the penultimate folio (no modern foliation) a single-column miscellany in a late thirteenth-century hand of 45 Latin plant names with vernacular (French or English) equivalents.
4 See Hunt *Plant Names*, pp. xx–xxi and James *Cat*, pp. 163 seq.
7 English in one hand.

1 Cambridge, Pembroke College 258.
2 C13–C14.
3 [λ] A MS of many volumes containing *Narrationes*, etc. Contains English as follows.
   (1) Fol. 129r the English quatrain beg. *Nou goth þe sonne under wode* appearing in the French text of Edmund Riche's *Speculum Ecclesie*.
   (2) Fol. 134v three couplets on three sorrowful things beg. *Eueri day me come ʒ tiþinge þre*.
   (3) Fol. 135v three lines on a thief beg. *þre þinges it ben þat I hold pris*.
   (4) Fol. 136r *Yis world hymn pleynez of mikel ontrewe / Ryt is ded ant yat is reweze / Falsnesse regnez ant is aboue / Nou is buried trew loue*.
   (5) Fol. 141v *Murie a tyme I telle in may / Wan bricte blosmen brekez on tre / Yeise foules singe nyt ant day / In ilche grene is gamen an gle*.
4 (1) *IMEV Suppl* 2320/A15.
   (2) *IMEV Suppl* 738.5 (cf. *IMEV Suppl* 695).
   (3) *IMEV Suppl* 3711.5.
   (4) CB Reg i 226. Wells *Suppl* 1, p. 975 (VII.14a). *IMEV* 3650. For variants see *IMEV* 2145 and 2146. See also Wenzel 1986, p. 191.

(5) Wells *Suppl* 1, p. 987 (XIII.9a). *IMEV* 2162. Edited: Theo Stemmler, *Die englischen Liebesgedichte des MS. Harley 2253* (Bonn, 1962), p. 20 and Wilson *Lost Lit*, p. 169.

Both (4) and (5) are printed in James *Cat*.

5 For other MSS containing item (1), including the English quatrain, see the Index of Texts in French. Other versions of item (4) appear in Oxford, Merton College 248, fol. 166v (item (36)); Oxford, Balliol College 227, fol. 258r; Bodley, Hatton 107, fol. 1v.

6 James says the MS might have been compiled by a parish priest: "The presence of St Hugh, rather prominent, suggests Lincolnshire".

1 Cambridge, Peterhouse 215.

2 C13b.

3 [γ] MS containing school texts and grammatical works in Latin, heavily glossed. Many of the glosses are in the vernacular. Most of the English glosses appear in Alexander of Villa Dei's *Doctrinale* on fols. 30v–59r.

4 James *Cat*, pp. 257–61. For contents see also Hunt *Teaching* 1, p. 72 and for the glosses, Hunt *Teaching* 2, pp. 23–26 and 5–9.

1 Cambridge, St John's College 15 (A.15).

2 C13a2–b1

3 [λ] Latin sermons, etc. of C13–C15. English on fol. 72r, two short pieces, (1) and (2), 21 lines in all:

(1) a version of the lyric *My Leman on the Rood* beg. *Wenne hic soe on rode idon*;

(2) a version of *Respice in Faciem*, beg. *Loke to þi louerd man þar hanget he arode*.

(3) Fol. 120v English translation of *Candet Nudatum Pectus* beg. *Hwyt was hys nakede brest and his blodi side*. The third line is missing in this copy.

4 CB Reg i 228.

(1) Wells *Suppl* 5, p. 1365 (XIII.107b). *IMEV* 3965. CB13 35A.

(2) Wells *Suppl* 1, p. 987 (XIII.114). *IMEV* 1943. CB14 2B.

For (3) see Wells *Suppl* 1, p. 987 (XIII.116), *IMEV* 4088 and Thomson *Candet* though he does not print this version.

5 A variant text of item (1) is in BL Royal 12 E i, fol. 194v. Cf. also CB13 36 and 37. A shorter version of (2) is to be found in Bodley 42, fol. 250r. For other versions of these and of *Candet Nudatum Pectus* see the Index of Middle English Texts A: Titles.

6 According to Thomson the hand at least is to be associated with the area between Cambridge and Bury St Edmunds.

7 English in one hand.

1 Cambridge, St John's College 62 (C.12).

2 C13b1 (*ca.* 1250–75, *OBMEV*).

3 [λ] Latin sermons, etc. English on fol. 126v: six rhyming lines, written as prose, on the memory of the passion beg. *Loverd þi passion. Who þe þenchet arist þar on* and continuing *teres hit tollet / and eyen hit bollet*.

4 CB Reg i 229. Wells *Suppl* 5, p. 1367 (XIII.136a). *IMEV* 1977. CB13 56B. *OBMEV* 268.

5 For other versions see under *teres tollet*, etc. in the Index of Middle English Texts B: Incipits.

7 English in one hand.

1 Cambridge, St John's College 111 (E.8).

2 C13b2.

3 [λ] Exerpta — mostly Latin religious verse and prose. English on fol. 106v: a version (incomplete) of *Stabat iuxta Christi crucem*, beg. *Stand wel moder vnder rode*. The English is written parallel with the Latin text and the words are accompanied by music. (French texts are on fols. 106r and 107r: poem on the Day of Judgement and a recipe.)

4 CB Reg i 229. Wells *Suppl* 1, p. 988 (XIII.129) (cf. *Suppl* 5, p. 1358 (IX.3)). Hartung 3 VII.1(r). *IMEV* 3211. CB13, p. 203 notes. D&H, pp. 152–53.
5 For other texts of *Stabat iuxta Christi crucem* see the Index of Middle English Texts A: Titles.
7 English in one hand.

1 Cambridge, St John's College 112 (E.9).
2 C13b2–C14a1 (*ca.* 1300).
3 [λ] *Veritas Theologica Distinctiones*, etc. in Latin. Fol. 400r contains twelve macaronic lines in Anglo-Norman and English linking the Abuses of the Age to Edward I.
4 Hartung 5 XIII.80. *IMEV* and *IMEV Suppl* 1857. Edited: James *Cat*, p. 146.
5 Another version is in Edinburgh, National Library of Scotland, Advocates' 19.2.1, the Auchinleck MS.
6 *Ex libris* inscription indicates the MS is from Durham Priory. Ker *Med Lib*, p. 62.

1 Cambridge, St John's College 120 (E.17).
2 C12b2 (?a1300, *MED Plan & Bibl*, 76b).
3 [γ] Sententiae, Abbreviatiae, etc. in Latin containing on fol. 216r a list of trees and their English equivalents.
4 Edited: James *Cat*, p. 155.

1 Cambridge, St John's College 145 (F.8).
2 C13.
3 [λ] Fragments (about 18 fols.) from a wrapper contain parts of *The Proverbs of Hending*; (also a page of French relating to the Virgin, and sermons, etc.)
4 CB Reg i 230. Wells *Suppl* 1, p. 973 (VII.6). *IMEV* 1669. Edited: G. Schleich, 'Zu den Sprichwörten Hendings', *Anglia* 52 (1928), 350–61. Cf. 'Die Sprichwörter Hendings und die Prouerbis of Wysdom', *Anglia* 51 (1927), 220–77.
5 Other MSS containing all or part of *The Proverbs of Hending* are listed in the Index of Middle English Texts A: Titles.
6 Accounts mention Northampton and Billing Manor near Northampton.

1 Cambridge, St John's College 255 (S.19).
2 C13–C14.
3 [λ] Sermon collection in Latin. On the lower margins of p. 534, a quatrain warning against death and beg. *Al þat ys shal com to was.*
4 Wenzel 1974, no. 4. James *Cat*: "English words and phrases are of fairly frequent occurrence". Sermons are listed by J.-B. Schneyer, *Repertorium der lateinischen Sermones des Mittelalters* 7 (Münster, 1976), pp. 202–212, but he makes no mention of English phrases.
7 There are at least two hands in the MS, one of C13 the other C13–C14: information from Richard Beadle.

1 Cambridge, Trinity College 43 (B.1.45).
2 C13b2 (*ca.* 1275–1300, *OBMEV*).
3 [λ] Latin except for fols. 19v–24r line 13, sermons in French and then English as follows.
  (1) Fol. 24r–v two verses beg. *Liþer lok and tuingling* and *Ne leue leuedi ne be þi wimpil neuere so Ielu.* Thereafter the sermon beg. *Bernardus. Quamdiu fuero* followed by a brief note in English (edited: Dobson *AR*, p. cxliii).
  (2) Fols. 41v–42r sermon beg. *Atte wrastling mi lemman iches and atte ston kasting i him for les.*
  (3) Fol. 42r *The Ten Commandments* in five rhyming couplets (each couplet written on a single line) beg. *Ne haue þou no god botin on.*
  (4) Fol. 73v verse beg. *Wanne mine eyhnen misten.*
4 See Dobson *AR*, pp. cxl–clxxii. James *Cat* 1, pp. 56–59. CB Reg i 234.

(1) *IMEV* 1917 and 2285. Wells *Suppl* 2, p. 1056 (V.3a) (cf. Wells *Suppl* 4, p. 1265 (V.3c)). *IPMEP* 552.
(2) Wells *Suppl* 2, p. 1057 (V.3b) and p. 1075 (XIII.1a). *IMEV* 445. *IPMEP* 432. *OBMEV* 274. *Sec Lyr* xxxix (and cf. CUL Ii.III.8, fol. 87r).
(3) Wells VI.15. Hartung 7 XX.42. *IMEV* 2286 (cf. 3684). CB13 70A (and cf. versions in CUL Ff.VI.15; Oxford, University College 96, fol. 109v and Cambridge, Emmanuel College 27, fol. 162r).
(4) Wells *Suppl* 1, p. 977 (VII.27). *IMEV* 3998. CB13 71. *OBMEV* 24.
Also edited: (fols. 24r and 42r) M. Förster, 'Kleine Mitteilungen zur mittelenglischen Lehrdichtung', *Archiv* 104 (1900), 293–309 (303–304) (with variants from Cotton Cleopatra C vi); (prose texts with Cleopatra version of the St Bernard sermon parallel to Trinity), M. Förster, 'Kleinere mittelenglische Texte', *Anglia* 42 (1918), 147–54. All the texts, both verse and prose also edited by Carleton Brown, 'Texts and the man', *Modern Humanities Research Association* vol. ii, no. 5 (1928), 97–111 (104–108). CB's texts in general not as scholarly as Förster's (Dobson). Dobson *AR*, p. cxliii fn. 5 provides corrections to Förster's text. Facsimile of fol. 24r–v in Dobson *AR*, opp. p. 110.

5 The verses on fol. 24r–v both appear in BL Cotton Cleopatra C vi, also the sermon that follows.
7 Dobson notes (*AR*, p. cliv) that the English texts on fols. 24r–v, 41r–v were written by scribe D of BL Cotton Cleopatra C vi whose language AM associates with NW Norfolk (AM *Havelok*). Dobson says that D, both in Trinity and Cleopatra, manifests two different scribal styles, one more formal (e.g. Cleo fols. 23r–v, 199, Trin 42r), one "semi-cursive" (e.g. Cleo fol. 57v, Trin 41v–42r). The hand of fol. 73v is different.
8 NW Norfolk.

1 Cambridge, Trinity College 108 (B.3.29).
2 C13.
3 [λ] MS of Isaias Glosatus (C12b2) containing on fol. 114r, in pencil, in a hand of C13 four lines attributed to King Alfred on the *Abuses of the Age*: [Ald man] witles / yung man recheles / wyman ssameles / betere ham were lifles.
4 Wells *Suppl* 1, p. 974. *IMEV* 1820. See James *Cat* 1, pp. 130–31.
5 Cf. the versions beg. *Bissop lorles*, etc. in BL Harley 913, item (2) and *King conseilles*, etc. in BL Cotton Cleopatra C vi, item (2).
6 MS from Christ Church, Canterbury. Ker *Med Lib*, p. 3.

1 Cambridge, Trinity College 323 (B.14.39). (Bound together with 324 (B.14.40) of C14–C15.)
2 C13b2 (1275–1300, *OBMEV*; after 1253, CB13, p. xx fn. 1).
3 [λ] Fols. 87. James *Cat* notes 43 pieces (some subdivided), in prose and verse, in Latin, Anglo-Norman and English. English is as follows.
 (1) Fol. 19r admonition to alms-giving in Latin and English; English beg. *vid word & wrid ic warne þe sire ode*.
 (1b) (Perhaps part of (1).) Fol. 19r six lines beg. *de marmien þu depis ezechiel / Biþenc þe nu suiþe wel*.
 (2) Fols. 20r–24r, *Life of St Margaret* beg. *Olde ant yonge i preit ou*.
 (3) Fol. 24r lyric in alternate French and English stanzas, English beg. *Louerd crist þou hauest us boust*.
 (4) Fol. 24v macaronic hymn to the BV beg. *Seinte mari moder milde*.
 (5) Fol. 24v macaronic song in praise of the BV beg. *For on þat is so feir ant brist*.
 (6) Fol. 25r hymn of the Five Joys beg. *Seinte marie leuedi brist*.
 (7) Fol. 25r four lines on Sir Eode beg. *bisete þine ponevis sire eode*.
 (8) Fol. 25v three lines against oath breaking: *Wose is ene firsuoren; he is ever firt / bote he come to amendement / lif & soule he wrt iscent*.
 (9) Fol. 25v lyric on the BV beg. *Ful feir flour is þe lilie*.

(10) Fols. 26r–27r Homily for the anniversary of St Nicholas consisting of English paraphrases of Biblical texts and beg. *Yc ou rede ye sitten stille.*
(11) Fol. 27r fragment of a debate between Body and Soul beg. *Nou is mon hol & soint.*
(12) Fol. 27v: *Bi þench þe wat þe wole bitiden yf þou so dest; ar þou biginne þat þou habbe god endinge.*
(13) Fol. 27v couplet: *Ic chule bere to wasscen doun iþe toun / þat was blac ant þat was broun.*
(14) Fol. 27v seven lines on penance beg. *Penaunce is in herte reusinge.*
(15) Fol. 28r lyric beg. *Say me viit in þe brom.*
(16) Fol. 28r three couplets on bequeathing worldly possessions beg. *Godefrey þe guede.*
(17) Fol. 28r two couplets beg. *A þeif of is treunesse to widnesse drou.*
(18) Fol. 28r ten lines beg. *A vidue pouere was & freo.*
(19) Fol. 28r four lines on the signs of death beg. *wenne þin eþen beit ihut.*
(20) Fol. 28r a couplet tag beg. *hic am michel of airas.*
(21) Fol. 28r a tag on lazy clerics beg. *longe scleparis ouerleparis.*
(22) Fol. 28v four short lines paraphrasing Latin 'Non humilis paruus' beg. *wen þe rede is god.*
(23) Fol. 28v proverbs: *Serue & sai leit & beit*, etc.
(24) Fol. 28v three six-line stanzas translating 'Gaude virgo mater christi' and beg. *Glade us maiden moder milde.*
(25) Fol. 29r *The Ten Commandments* beg. *Hawe on god in wrchipe.*
(26) Fols. 29v–32r *Debate of the Body and Soul* beg. *In an þestrei stude ic stod.*
(27) Fols. 32v–33r lyric on the Resurrection beg. *On leome is in þis world ilist.*
(28) Fol. 33v five couplets beg. *vuele men goid þe siechen.*
(29) Fol. 34r *The Bargain of Judas* beg. *Hit wes up-on a scereþorsday.*
(30) Fol. 35r–v (and parts of a draft in plummet on the lower margins of fols. 36r–38r, 41v–42r) story of the Magi and Herod beg. *Wolle ye iheren of twelte day.*
(31) Fols. 36r–42r *Old Testament History* beg. *Louerd asse þu ard on god.*
(32) Fol. 42r four lines on how to find Easter from St Benet's Day beg. *Ate feste of seint benedist.*
(33) Fol. 42v six lines on the health of body and soul beg. *liuis firist & licames hele.*
(34) Fol. 42v a prayer to the BV beg. *Leuedie ic þonke þe wid herte suiþe milde.*
(35) Fol. 43r–v *Doomsday* beg. *Wenne Hi þenche on domes dai.*
(36) Fols. 43v line 19–45v *The Latemest Day* beg. *Þene latemeste dai wenne we sulen farren.*
(37) Fol. 46r three line tag translating Latin 'Lento pede procedet divinitas' beg. *Godis wreche late arecheit.*
(38) Fol. 46r couplet beg. *Eueir asse mon liuit lengore.*
(39) Fol. 47r ten lines on the beasts produced by parts of the dead body beg. *Wose wartt wid pritte abeit amadde.*
(40) Fol. 47v lyric on mortality beg. *Wen þe turuf is þi tuur.*
(41) Fol. 47v three lines on the lowliness of Christ beg. *Of one stable was is halle.*
(42) Fol. 81v song in praise of the BV beg. *Nu þis fules singet.*
(43) Fols. 81v–82r *Orison to Our Lady* beg. *On hire is al mi lif ylong.*
(44) Fol. 83v fourteen lines paraphrasing 'Aspice mitissime conditor' beg. *þu þad madist alle þinc.*
(45) Fol. 83v meditation on the Passion beg. *Wose seþe on rode.*
(46) Fol. 84r address to the body on the bier beg. *Nu þu vnseli bodi.*
(47) Fol. 84r seven lines on the Old Testament worthies beg. *Abel was looset in treunesse.*
(48) Fols. 85r–87v *The Proverbs of Alfred* beg. *At siforde setin kinhis monie.*

4 CB Reg i 236–37. Hartung 6 XV.1. Described in James *Cat* 1, pp. 438–47 and CB13, pp. xx–xxii. See also, H.A. Person, *Cambridge Middle English Lyrics* (Seattle, 1962); R.T. Davies *Medieval English Lyrics* (London, 1963); Karl Reichl,

Religiöse Dichtung im englischen Hochmittelalter. Untersuchung und Edition der Handschrift B.14.39 des Trinity College in Cambridge (Wilhelm Fink Verlag, Munich, 1973) and K. Brunner, 'Zwei Gedichte aus der Handschrift Trinity College Cambridge 323 (B.14.39)', *EStn* 70 (1936), 221–43.

(1) Wells *Suppl* 5, p. 1364 (XIII.7a). *IMEV* 4211. CB13 14.
(1b) James *Cat*, p. 439.
(2) Wells V.52. *IMEV* 2672. Edited: Hickes's Thesaurus 1 (Oxford, 1705), p. 224; C. Horstmann, *Altenglische Legenden*, Neue Folge (Heilbronn, 1881), pp. 489–98 (cf. O. Cockayne, *Seinte Marherete*, EETS OS 13 (1866), pp. 34–43).
(3) Wells *Suppl* 5, p. 1367 (XIII.172a). *IMEV* 1949. CB13 15.
(4) Wells XIII.188. *IMEV* 2995. CB13 16.
(5) Wells XIII.189. *IMEV* 2645. CB13 17A.
(6) Wells XIII.210. *IMEV* 2992. CB13 18.
(7) *IMEV* 522. CB13, p. 176.
(8) James *Cat*, p. 440.
(9) Wells *Suppl* 5, p. 1368 (XIII.183a). *IMEV* 885. CB13 19.
(10) Wells *Suppl* 5, pp. 1350–51 (V.3d); Wells *Suppl* 6, p. 1457 (VII.13c) and cf. Wells *Suppl* 8, pp. 1669, 1673 (V.3d, VII.13c). *IMEV* 1405. Edited: Carleton Brown, 'An early mention of a St Nicholas play in England', *Studies in Philology* 28 (1931), 594–601.
(11) Wells IX.1 (and cf. Wells *Suppl* 4, pp. 1272–73). Hartung 3 VII.18(d). *IMEV* 2336. CB13 20.
(12) James *Cat*, p. 441.
(13) *IMEV Suppl* 1389.5. *OBMEV* 275.
(14) *IMEV* 2746.
(15) Wells *Suppl* 5, p. 1364 (XIII.11a). Hartung 3 VII.62. *IMEV* 3078. CB13 21A. D&W XXVII. *OBMEV* 28.
(16) *IMEV* 995.
(17) *IMEV* 98.
(18) *IMEV* 106.
(19) *IMEV* 4046.
(20) *IMEV Suppl* 1276.3.
(21) *IMEV* 1935.
(22) *IMEV Suppl* 4040.3.
(23) James *Cat*, p. 442. Cf. Bodley, Ashmole 1285 and *IMEV* 3200.
(24) Wells *Suppl* 5, p. 1364 (XIII.43a). *IMEV* 912. CB13 22.
(25) Wells *Suppl* 5, p. 1352 (VI.15). Hartung 7 XX.42. *IMEV* 1129. CB13 23.
(26) Wells IX.1. Hartung 3 VII.18(f). *IMEV* 1461 (cf. *IMEV* 2336).
(27) Wells *Suppl* 5, p. 1366 (XIII.133a). *IMEV* 293. CB13 24.
(28) *IMEV* 747 cited erroneously as fol. 93v.
(29) Wells V.48. *IMEV* 1649. CB13 25. *OBMEV* 30.
(30) Wells VIII.34. Severs 2 IV.43. *IMEV* 4170. CB13 26 and notes.
(31) Wells *Suppl* 5, pp. 1356–57 (VIII.1a). Severs 2 IV.50. *IMEV* 1946 and edited: Brunner, op. cit., *EStn* 70 (1936), 231.
(32) *IMEV* 426.
(33) *IMEV* 1924.
(34) Wells *Suppl* 5, p. 1368 (XIII.183b). *IMEV* 1836. CB13 27. *OBMEV* 29.
(35) Wells *Suppl* 1, p. 977 (VII.32). Hartung 3 VII.18(g). *IMEV* 3967. CB13 28A.
(36) Wells *Suppl* 5, p. 1356 (VII.36). Hartung 3 VII.18(h). *IMEV* 3517. CB13 29A.
(37) *IMEV Suppl* 1001.5.
(38) *IMEV Suppl* 733.3.
(39) *IMEV* 4119.
(40) Wells *Suppl* 5, p. 1356 (VII.37a). *IMEV* 4044. CB13 30. D&W XXXIV.
(41) Wells *Suppl* 5, p. 1364 (XIII.45a). *IMEV* 2644. CB13, p. 192.
(42) Wells XIII.205. *IMEV* 2366. CB13 31.
(43) Wells XIII.201. *IMEV* 2687. CB13 32A. Cf. D&H, pp. 130–31.
(44) Wells *Suppl* 5, p. 1365 (XIII.107a). *IMEV* 3696. CB13 33.
(45) Wells *Suppl* 5, p. 1366 (XIII.123). *IMEV* 4141. CB13 34.

(46) Hartung 3 VII.18(j). *IMEV* 2369. CB13 38.
(47) *IMEV* 109.
(48) Wells VII.5. *IMEV* 433. Edited: Arngart *P of A*; esp. vol. 1, pp. 7 and 130–33 and vol. 2, pp. 30–34. This text contains eight sections at the end not present in the J or M texts but probably once present in the C text, (Arngart *P of A* 1, pp. 111–15). Cf. also W.W. Skeat, *The Proverbs of Alfred* (Oxford, 1907); H.P. South, *The Proverbs of Alfred, Studied in the Light of the Recently Discovered Maidstone MS* (New York, 1931); R. Wülcker, 'Über die neuangelsächsischen Sprüche des Königs Aelfred', *Beiträge zur Geschichte der deutschen Sprache u. Literatur hrsg. v. H. Paul u. W. Braune* 1 (Halle, 1874), 240–62 and E. Ekwall, *Beiblatt zur Anglia* 21 (1910), 77, who points out that the metre of the last five sections of T differs from the rest in that they are throughout in rhyming couplets.

5 This MS shares texts with several others. Cf. especially BL Cotton Caligula A ix, Bodley, Digby 86 and Oxford, Jesus College 29. For correspondences with these and other MSS see the cross references to titles and incipits in the Indexes of Middle English Texts.

6 On fol. 83 appears a Latin epitaph of Bishop Robert Grosseteste of Lincoln (*ob.* 1253). The language, however, is not East Midland in character (see below).

7 At least four hands contribute to the MS.
Hand A wrote fols. 19r, 25v, 27r col. 2, i.e. (1), (1b), (9) and (11) (CB13 nos. 14, 19 and 20). (These contributions are perhaps rather later than the rest.)
Hand B wrote fols. 20r–25r, 26r–27r col. 1, 27v, 34r, 35r–v, i.e. (2)–(6), (10), (12)–(14), (29), (30) (CB13 nos. 15–18, 25, 26; *Life of St Margaret* and the sermon for the anniversary of St Nicholas).
Hand C (considered by Skeat to be a Norman scribe; see W.W. Skeat, *The Proverbs of Alfred* (Oxford, 1907), xiv seq.) wrote fols. 28r–29r, 32r–33r, 36r–46r, 47r–v, 81v–82r, 83v–84r, 85r–87v, i.e. (15)–(25), (26) last 30 lines, (27), (31)–(40), (43)–(47) (CB13 nos. 21–24, 27–30, 32–34, 38; the last 30 lines of *The Debate of the Body and Soul* (fol. 32r); *The Old Testament History* and *The Proverbs of Alfred*).
Hand D wrote fols. 29v–31v and possibly 81v, i.e. (26) and (42) (*The Debate of the Body and Soul* except the last 30 lines, and possibly CB13 no. 31, which may however be in yet another hand).
Fol. 25r last four lines, fol. 25v first four lines and fol. 33v, i.e. (7), (8) and (28) may be in hand B or in a different hand again.

8 MLS places in W Worcs (*LALME* LP 7721). AM places the language of *The Proverbs of Alfred* in NW Worcs ('*The Proverbs of Alfred*: notes on the possible dialectal value of the four versions' (1986) unpubl.).

1 Cambridge, Trinity College 335 (B.14.52).

2 C12b. *Poema Morale* (s. xii^2, Parkes *Orrm*, p. 124). Trinity Homilies (s. xii ex., Parkes *Orrm*, p. 124).

3 [λ] Fols. 91. The opening gathering, which contains the *Poema Morale*, is foliated; the rest of the MS is paginated 1 to 157.
(1) Fols. 2r–9v *Poema Morale* beg. *Ich am nu elder þan ich þas a þintre & a lore.*
(2) Pp. 1 (also marked 10)–153 Trinity Homilies. (Pp. 154, 155 are blank.)
(3) Pp. 156–57 sermon on Isaiah, in a third hand.

4 Ker, p. xix (not included in the main part of the catalogue). James *Cat* 1, p. 459. CB Reg i 237.
(1) Wells VII.25. *IMEV* 1272. Hall i VIII, ii 312–54.
(2) Wells V.13 (cf. Wells *Suppl* 2, p. 1058). *IPMEP* 159. Hall i XII, ii 427–38. Edited: Morris *OEH* 2, pp. 3–219.
(3) Edited: Morris *OEH* 2, pp. 217–19.
For language see, O. Strauss, 'Die Sprache der mittelenglischen Predigtsammlung in der Handschrift B.14.52 des Trinity College, Cambridge', *Wien. Beitr. z. engl. Philol.* 45 (1916). Cf. A. Rynell, *The Rivalry of Scandinavian and Native Synonyms in Middle English*, Lund Studies in English 13 (Lund, 1948), 266 seq. Cf. also,

Parkes *Orrm*; AM *Havelok*; and for the *Poema Morale*, Hill 1977, and references therein.
5 Trinity shares five sermons and the *Poema Morale* with Lambeth Palace Library 487, edited Morris *OEH* 1. Compare in Morris the sermons Trinity iv – Lambeth vii; T xxv – L xvii; T xxvi – L xiii; T xxx – L xvi; T xxxii – L xv. The parallel texts reveal numerous interesting differences including some of a lexical kind. *Poema Morale* survives in seven copies for which see the Index of Middle English Texts A: Titles where MSS containing short quotations from the text are also listed.
6 Bequest of Archbishop Whitgift *ob*. 1604.
7 The MS is in three hands (here labelled A, B and C) see N.R. Ker, 'The scribes of the *Trinity Homilies*', *MÆ* 1 (1932), 138–40.

Hand A, fols. 1r–9v, pp. 1–24 (Morris 3/1–35/6); 27 (Morris 37/15–39/1); 53/15–53 bottom (Morris 73/1–73/7); 58/6 (3rd word)–58 bottom (Morris 77/26–79/11); 114/13–118/11 (Morris 161/3–165/27); 121–123 (Morris 169/20–173/22); 128–133 (Morris 179/15–187/31); 137 (Morris 191/33–193/22); 139 (Morris 195/20–197/8); 142–143/1 (first 5 words) (Morris 199/27–201/18); 151/1 (Morris 213/27–215/15).

Hand B, pp. 25–26 (Morris 35/6–37/15) (except *teð forð* p.25 lines 7–8, Morris 35/36 cf. Ker 140, fn.); 28–53/14 (Morris 39/2–?72/26) (Ker gives all of 53 to A but AM thinks B goes on to end of line 14 of p. 53 of MS); 54–58/6 ... *hem clensen* (Morris 73/8–77/26); 59–114/13 (Morris 79/11–161/3) — note however that Sermon xxiv (pp. 101 bottom half–104 top half, Morris 141/9–145/16) is in a language different from the rest of B (and from A). The hand however is definitely B — 118/11–120 (Morris 165/27–169/20); 124–128 (Morris 173/22–179/15); 134–136 (Morris 187/31–191/33); 138 (Morris 193/22–195/20); 140–141 (Morris 197/9–199/26); 143/1–151/1 (Morris 201/18–213/27); 152–153 (Morris 215/15–217/21).

Hand C, pp. 156–157 (Morris 217/22–219 (end)).

8 See Hill 1977, p. 107 where MLS is cited as believing the language to have a London provenance but of a type "influenced by immigration, perhaps from East Anglia". The language of hand B is of a somewhat more northerly character than that of hand A. For a preliminary study of the language of the seven surviving copies of the *Poema Morale* see Laing 'Versions'.

1 Cambridge, Trinity College 598 (R.3.18).

2 C13a2–b1 (*ca*. 1250, Hunt *Teaching*).
3 [γ] Fols. 45r–54v sporadic vernacular glossing, mainly in French but some English, to the Latin text of the *Satyrae* of Persius.
4 Hunt *Teaching* 1, pp. 61–62, 64. See also Hunt *Teaching* 1, p. 160 for vernacular glosses to the Pseudo-Boethian *De disciplina scolarium* on fols. 1r–11v of the MS.

1 Cambridge, Trinity College 609 (R.3.29).

2 C13.
3 [γ] Grammatical texts in Latin with some vernacular glosses (very few in English) to texts on fols. 70r–81r and 137r–168r.
4 See Hunt *Teaching* 1, pp. 62, 63, 89–90.
6 *Ex libris* inscription indicates the MS is from Holme Cultram, Cumberland. Ker *Med Lib*, p. 102.

1 Cambridge, Trinity College 724 (R.5.33).

2 *C13.
3 [δ] Fol. 106v, English bounds of the parish of Bassaleg (= Basselech, Monmouth) in a Latin diploma of Robert de Haia and his wife Gundred (original 1100 x 24 Oct 1118).
4 Pelteret 58.
6 MS from Glastonbury Abbey. Ker *Med Lib*, p. 90. Diploma concerns Glastonbury, Somerset and places in Monmouthshire.

1 Cambridge, Trinity College 770 (R.7.28).
2 *C12a2–b1.
3 [λ] P. 26 Bede's Death Song in the text of Cuthbert's *Epistola de obitu Bedae* which here forms part of the annal for the year 734 in *Chronicon Fani Sancti Neoti* or *Annales Asserii*.
4 Ker 88. Edited: Dobbie 1937, p. 90; David Dumville and Michael Lapidge, *The Annals of St Neots with Vita Prima Sancti Neoti*, *The Anglo-Saxon Chronicle: a Collaborative Edition*, vol. 17 (Cambridge, 1985), p. 31.
5 For other MSS containing Bede's Death Song see the Index of Old English Texts.
6 The contents and character of script associate the MS with Bury St Edmunds. Ker, p. 134: "The manuscript was written by scribes of Bury St Edmunds". See also Ker *Med Lib Suppl*, p. 6.

1 Cambridge, Trinity College 987 (R.17.1).
2 C12a2–b1.
3 [γ] Continuous gloss to Eadwine's Psalter. The Psalms are in Hebrew, Roman and Gallican versions, the Roman version being glossed in OE and the Hebrew in French. The Canticles lack the Hebrew version and Roman after the first six. The gloss is word for word except fols. 164r line 25 – 170v where a metrical translation (in a different hand from the gloss before and after) replaces the gloss.
4 Ker 91. Ed. F. Harsley, *Eadwine's Canterbury Psalter*, EETS OS 92 (1889, repr. 1973). Facsimile (reduced): M.R. James, *The Canterbury Psalter* (1935). For fols. 281v–282r, how the Apostles made the Creed, see Hartung 7 XX.40.
6 Written at Christ Church, Canterbury. Ker *Med Lib*, p. 33.
7 For details of other hands, including later C12 hands, see Ker, p. 136. According to Ker, the Latin text is in the hand of Eadwine but not the OE gloss. The OE and French glosses were added soon after the Latin text was written. The main hand of OE is tall and narrow. Ker identifies another rounder hand from fols. 141–164 line 24, 170v line 11 – 172v, 253r–266v.

1 Cambridge, Trinity College 1105 (O.2.1).
2 *C12b2 (1175–1200, *OBMEV*; s. xii^2, Ker).
3 [δ] [λ] *Liber Eliensis* (Cartulary). *Historia Eliensis Insulae* (Latin) containing, in Book 2, English as follows.
   (1) Fol. 79r (Ker cites as fol. 93), no. 85 a version of the Confessor's Writ, beg. *Ædwardus cyning gret ælle mine biscopes*.
   (2) Fols 87v–88r, poem of four lines beg. *Merie sungen ðe muneches binnen ely*.
4 Davis 366.
   (1) Sawyer 1100. Edited (with commentary): Laing 'Anchor texts', esp. pp. 38–40.
   (2) Wells XIII.1. Hartung 5 XIII.8. *IMEV* 2164. Edited: Ker 93 and *OBMEV* 264.
5 Cf. CUL, EDC 1, *Liber Eliensis* (Ker 113) and for other Ely cartularies containing copies of the Confessor's Writ see the Index of Old English Texts.
6 MS from Ely. Ker *Med Lib*, p. 78. The *Historia* is preceded by a calendar with Ely obits (see B. Dickins, 'The day of Byrhtnoth's death and other obits from a twelfth-century Ely kalendar', *LSE* 6 (1937), 14–24) and is followed by lives of Ely saints.

1 Cambridge, Trinity College 1145 (O.2.41).
2 *C12.
3 [δ] *Collectio Privilegiorum Eliensis Ecclesie*. Contains (p. 105) the Confessor's Writ in a C12 version. Latin charters with English bounds are on pp. 86–95.
4 Ker, p. xiv fn. 2. Cf. Ker, p. 137 fn. Davis 364. Sawyer as follows: S 780, S 781, S 907, S 1100. Confessor's Writ edited (with commentary): Laing 'Anchor texts', esp. pp. 38–40.
5 For other Ely cartularies containing copies of the Confessor's Writ see the Index of Old English Texts.
6 MS from Ely. Ker *Med Lib*, p. 78.

1 Cambridge, Trinity College 1149 (O.2.45).
2 C13b2 (*ca.* 1275, *OBMEV*).
3 [λ] Miscellanea in Latin with scraps of English as follows.
  (1) P. 4 devotional instruction and prayers in Latin, French and English: *Louerd ihesu crist ich ʒe bid for ʒe vif wunde*, etc.
  (2) P. 351 Latin sayings in Leonine hexameters. The scribe's intention was to give the original vernacular proverbs in French or English; spaces are left for them but only eighteen are provided of which fifteen are English.
4 (1) Edited: James *Cat* 3, p. 153.
  (2) See Wells VII.2. Cf. *IMEV Suppl* 3318.8, 3502.5, 3792.5, 3894.6, 3927.6 and 4079.8. *OBMEV* 301. Edited: M. Förster, 'Frühmittelenglische Sprichwörter', *EStn* 31 (1902), 1–20. Cf. Wenzel 1978, p. 74.
6 The contents and liturgical evidence associate the MS with Cerne Abbey, Dorset. Ker *Med Lib*, p. 49.

1 Cambridge, Trinity College 1337 (O.7.9).
2 C12–C13.
3 [γ] Collection of religious and grammatical texts in Latin lightly glossed in the vernacular. All the glosses are of C13; there are very few in English.
4 James *Cat* 3, pp. 351–61. See Hunt *Teaching* 1, pp. 167–68, 178. Vernacular glosses edited: Hunt *Teaching* 2, pp. 37–52 (Hunt's MS T), 86–90.
6 *Ex libris* inscription indicates the MS belonged to Buildwas Abbey, Salop. Ker *Med Lib*, p. 14.

1 Cambridge, Trinity College 1435 (O.9.23).
2 C13.
3 [λ] Contains the final part (1187 – end) of Roger of Hoveden's *Chronicle* including a prophecy in English verse beg. *þan þu seches in here hert yreret*.
4 MS described, as MS I, by Stubbs *Hoveden* 1, p. lxxxiv. English printed Stubbs *Hoveden* 3, p. 68 fn. 1. Cf. Wilson 1943, p. 46 and Richter 1979, p. 74.
5 for other MSS containing this text and the English prophecy see the Index of Texts in Latin under Roger of Hoveden.

1 Cambridge, Trinity Hall, MS 1.
2 *C15a.
3 [δ] Thomas of Elmham, *Historia Abbatiae S. Augustine*.
  (1) Fols. 70v–71r (*olim* 56v–57r) English bounds to charter of Offa concerning land in Kent.
  (2) Fol. 78r (*olim* 64r) copy of a writ of King William I (*ca.* 1067) concerning St Augustine's, Canterbury.
4 Davis 198. There is a C18 transcript in BL Harley 686.
  (1) is Sawyer 140 (B 207, K 119 and iii 380).
  (2) is Pelteret 6. See C. Hardwick, *Historia Monasterii S. Augustini Cantuariensis, by Thomas of Elmham*, RS 8 (1858), pp. 332 and 347.
6 St Augustine's, Canterbury. Ker *Med Lib*, p. 42.

1 Cambridge University Library, Additional 3020.
2 *C14.
3 [δ] The Red Book of Thorney Abbey, vol. 1 (vol. 2 is CUL Add 3021). A general cartulary containing English (mostly in bounds only) on fols. 15r–18r.
4 Davis 964. There are excerpts from this MS in BL Add 5937 (C16), fols. 131–133v, from which Birch and Kemble's versions derive, and in BL Lansdowne 994, fols. 72–115v. Sawyer as follows: fols. 15r–v S 931 (K 1308); fols. 15v–16 S 847; fol. 16r S 943; fol. 16v S 437 (B 712, K 1114); fol. 17r S 948 (B 809, K 1153); fol. 17r–v S 556 (B 893, K 1167); fols. 17v–18 S 595 (B 940, K 1180) — all the above are Latin with English bounds; fol. 18r S 1523 (English). S 1523 is also in Kemble 1329 (from BL Add 5937). This is the source of Whitelock 23, the will of Mantat the

anchorite, which relates to Thorney. Edited (by "M") in 'Saxon charters to Thorney Abbey in Cambridgeshire', *Collectanea Topographica et Genealogica* 4 (1837), 54–59. See also C. Hart, *The Early Charters of Eastern England* (Leicester, 1966), where all the above are printed from this MS (pp. 150–65, 186–205). Sawyer 847 edited (bounds only): J.E.B. Glover *et al.*, *The Place-Names of Surrey*, (English Place-Name Society 11, 1934), p. 90 n.
5 Cf. BL Add 5937 for C16 transcripts, and CUL Add 3021, below.
6 Thorney Abbey, Cambridgeshire.
7 English in two hands. The first provides only three and a half lines at the foot of fol. 15r. The second, which appears to be the same hand as the surrounding Latin text, provides the rest.

1 Cambridge University Library, Additional 3021.

2 *C14.
3 [δ] The Red Book of Thorney Abbey, vol. 2 (vol. 1 is CUL Add 3020). A general cartulary. English on fol. 372r.
4 Davis 964.
5 A version of the same text is found in two copies in *Cartularium Monasterii de Rameseia*, ed. W.H. Hart and P.A. Lyons, RS 79 (1884–93), vol. 1, p. 188 and vol. 3, p. 38: see PRO E 164/28. Cf. also CUL Add 3020 and BL Add 5937.
6 Thorney Abbey, Cambridgeshire.
7 English in one hand.

1 Cambridge University Library, Additional 3041.

2 *C16.
3 [δ] Fols. 282v–283 copy of a grant of privilege by Æthelred to the church of St Peter, Gloucester in a collection of Saints' Lives by the Cornish recusant Nicholas Roscarrock (*ob.* 1633).
4 Sawyer 74 (nothing else in English cited by Sawyer from this MS). Edited: Finberg 1964, pp. 252–53.
6 Gloucester.
7 The transcript is written in a laborious imitation of an Anglo-Saxon hand and is followed by a literal translation.

1 Cambridge University Library, Additional 4220.

2 *C15 (after 1420, Thomson).
3 [δ] Cellarer's Register of Bury St Edmunds. Fol. 61 contains copies in English of two writs of King Edward relating to Bury St Edmunds, Suffolk.
4 Davis 110. Sawyer 1068 (cf. Har 8 edited from earlier texts); 1069 (cf. Har 9 from BL Harley 638, q.v. and K 832 from CUL Ff.II.33). Nothing else is cited by Sawyer. Neither text seems to have been printed anywhere from this MS. See also Thomson *Archives*, p. 151–52, no. 1300.
6 Bury St Edmunds, Suffolk.

1 Cambridge University Library, Additional 4407, art. 19.

2 C14a2–b1.
3 [λ] Four fragmentary leaves each side of which is marked with an index letter, a–h.
 (1) Sides a,b and c three fragments of the *Elegy on the Death of Edward I*.
 (2) Sides d, e and f fragments of *Havelok*, lines 174–183, 341–351, 356–364, 537–551.
 (3) Side g a fragment containing 23 lines of an elegiac poem otherwise unknown and beg. *On folie was myn silwyr leyd*.
 (4) Side h lines 2–6 and 15–36 of *The Proverbs of Hending*.
4 (1) *IMEV* 205.
 (2) Wells I.5; Severs 1.1.5; *IMEV* 1114. Edited: G.V. Smithers, *Havelok* (Oxford, 1987), pp. 6, 12, 18. See pp. xiv–xvi for a description of the MS fragments and for further refs. Cf. also W.W. Skeat, *The Lay of Havelok the Dane*, 2nd edn. rev. K. Sisam (Oxford, 1915), and 'A new "Havelok" MS', *MLR* 6 (1911), 455–57.

(3) *IMEV Suppl* 2685.5. Edited (in part): W.W. Skeat, 'Elegy on the death of King Edward I', *MLR* 7 (1912), 149–52 (151).
(4) *IMEV Suppl* 2078.
5 The full text of *Havelok* is in Bodley, Laud Misc. 108. Complete versions of the *Elegy on the Death of Edward I* and *The Proverbs of Hending* appear in BL Harley 2253. For other MSS containing all or part of *The Proverbs of Hending* see the Index of Middle English Texts.
7 One hand.
8 AM places in W Norfolk; see AM *Havelok*.

1 Cambridge University Library, Additional 6006.
2 *C13b (after 1265, Thomson).
3 [δ] *Liber de Consuetudinibus*, Bury St Edmunds. Fol. 51 contains a text also found in CUL Ff.II.33; fols. 73–76, list of benefactions to Bury St Edmunds.
4 Davis 123. Edited: Robertson CXIX, from CUL Ff.II.33. See also Thomson *Archives*, pp. 139–41, no. 1292. See also AM *Havelok*, 41 seq. and fn. 12.
5 Cf. other Bury St Edmunds cartularies and registers: CUL Ee.III.60; Ff.II.33; Gg.IV.4; Mm.IV.19; BL Add 14847; Harley 743.
6 Pressmark and *ex libris* inscription of the Abbey of Bury St Edmunds, Suffolk. Ker *Med Lib*, p. 16.

1 Cambridge University Library EDC 1 (*olim* Ely Cathedral, Dean and Chapter Muniments, *Liber Eliensis*).
2 *C13b.
3 [λ] [δ] *Historia Eliensis Insulae* (Latin) contains English as follows.
(1) fol. 72r, poem beg. *Merie sungen ðe muneches binnen ely*.
(2) fol. 77r, a writ of Edward the Confessor to Abbot Wulfric of Ely (The Confessor's Writ), beg. *Ædward cyninc gret ealle mine biscopas*.
Fols. 42v–43, 55r–v and 62r–v contain three Latin charters (Sawyer 780, 781, 907) but in this MS they lack the English bounds cited in Sawyer.
4 Davis 367. Ker 113. Ker *Med MSS* 2, p. 624–25. Edited: E.O. Blake, *Liber Eliensis*, Royal Historical Society, Camden Third Series 92 (1962).
(1) Hartung 5 XIII.8. Cf. *IMEV* 2164. Edited Ker 113, p. 150.
(2) Sawyer 1100 Latin and English versions (Blake, p. 164). Also edited (with commentary): Laing 'Anchor texts', esp. pp. 38–40.
5 For other texts of the same, see Cambridge, Trinity College 1105 (O.2.1) (Ker 93), and for other Ely cartularies containing copies of the Confessor's Writ see the Index of Old English Texts.
6 Written at the Benedictine Abbey of Ely. Ker *Med Lib*, p. 78; the press mark reading is corrected in Ker *Med MSS* 2, p. 625.

1 Cambridge University Library Ee.III.60.
2 *C14a2 (begun 1333).
3 [δ] Pinchbeck (or Vestry) Register of the Abbey of Bury St Edmunds. Contains charters in debased OE as follows: fols. 125v–126v, 127r, and 161. Fols. 320–326, list of benefactions to Bury St Edmunds.
4 Davis 119. For charters see Sawyer as follows: S 980, S 1045, S 1084, S 1075, S 1085, S 1069; and (fol. 161, not in Sawyer) Kemble 944. Edited: Lord Francis Hervey, *The Pinchbeck Register Relating to the Abbey of Bury St Edmunds* 1 (Brighton, 1925), pp. 294–95, 296, 360. Cf. Robertson CXIX and Thomson *Archives*, pp. 123–26, no. 1280. See also AM *Havelok*, 41 seq. and fn. 12.
5 Shares texts with CUL Add 6006 and Gg.IV.4. Cf. also CUL Ff.II.33, Mm.IV.19, BL Add 14847 and Harley 743.
6 Bury St Edmunds, Suffolk.

1 Cambridge University Library Ee.V.21.
2 *C15b.

3 [δ] *Liber Statutorum*. English on fols. 97r and 128r–v. Two versions of a writ of King Edward and two versions of a writ of King William, granting rights and privileges to St Paul's Church, London.
4 Davis 605. Sawyer 1104 and Pelteret 27.
5 For C13 versions of Sawyer 1104 see London, St Paul's DC, A Box 69, dorse; St Paul's DC, W.D.1, fol. 1 and cf. St Paul's DC, Liber B, fol. 21v (lost). For C13 versions of Pelteret 27 see London, Guildhall 25272, m. 2, no. 13; Guildhall 25501, IIa no. 9; Guildhall 25504, fols. 16v–17r.
6 London.

1 Cambridge University Library Ff.I.27.
2 *C12b2 (Ker s. xii ex.).
3 [λ] On p. 202 appears a version in OE of the poem on Durham headed *De Situ Dunelmi* and beg. *Is ðeos burch breome geond Breotenrice*. There are 21 lines; two and a half lines have been erased at the end.
4 Ker 14. Wells X.25. Hartung 5 XIII.9. *IMEV Suppl* 1608.5. Murakami, p. 89, no. 20.
5 Also found in BL Cotton Vitellius D xx (q.v.), now no longer extant.
6 Cambridge, Corpus Christi College 66, which appears to contain no OE, and CUL Ff.I.27 were formerly parts of the same manuscript from the Cistercian abbey of Sawley, Yorks. Ker *Med Lib*, p. 177.

1 Cambridge University Library Ff.II.33.
2 *C13b2 (probably *ca.* 1300).
3 [δ] Sacrist's Register of Bury St Edmunds, originally in two separate volumes bound together *ca.* 1400. Fols. 1–90 (volume 1) has copies of 47 pre-Conquest documents relating to the Abbey of Bury St Edmunds consisting of royal grants (including vernacular writs and privileges) and wills. Most of these texts are in the vernacular though some are in Latin with English bounds. English appears on (at least) fols. 20r–24r, 27v–28r, 45r–50r.
4 Davis 117 and pp. 13–17. See Sawyer as follows: S 507 (B 808, K 404 and iii 423); S 980 (K 735); S 1045 (K 895); S 1069 (K 832); S 1078 (Har 18, K 883); S 1084; S 1072 (K 892); S 1079 (K 884); S 1071; S 1068 (Har 8, K 868); S 1083 (Har 23, K 881); S 1082 (Har 22, K 882); S 1077 (Har 17, K 878); S 1073 (Har 13, K 852); S 1085; S 1075 (K 879); S 1046; S 1081 (Har 21, K 877); S 1080 (Har 20, K 880); S 1074 (Har 14, K 851); S 1076 (Har 16, K 876); S 1490 (K 970, Whi 28); S 1528 (B 1017, K 960, Whi 25); S 1521 (K 931, Whi 29); S 1516 (K 921, Whi 33); S 1519 (K 1339, Whi 34); S 1483 (Whi 2); S 703; S 1494 (B 1354); S 1486; S 1526 (B 1008, K 957, Whi 1); S 1489; S 1527 (B 1020, K 959, Whi 24); S 1499 (Whi 35); S 1468 (Rob 97); S 1531 (Whi 31); S 1470 (K 1340, Rob 100); S 1219 (B 1013, K 1349, Rob 73); S 1525 (B 1014–15, K 946–47, Whi 37–8); S 1537 (K 979, Whi 27); S 1224 (K 978, Rob 92); S 1225; S 1529 (K 980, Whi 36); S 1501. For charters on fols. 24r, 27v and 28r see Pelteret 5, 18–20. Cf. AM *Havelok*, 41 seq., and, for other texts, fn. 12. A recent study of the language of the wills in this MS is to be found in Lowe *Thesis*, esp. pp. 75–104; transcripts pp. 232–39 and Lowe 'Cartularies'. For printed texts from this and associated MSS see, F.E. Harmer, *Select English Historical Documents of the Ninth and Tenth Centuries* (Cambridge, 1914); Whitelock, *Wills*; Robertson, *Charters*. Whitelock says Will no. 14 (BL, Harley Charter 43 C 4 of C11a) is probably the original for Ff.II.33, fol. 46v. AM thinks not (see below) and cf. Whitelock, p. 181 on Will no. 26 (Sawyer 1489). See also D.C. Douglas, *Feudal Documents from the Abbey of Bury St Edmunds* (Oxford, 1932) and Thomson *Archives*, pp. 148–49, no. 1296.
5 This MS and BL Additional 14847 probably descend from a common lost MS also produced in Bury St Edmunds, but written by a scribe from at least 20 miles further north (AM *Havelok*, 42). But note that Kathryn Lowe ('Cartularies') presents evidence that the writs were copied from a common exemplar but that the scribe copying the wills of Add copied them directly from Ff. The MSS share the following material: Ff 24r, Add 32v; Ff 27v–28r, Add 38r; Ff 45 (2), Add 15 (2); Ff 45, Add

15v; Ff 45v, Add 20; Ff 46, Add 16v; Ff 48, Add 18; Ff 48v, Add 18v; Ff 49–50, Add 19r–v. Cf. also CUL Ee.III.60; Gg.IV.4; Mm.IV.19; CUL Add 6006 and BL Harley 743.
6 Bury St Edmunds, Suffolk.
7 English in one hand.
8 MS probably *ca*. 1300 but contains "modified OE": in so far as the forms have been changed from OE they probably represent E Anglian language at a mid or latish C13 stage rather than *ca*. 1300. The remarkably close agreement of this MS and BL Add 14847 suggests that the common original "had already given the texts a strongly late thirteenth-century flavour." (AM).

1 Cambridge University Library Ff.IV.35.
2 *C15 (temp H VI).
3 [δ] Registrum Rubeum Vestiarii, part II. Fol. 23v contains copies of writs of King Edward regarding Bury. Said to be incomplete.
4 Davis 121. Sawyer, p. 46 and items 1078, 1084, 1079. Cf. Thomson *Archives*, pp. 131–32, no. 1285.
6 Bury St Edmunds, Suffolk.

1 Cambridge University Library Ff.VI.15.
2 C14a1.
3 [λ] Latin MS with material dating from C12 to C15a and containing on fol. 21r a ten-line verse in English on *The Ten Commandments* beg. þu salt hauen na god buten An.
4 CB Reg i 182. Wells VI.15. Hartung 7 XX.42. *IMEV* 3684. Edited: Morris *OE Misc*, p. 200. See also CB13 70 notes and Laing *Thesis* 1, pp. 14–15.
5 Different versions of *The Ten Commandments* appear in a number of other MSS for which see the Index of Middle English Texts A: Titles.
6 There is an account on fol. 245v of the sighting of two "ingentes dracones" on the feast of St Augustine, 1408 near Saxfleet in Spaldington, Yorks. This is presumably the source of the dating of the MS in James *Cat* as C15 but it forms part of later additions to the earlier chronicle. The MS also has associations with Lincs. It contains a chronicle with original entries up to 1308 and is marked for continuations to 1399, of which those up to 1342 have been supplied with several notes relating specifically to Louth Park Cistercian Abbey. See also Ker *Med Lib*, p. 127.
7 English in one hand.
8 The hand and language of the English poem suggest a date early in the fourteenth century. The language looks northerly but not far northern; it fits well in the Louth Park area.

1 Cambridge University Library Gg.I.1.
2 C14a1 ("First third of the fourteenth century", Foster).
3 [λ] [γ] 44 articles of which 38 are in French, three in Latin and three in English, viz.
(1) Fols. 122r–134v *The Northern Passion*.
(2) Fols. 328v–345v English verses in Pierre Langtoft's *Chronicle*.
(3) Fols. 476v–479v *The Proverbs of Hending*.
Also (4) the ME glosses to *Le Tretiz* of Walter de Bibbesworth on fols. 279v–294r;
(5) fol. 489v two English couplets preceded by three French lines on the Evil Times of Edward II.
4 CB Reg i 183.
(1) Wells V.18. *IMEV* 1907. Edited: W. Heuser and F.A. Foster, *The Northern Passion*, EETS OS 183 (1930, repr. 1971). Cf. EETS OS 147 (1916 for 1913), pp. 9, 22, 38; also P. Meyer, *Romania* 15 (1886), 283–340.
(2) Hartung 5 XIII.23. *IMEV* 310/A2, 313/A2, 814/A3, 848, 2686/A2, 2754/A3, 3352/A3. Edited: Thomas Wright, *The Political Songs of England*, Camden Society vi (1839), pp. 286–318.

(3) Wells VII.6 and Wells *Suppl* 1, p. 973. *IMEV* 1669. Edited: H. Varnhagen, 'Zu mittelenglischen Gedichten', *Anglia* 4 (1881), 180–210 (182–91).
(4) Edited: Annie Owen, *Le Traité de Walter de Bibbesworth sur la langue française* (Paris, 1929; repr. Geneva, 1977). Corrections to this edition may be found in W. Rothwell, 'A mis-judged author and a mis-used text: Walter de Bibbesworth and his "Tretiz"', *MLR* 77 (1982), 282–93; see also W. Rothwell, *Walter de Bibbesworth Le Tretiz*, Anglo-Norman Text Society, Plain Text Series 6 (London, 1990) where other MSS of early C14 are listed. The original work was probably of mid C13. Cf. BL Sloane 809 for a text of C13b2.
(5) *IMEV* and *IMEV Suppl* 4235. Hartung 5 XIII.15.
5 For other MSS containing all or part of *The Proverbs of Hending* see the Index of Middle English Texts A: Titles. Other early copies of *Le Tretiz* by Walter de Bibbesworth are found in BL Sloane 809 and Bodley Selden Supra 74.
7 One hand — the scribed is a literatim copyist.
8 The language of (1) and (3) is MHE. The language of (2) appears to be NME.

1 Cambridge University Library Gg.IV.4.
2 *C15a2 (after 1425, Thomson).
3 [δ] Bury St Edmunds Register of Evidences. Contains debased OE material on fols. 94r, 98r, 101v–102v, 220r, 270r–271r, 304r–v.
4 Davis 109. See Sawyer as follows: fol. 94r S 507; fols. 101v–2 (cf. fol. 270r–v below) S 980; fol. 102r–v (cf. fols. 270v–71 below) S 1045; fol. 102v (cf. fol. 271r below) S 1084, S 1075, S 1085, S 1069; fol. 270r–v S 980; fols. 270v–71 S 1045; fol. 271r S 1084, S 1075, S 1085, S 1069; fol. 304r–v S 703. Fol. 98r is Pelteret 19. See Thomson *Archives*, pp. 150–51, no. 1299. See also AM *Havelok*, 41 seq. and fn. 12.
5 Cf. other Bury St Edmunds cartularies and registers, CUL Add 6606, Ee.III.60, Ff.II.33, Mm.IV.19, BL Add 14847 and Harley 743.
6 Bury St Edmunds, Suffolk.
8 The language looks very late and the texts are somewhat garbled.

1 Cambridge University Library, Gg.IV.27(2).
2 C13a2–C14a1 (c1300, *MED Plan & Bibl*, p. 41; *ca.* 1250–60, Wells I.1).
3 [λ] (1) Fols. 1r–5v *Floriz and Blauncheflur* (begins abruptly).
(2) Fols. 6r–13r *King Horn*. See also Rosamund Allen, 'The date and provenance of *King Horn*: some interim reassessments' in *Medieval English Studies presented to George Kane*, ed. E.D. Kennedy, R. Waldron and J.S. Wittig (Woodbridge, 1988), pp. 99–125.
(3) Fols. 13v–14v *Assumpcion de nostre dame* (corresponds to *Cursor Mundi* lines 20065–20848; ends abruptly).
4 (1) Wells I.99. Severs 1 I.96. *IMEV Suppl* *2288.8 (*olim IMEV* *45). D&W IX.
(2) Wells I.1. Severs 1 I.1. *IMEV* 166.
(3) CB Reg i 186. Wells V.78. Severs 2 V.318. *IMEV* 2165.
Edited: J.R. Lumby, *King Horn, Floriz and Blauncheflur, The Assumption of Our Lady*, EETS OS 14 (1866, rev. G.H. McKnight, 1901, repr. 1962); F.C. De Vries, *Floris and Blauncheflur* (Gröningen, 1966), see esp. p. 3 seq.; J. Hall, *King Horn. A Middle English Romance* (Oxford, 1901), see esp. p. x; W.H. French and C.B. Hale, *Middle English Metrical Romances* (New York, 1930), pp. 25–70. Facsimile of one page, with commentary, in M.B. Parkes and Richard Beadle, *The Poetical Works of Geoffrey Chaucer. A Facsimile of Cambridge University Library MS Gg.4.27*, 3 vols. (Cambridge, 1979–80), vol. 3, pp. 68–69.
5 For other MSS containing these texts see the Index of Middle English Texts A: Titles.
7 MS in one hand.
8 The language of this MS is placed in *LALME* as LP 6800 in West Berks.

1 Cambridge University Library Hh.VI.11.
2 C13–C14.

3 [λ] Latin MS (imperfect) containing English as follows.
   (1) Fol. 67r four short lines translating a Latin version and beg. *I am Rose wo is me*.
   (2) Fol. 70v *Pater Noster* in eight 7-stress verses.
   (3) *Ave Maria* in three short couplets.
4 CB Reg i 194.
   (1) *IMEV* 1279.
   (2) Wells VI.11 and *IMEV* 2705.
   (3) Wells XIII.179. Hartung 7 XX.37. *IMEV* 1067.
   Pater Noster and *Ave Maria* edited: *Rel Ant* i 169.
5 For other EME versions of these ecclesiastical texts see the Index of Middle English Texts A: Titles.
6 Given by Frater R. de Alneye to the "Armoriolus" of Ramsey monastery, Hunts. Ker *Med Lib*, p. 153.
7 Items (2) and (3) are in the same hand.

1 Cambridge University Library Ii.I.33.

2 *C12b.
3 [λ] Parts of *Genesis* in a version unique to this MS (chaps iv–v, x–xi, xxiii–xxiv). Also Homilies and Lives of the Saints for the most part by Ælfric.
4 Ker 18. See S.J. Crawford, *The Old English Version of the Heptateuch*, EETS OS 160 (1922 for 1921; repr. with additional material, ed. N.R. Ker 1969). The MS is also described in Pope *Ælfric*, pp. 35–39.
6 William Schipper, 'A composite Old English homiliary from Ely: Cambr. Univ. Libr. MS Ii.1.33', *TCBS* 8 (1983), 285–98, associates the MS with Ely.
7 Ker: "Probably in two main hands, (1) ff. 2–36v, 120v–227v, (2) ff. 37–120v, but there are changes in the appearance of the script at ff. 29, 53 and about f. 120 and additions in a blank space on f. 60v. The manuscript was probably compiled gradually (cf. the signatures [see p. 23]): ff. 37–120v look rather earlier than the rest, and annotations on these leaves are perhaps in hand (1)".
8 For language see Pope *Ælfric*, pp. 38–39. He points out that both scribes are conservative, especially Ker's hand (2), faithfully preserving W-S spellings of the eleventh century. The language of *Genesis* has a mixture of forms including south-eastern spellings. These do not appear in the other texts whose language "has a prevailingly southern look".

1 Cambridge University Library Kk.III.18.

2 C13a2 (tremulous hand: see Ker 'Date').
3 [γ] Bede's *Historia ecclesiastica* in a hand of C11b but lightly glossed throughout in the Worcester tremulous hand. Many of the glosses have subsequently been erased. No English glosses are cited by Ker or Franzen.
4 Ker 23. Franzen 1991, p. 63.
5 For other MSS containing glosses by the tremulous hand see Franzen 1991, Ker, p. lvii and the entry for Worcester Cathedral, Dean and Chapter Library F 174.
6 Written at Worcester. Ker *Med Lib*, p. 206.
7 Latin glosses in the Worcester tremulous hand.

1 Cambridge University Library Mm.I.18.

2 C13b2 ("not later than about 1300, and possibly the last quarter of the thirteenth century", Robbins).
3 [λ] A composite MS with material dating from between C12 and C15 and labelled "Miscellanea". Fol. 62r (*olim* 58r) 'The Cambridge Prologue'. A prologue in French (22 lines) followed by English (22 lines) to a play no longer extant.
4 *IMEV* and *IMEV Suppl* 2360. Hartung 5 XII.4. Edited: N. Davis, *Non-Cycle Plays and Fragments*, EETS SS 1 (1970), pp. 114–15; and R.H. Robbins, 'An English mystery play fragment ante 1300', *MLN* 65 (1950), 30–35. Facsimile in N. Davis, *Non-Cycle Plays and the Winchester Dialogues*, Leeds Texts and Monographs Medieval Drama Facsimiles 5 (1979), p. 3 no. 1.

7 English in one hand.
8 Davis (1970) suggests (pp. cxi–cxv) that the language may be MHE; but see the entry in *LALME* 1, p. 68 (MS designation erroneously given as CUL Mm.I.1.1): "there is too little text for proper comparison. One or two of its features are not known in MHE, though it is possible that they are very early forms that were later displaced; there is very little MHE writing co-aeval with this text".

1 Cambridge University Library Mm.IV.6.
2 C13.
3 [λ] Lives of saints in Latin including, fols. 37r–53r, the "Anonymous A" version of the *Life of St Edmund* said to contain his last words in English.
4 See Lawrence *St Edmund*, p. 50. Cf. Wilson 1943, p. 59.
5 Cf. refs. to other C13 versions of this work in the Index of Texts in Latin.

1 Cambridge University Library Mm.IV.19.
2 *C12b2–C13a1.
3 [δ] *Nigrum Registrum de Vestiario* of Bury St Edmunds. Contains texts in debased OE on (at least) fols. 83r–91r, 93v, 105v, 119v–120r.
4 Davis 118. Sawyer as follows: S 507 (B 808); S 980; S 703; S 1072 (Har 12). Fol. 93v is Pelteret 19. See D.C. Douglas, *Feudal Documents from the Abbey of Bury St Edmunds* (Oxford, 1932) and Thomson *Archives*, pp. 119–21, no. 1277. See also AM *Havelok*, 41 seq. and fn. 12.
5 Cf. other Bury St Edmunds cartularies and registers, CUL Add 6606, Ee.III.60, Ff.II.33, Gg.IV.4, BL Add 14847 and Harley 743.
6 Bury St Edmunds, Suffolk.
8 Language of the same general character as Ff.II.33 and BL Add 14847. It uses *-cht* in e.g. "right". Said by Sawyer, p. 46 to be C12 but English looks more likely to be of C13.

1 Cambridge University Lbrary Mm.IV.28.
2 C12b2–C13a1 (*ca.* 1200).
3 [λ] MS of *Vitas patrum* (C12a2). Contains in a blank space on the recto of the last leaf (fol. 149) the first stanza of Godric's Hymn A.
4 CB Reg i 199. Wells *Suppl* 1, p. 986 (XIII.27). *IMEV* 2988. Ker 28. Hall ii 241. Murakami, p. 105, no. 38. See also D&H, p. 105 and Zupitza 'Godric'.
5 For other MSS containing one or more of Godric's Hymns see the Index of Middle English Texts A: Titles.
6 MS from Biddlesden Priory ("de Bethlesdena"), Bucks. where it was probably at the turn of C12. Ker *Med Lib*, p. 10.
7 English in one hand.

1 Cambridge University Library Oo.VI.110.
2 C13b.
3 [γ] Fols. 1r–83r grammatical texts in Latin with vernacular glosses, mostly French but some English. The rest of the MS is of C15.
4 See Hunt *Teaching* 1, pp. 87 and 395 and Ker *Med Lib*, p. 16 fn. 1. Vernacular glosses edited: Hunt *Teaching* 2, pp. 21–23, 159–71.

1 Canterbury, Dean and Chapter Library, Ch. Ant. C. 14 and C. 18A.
2 C12b1–2.
3 [δ] Two versions of a writ of King Henry II (1154 x 1161/1172 x 1189) concerning lands near Canterbury. Purported originals.
4 Pelteret 54. See Harmer, pp. 174–75.
5 For other purported originals see BL Stowe Charter 44 and Lambeth Palace, Cart. Misc. XI/2. A C13 version in English is in Canterbury, D & C, Register E, fol. 54r (*olim* 22r), no. 113. A C13–C14 English version is in Lambeth Palace 1212, fol. 99v.
6 Canterbury, Kent.

1 Canterbury, Dean and Chapter Library, Ch. Ant. C. 17, C. 18 and C. 20.
2 C12b1 (Feb 1155).
3 [δ] Writ of Henry II confirming Theobald, Archbishop of Canterbury, and the monks of Christ Church in their lands and privileges of jurisdiction. ? Originals.
4 Pelteret 51. See L.V. Delisle, 'Recueil de 109 chartes originales de Henri II Roi d'Angleterre et Duc de Normandie rassemblées et photographiées par le Rev. H. Salter', *Bibliothèque de l'Ecole des Chartes* 69 (1908), 541–80.
5 For more information and refs. to copies of the same see the entry for BL Harley Charter 111 B 49.

1 Canterbury, Dean and Chapter Library, Ch. Ant. C. 46.
2 C13a1–b1 (1224–53).
3 [δ] *Inspeximus* of Robert of Battle, Abbot of St Augustine's Abbey, Canterbury. Writ of King Stephen (1138 x 1154) concerning lands near Canterbury.
4 Pelteret 50.
5 Cf. Canterbury, Dean and Chapter Library, Ch. Ant. C. 1310(1)

1 Canterbury, Dean and Chapter Library, Ch. Ant. C. 1310 (1) and (3) (damaged).
2 C14a1.
3 [δ] Copies of a writ of King Stephen (1138 x 1154) and a writ of King Henry II (Feb 1155) both concerning lands near Canterbury.
4 Pelteret 50 and 51.
5 For an earlier version (1224–53) of King Stephen's writ, see Canterbury, Dean and Chapter Library, Ch. Ant. C. 46. For a fuller account of the writ of Henry II, see BL Harley Charter 111 B 49.
6 Canterbury, Kent.

1 Canterbury, Dean and Chapter Library, Ch. Ant. F. 47.
2 *C15.
3 [δ] Copies of two writs of King Edward to St Augustine's, Canterbury.
4 Sawyer 1092 and 1091.
5 See BL Cotton Claudius D x for earlier copies (C13) of the same charters.
6 Canterbury, Kent.

1 Canterbury, Dean and Chapter Library, Ch. Ant. R. 51.
2 *C13.
3 [δ] English bounds to a copy of a grant by King Edward of Ottery St Mary, Devon.
4 Sawyer 1033. Facsimile in F. Rose-Troup, 'The Anglo-Saxon charter of Ottery St Mary', *Transactions of the Devonshire Association* 71 (1939), 201–220.

1 Canterbury, Dean and Chapter Library, C 204.
2 *C13.
3 [δ] Copy of a writ of King Edward to Christ Church Canterbury.
4 Sawyer 1089.
5 Cf. Reg A, fol. 148v, Reg E, fol. 53v, Reg I, fol. 58r–v.
6 Canterbury, Kent.

1 Canterbury, Dean and Chapter Library, Register A.
2 *C13b2.
3 [δ] Copies of 21 charters in English and Latin and including eight wills in the vernacular. Also contains six C15 transcripts of A-S charters. English on fols. 141r–144v (*olim* 151r–154v), 148v–149r (*olim* 158v–159r).
4 Davis 169. See Sawyer as follows: S 1202 (B 530); 1506 (B 1011, K 478); S 1501; S 939; S 1503; S 1465; S 1471 (K 773); S 1535 (K 782); S 1234 (K 799, Rob 116); S 959; S 1089. Fols. 148v–149r see Pelteret 22, 48 and 54 (Latin only).

5 J.B. Sheppard, *Eighth Report of the Royal Commission on Historical Manuscripts* (London, 1881), Appendix, 315–35 (p. 331), suggests that Register A was a "more roughly executed counterpart" of Register E. Kathryn Lowe argues that both Registers derive from a single exemplar, now lost; see Kathryn A. Lowe, 'A new edition of the will of Wulfgyth', *N&Q* 234 (1989), 295–98. Cf. shared charters in Reg E as follows: A fol. 144r = E fol. 44v (Rob 82); A fol. 143r = E fol. 43v (Rob 86); A fol. 143r = E fol. 44r (Rob 101); A fol. 143v = E fol. 44v (Rob 116). For a study of the language of the wills in this MS, see Lowe *Thesis*, esp. pp. 127–43, transcripts pp. 252–65 and Lowe 'OE wills'.
6 Canterbury, Kent.
8 Kathryn Lowe's observations on the language of the vernacular wills suggest that the scribe of Register A was a more careful copyist than that of Register E and made little modification to the language of the common exemplar. The common exemplar itself was probably for the most part an accurate representation of the OE models underlying it.

1 Canterbury, Dean and Chapter Library, Register C.

2 *C15.
3 [δ] English on fol. 148v (OE and ME versions).
4 Davis 171. See Sawyer 1202. Note that Kemble refers to Register C, fols. 9v and 11v as the source for his nos. 301 and 799. These references should, however, now read Register E, fols. 42v and 44v, q.v. It seems that earlier printed versions refer to the numbering of the Registers by Samuel Norris in his eighteenth-century catalogue or possibly to the (not identical) numbering in the 1805 catalogue by Cyprian Rondeau Bunce. See Lowe *Thesis*, p. 130 fn. 78.
6 Canterbury, Kent.

1 Canterbury, Dean and Chapter Library, Register E.

2 *C13b2 (1284–1331 — priorate of Henry of Eastry).
3 [δ] 21 charters in English and Latin. English on fols. 42v–45r (*olim* 9v–12r), 53v–54r (*olim* 21v–22r).
4 Davis 168. Sawyer as follows: S 1202 (B 530, K 301); S 1506; S 1501; S 939; S 1503; S 1465; S 1471 (K 773; Thorpe 354–57); S 1535 (fol. 44r–v. Will of Wulfgyth = Whitelock 32, the source of which she gives as Reg C, v, fol. 11; see note on catalogues under the entry for Register C above); S 1234; S 959; S 1089. Fols. 53v–54r, see Pelteret 22, 48 and 54.
5 J.B. Sheppard, *Eighth Report of the Royal Commission on Historical Manuscripts* (London, 1881), Appendix, 315–35 (p. 331), suggests that Register A was a "more roughly executed counterpart" of Register E. Kathryn Lowe argues that both Registers derive from a single exemplar, now lost; see, Kathryn A. Lowe, 'A new edition of the will of Wulfgyth', *N&Q* 234 (1989), 295–98. Cf. shared charters in Reg E as follows: A fol. 144r = E fol. 44v (Rob 82); A fol. 143r = E fol. 43v (Rob 86); A fol. 143r = E fol. 44r (Rob 101); A fol. 143v = E fol. 44v (Rob 116). For a study of the language of the wills in this MS, see Lowe *Thesis*, esp. pp. 127–43, transcripts pp. 252–65 and Lowe 'OE wills'.
6 Canterbury, Kent.
8 According to Kathryn Lowe ('OE wills') the scribe of Register E made somewhat more modification to the language of his copy than the scribe of Register A. He occasionally omits words or phrases apparently unfamiliar to him and sometimes replaces obsolete words with more modern equivalents.

1 Canterbury, Dean and Chapter Library, Register I.

2 *C13b.
3 [δ] Fols. 58r–v, 59v, 61r–62r and 65v contain copies of two writs of King Edward, a writ of William I, three of Henry I and one of Henry II to Christ Church Canterbury.
4 Sawyer 1088, 1089; Pelteret 22, 46 and 47 (Latin with English rights clauses) 48, 54.

6 Canterbury, Kent.

1 Cardigan, Earl of. See Private: Cardigan, Earl of, Sturmy House, Sevenake Forest.

1 Carlisle, Cumbria Record Office: D/Lons/L Medieval deeds C1 (*olim* Lowther Castle, Westmorland, Gospatric's Writ).
2 *C13.
3 [δ] Copy of the Writ of Gospatric concerning lands in Allerdale, Cardew and Cumdivock, Cumbria. Original writ (not extant) probably 1041 x 1064 (1041 x 1055).
4 Edited: Harmer 121, commentary pp. 419–23. For details of other editions see Harmer, p. 531. See also Murakami, p. 76, no. 5. Facsimile: F. Liebermann, 'Drei nordhumbrische Urkunden um 1100', *Archiv* 111 (1903), 275–84 (for which see also Pelteret 64 and 148).
6 Cumbria.
7 One hand of C13.
8 The document is of great interest linguistically because its vocabulary combines elements of Celtic, English and Scandinavian, a mixture which is also apparent in the personal names and place-names mentioned in the text. See Harmer, p. 419.

1 Chichester, Diocesan Record Office, Episc. VI/1/1 ('Liber A' or 'vol. XVII').
2 *C14.
3 [δ] Fols. 23r–v and 24r–v contain two Latin charters with English bounds.
4 Davis 236. Sawyer 1291 (B 997, *Mon Angl* vi 1166 no. 18 and thence K 464); S 403 (B 669, *Mon Angl* vi 1165 no. 15 and thence K 350). Also edited: E.E. Barker, 'Sussex Anglo-Saxon charters', *Sussex Archaeological Collections* 88 (1949), 82–85 and *Sussex Archaeological Collections* 87 (1948), 139–45. Sawyer also notes Chichester, DRO, Episc. VI/1/2, which is Register B XVIII referred to by Birch and Kemble, (see Sawyer nos. 43, 403, 1291, 872 and Davis 235) but this MS lacks the English bounds.
5 The exemplar for these texts is perhaps Episc VI/1/6, below.
6 Chichester, Sussex.
7 These entries are in one hand.
8 The scribe clearly has little or no knowledge of A-S. Letter-shapes are confused. OE long s is written r, OE ᵹ is written s, OE p is written y, etc.

1 Chichester, Diocesan Record Office, Episc. VI/1/6 ('Liber Y').
2 *C13b1 (*ca.* 1250–60, Davis).
3 [δ] English bounds to Latin charters, fols. 72r–74v.
4 Davis 248. Sawyer as follows: S 403 (B 669); S 872; S 1291 (B 997). Edited: W.D. Peckham, *The Chartulary of the High Church of Chichester*, Sussex Record Society 16 (1942–1943); also E.E. Barker, 'Sussex Anglo-Saxon charters', *Sussex Archaeological Collections* 87 (1948), 139–45 and *Sussex Archaeological Collections* 88 (1949), 86–88, 103–105.
5 This MS may be the exemplar for Episc. VI/1/1, above.
6 Chichester, Sussex.
7 These entries are in a single hand.
8 The scribe makes some attempt to imitate A-S script, but OE p is written y. There are a few forms of interest.

1 Dresden, Sächsische Landesbibliothek Dc. 187 + 160 + 186 + 185. (Once, in this order, formed a single vol. with a later medical MS, now Dresden MS.C. 309.)
2 *C12a2–b1 (s. xii med., Ker).
3 [γ] Glosses and names of herbs in a MS containing medical texts in Latin.
(1) Dc. 187, fols. 7 seq. ten names and glosses to names of herbs.

(2) Dc. 187, fols. 30 seq. glosses to diseases and parts of the body.
  (3) Dc. 186, fols. 1 seq. 27 glosses to herb recipes.
  (4) Dc. 185, fols. 27–39 ten names and glosses to names of herbs.
  (5) Dc. 185, fol. 39v names of herbs in recipes.
4 Ker 102. Edited: H.D. Merritt, *Old English Glosses*, the Modern Language Association of America, General Series 16 (1945), no. 73; M. Manitius, 'Angelsächsische Glossen in Dresdner Handschriften', *Anglia* 24 (1901), 428–35, corrected by H. Varnhagen in *Commentariorum Hermanni Varnhagen de glossis nonnullis anglicis* (Erlangae, 1902) (includes facsimile).

1 Dublin, Trinity College 270 (D.4.9).
2 C13–C14.
3 [γ] Collection of grammatical works in Latin by John of Garland, Alexander Neckham, Adam of Petit Pont, *et al*. The texts are heavily annotated and glossed including vernacular glosses most of which are French but some are English.
4 For a description of the contents of the MS see Hunt *Teaching* 1, pp. 87 and 166–67. Vernacular glosses edited: Hunt *Teaching* 1, pp. 42–43, 44, 156; *Teaching* 2, pp. 15–21 (Hunt's MS T), 26–34 (Hunt's MS T), 37–52 and 54–55 (Hunt's MS D), 65–84 (Hunt's MS D), 125–149 (Hunt's MS D and D* — two copies of the same text).

1 Dublin, Trinity College 301 (C.3.19).
2 C13b2 (Wenzel 1986).
3 [λ] Theological miscellany with Latin sermons containing in English on fol. 194r a version of *Stabat iuxta Christi crucem* beg. *Stond wel moder*.
4 *IMEV Suppl* 3211. See Wenzel 1986, p. 51.
5 For refs. to other texts of *Stabat iuxta Christi crucem* see the Index of Middle English Texts A: Titles.
7 English in one hand.

1 Dublin, Trinity College 347 (C.5.8).
2 C13b2 (Wenzel 1986).
3 [λ] Sermons and preaching material in Latin, containing on fol. 199v, in a copy of Peraldus's *Summa de Vitiis*, several vernacular verses. Two are in English beg. *Of my husband giu I noht* and *Lete þe cukewald syte at hom*.
4 See Wenzel 1986, pp. 216–17.

1 Dublin, Trinity College 432 (D.4.18), part I.
2 C13.
3 [λ] A composite MS, the first two parts of which (fols. 1–22 and fols. 23–58) contain French religious verse and Latin commentaries in hands of the thirteenth and fourteenth centuries. On the bottom margin of fol. 22r is a version in C13 English of the lyric, titled in CB13 *My Leman on the Rood*, as follows: *Whanne i þe o rode i-se / ihu mi leman. / whu þi moder stant te bi / wepende And Iohan. / wel oute ihc wit herte wepen / and mi neb wit teres weten / if ihc one luue kan / for nis non nu man o liue. / þat wolde þolien of det þe pine / for luue of senful man.*
4 *IMEV* 3966. Cf. CB13 35A and B, 36 and 37. For later Middle English in the second part of the MS see Hamer 'MS index' and the entry in *LALME* 1, p. 77.
5 There are several different versions of the lyric; for refs. see the Index of Middle English Texts A: Titles under *My Leman on the Rood*.
6 *Ex libris* inscription associates part II of the MS (fols. 23–58) with Priory of Belvoir, Lincs. Ker *Med Lib*, p. 9.
7 English in one hand.

1 Dublin, Trinity College 492 (E.2.23).
2 *C12.
3 [λ] Bede's *Historia Ecclesiastica* including on fol. 176 Bede's Death Song in the text of Cuthbert's *Epistola de obitu Bedae*.

4 Ker 104.
5 For other MSS containing Bede's Death Song see the Index of Old English Texts.
6 Pressmark of the Abbey of Bury St Edmunds, Suffolk. Ker *Med Lib*, p. 19.

1 Durham Cathedral, Dean and Chapter Library A.III.12.

2 C13a2–b (*ca.* 1225–50, *OBMEV*; not later than 1231, Thomson). There is some confusion about the palaeographical dating; Carleton Brown (CB14 1A notes, p. 241) refers to the hand as "early fourteenth century" and then cites, with no further elucidation, Thomson's dating of *ca.* 1230. See further notes on the hand, below.

3 [λ] 21 Latin theological tracts written in at least a dozen hands before and up to the time of Bertram of Middleton, Prior of Durham 1244–58. Fol. 49r contains, on an inserted strip of vellum, the Latin text, followed by an English translation, of *Candet Nudatum Pectus*. The translation begins *Wyth was hys nakede brest and red of blod hys syde*. The inserted strip formed one part of a rotulus now in two pieces. The other piece is bound in as fol. 58 and contains two *Questiones* and part of a quotation from St Augustine.

4 CB Reg i 444. Wells XIII.116. *IMEV* 4088. CB14 1A; *OBMEV* 4. Murakami, pp. 110–11, no. 44. Edited: F.J. Furnivall, *Political, Religious and Love Poems*, EETS OS 15 (1866, repr. 1962), p. 243 (from an inaccurate transcript by Rev. W. Greenwell). Also edited: Thomson *Candet*.

5 For other copies of *Candet Nudatum Pectus* see the Index of Middle English Texts A: Titles.

6 *Ex dono* inscription from prior Bertram of Middleton to Durham Cathedral. Ker *Med Lib Suppl*, p. 20.

7 English in one hand. Thomson (*Candet*, p. 101) states that the English translation is in the same hand as the Latin text of the *Candet Nudatum Pectus*. He then (p. 102) presents palaeographical evidence to suggest that the hand should be dated between 1220 and 1240. The hand that writes the English translation is, however, quite different from that of the Latin text. The characteristics cited by Thomson apply in each case either to the Latin text or to the English but never to both. Moreover the letter-shapes in the two scripts are in almost every case formed in a different manner. The combination of characteristics in the hand of the English text suggests to me a date in the second half of the thirteenth century rather than one as late as the fourteenth.

8 The language does not look northern.

1 Durham Cathedral, Dean and Chapter Library B.I.18.

2 C13 (Wenzel 1986); C14 (Ker *Med Lib*).

3 [λ] Verses in English as follows.
  (1) Fol. 37r–v one six-line stanza from the *Proverbs of Hending* beg. *Riche and pouer yunge and halde*.
  (2) Fol. 56v couplet on Christ's love for mankind beg. *So lange ik aue lefman stonden at þe yathe*.
  (3) Fol. 56v couplet paraphrasing 'Ubi amor ibi oculus' and beg. *þer I luuie þer leik i noth*.
  (4) Fol. 85v repeat of no. (3) with a different second line.
  (5) Fol. 116v couplet beg. *Barred girdel wo þe be*.
  (6) Fol. 116v a proverb.
  (7) Fol. 117r quatrain regretting lechery beg. *Were þat his don / for to done*.

4 Wenzel 1974, nos. 8, 51, 53, 65, 80, 87. See also Wenzel 1978, p. 94 and Wenzel 1986, pp. 119, 226, 240. For (1) cf. *IMEV* 2817; (2) cf. *IMEV Suppl* 3167.3. For a variant of (7) see *IMEV Suppl* 3897.5.

5 See the entries under BL Harley 3823 and Berlin-Dahlem, Stiftung Preussischer Kulturbesitz, Staatsbibliothek, MS theol. lat. for some of the same verses. For refs. to other MSS containing all or part of *The Proverbs of Hending* see the Index of Middle English Texts A: Titles.

6 Inscription of ownership associates MS with Durham Cathedral. Ker *Med Lib*, p. 65; Ker *Med Lib Suppl*, p. 22.

1 Durham Cathedral, Dean and Chapter Library C.IV.26.
2 C13b2.
3 [γ] Collection of grammatical works by John of Garland *et al.* with marginal commentary and interlinear vernacular glosses of C13b, French and English.
4 Contents listed Hunt *Teaching* 1, pp. 86–87 and 395–96. Vernacular glosses edited: Hunt *Teaching* 2, pp. 15–21, 26–33 (Hunt's MS D).

1 Durham, Prior's Kitchen, Cartularium Vetus.
2 C13.
3 [δ] Fol. 134v copy of a writ of Ranulf Flambard, bishop of Durham granting lands near the mouth of the Tweed to St Cuthbert's Church.
4 Pelteret 64.
5 For an earlier version see next entry. For later versions see Pelteret.
6 Durham.

1 Durham, Prior's Kitchen, Dean and Chapter Muniments 2.1, Pontificalium, no. 9.
2 C11–C12.
3 [δ] Writ of Ranulf Flambard, bishop of Durham granting lands near the mouth of the Tweed to St Cuthbert's Church.
4 Pelteret 64. *New Pal Soc*, First Series, vol. 1, plate 45[c].
5 A C13 copy is in Prior's Kitchen, Cartularium Vetus, fol. 134v.
6 Durham.

1 Durham University Library, Cosin V.II.8.
2 C13a2–b1 (AID, pers. comm.).
3 [λ] Sermon cycles in Latin. On fol. 58ra is a short quotation from a ME lyric: *That mi lef askes wit sare weping, ne mai ic it werne for nane kinnes thing.*
4 Wenzel 1986, p. 222.
6 MS from Durham Cathedral. Ker *Med Lib*, p. 72; Ker *Med Lib Suppl*, p. 29.

1 Durham University Library, Cosin V.III.2.
2 C13a1 (AID, pers. comm.).
3 [λ] Sermon collection in Latin. On fol. 127ra is a short quotation from a ME lyric: *Luue bendes me bindet.* On fol. 127va is a version of lines 143–44 of the *Poema Morale*: *suete bet swines brede ant of wilde dere. harde ye hus abiet hat haruore gift hiis swire.*
4 Wenzel 1986, p. 222.
5 The *Poema Morale* survives in seven main versions for which see the Index of Middle English Texts A: Titles where other MSS containing short quotations from the text are also listed.
7 English in one hand.

1 Durham University Library, Cosin V.V.15.
2 C14a1 (AID, pers. comm.).
3 [λ] Fol. 39r contains the English quatrain which is introduced into the French text of the *Speculum Ecclesie* by Edmund Riche: *Nu gos ye sonne vndre wode, / me reuez marie yi faire roude. / Nu goht sonne vndre tre, / me reueht marie yi son and te.*
4 CB Reg i 446. Wells *Suppl* 1, p. 988 (XIII.127a). *IMEV* 2320/A12.
5 For other MSS containing this text and the English quatrain see the Index of Texts in French.
7 English in one hand.

1 Edinburgh, Royal College of Physicians: MS of *Cursor Mundi*.
2 C13b2–C14a1.

3 [λ] (1) Fols. 37r–50v; 1r–15v *Cursor Mundi* (imperfect and wrongly ordered).
(2) Fols. 16r–36v Prologue and first thirteen items of the *Northern Homily Collection*.
4 See *LALME* 1, p. 88. CB Reg i 508–510. Ker *Med MSS* 2, pp. 539–40. Murakami, pp. 114–15, no. 49.
(1) Wells VI.1. Hartung 7 XX.31. *IMEV* 2153 and cf. *IMEV* 104, 1885, 3208, 3976. Edited as Appendix 1 to Part v of R. Morris, *Cursor Mundi*, EETS OS 68 (1878), pp. 1587–1637. See also description by H. Hupe in Part vii, EETS OS 101 (1893), pp. 62–63.
(2) Wells V.18 (p. 289). For individual entries in *IMEV* see Hamer 'MS index'. Edited: J. Small, *English Metrical Homilies* (Edinburgh, 1862).
7 Hand A: fols. 1r–15v.
Hand B: fols. 16r–36v.
Hand C: fols. 37r–50v.
8 Yorks. *LALME* LP 14 and LP 375.

1 Edinburgh University Library 107.

2 C13b2.
3 [λ] On fol. 89rA appears an English translation of a Latin verse 'O homo securum habeas accessum' and beg. *Cum þu man ne dred þe nast*.
4 See Wenzel 1974, no. 9 (Note: English on fol. 89r not 88v as in Wenzel). For a different translation of the verse see *IMEV* 2074.
7 English in one hand.

1 Ely Cathedral, Dean and Chapter Muniments, *Liber Eliensis*: now lodged in CUL as Cambridge University Library EDC 1, q.v.

1 Exeter, Dean and Chapter Library 1705.

2 *C14.
3 [δ] Grant of land (Latin) by King Athelstan to the monastery of SS. Mary and Peter. Has English bounds which are the same as those in D and C 1706 below.
4 Sawyer 390.
6 Exeter, Devon.

1 Exeter Cathedral, Dean and Chapter Library 1706.

2 *C15.
3 [δ] Grant of land at Stoke Canon, Devon by King Athelstan to the minster of St Mary, Exeter. Text contains English bounds only.
4 Sawyer 389.
6 Exeter, Devon.

1 Exeter Cathedral, Dean and Chapter Library 2570.

2 C15 (transcript of a lost C13 MS).
3 [δ] A ME version of the gifts of Bishop Leofric to Exeter.
4 Pelteret 91. The relationship of this text to the Anglo-Saxon copies is discussed by M. Förster in *The Exeter Book of Old English Poetry*, with introductory chapters by R.W. Chambers, Max Förster and Robin Flower (1933), p.14; text printed, p. 30. Cf. also Robertson, pp. 226 and 473.
6 Exeter, Devon.

1 Exeter Cathedral, Dean and Chapter Library 3514.

2 C13a2–b.
3 [λ] A miscellany of English history in Latin. On pp. 19–21 appears the 'insular version' of Cuthbert's *Epistola de obitu Bedae* including Bede's Death Song.
4 MS described Ker *Med MSS* 2, pp. 822–24. Cf. Dobbie (1937), pp. 119–27.
5 For other MSS containing Bede's Death Song see the Index of Old English Texts.

1 **Exeter Cathedral, Dean and Chapter Library 3672.**
2 *C15a.
3 [δ] P. 94 grant of land at Culmstock, Devon by King Athelstan to the minster of SS. Mary and Peter, Exeter. Text contains English bounds only.
4 Davis 387. Sawyer 386.
6 Exeter, Devon.

1 **Exeter, Devon Record Office, W 1258/D 84/3 (*olim* Woburn Abbey, Duke of Bedford, Muniments, Table 3, Drawer A.3).**
2 C13.
3 [δ] Fols. 7r–8r copy of a diploma of *ca.* 1174 x 1184 concerning places in Devon. Latin with English bounds.
4 Pelteret 59. Edited: H.P.R. Finberg, 'Some early Tavistock charters', *EHR* 62 (1947), 363, no. xxix. See also Finberg, 'The bounds of Abbotsham', *Devon and Cornwall Notes and Queries* 22 (1944), 201.
6 Devon.

1 **Glasgow University Library, Hunterian 292 (U.6.10).**
2 C13a2–b1 (*ca.* 1250).
3 [γ] Fols. 18–21 four folios inserted into a copy of the *Prior and Posterior Analytics* of Aristotle and containing part of a glossary in Latin and Anglo-Norman which includes a few English words.
4 See John Young and P. Henderson Aitken, *A Catalogue of the Manuscripts in the Library of the Hunterian Museum in the University of Glasgow* (Glasgow, 1908). Edited: Hunt *Teaching* 1, pp. 400–19; and in part Paul Meyer, *Documents manuscrits de l'anciennne littérature de la France conservés dans les Bibl. de la Grande-Bretagne* (Paris, 1871), pp. 120–26 and A. Ewart, 'The Glasgow Latin-French glossary', *MÆ* 25 (1957), 154–63.

1 **Gloucestershire Record Office, D 4431, no. 27931.**
2 *C13b2.
3 [δ] A heading to an exemplification of grants of privileges and property to the Abbey of Fécamp, drawn up in 1293, purporting to assign grants to the authority of King Ælfred. *[?W]ytey alle myn yenes þat ich Alfred King habbe hy iȝune Stening Mine goude mete hom to seinte Trinitote of Fescampe al so fair and al so goud al so he me an and stod.*
4 Communicated by D.J.H. Smith, county and Diocesan Archivist, Gloucestershire Record Office. Description and transcript supplied by MB.

1 **Göttingen University Library, MS Theol. 107r.**
2 C14a1.
3 [λ] (1) Fols. 1–165r *Cursor Mundi.*
   (2) Fol. 165r–v the *Creed* and its exposition beg. *Trou in godd fadir all-mighti.*
   (3) Fols. 165v–167v *The Lord's Prayer* and its exposition beg. *[F]Adir vr þt es in heuen.*
   (4) Fol. 167v *Prayer to the Trinity* beg. *[F]adir and sune and hali gast.*
   (5) Fols. 168r–169r *A Prayer for the Hours of the Passion* beg. *Iesu þt wald efter midnight.*
   (6) Fol. 169r *A Song of the Five Joys of Our Lady* beg. *[H]Aile be þu mari maiden bright.*
   (7) Fol. 169r–v *The Book of Penance. Prologue* beg. *[D]rightin dere wid blisful beildes.*
4 CB Reg i 517–18. Murakami, pp. 113–15, nos. 47–48. Edited: R. Morris, *Cursor Mundi*, EETS OS 57, 59, 62, 66, 68, 99, 101 (1874–1878, 1892–1893).
   (1) Wells VI.1. Hartung 7 XX.31. *IMEV* 2153 and cf. *IMEV* 1885, 3208, 3976. For an interpolation on fol. 114v see also Hartung 3 VII.2(b) and *IMEV* 1786.
   (2) *IMEV* 959.

(3) *IMEV* 788.
(4) Wells *Suppl* 3, p. 1180 (XIII.138b). *IMEV* 780.
(5) Wells *Suppl* 3, p. 1179–80 (XIII.138a). Hartung 7 XX.227. *IMEV* 1775.
(6) Wells XIII.214. *IMEV* 1029. CB14 31.
(7) *IMEV* 694.
7 MS in one hand.
8 To fol. 75rA (*ca.* line 11000), the text depends on an exemplar in non-northern language; from *ca.* line 11000 on, the language is thoroughly and consistently northern (probably WRY), whereas in the earlier section, forms of probably SE Lincs origin (Crowland area) are well established. See *LALME* 1, p. 89 and Laing *Thesis* 1, pp. 23–26.

1 Heiligenkreuz, Stiftsbibliothek 12.
2 *C12b2.
3 [λ] The earliest MS of *The Austrian Legendary*. On fols. 170v–171r Bede's Death Song appears in the text of Cuthbert's *Epistola de obitu Bedae*.
5 For other MSS containing Bede's Death Song see the Index of Old English Texts.
4 Ker App. no. 13. Murakami, pp. 101–102, no. 33. Edited: Dobbie 1937, p. 57.
7 Written by a foreign scribe.

1 Hereford Cathedral Library P.i.17.
2 C12–C13.
3 [γ] 57 Glosses to Aldhelm's *De laude virginitatis*.
4 Ker 120. Edited: A.S. Napier, *Old English Glosses*, Anecdota Oxoniensa, Medieval and Modern Series 11 (1900), no. 3.
6 Ker, p. 157: "The MS is from Cirencester: 'Liber ecclesie beate marie cirencestrie'".

1 Hereford Cathedral Library P.v.5.
2 C13a1 (main hand *ca.* 1200, Hunt *Teaching* 1, p. 376).
3 [γ] Fols. 1r–172v the *Panormia* or *Liber derivationem* by Osbern of Gloucester (Latin) containing interlinear glosses and marginal notes. There are some vernacular glosses of which a few are English.
4 Vernacular glosses edited: Hunt *Teaching* 1, pp. 376–78.
6 *Ex libris* inscription on the first flyleaf indicates that the MS was from the abbey of Valles Dore in Herefordshire. Ker *Med Lib*, p. 58 and Hunt *Teaching* 1, p. 374.
7 Some of the glosses are in the main hand. Others may be later.

1 Hereford, Diocesan Registry, Registrum Ricardi de Swinfield.
2 *C14a.
3 [δ] Fol. 152 copy of a writ of King Edward declaring that he has granted to his clerks at Bromfield, Salop, judicial and financial rights over their lands.
4 Sawyer 1162. Edited: W.W. Capes, *Charters and Records of Hereford Cathedral* (Cantilupe Society, Hereford, 1908), p. 2; W.W. Capes, *The Register of Richard de Swinfield, Bishop of Hereford (1283–1317)* (Cantilupe Society, Hereford, 1909; also issued by the Canterbury and York Society), p. 425; F.E. Harmer, 'A Bromfield and a Coventry writ of King Edward the Confessor', *The Anglo-Saxons*, ed. P. Clemoes (London, 1959), pp. 101–102.
6 Hereford.

1 Henry E. Huntington Library (San Marino, California), HM 25782.
2 C13b2 (after 1286).
3 [γ] Fol. 7r–v French/English legal glossary.
4 See *IMEP* I, A3, pp. 62–63.
5 *IMEP* cites many other MSS with such glossaries, viz.: BL Add 32085, fol. 111; BL Harley 858, fol. 49; BL Stowe 386, fol. 70; Bodley, Rawlinson C 668A, fol. 87; Cambridge, Corpus Christi College 297, fol. 168v; Sidney University Library, Richardson Dep. (Sinclair 93), fol. 84v.

1 Henry E. Huntington Library (San Marino, California), HM 25904.
2 *C13–C14.
3 [λ] A royal saucery account for a Wednesday; the commodities purchased are given in English.
4 See *IMEP* I, B1, p. 61.

1 Kansas University Library Y 103. See Cambridge, Corpus Christi College 557.

1 Kansas University Library Y 104. See Oxford, Bodleian Library, Hatton 115.

1 Kilkenny Corporation Archives, *Liber Primus Kilkenniensis*.
2 C13b2–C14a1.
3 [λ] Fol. 1r (flyleaf) contains part of the Prologue to the *South English Legendary*: ten long verses on Christ shedding his blood on the earth of man's heart and beg. *þat ful uneþe eny more me miȝt þer on bringe.*
4 Wells *Suppl* 7, p. 1578 (VII.38a). *IMEV Suppl* *3634.1 (*olim IMEV* *53). Görlach *SEL*, p. 113. Edited: St J.D. Seymour, 'Three medieval poems from Kilkenny', *Proceedings of the Royal Irish Academy* 41, Section C (1932–1934), 205–208 and F.E. Richardson, 'A Middle English fragment from the First Book of Kilkenny', *N&Q* 207 (1962), 47–48.
5 For other early MSS containing parts of the *South English Legendary* see the Index of Middle English Texts A: Titles.
6 Fol. 1v contains Latin documents relating to the affairs of the borough of Kilkenny, 1378–1383.
8 Seymour (following Mabel Day): "it belongs to the SW Midland dialect".

1 Klosterneuburg (Lower Austria), Stiftsbibliothek 708.
2 *C13–C14.
3 [λ] Latin MS containing saints' lives. Bede's Death Song appears in Cuthbert's *Epistola de obitu Bedae* (fols. 371v–373v).
4 Murakami, p. 101, no. 32. Edited: Dobbie 1937, p. 59.
5 For other MSS containing Bede's Death Song see the Index of Old English Texts.
6 Continental.

1 Klosterneuburg (Lower Austria), Stiftsbibliothek 787.
2 *C13a.
3 [λ] Latin MS containing tracts by St Augustine and works by Bede. Bede's Death Song appears in Cuthbert's *Epistola de obitu Bedae* (fols. 182–184).
4 Murakami, pp. 100–101, no. 31. Edited: Dobbie 1937, p. 57.
5 For other MSS containing Bede's Death Song see the Index of Old English Texts.
6 Continental.

1 Leicester Museum 18 D 59.
2 C14a1 (c1310–20, Görlach *SEL*, p. 113).
3 [λ] A parchment bifolium containing parts of the fifth quire of the *South English Legendary* and used as binding for fols. 1–10, the accounts of Wyggeston Hospital Charity, Leicester for 1567.
4 Görlach *SEL*, pp. 113–14.
5 According to Görlach the text and orthography resemble those of Cambridge, Corpus Christi College 145 and BL Egerton 2891. For other early MSS containing parts of the *South English Legendary* see the Index of Middle English Texts A: Titles.
7 *SEL* text in one hand.

1 Lincoln Cathedral Chapter Library 132.
2 C13b.

3 [γ] Latin MS containing works of grammatical instruction heavily glossed. All the texts contain vernacular glosses almost entirely in French but a few in English.
4 See R.M. Thomson, *Catalogue of the Manuscripts of Lincoln Cathedral Chapter Library* (Cambridge, 1989), pp. 100–102. Contents also described Hunt *Teaching* 1, pp. 71–72. Vernacular glosses edited: Hunt *Teaching* 1, pp. 37, 43, 146–47, 150–51 and *Teaching* 2, pp. 3–5, 37–52 and 55–57, 65–81 and 84–85, 125–45 and 149–53 (Hunt's MS L). For C14 and C15 verses on fol. 100r–v see Thomson, op. cit., p. 102, *IMEV* 3895 and *IMEV Suppl* 2830.5.

1 Liverpool, Athenaeum, Gladstone 27.
2 C13.
3 [γ] *Statuta Angliae* in Latin and French. On fols. 74v–75r appears an OE/Latin legal gloss.
4 Ker *Med MSS* 2, pp. 147–51 (art. 36).

1 London, British Library, Additional 4936.
2 *C18.
3 [δ] Fols. 179r–v and 179v–80 transcripts of two writs of King Edward relating to Ramsey Abbey.
4 Sawyer 1110; Sawyer 1109 (K 853, printed from this MS — see Kemble vi, p. viii). Also edited *Mon Angl* ii 560.
6 Ramsey Abbey, Hunts.

1 London, British Library, Additional 5819.
2 *C18.
3 [δ] Fols. 3v–5 Latin and English versions of the Ely privilege: King Edgar to Ely Abbey. Abstracts made by William Cole.
4 Sawyer 779 (K 563, printed from this MS and from BL Cotton Augustus ii 13 (C15)).
5 For medieval copies of this text see the Index of Old English Texts. Other late copies are to be found in Bodley, Dodsworth 97, fols. 68r–71v, PRO C56/8, 56/35, 56/97 and 56/107 for which see Sawyer.
6 Ely Abbey.

1 London, British Library, Additional 5937.
2 *C16.
3 [δ] Fols. 131–133v abstracts from CUL Add 3020.
4 Sawyer as follows: S 931 (K 1308); S 437 (B 712, K 1114); S 556 (B 893, K 1167); S 595 (B 940, K 1180); S 1523 (K 1329, Whi 23); all apparently printed from this MS. Also edited (by "M."), 'Saxon charters to Thorney Abbey, in Cambridgeshire', *Collectanea Topographica et Genealogica* 4 (1837), pp. 54–59.
5 Cf. CUL Add 3020 for the originals from which these abstracts were made.
6 Thorney Abbey, Cambridgeshire.

1 London, British Library, Additional 8092.
2 C13.
3 [γ] Grammatical treatises in Latin including on fols. 11v–16r Adam of Petit Pont's *De Utensilibus* glossed in the vernacular, both French and English.
4 See Hunt *Teaching* 1, p. 166. Vernacular glosses edited: Hunt *Teaching* 2, pp. 37–53 (Hunt's MS A).
7 According to Hunt, the text is glossed in two hands contemporary with the main text.

1 London, British Library, Additional 9822.
2 *C15.
3 [δ] Ely "Liber A". Fols. 13r–14v. Latin and English versions of the Ely privilege: King Edgar to Ely Abbey.
4 Davis 378. Sawyer 779. Probably not printed anywhere from this MS.

5 For other medieval copies of this text see the Index of Old English Texts. Cf. also BL Add 5819 for a C18 copy by William Cole. The earliest surviving text is BL Stowe Charter 31, C11b2. The English version may have been written by Ælfric. See AM 'Wulfstan', p. 113 and n. 8 (pp. 128–29) (repr. 1989, pp. 115, 130–31) and Pope 'Ely Privilege'.
6 Ely Abbey.
7 English in one hand.
8 Garbled OE.

1 London, British Library, Additional 11579.
2 C14a1 ("early fourteenth century", CB14 1 (notes); *ca*. 1300–1325, *OBMEV*).
3 [λ] Miscellanea in Latin, French and English. Lyrics and other odd scraps of English appear as follows.
  (1) Fol. 24v nine irregular lines written as prose in a sermon collection and beg. *Nw ych habbe þat y nolde*.
  (2) Fol. 26v four lines beg. *þw wreche gost wid mud y det*.
  (3) Fol. 26v four short lines translating Latin 'Sic in te diligo' and beg. *þyf* [? *þys*] *yc loue in þe*.
  (4) Fol. 29r five lines on sin and repentance beg. *Let for þy senne*.
  (5) Fol. 29r lyric beg. *Sey wist y þe brom*.
  (6) Fols. 35v–36r Latin version followed by the English translation of *Candet Nudatum Pectus* beg. *þwit was his naked brest. and red blodi his side*.
  (7) Fols. 36r–v Latin, French and English versions of *Respice in Faciem*. English begins *Man folwe sentt Bernardes trace*.
  (8) Fols. 72v–73r quotes (in a Latin homily) the greater part of the first stanza of the lyric *Long Life* or *Man may longe liues wene*. It is in a garbled order and with line 1 contaminated by *The Proverbs of Alfred*, lines 108–109 (Arngart *P of A*, lines 153–156).
  (9) Fols. 97v, 98v, 102r proverbs and jingles in English appearing in Latin fables by Odo of Cheriton. Fol. 97v *Selde comet the lattere the betere*. Fol. 98v *Of aye ich the brouste of athele ich ne miste*. Fol. 102v *They thou the vulf hore hod to preste / They thou him to skole sette salmes to lerne / Hevere bet hise geres to the grove grene*.
  (10) Fol. 117r three lines beg. *I senege ilch dai*.
  (11) Fols. 141r–143r Sentence of Cursing; seven articles followed by six further curses.
4 CB Reg i 393. Wells *Suppl* 1, p. 978 (VII.51).
  (1) *IMEV* 2328.
  (2) *IMEV* 3701.
  (3) *IMEV Suppl* 1415.5.
  (4) *IMEV Suppl* 1863.8.
  (5) Wells *Suppl* 5, p. 1364 (XIII.11a). Hartung 3 VII.62. *IMEV* 3078. CB13 21B. T. Wright, *Latin Stories*, Percy Society 8 (1843), p. xxii.
  (6) Wells *Suppl* 1, p. 987 (XIII.116). *IMEV* 4088. See also Thomson *Candet* and CB14 1 (notes).
  (7) Wells *Suppl* 5, p. 1366 (XIII.115a). *IMEV* 2051. CB13 69.
  (8) Wells VII.46 (cf. Wells *Suppl* 6, p. 1456 (VII.5)). *IMEV* 2098 and 2070. Printed versions of the complete lyric are in CB13 10 (entitled *Death's Wither-Clench*) and D&H, p. 122.
  (9) Edited: T. Wright, op cit. nos. li, liv, lix and notes. *IMEV* 3513. *OBMEV* 278. Cf. also Wilson *Lost Lit*, pp. 124–25 and B.J. Whiting's review of CB13, *Speculum* 9 (1934), 219 fn. 2.
  (10) Wells *Suppl* 1, p. 986 (XIII.32a). *IMEV* 1366.
  (11) Hartung 7 XX.229. *IMEP* V, p. 38. Cf. *IPMEP* 122 and O.S. Pickering, 'Notes on the sentence of cursing in Middle English, or a case for the Index of Middle English Prose', *LSE* NS 12 (1981), 229–44.

5 For item (5) cf. Cambridge, Trinity College 323 item (15). For other copies of *Candet Nudatum Pectus*, *Respice in Faciem* and *Long Life*, see the Index of Middle English Texts A: Titles.
7 See D&H, p. 123 where Dobson, referring to item (8), says: "Some corrections have been made to the English words, apparently in a different hand".

1 London, British Library, Additional 14408.
2 C14a1.
3 [λ] Fols. 74r–81v fragments of *Guy of Warwick*. Four mutilated leaves, containing originally 50–56 lines to a column of which 48–52 remain, but many of these are almost obliterated.
4 Wells I.6. Severs 1.I.7. *IMEV Suppl* *4194.5 (*olim IMEV* *76). Edited: Maldwyn Mills and Daniel Huws, *Fragments of an Early Fourteenth-Century Guy of Warwick*, Medium Ævum Monographs NS 4 (Oxford, 1974).
5 Once part of the same manuscript as similar binding fragments in Aberystwyth, National Library of Wales 572.
7 One hand — same as NLW 572, q.v.
8 NME.

1 London, British Library, Additional 14847.
2 *C13b2 (1280–1294 (when William of Hoo was sacrist), with later additions, Thomson).
3 [δ] White Register of Bury St Edmunds. Contains copies of 40 pre-Conquest charters consisting of royal grants (including vernacular writs and privileges) and wills. English appears on (at least) fols. 15r–19v, 27r–28r, 30r–31v, 32v, 38r.
4 Davis 96. For charters (mostly English, some Latin with English bounds), see Sawyer as follows: S 1490; S 1528 (B 1017); S 1521; S 1516; S 1519 (K 1339); S 1483 (B 1012, K 1222, Whi 2); S 703; S 1526; S 1489; S 1527 (B 1020); S 1531; S 1470 (K 1340); S 1219 (B 1013, K 1349); S 1525 (B 1016); S 1537 (B 1162); S 1225 (B 1019); S 1045; S 1070 (K 1342, Har 10); S 1078; S 1084; S 1072; S 1079; S 1071; S 1068; S 1083; S 1082; S 1077; S 1073; S 1085; S 1075; S 1046 (K 1346); S 1081; S 1080; S 1074; S 1076. Not listed by Sawyer as from this MS but noted in Lowe 'Cartularies' are S 507 on fol. 27r and S 980 on fols. 27v–28r. Cf. S 995 (Latin) on fols. 28v–29v. Fol. 32v Pelteret 19; fol. 38r Pelteret 5, 18, 20. See Whitelock, pp. 103–104; will nos. 2, 24–27, 29, 31, 33 and 34, which she prints from CUL Ff.II.33, are also preserved in this MS. Cf. Thomson *Archives*, pp. 121–23, no. 1278. See also AM *Havelok*, 41 and fn. 12.
5 This MS and CUL Ff.II.33 probably descend from a common lost MS (Whitelock, p. 104) also produced in Bury St Edmunds, but written by a scribe from at least 20 miles further north (AM *Havelok*, 42). But note that Kathryn Lowe ('Cartularies') presents evidence that the *writs* were copied from a common exemplar but that the scribe copying the *wills* of Add copied them directly from Ff. The MSS share the following material: Ff 24r, Add 32v; Ff 27v–28r, Add 38r; Ff 45 (2), Add 15 (2); Ff 45, Add 15v; Ff 45v, Add 20; Ff 46, Add 16v; Ff 48, Add 18; Ff 48v, Add 18v; Ff 49–50, Add 19r–v. Cf. also CUL Ee.III.60; Gg.IV.4; Mm.IV.19; CUL Add 6006 and BL Harley 743.
6 Bury St Edmunds, Suffolk.
7 Kathryn Lowe ('Cartularies') notes that in this MS the royal grants are separated from the wills by seven folios (19v–27) and are written in a different, contemporary hand. In Lowe's view, the scribe copying the writs in this MS had more difficulty understanding his OE exemplar than did the scribe of the wills. On the other hand, the scribe of the wills omits more material in his copy than does the scribe of the writs.
8 MS probably *ca.* 1300 but contains "modified OE": in so far as the forms have been changed from OE they probably represent E Anglian language at a mid or latish 13C stage rather than *ca.* 1300. The remarkably close agreement of this MS and CUL Ff.II.33 suggests that the common original "had already given the texts a strongly late thirteenth-century flavour" (AM). Occasionally Add preserves a superior reading but in general is "greatly inferior to Ff" (Whitelock, p. 104). Kathryn Lowe notes that the

scribe of the wills modernises the language of his text more than does either the scribe of the writs or the scribe of Ff.II.33.

1 London, British Library, Additional 14850.
2 *C15a2 (after 1436, Thomson).
3 [δ] Fol. 85 copy of a grant of land by Ulfketel to Bury.
4 Davis 104. Sawyer 1219. This version not printed. Cf. Thomson *Archives*, p. 161, no. 1315.
5 Cf. CUL Ff.II.33, fol. 49v and BL Add 14847, fol. 19v.
6 Bury St Edmunds, Suffolk.

1 London, British Library, Additional 15236.
2 C13b2–C14a1 (*ca.* 1300, Hunt).
3 [γ] (1) Fols. 2r–9r, *synonyma* with English, French and Irish glosses to the Latin names of plants.
(2) Fols. 9r–11v, two lists of herbs alphabetically arranged.
(3) Fols. 11v–13v, non-alphabetical list of *synonyma*; 14r–22r, a similar list with fewer vernacular versions. A slightly later list of the same kind is on fols. 172v–187v.
4 See Hunt *Plant Names*, pp. xix–xx; Hunt *Pop Med*, pp. 217–63 and cf. T. Hunt, 'The botanical glossaries in MS London B.L. Add. 15236', *Pluteus* 4 (1986).
7 Hand A: fols. 2r–13v. Hand B: fols. 14r–22r. Hand C: fols. 172v–187v.

1 London, British Library, Additional 15350.
2 *C12a–C14b.
3 [δ] Codex Wintoniensis. Cartulary of the Benedictine Cathedral Priory of St Peter, St Paul and St Swithin (Old Minster), Winchester. English on fols. 6r–8v, 10r, 13v–23v, 24v–65r, 66r–120r. Contains copies of more than 200 pre-Conquest charters. The original cartulary, comprising the present gatherings 2–14 and believed to have been written during the episcopate of Henry of Blois (1130–1150), contains transcriptions of 185 documents from before 1086. Supplementary material down to *temp* Henry II has been added with some C14 notes of later charters at the beginning and end (fols. 3–8, 116r–120). See especially fols. 7v, 116v–117r, (vision of the monk Eadwine and charter granting land in Winchester for the foundation of New Minster) and 119v. Thirty-four of the documents (including eight wills) are in the vernacular throughout. The rest are in Latin but most have bounds in English.
4 Davis 1042. Ker, p. xiv fn. 2 and, for fols. 116v–117r, p. 274 seq. (Cf. Sawyer 1428). For fol. 119v, see *Regesta* 1, 268. Sawyer as follows: S 946 (Har 107, K 642); S 1820–21 (B 1160–61); S 889 (K 1291); S 836 (K 626); S 1154 (Har 112, K 891); S 1559; S 1376 (K 1347, Rob 53); S 1443 (B 605, K 1087); S 1449 (B 1163, K 594, Rob 49); S 817 (B 1148, Rob 38); S 229 (B 27, K 985); S 275 (B 391, K 1036); S 393 (B 690, K 1108); S 540 (B 863); S 891 (K 698); S 635 (B 962, K 1188); S 522 (B 832); S 861 (K 655); S 640 (B 1004, K 1209); S 696 (B 1071, K 1232); S 242 (B 102, K 997); S 589 (B 938, K 1189); S 1557 (B 939); S 284 (B 398, K 1039); S 596 (B 960, K 1186); S 443 (B 727, K 374); S 806 (2 versions) (B 1220, K 598, Rob 45); S 697 (B 1072); S 1242 (Har 108, K 717); S 352 (cf. another version below); S 1819; S 1571; S 311; S 254 (cf. another version below); S 1572; S 1006 (K 774); S 440 (B 729, K 1117); S 475 (B 770, K 1140); S 680 (B 1051, K 1225); S 565 (B 905, K 1170); S 487 (B 787, K 1145); S 258 (B 179, K 1006); S 383 (B 628, K 1095); S 412 (B 674, K 1102); S 811 (B 1319, K 597); S 718 (B 1114, K 1243); S 754 (B 1200, K 535); S 417 (B 689, K 1107); S 619 (B 982, K 1190); S 283 (B 377, K 1031); S 613 (B 974, K 1187); S 970 (K 752); S 465 (B 763, K 1136); S 638 (B 983, K 1185); S 763 (B 1217, K 544); S 486 (B 788, K 1146); S 1391 (K 768, Rob 98); S 1503 (cf. another version below); S 771 (B 1230, K 556); S 1001 (K 775); S 517 (B 810, K 1154); S 523 (B 830, K 1156); S 790 (B 1292, K 578); S 856 (K 648); S 672 (B 1183, K 1273); S 1503 (cf. first version above); S 511 (B 765, K 1139); S 488 (B 786, K 1144); S 571 (B 931, K 1174); S 1512 (B 931, K 628, Whi 7); S 352 (cf. first version above) (B 549, K

1064); S 441 (B 730, K 1116); S 536 (B 864, K 1161); S 381 (B 629, K 1096); S 693 (B 1077–78, K 1231, Rob 33); S 377 (2 versions) (B 625–26, K 1094, 1092); S 382 (B 627, K 1093); S 254 (cf. first version above) (B 158, K 1002); S 1581; S 1287 (B 617, K 1086, Rob 15); S 1524 (K 943, Whi 5); S 1285 (B 599, K 1079); S 274 (B 392, K 1037); S 444 (B 731, K 1118); S 385 (B 622, K 1088, Rob 20); S 636 (cf. another version below); S 310 (B 475, K 1051); S 345 (B 550, K 1065); S 1012 (K 776); S 598 (B 976, K 1192); S 653 (B 1027, K 1211); S 840 (2 versions) (K 633); S 803 (B 1314, K 589); S 532 (B 865, K 1163); S 400 (B 663, K 1101); S 359 (B 594, K 1077, Rob 110); S 695 (B 1076, K 1230); S 748 (B 1199, K 533); S 723 (B 1119, K 1246); S 802 (B 1315, K 590); S 574 (B 987, K 1155); S 1275 (B 543, K 1062, Rob 14); S 272 (B 390, K 1035); S 1403 (B 390 last 13 lines, K 949, Rob 107); S 1513 (B 566, K 1070, Rob 17); S 848 (K 636); S 846 (K 638); S 636 (cf. first version above); S 1009; S 1008; S 860 (K 650); S 1007 (K 780); S 416 (B 679); S 1533; S 676 (B 1037, K 1220); S 800 (cf. another version below) (B 1316, K 592); S 715 (B 1118, K 1245); S 942 (K 712); S 944 (K 713); S 312; S 313; S 1588 (B 479); S 868 (K 664); S 1504 (B 819, K 1173); S 831 (K 611); S 362 (B 595, K 1078); S 962 (K 743); S 351 (B 740, K 1121); S 309 (B 473, K 1055); S 340 (B 520, K 1061); S 304 (B 468, K 1054); S 273 (B 389, K 1033); S 378 (B 624, K 1091); S 585 (B 948, K 1184); S 427 (B 706, K 1110, Rob 25); S 1485 (B 1174, K 593, Whi 9); S 1444 (B 619); S 376 (B 621, K 342 and iii 404–405); S 837 (K 624); S 430 (B 707, K 1111); S 604 (B 979, K 1193); S 1476 (B 980, K 1337, Rob 114); S 446 (B 742, K 1122); S 600 (B 953, K 1181); S 276 (B 393, K 1038); S 575 (B 902, K 1178); S 503 (B 796, K 1148); S 317 (B 491, K 1056); S 867 (K 658); S 463 (B 758, K 1131); S 606 (B 959, K 1182); S 960 (K 739); S 675 (B 1042, K 1219); S 874 (cf. another version below) (K 673); S 608 (B 969, K 1183); S 467 (B 764, K 1137); S 994; S 336 (B 508, K 1059); S 849 (K 640); S 683 (B 1054, K 1227); S 354 (B 565, K 1069); S 1277 (B 544, K 1063); S 857 (K 652); S 835 (K 622); S 699 (B 1068, K 1229); S 1013; S 925 (K 720); S 972 (K 750); S 820 (B 1307, K 595); S 976 (K 753); S 1428 (K 922); S 1558; S 804; S 874 (cf. first version above); S 325 (B 493, K 1057); S 449 (K 1120); S 547 (B 875, K 1162); S 800 (cf. first version above); 938 (K 1284). Many of the above have English only in bounds. Other charters noted by Sawyer are Latin only. Fol. 27r contains a record of dues rendered to the manor of Taunton, Somerset (1066 x 1086), Pelteret 144. For fol. 119v see Pelteret 32. For collation to originals, see A.R. Rumble, 'The structure and reliability of the Codex Wintoniensis', Diss. Ph.D., University of London (1980), unpubl. and 'The purposes of the Codex Wintoniensis', *Proceedings of the Battle Conference on Anglo-Norman Studies IV – 1981*, ed. R. Allen Brown (Woodbridge, 1982), pp. 153–67, 224–32. For a study of the language of the wills in this MS see Lowe *Thesis*, esp. pp. 105–26, transcripts pp. 240–51 and Lowe 'OE wills'. Cf. also C.R. Hart, 'The *Codex Wintoniensis* and the king's *Haligdom*', in *Land, Church and People: Essays Presented to H.P.R. Finberg*, Agricultural History Review 18 Supplement (1970), pp. 7–38.

5 For texts on fols. 116v–117r cf. BL Stowe 944, fols. 40r–v and 57r–v.
6 Winchester, Hants.
8 Kathryn Lowe's observations on the language of the C12 copies of the vernacular wills in the MS suggest that the copying scribe has modified his West-Saxon originals very little. Lowe compares the language of the cartulary copies of some of the vernacular wills with their known, single sheet exemplars. She sees almost no changes in vocabulary but observes "minor syntactic changes" and a tendency to "replace late phonological forms with earlier ones".

1 London, British Library, Additional 15667.
2 *C13a2–b1.
3 [δ] Malmesbury Cartulary. Bounds in English on fols. 12r–13r, 33r, 34v–36v, 38. But apparently only odd words in English couched in Latin text.
4 Davis 643. Sawyer as follows: S 1577; S 1552 (B 673); S 1578; S 1585 (B 672); S 862.
5 For S 1577, cf. PRO E 164/24, fol. 132r–v.

6 Malmesbury, Wilts.
7 Fols. 12r–13r probably in three different hands. Fols. 33r–38r all one hand.

1 London, British Library, Additional 23986 (roll).
2 C13b2 (*ca.* 1275–1300, *OBMEV*; *ca.* 1300, D&W).
3 [λ] On the verso of the roll, *Interludium de Clerico et Puella*, an interlocutory poem in 84 lines, imperfect at the end.
4 Wells XIV.4. Hartung 5 XII.6. *IMEV* and *IMEV Suppl* 668. Edited: W. Heuser, 'Das Interludium De Clerico et Puella und das Fabliau von Dame Siriz', *Anglia* 30 (1907), 306–19; *OBMEV* 27; BSD XV; D&W XXXVIII. Cf. AM *Havelok*, 39 and Laing *Thesis* 1, pp. 16–19. Facsimile in N. Davis, *Non-Cycle Plays and the Winchester Dialogues*, Leeds Texts and Monographs Medieval Drama Facsimiles 5 (1979), p. 9, no. 2.
7 One hand.
8 Probably Lincs language.

1 London, British Library, Additional 25031.
2 C13 (a1300, *MED Plan & Bibl*, p. 102).
3 [λ] On fol. 5v *The Ten Commandments* in ten lines of English verse beg. *þu schald o god louien and heren.*
4 CB Reg i 404. Wells *Suppl* 1, p. 969 (VI.15). Hartung 7 XX.42. *IMEV* 3689.
6 MS is from Worcester. Ker *Med Lib*, p. 206. On fol. 9 is the heading of a letter from Stephen, Archbishop of Arles (1349–1350), papal chamberlain, to the inhabitants of the city and see of Worcester. On fol. 25v in writing of C14 appears "Obiit Robertus Dymhok, pater Ade de Cyrecestria".

1 London, British Library, Additional 27909.
2 C13a.
3 [λ] Fol. 2r a 44-line lyric, written as prose, beg. *Leuedi sainte marie moder and meide.*
4 CB Reg i 405. Wells XIII. 200. *IMEV* 1839. CB13 2. For a suggestion as to how the stanzas of this poem might be reordered to make better sense see Thomas G. Duncan, 'Textual notes on two Early Middle English lyrics', *NM* 93 (1992), 109–120.
5 Echoes phrases from the *Poema Morale* (see CB 13, pp. xvi–xvii); but there are apparently no other versions in this form.
7 English in one hand.
8 Still uses *p*.

1 London, British Library, Additional 29436.
2 *C13a2–b1 (after 1242).
3 [δ] Winchester Cartulary. Three Anglo-Saxon charters on fols. 10r–v. Post-Conquest vernacular charters on fols. 10v, 10v–11r, 11v, 13v–14r.
4 Davis 1043. For A-S charters see Sawyer 1151–53 (Harmer 109–11). For post-Conquest charters see Pelteret 31, 34, 35, 45. The C13 part is fols. 10–48. This is bound with later material from C13–C15.
6 Winchester, Hants. Ker *Med Lib*, p. 200.
7 English in one hand.
8 There appears to be very little modification of the OE in the material printed by Harmer.

1 London, British Library, Additional 33182.
2 *C16.
3 [δ] Fol. 8v copy of a Latin charter with English bounds: King Eadwulf grants lands in Sussex to Hunlaf his *comes*, *ca.* AD 765.
4 Sawyer 50.
5 Cf. London, Lambeth Palace Library 1212, p. 382.
6 Sussex.

1 London, British Library, Additional 38131.
2 *C14a1.
3 [δ] Copy and translation of AD 1314 into ME and Latin of a Writ of William I in French and English to the bishop, portreeve and burghers of London.
4 Pelteret 8.
6 London.

1 London, British Library, Additional 40000.
2 C12–C13.
3 [γ] A gospel book written in continental minuscule C10a, containing 42 OE glosses of C10a and two glosses of C11, used *ca*. 1100 and later as a Liber Vitae of the abbey of Thorney. Contains on fol. 10r–v name lists relating to Thorney Abbey with OE datable to C12–C13.
4 Ker 131. Edited in part (Scandinavian influenced language) by E. Jørgensen, 'Bidrag til ældre nordisk Kirke- og Literaturhistorie', *Nordisk Tidschrift för Bok- och Biblioteksväsen* 20 (1933), 186 seq.
6 MS was at Thorney Abbey, Cambs by *ca*. 1100. See Ker, p. 163 and Ker *Med Lib*, p. 189.

1 London, British Library, Additional 41476.
2 C13b.
3 [γ] Grammatical treatises in Latin including on fols. 22r–45v, John of Garland's *Accentarium* heavily glossed in the vernacular. The glosses are mostly French but some English. A few vernacular glosses are also to be found in an incomplete copy of Persius *Satyrae* on fols. 3r–9v.
4 Vernacular glosses printed: Hunt *Teaching* 1, pp. 148–50; *Teaching* 2, p. 12.

1 London, British Library, Additional 42055.
2 *C15 (after 1435, Thomson).
3 [δ] Fol. 1 copy of a grant by Thurketel to Bury St Edmunds.
4 Davis 100. Sawyer 1225. Cf. Thomson *Archives*, p. 158, no. 1310.
5 Same text as CUL Ff.II.33, fol. 50 and BL Add 14847, fol. 19v. This version is not printed.
6 Suffolk.

1 London, British Library, Additional 45951.
2 *C15 (*ca*. 1440, Thomson).
3 [δ] Fol. 1 copy of the Will of Thurketel.
4 Davis 103. Sawyer 1527.
5 Same text as CUL Ff.II.33, fol. 48v and BL Add 14847, fols. 18v–19. This version is not printed. Cf. Thomson *Archives*, p. 160, no. 1314.
6 Mentions Bury St Edmunds and other places in Suffolk and in Norfolk.

1 London, British Library, Additional 46487.
2 *C12a2 (c.1146, Davis) .
3 [δ] Sherborne Cartulary. Charters in English (some bounds only) on fols. 4v–13v, 16v, 18v–20v, 23r–v, 24v–25r, 26r–31v.
4 Davis 892. Ker, p. xiv fn. 2. Sawyer as follows: fols. 4v–6r S 933 (K 1309); fols. 6r–7v S 975 (K 1322); fols. 7v–9r S 290; fols. 9r–10v S 422 (B 695); fols. 10v–11 S 813 (B 1308, Rob 50); fols. 11r–12r S 516 (B 894); fols. 12r–13v S 423 (B 696); fol. 16v S 1422 (K 1302, Rob 74); fols. 18v–20v S 333 (B 510, Rob 11); fol. 23r–v S 1474 (K 1334, Rob 105); fols. 24v–25, 26r–27v (2 versions) S 969 (K 1318); fols. 27v–29 S 910 (K 1301); fols. 29r–30 S 998 (K 1332); fol. 30r–v S 601 (B 952); fol. 31r–v S 1032 (K 1341, Rob 120). Fols. 7v–9, edited: Finberg 1964, no. 567, pp. 160–3. See Finberg also for comment on the other charters in this MS.
6 Sherborne Abbey, Dorset. Ker *Med Lib*, p. 179.

1 London, British Library, Additional 53710.
2 *C14.
3 [δ] Fols. 222v–223v copies of two charters with English bounds, relating to places in Kent. Fol. 224 copy of a charter in English relating to Fordwich, Kent.
4 Sawyer 501, 300, 1092. Edited: R. Twysden, *Historiae Anglicanae Scriptores X* (1752), cols. 2125–28. Cf. BL Cotton Claudius D x, fols. 62r–63v and 175.
6 MS from St Augustine's, Canterbury, Kent. Ker *Med Lib Suppl*, p. 12.

1 London, British Library, Additional 61901 (*olim* Bradfer-Lawrence, H.L., MS 3).
2 C14a2–b1.
3 [δ] [λ] The Beverley Cartulary. MS in Latin except for
  (1) fol. 69r–v, a Middle English rhyming version of the charter of King Athelstan;
  (2) fols. 87v–88v, writs of Edward the Confessor and William I cited in an inspeximus of Richard II.
4 Davis 49. The MS is described by Ian Doyle, in Appendix 1 (pp. 20–21) of Richard Morris and Eric Cambridge, 'Beverley Minster before the early thirteenth century' in *Medieval Art and Architecture in the East Riding of Yorkshire* (British Archaeological Society, 1989), pp. 9–32. The contents of the MS are listed in Appendix 2 (pp. 22–27).
For (1) see Sawyer 451 cf. *IMEV* 3300.
For (2) see Sawyer 1067 and Pelteret 14 (though the version he cites on fol. 70v is in Latin only).
The rhyming charter of King Athelstan was probably concocted in the early fourteenth century. See J.R. Witty, 'The rhyming charter of Beverley', *TYDS* 22 (1921), 36–44.
5 This MS is the source for the C16 transcript, BL Harley 560 (of which BL Cotton Otho C xvi, fols. 65–102 is itself an incomplete transcript). Other copies of the rhyming charter of King Athelstan are BL Cotton Charter iv 18 and BL Lansdowne 269, fol. 97r–v. The Beverley Cartulary version has six more lines than the Cotton Charter version.
6 MS from Beverley, ERY.

1 London, British Library, Arundel 57.
2 C13–C14.
3 [λ] (1) Fol. 2r–4r (modern foliation) Author's Preface and Table of Contents to *Ayenbite of Inwit* including a prayer beg. *Zuete iesu þin holy blod*; introductory invocations in three long couplets beg. *Holy archan[g]le Michael* and two couplets beg. *Lord ihu almiȝti kyng* followed by personal lines beg. *Blind and dyaf and alsuo domb.*
(2) Fols. 13r–94r (*olim* 1r–82r) *Ayenbite of Inwit*, written by Dan Michel of the Northgate and including a rhyming introduction beg. *þis boc is ywrite uor englisse men þet hi wyte* and on fol. 51v (*olim* 39v) a stanza of the lyric *Long Life* beg. *Mon may longe his lyues wene* and on fol. 94r an ending couplet followed by the rhyming conclusion beg. *Nou ich wille. þet ye ywyte hou hit is y-went.*
(3) Fol. 94r (*olim* 82r) *Pater Noster* beg. *Vader our þet art ine heuenes*; *Ave Maria* beg. *Hayl Marie / of þonke uol* and *Creed* beg. *Ich leue ine god / uader almiȝti.*
(4) Fols. 94v–96v (*olim* 82v–84v) translation of Pseudo-Anselm beg. *Uor to sseawy þe lokynge of man wyþ-inne.*
(5) Fol. 96v (*olim* 84v) treatise on the difference between men and beasts beg. *Nammore ne is be-tuene ane manne / and ane beste.*
(6) Fol. 96v *Ave Maria* beg. *Hayl godes moder Marie / Mayde uol of þonke.*
(7) Fol. 96v another version of *Ave Maria* beg. *Mayde and moder mylde, uor loue of þine childe.*
4 CB Reg i 259. Edited: R. Morris, *Dan Michel Ayenbite of Inwyt*, EETS OS 23 (1866), rev. P. Gradon (1965) and EETS OS 278 (1979). Facsimile of one fol. *Pal Soc*, Parts ix–xiii, Plate 197.

(1) *IMEV Suppl* 3238.5, 1227, 1961.3, 539.5.
(2) Wells VI.4. Hartung 7 XX.4. *IPMEP* 55. Joliffe *Checklist* A.1(a) and I.11. For the rhyming intro. see *IMEV* 3579. For the verse on fol. 51v see Wells *Suppl* 1, p. 966 (VI.4) and *IMEV* 2070. For the couplet see *IMEV Suppl* 3578.5 and for the conclusion *IMEV Suppl* 2331.
(3) Wells VI.11 no. 7 and XIII.177. *IPMEP* 171, 279 and 316.
(4) Hartung 7 XX.134. *IPMEP* 219.
(5) Hartung 7 XX.164. *IPMEP* 473. Joliffe *Checklist* D.11.
(6) Not listed in *IMEV*.
(7) Wells *Suppl* 3, p. 1171 (VI.4). *IMEV* 2034.
For the prophecy of Thomas of Erceldoune on fol. 8v in a later hand see Hartung 5 XIII.289 and *IMEV* 3762.
6 Written at St Augustine's, Canterbury *anno* 1340, by which time Dan Michel was an old man of 70 years or more (see Gradon, EETS OS 278, p. 12). The language therefore is probably representative of the late 13th century rather than of the mid 14th. *Ex libris* inscription indicates MS belonged to the Abbey of St Augustine. See Ker *Med Lib*, p. 42.
7 The hand of Dan Michel.
8 Language of Canterbury, Kent. *LALME* LP 5890.

1 London, British Library, Arundel 60.
2 C13–C14.
3 [γ] *Psalterium*. Margins of fols. 8v, 9, 10v, 11 contain about 87 pencilled Latin lemmata and English glosses, only partly legible.
4 Ker 134, section 5.
6 Liturgical evidence associates the MS with Hyde Abbey, Hants. Ker *Med Lib*, p. 103.

1 London, British Library, Arundel 69.
2 C13a1.
3 [λ] Contains Roger of Hoveden's *Chronicle* including scraps of proverbs and a prophecy in English.
4 MS described as MS B by Stubbs *Hoveden* 1, pp. lxxx–lxxxii. English printed (from BL Royal 14 C ii): Stubbs *Hoveden* 2, pp. 224, 229–30 and (from Bodley, Laud Misc. 582): Stubbs *Hoveden* 3, p. 68. Stubbs provides variants from this MS (B). See also Wilson 1943, p. 46 and Richter 1979, p. 74.
5 According to Stubbs the first part of this MS is a copy of BL Royal 14 C ii, q.v. For other MSS containing Roger of Hoveden's *Chronicle* including the prophecy in English see the Index of Texts in Latin.
6 *Ex libris* inscription indicates the MS belonged to the Cistercian Abbey of Netley, Hants. See Ker *Med Lib*, p. 133. Stubbs considered the MS to be probably of Bury St Edmunds but this ascription is rejected by Ker (*Med Lib*, p. 22).

1 London, British Library, Arundel 178.
2 C16.
3 [δ] Crowland charters. Sawyer reports no English but spelling of names is interesting, not less because the charters are probably spurious.
4 See especially Sawyer 200 (B 461, K 265): confirmation of land by Berhtwulf, King of Mercia to Siward, abbot of Crowland — contains many Norse names. Cf. Kemble 297, 320. Edited: W. de Gray Birch, *The Chronicles of Croyland Abbey* (Wisbech, 1883).
6 Crowland Abbey.

1 London, British Library, Arundel 248.
2 C13b2.
3 [λ] Religious verse and prose mostly in Latin with some French. Only English on fols. 154r–155r.

(1) 154r *Angelus ad Virginem* (in Latin and English). English begins *Gabriel fram evene-king*.
(2) 154r a verse on the crucifixion beg. *þe milde Lomb isprad o rode*.
(3) 154r A verse on the vanity of the world beg. *[w]orldes blis ne last no throwe*.
(4) 154v–155r a version of *Stabat iuxta Christi crucem* beg. *Iesu cristes milde moder*.
4 CB Reg i 260.
(1) Wells XIII.42. *IMEV* 888. CB13 44 (English only). *OBMEV* 39. D&H, p. 176 (Latin and English).
(2) Wells XIII.128. *IMEV* 3432. CB13 45. D&H, p. 173.
(3) Wells XIII.31. *IMEV* 4223. CB13 46A. D&H, p. 136.
(4) Wells XIII.127. *IMEV* 1697. CB13 47. D&H, p. 161.
See CB13, pp. xxv–xxvi for a note on these lyrics and for the MS see D&H, p. 162.
5 For item (3) cf. Bodley, Digby 86 item (15) and Bodley, Rawlinson G 18. For MSS containing another version of *Stabat iuxta Christi crucem* beg. *Stand wel moder vnder rode* see the Index of Middle English Texts.
6 Dobson says (D&H, p. 162) the MS was written (in several hands) towards the end of the thirteenth century; "it is a collection made by and for clerics". He also suggests that it might have belonged to a Franciscan house.
7 The scribe of the English lyrics is considered by Dobson to be Anglo-Norman; the scribe misuses þ and shows confusion in the use of *h* and *ch*.
8 Dobson thinks items (1) and (4) were probably composed in East Anglia. AM considers (pers. comm.) that they must be from the southern part of that area. NB (4) line 34 has *hoschet* "asks".

1 London, British Library, Arundel 288.
2 C13b.
3 [λ] Religious verse and prose mainly in French. On fol. 118v in the French text of Edmund Riche's *Speculum Ecclesie* appears the usual English quatrain *Nou goþ sunne under wode / me reuweþ marie þy faire rode. / Nou goþ sunne under tre. / me reweþ marie sone and the*.
4 CB Reg i 262. Wells *Suppl* 1, p. 988 (XIII.127a). *IMEV* 2320/A9. See notes to CB13 1: "This English quatrain is introduced in the text of abp. Edmund's *Speculum Ecclesie*, a treatise probably composed 1239–40, since it was dedicated to the monks at Pontigny, where St Edmund was buried in 1240 only a few months after he left England. Numerous MSS of the *Speculum* exist in French, Latin and English".
5 For other MSS containing this text and the English quatrain see the Index of Texts in French.
7 English in one hand.

1 London, British Library, Arundel 292.
2 C13b2 (*ca.* 1275–1300, *OBMEV*).
3 [λ] Miscellaneous contents in English, Anglo-French and Latin. English appears as follows.
(1) Fol. 3r *Creed* in eleven couplets beg. *I leue in godd almicten fader*.
(2) Fol. 3r–v *Pater Noster* in twelve lines beg. *Fader ure ðatt art in heuene blisse*.
(3) Fol. 3v *Ave Maria* beg. *Marie ful off grace weel de be*.
(4) Fol. 3v *In manus tuas* beg. *Louerd godd in hondes tine*.
(5) Fol. 3v six lines on *Three Sorrowful Things* beg. *þanne i ðenke ðinges ðre*.
(6) Fol. 3v five couplets on mortality beg. *If man him biðocte*.
(7) Fols. 4r–10v *The Bestiary*.
(Later English on fols. 71v–72r (*ca.* 1350), *Uncomly in cloistre I cowre ful of care*, Wells XIII.32, *IMEV* 3819, *OBMEV* 80; and fol. 72v (*ca.* 1400–1425), *Swarte smeked smithes smatered with smoke*, Wells IV.41, *IMEV* 3227, *OBMEV* 142.)
4 CB Reg i 262.
(1) Wells VI.11. Hartung XX.38. *IMEV* 1326.
(2) Wells VI.11. *IMEV* 787.
(3) Wells VI.11; XIII.175. Hartung 7 XX.37. *IMEV* 2100.

(4) Wells VI.11. *IMEV* 1952.
(5) Wells VII.37. *IMEV* 3969. CB13 12B. *OBMEV* 271.
(6) Wells VII.17. *IMEV* 1422. CB13 13. *OBMEV* 25.
  Edited: R.M. Garrett, 'Religious verses from MS. Arundel 292', *Archiv* 128 (1912), 368 seq.
(7) Wells II.24. *IMEV* 3413. Hall i XXI, ii 579–626. D&W XI. BSD XII. *OBMEV* 26.
  Edited: Morris *OE Misc*, pp. 1–25.
5 For similar ecclesiastical texts see Cambridge, Emmanuel College 27 (I.2.6) and further refs. in the Index of Middle English Texts A: Titles. For item (5) cf. London, Lambeth Palace Library 499 item (4) and Oxford, New College 88 item (1). *The Bestiary* is unique to this MS.
6 MS has a C14 press-mark of Norwich Cathedral Priory and formerly contained an item on the fire of 1272 there. Ker *Med Lib*, p. 138.
7 The English on fols. 3r–10v is all in one hand.
8 Language of W Norfolk (cf. Cambridge, Corpus Christi College 444, *Genesis and Exodus* and see AM *Havelok*, 40–41 and fn. 11.)

1 London, British Library, Arundel 394.

2 C13b.
3 [γ] School texts in Latin including on fols. 1r–42r an acephalous copy of the *Graecismus* of Eberhard of Bethune and on fols. 44r–93v John of Garland's revision of Alexander of Villa Dei's *Doctrinale*. Both these texts are glossed in the vernacular, French and English.
4 Contents listed Hunt *Teaching* 1, p. 86. Vernacular glosses edited: Hunt *Teaching* 2, pp. 15–33 (Hunt's MS A).

1 London, British Library, Campbell Charter xxi 6.

2 C12a1 (February?, 1123)
3 [δ] One of three surviving originals of the writ granted to William of Corbeil and the monks of Christ Church, Canterbury by Henry I in 1123.
4 Pelteret 48. Edited: Edward Lye, *Dictionarium Saxonico et Gothico-Latinum*, ed. Owen Manning, 2 vols. (London, 1772), vol. 2 appendix 2, no. 6, perhaps from this MS. Reproduced in *Facsimiles of Royal and other Charters in the British Museum. Vol. 1. William I – Richard I*, ed. George F. Warner and Henry J. Ellis (London, 1903), plate v.
5 BL Stowe Charter 43 and Lambeth Palace, Cart. Misc. X/109 are the other originals of this text. Cf. BL Campbell Charter xxix 5 and Cotton Charter vii 1 which are similar in form and BL Harley Charter III B 49 which is said to be based on them (Hall ii 264).
7 Written in the same hand as Canterbury, D&C Library, Ch. Ant. C. 9. See Pelteret 47.
8 Hall says the dialect is mainly southern with some Kentish forms.

1 London, British Library, Campbell Charter xxix 5.

2 C12a1 (?1107).
3 [δ] One of three originals of the bilingual writ granted to S Anselm and Christ Church, Canterbury by Henry I, *ca.* 1107.
4 Pelteret 46. Reproduced in M.T. Clanchy, *From Memory to Living Record* (London, 1979), Plate iii.
5 Also extant in BL Cotton Charter vii 1 and Lambeth Palace, Cart. Misc. XI/1. For a fuller note see the entry for the former. Cf. also, BL Harley Charter III B 49 (Hall ii 264) and Campbell Charter xxi 6.

1 London, British Library, Cotton Augustus ii 8.

2 *C15.
3 [δ] Copy of a charter of King Cnut to Bury St Edmunds Abbey. AD 1021 x 1023.
4 Sawyer 980. Cf. Thomson *Archives*, p. 45, no. 2.
5 Cf. the entry for CUL Ff.II.33 and other Bury St Edmunds cartularies listed there.

6 Bury St Edmunds, Suffolk.

1 London, British Library, Cotton Augustus ii 13.
2 *C15.
3 [δ] Fols. 13r–v Latin and English versions of the Ely privilege: King Edgar to Ely Abbey.
4 Sawyer 779 (K 563).
5 For other medieval copies of the same see the Index of Old English Texts. Cf. also BL Add 5819 for a C18 copy by William Cole. The earliest surviving text is BL Stowe Charter 31, C11b2. The English version may have been written by Ælfric. See AM 'Wulfstan', p. 113 and n. 8 (pp. 128–29) (repr. 1989, pp. 115, 130–31) and Pope 'Ely Privilege'.
6 Ely Abbey.
7 English in one hand.

1 London, British Library, Cotton Augustus ii 81.
2 *C12.
3 [δ] Copy of a writ of King Edward declaring that Leofsi Duddesunu has given land at Wormley, Herts, to Westminster Abbey with his permission. AD 1053 x 1066.
4 Sawyer 1134 (Har 90, K 866). *BM Facs* iv 40.
5 Cf. BL Cotton Faustina A iii.
6 Herts.

1 London, British Library, Cotton Caligula A ix.
2 C13b2.
3 [λ] Part I, fols. 3r–194v Laʒamon's *Brut* (Laʒamon A). Part II, fols. 195–261v, originally a separate MS containing French and English verse.
 (1) Fols. 233r–246r *The Owl and the Nightingale* beg. *Ich pas in one sumere dale*
 (2) Fol. 246r–v *Long Life* or *Death's Wither-Clench* beg. *NON* [for *Mon*] *mai longe liues pene*
 (3) Fol. 246v *An Orison to Our Lady* beg. *ON hire is al mi lif ilong*.
 (4) Fol. 246v *Will and Wit* beg. *Hpenne-so wil pit ofer-stieð*.
 (5) Fols. 246v–247r *Doomsday* beg. *Hpenne ich penche of domes-dai*.
 (6) Fols. 247r–248v *The Latemest Day* beg. *Ihereð of one þinge*.
 (7) Fol. 248v *The Ten Abuses* beg. *Hpan þu sixst onleoð king þat is pilful*.
 (8) Fols. 248v–249r *Litel Soth Sermun* beg. *Herknied alle gode men*.
French pieces: fols. 195r–216r *Saint Josaphat*; fols. 216v–229v *The Seven Sleepers*; fols. 229v–232v prose chronicle; fols. 249r–261v *Le Petit Plet*.
4 Part 1 Wells III.3 (and cf. Wells *Suppl* 2, p. 1052 and Wells *Suppl* 9, p. 1805). Hartung 8 XXI.3. *IMEV* 295. Hall ii 450–79. Edited: F. Madden, *Laʒamon's Brut*, 3 vols. (London, 1847); G.L. Brook and R.F. Leslie, *Laʒamon's Brut*, EETS OS 250, 277 (1963 for 1961 and 1978). Extracts printed Hall i XIV, BSD X, D&W VI, *OBMEV* 1 and G.L. Brook, *Selections from Laʒamon's Brut* (Oxford, 1963).
For contents of part II and correspondences of texts with Oxford, Jesus College 29, see CB 13, pp. xxiii–iv. See also CB Reg i 266 and Morris *OE Misc*, pp. 156–90.
 (1) Wells IX.8. Hartung 3 VII.45. *IMEV* and *IMEV Suppl* 1384. Hall i XX, ii 553–79. BSD I. D&W X (facsimile of fol. 233r opp. p. 52). Edited (all under the title *The Owl and the Nightingale*): J.E. Wells (Boston and London, 1907); J.W.H. Atkins (Cambridge, 1922); J.H.G. Grattan and G.F.H. Sykes, EETS ES 119 (1935); E.G. Stanley (Nelson's Medieval and Renaissance Library, 1960).
 (2) Wells VII.46. *IMEV* 2070. See also CB13 10 (notes) and D&H, pp. 122–23.
 (3) Wells XIII.201. *IMEV* 2687. CB13 32B. D&H, p. 130 seq.
 (4) Wells VII.13. *IMEV* 4016. CB13 39.
 (5) Wells VII.32. Hartung 3 VII.18(g). *IMEV* 3967. CB13 28B.
 (6) Wells VII.36. Hartung 3 VII.18(n). See *IMEV* 3517. CB13 29B.
 (7) Wells VII.12. *IMEV* 4051.
 (8) Wells V.3. *IMEV* 1091.

For date see Ker in EETS OS 251 (cited below) and the review by E.G. Stanley, *N&Q* 209 (1964), 191–93. Malcolm Parkes (pers. comm.) says there are marked palaeographic resemblances with two datable MSS: (a) BL Royal 3 D vi (between 1283 and 1300); (b) BL Add 24686 (*ca.* 1284) and refers to Watson *BL*, pls. 169, 171. For evidence on the spelling of the copyist see G.L. Brook, 'A piece of evidence for the study of Middle English spelling', *NM* 73 (1972), 25–28. (Note that *IMEV* 1105/C3 cited as being from fol. 14r of this MS should refer to BL Cotton Caligula A xi, fol. 14r.)
Facsimile of *The Owl and the Nightingale*, ed. N.R. Ker, EETS OS 251 (1963 for 1962), contents listed p. xi.

5 Cf. Oxford, Jesus College 29 for many of the same texts, including *The Owl and the Nightingale*. For Laȝamon B, see BL Cotton Otho C xiii. For texts shared with other MSS see the Index of Middle English Texts A: Titles.

7 The two parts of the MS are in different hands, probably contemporary. The hand of part II is similar to that of part I but is more skilled. Part I, Laȝamon, is said by Madden to be in two hands. Using the old foliation he suggests that hand B takes over from hand A at fol. 16v and that A reappears at fol. 86 "for two and a half pages" after which the second hand recurs. This opinion is endorsed in *New Pal Soc*, First Series, vol. 1, plate 86. Here it is stated (using the new foliation) that the first hand breaks off at fol. 18v col. 2 line 6 and recurs on fols. 88–89 col. 1 line 11. There has also been some suggestion that fols. 26v–27r line 6 may be in another hand. My own belief, and that of AM, is that the entire text is in one hand. There is a great deal of variability in the cut of the pen and in the neatness of the script and this is mainly responsible for the appearance of hand changes where they have been noted. There is also variation in the formation of some letter shapes, especially *g* and *a*. But extremes of difference must be looked at in the context of all the variant forms of those letters represented in the text. The extremes are not confined to those stretches said to be in different hands but are often found in close proximity to each other. AM considers this view to be strongly supported by there being no sign of any concomitant change of language at any of the alleged points of change of hand.

8 Language of part I, Laȝamon, is of NW Worcs. The orthography, especially of the vowels, is very variable as though the system had not yet settled into a coherent form.

1 London, British Library, Cotton Caligula A xv.

2 C12a.

3 [λ] Part A, art. *r*, fols. 133–137. Fragments of a chronicle, (I), relating to Christ Church, Canterbury (Ker, p. 175). Last entry in English is for 1130.

4 Ker 139. Hartung 8 XXI.2. Edited: F. Liebermann, *Ungedruckte Anglo-Normannische Geschichtsquellen* (Strasbourg, 1879), pp. 1–8.

6 Part A of the MS was written at Christ Church, Canterbury. Ker, p. 176 and Ker *Med Lib*, p. 35.

1 London, British Library, Cotton Charter iv 18.

2 C14a2–b1 (not C16 as in Sawyer).

3 [δ] [λ] Contains a text of the Middle English rhyming version of King Athelstan's grant of privileges to St John's, Beverley.

4 Sawyer 451 (B 1339). *IMEV* 3300. Probably concocted in the early fourteenth century. See J.R. Witty, 'The rhyming charter of Beverley', *TYDS* 22 (1921), 36–44. This version of the charter has six fewer lines than that in BL Add 61901. See Ian Doyle, in Appendix 1 (pp. 20–21) of Richard Morris and Eric Cambridge, 'Beverley Minster before the early thirteenth century' in *Medieval Art and Architecture in the East Riding of Yorkshire* (British Archaeological Society, 1989), pp. 9–32.

5 Other MSS containing versions of this charter are BL Add 61901, Harley 560 and Lansdowne 269.

6 Beverley, Yorks; 'Carta adelstani facta sancto Johanni Beuerl' in a hand of C15.

7 AID: "written as continuous though punctuated prose; by a good cursive hand of the middle of the 14th century in charter format".

8 The language is northern. The scribe uses y for þ.

1 London, British Library, Cotton Charter vii 1.
2 C12a1 (?1107).
3 [δ] One of three originals of the bilingual writ granted to S. Anselm and Christ Church, Canterbury by Henry I, *ca.* 1107.
4 Pelteret 46. Edited: G. Hickes, *Antiquae Literaturae Septentrionalis Libri Duo* 1 (Oxford, 1705), xvi; and (from Hickes) *Mon Angl* i 111.
5 Also extant in Campbell Charter, xxix 5 and Lambeth Palace, Cart. Misc. XI/1. Cf. also Harley Charter 111 B 49 (Hall ii 264) and Campbell Charter xxi 6.

1 London, British Library, Cotton Charter viii 15.
2 *C14.
3 [δ] Copy of a writ of William I to his thegns in Wiltshire and Hampshire concerning lands in Wilts. Written at London.
4 Pelteret 32. Another copy of the same is in BL Add 15350, fol. 119v.
6 London.

1 London, British Library, Cotton Claudius B iv.
2 C12a2–b1.
3 [γ] Mid-twelfth-century notes (English and Latin) added to *Hexateuch* of C11a.
4 Ker 142. Edited: S.J. Crawford, 'The late Old English notes of MS. (British Museum) Cotton Claudius B.iv', *Anglia* 47 (1923), 124 seq.
6 MS associated with St Augustine's, Canterbury, Kent. Ker *Med Lib*, p. 43.
7 The C12 annotations are in two hands only one of which uses English.
8 Ker, p. 179, indicates that the orthography of the English text is "strange" and the dialectal forms are Kentish. The same hand added a few words to the text, e.g. fol. 39 *abrhames breþer*, fol. 80v & *ane dohter* (Crawford, op. cit., pp. 147, 227), and put in a very large number of additional accents, usually acute, but *c*-shaped on *god* ("God") and its case-forms, and on a few other short vowels. These accents occur also in the added notes, e.g. on fol. 15v, where they are evidently original.

1 London, British Library, Cotton Claudius B vi.
2 *C13b2.
3 [δ] Abingdon Cartulary. Charters, mostly in Latin with English in bounds only, on fols. 10v–11r, 16r–19, 20v–24v, 25v–32v, 33v–42v, 44v–68v, 69v–71r, 72r–83v, 85v–87r, 90v–93v, 95v–105r, 106r–107v, 108v–111r, 113r–115r, 116r–117r.
4 Davis 4. See J. Stevenson, *Chronicon Monasterii de Abingdon*, 2 vols, RS 2 (1858), where many texts are printed. Sawyer as follows: S 202 (B 466, K 268 and iii 393–94); S 355 (B 581, K 326 and vi 228); S 999 (K 767); S 369 (B 601, K 1080); S 404 (B 667); S 1208 (B 688, K 1129, Rob 22); S 413 (B 675, K 1103); S 1604 (B 676, K 1105); S 411 (B 682); S 396 (B 659, K 1099); S 448 (B 743, K 1223); S 1567 (B 760, K 1135 and v 263–64); S 471 (B 761, K 1133); S 461 (B 762, K 1134); S 480 (B 777, K 1141); S 491 (B 789, K 1147); S 494 (B 798, K 1150); S 496 (B 801, K 1151); S 482 (B 778, K 1142); S 500 (B 802, K 1152); S 567 (B 906, K 1171); S 542 (B 866, K 1164); S 335 (B 505); S 529 (B 833, K 1158); S 525 (B 834, K 1159); S 552; S 561 (B 899, K 1168); S 558 (B 892); S 560 (B 900, K 1169); S 564 (B 908, K 1172); S 577 (B 1022, K 1177); S 559 (B 895); S 578 (B 888, K 1175); S 605 (B 924); S 663 (B 1002, K 1216); S 607 (B 919, K 1208); S 583 (B 981, K 1194); S 617 (B 964, K 1195); S 618; S 611 (B 966); S 587; S 597 (cf. another version below) (B 949, K 1196); S 622 (B 963, K 1198); S 591 (B 942, K 1199); S 594; S 614 (B 971, K 1200); S 1292 (B 972, K 1201, Rob 31); S 590 (B 932, K 1202); S 621 (B 955, K 1203); S 588 (B 946, K 1205); S 624; S 620 (B 984, K 1204); S 603 (B 977, K 1206); S 620; S 597 (cf. first version above) (B 941, 950, K 1191, 1197); S 639 (B 1005, K 1210); S 654 (B 1028, K 1212); S 650 (B 1032, K 1213); S 651 (B 1035, K 1214); S 657 (B 1034, K 1215); S 673 (B 1047, K 1221); S 734 (B 1169, K 1255); S 1541 (B 1170, K 1255); S 757 (B 1222, K

1261); S 1569 (B 1223); S 682 (B 1058, K 1228); S 759 (B 1224, K 1262); S 760 (B 1225, K 1263); S 713 (cf. another version below) (B 1121, K 1247); S 725 (B 1143, K 1252); S 737 (B 1189, K 1257); S 698 (B 1075, K 1233); S 722 (B 1123, K 1248); S 705 (B 1093, K 1238); S 678 (B 1036, K 1218); S 761 (B 1227, K 1265); S 756 (B 1213, K 1266); S 689 (B 1080, K 1235); S 758 (B 1221); S 708 (B 1124, K 1249); S 724 (B 1142, K 1253); S 688 (B 1067, K 1236); S 714 (B 1125, K 1250); S 690; S 829 (K 1277); S 828 (K 1276); S 843 (K 1279); S 896 (K 703); S 918 (K 1305); S 833 (B 1096, K 1241); S 852 (K 1281); S 883 (K 1289); S 855 (K 1282); S 858 (K 1283); S 887 (K 1292); S 902 (K 1296); S 901 (K 1295); S 1488 (K 716, Whi 18); S 915 (K 1303); S 927 (cf. another version below) (K 1307); S 934 (K 1310); S 967 (K 751); S 964 (K 746); S 993 (K 762); S 1020 (cf. another version below) (K 792); S 1023 (K 796); S 1065 (K 888); S 1066 (K 840); S 1022 (K 793); S 1025 (K 800); S 1020 (cf. first version above); S 927 (cf. first version above); S 713 (cf. first version above) (B 1122, K 1247).

5 Cf. BL Cotton Claudius C ix, an earlier cartulary which contains many of the same texts.
6 MS from Abingdon Abbey, Berks. Ker *Med Lib*, p. 3.
8 Language apparently very little modernised.

1 London, British Library, Cotton Claudius C ix.
2 *C12b1 (before 1170, Davis).
3 [δ] Abingdon Cartulary. Charters, mostly in Latin with English in bounds only, on fols. 108v–112v, 113v–123v, 126v–127v, 129v–134v, 196r–202v.
4 Davis 3. Ker, p. xiv fn. 2. See J. Stevenson, *Chronicon Monasterii de Abingdon*, 2 vols., RS 2 (1858), where many texts are printed. Cf. F.M. Stenton, *The Early History of the Abbey of Abingdon* (Reading, 1913), who dates the MS C13a. Sawyer as follows: S 335 (B 504); S 355; S 404; S 1208; S 567; S 558 (B 892); S 605 (B 924); S 663; S 583; S 607; S 614; S 587; S 622; S 594; S 590; S 617; S 618; S 611; S 482; S 673; S 756; S 682; S 689; S 690; S 688; S 708; S 724; S 734; S 758; S 757; S 759; S 760; S 732; S 761; S 829; S 896; S 918; S 901; S 964; S 993; S 1065 (Har 4, K 888); S 1066 (Har 5); S 1025; S 1023; S 1020; S 713; S 927. Of the above charters all but thirteen appear again in the later part of the MS as follows: S 1208 (Rob 22); S 577; S 552; S 597 (B 949); S 529; S 650; S 591; S 639; S 471; S 1542 (B 633); S 494; S 1540; S 1545 (B 523); S 1546 (B 684); S 1567; S 413; S 491; S 369; S 858; S 828; S 1544 (B 1261); S 1216 (B 1262, Rob 51); S 705; S 843; S 855; S 1574 (B 947); S 967; S 1569. Fols. 196r–202v also contain the boundaries of the following charters listed above: S 567, S 673, S 756, S 682, S 689 (B 1144), S 700, S 724, S 734, S 758, S 759, S 757, S 760, S 558, S 587, S 605 (B 924), S 673, S 663, S 607, S 614, S 622, S 482, S 594, S 590, S 611, S 617, S 618, S 355, S 335 (B 505), S 713 (B 1121), S 896, S 404 (B 668), S 1023, S 964, S 1025.
5 Cf. BL Cotton Claudius B vi, a later Abingdon Cartulary which contains many of the same texts.
6 MS from Abingdon Abbey, Berks. Ker *Med Lib*, p. 3.
8 Language is probably too early to be very useful, but may be compared with parallel texts in Cotton Claudius B vi.

1 London, British Library, Cotton Claudius D iii.
2 C13a.
3 [λ] Benedictine Rule: copy in alternate chapters of Latin and ME of the beginning of C13. English on fols. 52r–54v, 55r–v, 58r–60r, 61r–v, 62v–67v, 68v–82r, 83v–92r, 93r–95v, 96v–103v, 104v–112v, 113v–115v, 116v–118v, 119v–126r, 127r–v, 128v–130r, 131r–138r.
4 Ker, p. xix fn. 2. Wells VI.41. Severs 2 VI.2. *IPMEP* 98. Edited: A. Shröer, *Die Winteney-version der Regula S. Benedicti* (Halle, 1888). For Latin and OE versions of the Rule see Mechthild Gretsch, *Die Regula Sancti Benedicti in England und ihre Altenglische Übersetzung*, Texte und Untersuchungen zur Englischen Philologie 2 (Munich, 1973); and for this MS see p. 194 seq.

6 This is a version of the rule adapted for nuns and seems to have been written for the Cistercian House of Wintney in NE Hampshire (9 miles ENE of Basingstoke). On fol. 156r in a hand somewhat later than the rest is written "Anno ab incarnatione domini millesimo ducentesimo tricesimo quarto. Dedicata est ecclesia de Winteneia". See also Ker *Med Lib*, p. 204.
8 Hampshire English of the EME period.

1 London, British Library, Cotton Claudius D vi.
2 C13b2–C14a1.
3 [λ] Contains historical works in Latin by Matthew Paris, William Rishanger and others including *Annales Angliae et Scotiae*. In a passage referring to the capture of Berwick in 1296 by Edward I appears a quotation of the Scots' abuse to Edward: *Kyng Edward wanne þu havest Berwic, pike þe, wanne þu havest geten, dike þe.*
4 Edited: H.T. Riley, *Willelmi Rishanger Chronica et Annales*, RS 28 (1865), p. 373. Cf. Richter 1979, p. 122.
5 This quotation, which is the only English given in this MS, corresponds to the five lines found in many early chronicles and most MSS of the prose *Brut* beg. *What wenes kinge Edward with his longe shankes*. The reply of the English is to be found in Pierre Langtoft's *Chronicle* as the first of a series of verses quoted in English. It begins: *Piket hym and diket him / on scorne saiden he.* See *IMEV* and *IMEV Suppl* 3918.5 and 2754.
6 MS from St Albans. Ker *Med Lib*, p. 166.

1 London, British Library, Cotton Claudius D vii.
2 C13a2.
3 [λ] Fol. 181v contains a saw in a Lanercost Chronicle (*sub anno* 1244): *Wille Gris, Wille Gris, Thinche twat you was, and qwat you es.*
4 Wells *Suppl* 2, p. 1065 (VII.25a). *IMEV* and *IMEV Suppl* 4174. Cf. also Wenzel 1978, p. 73; Wilson 1943, p. 51. Edited: J. Stevenson, *Chronicon de Lanercost* (Edinburgh, 1839), p. 52.
5 For similar lines cf. Cambridge, Gonville and Caius College 351/568 item (1).
6 Lanercost, Cumberland. Ker *Med Lib*, p. 108.

1 London, British Library, Cotton Claudius D x.
2 *C13.
3 [δ] Canterbury Cartulary, the 'Red Book'. English charters on fols. 62r–63v, 104r, 175r, 307r.
4 Davis 193. Sawyer as follows: S 501 (B 797, K 1149); S 300 (B 549, K 1049); S 1092 (cf. another version below); S 1239; S 1092 (Har 39, K 854); S 518 (B 1345).
6 Canterbury, Kent.
7 Fols. 62r–63v are in one hand, fols. 104r, 175r and 307r are in another hand.
8 The language is only slightly modernised but is of some interest.

1 London, British Library, Cotton Cleopatra B i.
2 C13.
3 [λ] Composite MS containing on fols. 24r–28v the *Life of St Edmund* by Eustace of Faversham which quotes in English Edmund's last words: *Man seid gamen god an uombe, and ich sigge game god on herte.*
4 See Lawrence *St Edmund*, p. 218 fn. 1.
5 For other C13 MSS containing this version of the *Life of St Edmund* see the Index of Texts in Latin. Cf. also the "Anonymous A" version which also quotes Edmund's last words.

1 London, British Library, Cotton Cleopatra B vi.
2 C13a2–b1 (1250, *OBMEV*).
3 [λ] Rhetorical and grammatical treatises in Latin except: fol. 204v (*olim* 201v) four short poems in English, written as prose and the *Creed* in prose.
(1) Twelve lines beg. *[B]Idde huue with milde steuene.*

(2) *Pater Noster* beg. *[V]Re fadir þat hart in heuene.*
(3) *Ave Maria* beg. *[H]eil marie. ful of grace.*
(4) Prayer to the BV and Jesus beg. *[M]aidin and moder þat bar þe heuene kinge.*
(5) *Creed* in prose beg. *[H]I true in god fader hal-michttende.*
4 CB Reg i 266. *Rel Ant* i 22. Murakami, pp. 108–109, no. 42.
(1) Wells XIII.136. Hartung 7 XX.203. *IMEV* 519. CB13 67. *OBMEV* 11.
(2) Wells VI.11. *IMEV* 2706.
(3) Wells XIII.176. Hartung 7 XX.37. *IMEV* 1062.
(4) Wells XIII.183. *IMEV* 2037. CB13 68.
(5) *IPMEP* 316.
5 For similar ecclesiastical texts see Cambridge, Emmanuel College 27 (I.2.6) and further refs. in the Index of Middle English Texts A: Titles.
7 English in one hand.
8 Important as one of the earliest surviving texts in Northern Middle English.

1 London, British Library, Cotton Cleopatra C vi.
2 C13a2 (1225–1230 for main hand (A), Dobson *AR*; 1240, Hall).
3 [λ] *Ancrene Riwle* MS C. Also contains consecutive English by Hand D (see Dobson *AR*, pp. cxl–clxxii) as follows.
(1) Fol. 22v (*olim* 21v) jingle beg. *Liþer lok and tuinkling.*
(2) Fol. 23r (*olim* 22r) verses on the *Abuses of the Age* beg. *King conseilles / Bissop lore les.*
(3) Fol. 57v (*olim* 56v) verses beg. *Ne be þi winpil* [for *wimpil*] *neuere so Ielu.*
(4) Fol. 57v (*olim* 56v) sermon beg. Bernardus. *Quamdiu fuero.*
4 CB Reg i 267. *Ancrene Riwle* Wells VI.40. Severs 2 VI.1. Hall ii 356. *IPMEP* 559. Edited: Dobson *AR*. See also Dahood *AW*. For a six-line verse inserted into *Ancrene Riwle* on fol. 105v see Wells *Suppl* 1, p. 975 (VII.15) and *IMEV* 3568. A proverbial saying: *Ach eauer is þe ech3e to þe wodele3e* appears on fol. 39r (*olim* 38r). See Wells *Suppl* 7, p. 1583 (XIII.1b), *IMEV Suppl* 734.5.
For (1) see Dobson *AR*, p. 45 fn. 15, Wells VII.12 and *IMEV* 1917.
For (2) see Dobson *AR*, p. 46 fn. 7, *IMEV* 1820 and *IMEV Suppl* for nine other versions.
For (3) see Dobson *AR*, p. 46 fn. 7, Wells *Suppl* 9, p. 1830 (VII.22) and *IMEV* 2285 but citing the wrong folio (fol. 22r).
For (4) see Dobson *AR*, pp. 110–11. Wells *Suppl* 2, p. 1057 (V.3a). *IPMEP* 552. Facsimile of fol. 190r in *Pal Soc*, Second Series, vol. 1, plate 76. Facsimile of fol. 57v with transcription (Hand D) in Dobson *AR*, pp. 110–111.
5 For other EME texts of *Ancrene Riwle* see the Index of Middle English Texts A: Titles. Later ME versions are found in Cambridge, Magdalene College, Pepys 2498; BL Royal 8 C i; Bodley, Eng. poet. a. 1, the Vernon MS. Cf. Cambridge, Trinity College 43 (B.1.45) for shared verses. Hand D also contributed to the latter MS.
6 *Ex libris* inscription indicates that the MS belonged to Canonsleigh Abbey, Devon. Ker *Med Lib*, pp. 28–29.
7 On hands see esp. Dobson *AR*, p. xlvi seq.
Hand A: the main scribe who copied the whole text of *Ancrene Riwle*, was apparently not trained in the AB orthographic tradition but his language belongs not far distant from the place of origin of AB language.
Hand B: a contemporary corrector of the MS, identified by Dobson as the original author of *Ancrene Wisse* (see p. xciii seq.), writes essentially AB language but at a less developed stage.
[Hand C: Dobson does not use the term "hand C" because the MS itself is sometimes referred to as C.]
Hand D: a slightly later corrector; see Dobson *AR*, p. xlvii.
8 On language of A see Dobson *AR*, pp. lxxii–xciii and cf. Smith 'Tradition'. For a comparison of the language of Scribe B with that of AB language proper, as defined by the language of Cambridge, Corpus Christi College 402, see Dobson *AR*, pp. xciii–cxl (esp. cxxx–cxl). Provenance almost certainly the eastern periphery of AB

area. Dobson suggests Worcester; Smith prefers N Worcs. Hand D Dobson associates with Lincs; AM believes it to be Norfolk, very probably NW Norfolk "perhaps not very far south of King's Lynn" (see AM *Havelok*, 36–49). For D's contribution and other work by him see Dobson *AR*, p. cxliii seq. and cf. the entry for Cambridge, Trinity College 43 (B.1.45).

1 London, British Library, Cotton Domitian i.
2 C13a2.
3 [λ] A composite MS containing on fols. 111v–135v the *Descriptio Kambriae* of Giraldus Cambrensis. On fol. 122r–v appear instances of alliterative lines in English: *Godes to gedere gamen and wisdom*; *Ne halt nocht alsor isaid ne al sorghe atwite*; and *Betere is red thene rap and liste thene lither streingthe.*
4 Edited: J.F. Dimock, *Giraldi Cambrensis Opera* 6, RS 21 (1868), p. 188. Cf. Wilson *Lost Lit*, p. 161; Richter 1979, p. 96.

1 London, British Library, Cotton Domitian ix.
2 C12a1.
3 [λ] Fol. 9r–v prose fragment of a chronicle dealing with years 1113–1114.
4 Ker 150. Wells III.2. Hartung 8 XXI.1. Edited: Julius Zupitza, 'Fragment einer englischen Chronik aus den Jahren 1113 und 1114', *Anglia* 1 (1878), 195–7. See also 'Zu Anglia 1 5 ff., 195 ff. u. 286 f.', *Anglia* 3 (1879–1880), 32–33.

1 London, British Library, Cotton Domitian x.
2 C13a.
3 [δ] Fols. 90–208 Rochester Cartulary. On fols. 103r–104r, 107r–108v, 112r–114r (nos. iii, xi, xv, xxv) are copies of bilingual diplomas, Latin with English rights clauses, of Kings William II, Henry I and Henry II, concerning land in Rochester and other places in Kent.
4 Davis 818. Pelteret 42, 49, 52, 55.
5 For other C13 versions see Maidstone, Kent County Archives Office, DRc/T60/1, 3, 5, 6 and DRc/T53; DRb/Ar 1/17, fol. 82v; DRb/Ar 2, fols. 13v–14r.
6 Rochester, Kent.
7 English in one hand.

1 London, British Library, Cotton Domitian xv.
2 *C15.
3 [δ] Ely Register. English on fols. 97r–101v: Latin and English versions of the Ely privilege, King Edgar to Ely Abbey.
4 Davis 363. Sawyer 779.
5 For other medieval copies of the same see the Index of Old English Texts. Cf. also BL Add 5819 for a C18 copy by William Cole. The earliest surviving text is BL Stowe Charter 31, C11b2. The English version may have been written by Ælfric. See AM 'Wulfstan', p. 113 and n. 8 (pp. 128–29) (repr. 1989, pp. 115, 130–31) and Pope 'Ely Privilege'.
6 MS from Ely Abbey. Ker *Med Lib*, p. 78.
7 English in one hand.

1 London, British Library, Cotton Faustina A iii.
2 *C13.
3 [δ] Cartulary of privileges, etc. Copies of charters in English on fols. 103r–113v, 259r.
4 Davis 1011. Sawyer as follows: S 1148 (K 862); S 1139 (K 865); S 1142 (K 855); S 1141 (K 886); S 1132 (Har 88, K 860); S 1136 (K 846); S 1129 (K 845); S 1120 (K 828); S 1122 (K 827); S 1135 (864); S 1123 (K 826); S 1134; S 1118 (Har 74, K 869); S 1128 (Har 84, K 859); S 1117 (K 870); S 1130 (K 858); S 1121 (K 843); S 1124 (K 873); S 1138 (K 863); S 1140 (K 842); S 1146 (K 829); S 1126 (K 889); S 1149 (K861); S 1119 (K 872); S 1127; S 1150 (K 857); S 1144 (K 830). Pelteret 2, 12–13, 15, 21, 24, 38, 65.

5 Cf. Westminster Abbey Muniment Book 11 for many of the same charters, for which see Harmer.
6 Westminster Abbey.
7 Fols. 103r–113v are in one hand (except for the last four words of English on fol. 113v), fol. 259r is in another hand.
8 The language of these texts is only slightly modernised but is of some interest.

1 London, British Library, Cotton Faustina A x.
2 C12b.
3 [γ] Annotations in Latin, English and French made to a MS in two parts (C11b and C12a) containing Ælfric's *Grammar* and *Glossary* and the *Rule of St Benedict*.
4 Ker 154. See Hunt *Teaching* 1, pp. 24–26, 100–111 and J. Zupitza, *Ælfric's Grammatik und Glossar* (Berlin, 1880; repr. with preface by H. Gneuss, Darmstadt, 1967).

1 London, British Library, Cotton Galba A xix.
2 C12b2–C13a1.
3 [λ] Fragments of *The Proverbs of Alfred*. Three leaves survive from the fire of 1731. These can be supplemented by transcripts of James, Wanley and Spelman, i.e. Bodley, James 6, pp. 68–9: 120 lines of transcript (not continuous text); Wanley's *Catalogue of Ancient Manuscripts* publ. 1705 as vol. 2 of Hickes' *Thesaurus linguarum septentrionalium*, p. 231b: transcript of lines 1–30; Sir John Spelman's (1594–1643) *Life of Alfred* (orig. Bodley e Mus 75): transcript of lines 1–94.
4 Wells VII.5. *IMEV* 433. Hall ii 286. Best edition: Arngart *P of A*; see especially vol. 2, pp. 11–25 and 57–64. Also edited: N.R. Ker, *MÆ* 5 (1936), 115–120. For a different opinion on the date of the MS see Betty Hill, 'Early English fragments and MSS Lambeth Palace Library 487, Bodleian Library Digby 4', *Proceedings of the Leeds Philosophical and Literary Society* 14 (1972), 269 seq. On language see Arngart *P of A* 1, pp. 135–36.
5 Ker (1936) indicates that *The Proverbs of Alfred* were once part of Bodley, Digby 4, q.v. See also Ker *Med Lib*, pp. 36, 38. *The Proverbs of Alfred* survive in four main versions, including the fragments in Coton Galba A xix, for which see the Index of Middle English Texts A: Titles where MSS containing short quotations from the text are also listed.
6 MS from Christ Church, Canterbury. Ker *Med Lib*, p. 36.
8 AM provisionally assigns the language to somewhere in the area of (and not further south than) N Bucks, SW Beds and W Herts. (Angus McIntosh, 'The Proverbs of Alfred: notes on the possible dialectal value of the four versions' (1986), unpubl.)

1 London, British Library, Cotton Galba E ii.
2 *C13b2 (1272–1302, Davis).
3 [δ] Cartulary of Benet Holme (St Benet of Hulme), Norfolk. English on fols. 30r–v in final clauses of two writs and in the rights clause of the second.
4 Davis 497. Sawyer 984 (K 740); 1055 (K 785). See also J.R. West, *St Benet of Holme 1020–1210*, Norfolk Record Society 2, 3 (1932).
6 Benet Holme, Norfolk.
7 English in one hand.

1 London, British Library, Cotton Galba E iv.
2 C13b2–C14a1 (1285–1331, Wells).
3 [γ] Fol. 46, English–French Legal Gloss.
4 Davis 182. Wells X.20. Edited: M. Förster, 'Ein englisch–französisches Rechtsglossar' in *Beiträge zur romanische und englischen Philologie* (Halle a. S., 1902), pp. 205–212.
5 Another version of this glossary is in BL Cotton Julius D vii, fol. 127. For a list of many other MSS containing OE feudal and legal terms see J. Hall, *The Red Book of the Exchequer* 1, RS 99 (1896), pp. cxiii–cxv.

6 *Ex dono* inscription associates the MS with Christ Church, Canterbury. Ker *Med Lib*, p. 36.
7 English in one hand.

1 London, British Library, Cotton Julius A ii, fols. 136–144.
2 *C12a2–b1 (s. xii med., Ker).
3 [λ] (1) Fols. 136r–137r metrical prayer beg. *Æla drihten leof. æla dema god*.
  (2) Fols. 137v–140r dialogue between Adrian and Ritheus.
  (3) Fol. 140v notes on the two thieves, measurements of Noah's ark, etc.
  (4) Fols. 141r–144v free translation of some of the Distichs of Cato.
4 Ker 159.
  (1) Edited: E. van K. Dobbie, *The Anglo-Saxon Minor Poems*, The Anglo-Saxon Poetic Records 6 (1942), p. 94.
  For (2)–(4) see Hartung 3 VII.70; J.M. Kemble, *The Dialogue of Salomon and Saturnus* Ælfric Society (1848), pp. 198, 258; Max Förster, 'Zu Adrian und Ritheus', *EStn* 23 (1897), 431 and 433 and 'Zur altenglischen Quintinus-Legende', *Archiv* 106 (1901), 342. Cf. also Wells VII.8.
5 Bodley, Junius 45 contains a transcription by Junius of fols. 137v–144v which is valuable for readings on fols. 140r–141r, 143r–144r which were damaged in the Cottonian fire.
7 One hand for which see Ker 159.

1 London, British Library, Cotton Julius A v.
2 C13b2–C14a1 (*ca.* 1300)
3 [λ] Fols. 180r–181v (*olim* 175r–176v) an early form of Thomas Erceldoune's Prophecy relating to the Scottish wars, in a part of the MS (fols. 171–187) which really belongs to BL Royal 20 A ii (*teste* Prof. M.D. Legge). MS also contains Langtoft's Chronicle, in which there is English on fols. 143r, 145v, 147r–150v, 168v.
4 For the prophecy see Wells IV.24; Hartung 5 XIII.292 and *IMEV* and *IMEV Suppl* 379. For the verses in Langtoft's *Chronicle* see Wells III.7; Hartung 5 XIII.23 and *IMEV* 310/A3, 313/A3, 814/A4, 841/A4, 2686/A3, 2754/A4, 3352/4. Edited: T. Wright, *Chronicle of Pierre de Langtoft* 2, RS 47 (1866–1868), p. 245 seq. Cf. *OBMEV* 33 and Murakami, pp. 91–92, nos. 23 and 24.
7 Fols. 180r–181v in one hand.
8 NME.

1 London, British Library, Cotton Julius D ii.
2 *C13a2–b1.
3 [δ] A composite MS containing on fols. 39v–133v a Canterbury Cartulary. MS in Latin but possibly has English bounds on fol. 133v.
4 Davis 192. Sawyer 140.
6 Contents associate the MS with St Augustine's, Canterbury, Kent. Ker *Med Lib*, p. 43.

1 London, British Library, Cotton Julius D vii.
2 C13a2–b1 (*ca.* 1250, Wells).
3 [γ] Fol. 127 English–French Legal Gloss.
4 Wells X.20. Hunt *Teaching* 1, p. 55.
5 Cf. BL Cotton Galba E iv.
6 Contents associate the MS with St Albans Abbey, Herts. Ker *Med Lib*, p. 166.
7 English in one hand.

1 London, British Library, Cotton Nero A xiv.
2 C13a2.
3 [λ] (1) Fols. 1–120v *Ancrene Riwle*.
  (2) Fols. 120v–123v *On God Ureison of Ure Lefdi*.
  (3) Fols. 123v–126v *On wel swuþe god Ureison of God Almihti*.

(4) Fols. 126v–128r *On Lofsong of Ure Lefdi*.
(5) Fols. 128r–131r *On Lofsong of Ure Louerde*.
(6) Fol. 131r–v *þe Lesse Crede*.
4 CB Reg i 274.
   (1) Wells VI.40. Severs 2 VI.1. *IPMEP* 559. Hall i IX, ii 355 and 388–407. D&W XVII. Edited: Mabel Day, *The English Text of the Ancrene Riwle*, EETS OS 225 (1952). See also Roger Dahood *AW*. For a six-line verse inserted into *Ancrene Riwle*, fol. 64r, see Wells *Suppl* 1, p. 975 (VII.15) and *IMEV* 3568. A proverbial saying *Auh euer is ðe eie to ðe wude leie þerinne is þet ich luuie* appears on fol. 23v (see Wells *Suppl* 7, p. 1583, *IMEV Suppl* 734.5).
   (2) Wells XIII.207. *IMEV* 631. Hall i XVIII, ii 531–43. CB13 3.
   (3) Wells XIII.170. *IPMEP* 419.
   (4) Wells XIII.206. *IPMEP* 617.
   (5) Wells XIII.172. *IPMEP* 416.
   (6) Wells VI.14. Hartung 7 XX.38. *IPMEP* 316.
   (2)–(6) edited: Morris *OEH* 1, pp. 200–17.
   For contents see W. Meredith Thompson, *þe Wohunge of Ure Lauerd*, EETS OS 241 (1958 for 1955, repr. 1970), pp. xi–xii; texts edited pp. 5–18.
5 For other EME texts of *Ancrene Riwle* see the Index of Middle English Texts A: Titles. Later ME versions are found in Cambridge, Magdalene College, Pepys 2498; BL Royal 8 C i; Bodley, Eng. poet. a. 1, the Vernon MS. For item (3) cf. London, Lambeth Palace Library 487 item (3). For item (4) cf. BL Royal 17 A xxvii item (5).
6 Names on the first flyleaf show C16 connections with places in Gloucs.
7 Two hands, A: fols. 1r–120v, B: fols. 120v–end.
8 In the opinion of MLS (pers. comm.) the language is S Worcs not far from the Gloucs border. It could conceivably belong to N Gloucs, but going on the later evidence it seems to have more in common with Worcs than Gloucs in an area where there are later some crucial divides. Cf. Smith 'Tradition', esp. pp. 60–62.

1 London, British Library, Cotton Nero D i.
2 *C13.
3 [δ] Fols. 149–161 two C13 quires containing a St Albans Cartulary. Latin MS with some English on fols. 150v–151r, 154v. Apparently only odd words of English of formulae such as *saca et soca, on strande et stream*, etc.
4 Davis 831. Cf. Sawyer 916 (K 1304). See also H.R. Luard, *Matthew Paris, Chronica Majora* 6 *Additamenta*, RS 57 (1882), pp. 28–40.
6 MS from St Albans Abbey, Herts. Ker *Med Lib*, p. 166.
7 Most of the MS in the hand of Matthew Paris. See Vaughan 1953, p. 390.

1 London, British Library, Cotton Nero D v.
2 C12b1 (before 1259).
3 [λ] Fol. 150v contains St Godric's Hymn A in a copy of Matthew Paris *Chronica maiora*.
4 CB Reg i 275. Wells *Suppl* 1, p. 986 (XIII.27). *IMEV* 2988. Hall ii 241. D&H, p. 105. Edited: Zupitza 'Godric'.
5 This derives from Cambridge, Corpus Christi College 26, q.v. and like it, was corrected by Matthew Paris himself. It is therefore likely to be a St Albans product also. See Vaughan 1953, p. 392. Cf. BL Harley 1620. For other MSS containing copies of one or more of Godric's Hymns see the Index of Middle English Texts A: Titles.
6 MS from St Albans Abbey, Herts. Ker *Med Lib*, p. 166.
7 English in one hand.

1 London, British Library, Cotton Otho B v, part II.
2 C14a1.
3 [λ] Fol. 32v contains Godric's Hymn A in a MS of Roger of Wendover *Flores Historiarum*.

4 CB Reg i 275. Wells *Suppl* 1, p. 986 (XIII.27). *IMEV* 2988. Hall ii 241. D&H, p. 105. Edited: Zupitza 'Godric'.
5 For other MSS containing copies of one or more of Godric's Hymns see the Index of Middle English Texts A: Titles.
7 English in one hand.

1 **London, British Library, Cotton Otho B x.**
2 C13a2 (tremulous hand: see Ker 'Date').
3 [γ] MS of C11 badly burnt in the fire of 1731. Only two badly damaged leaves remain. On fols. 29 and 30 glosses to *Judith and Holofernes* and to *Malchus* in the Worcester tremulous hand. No English glosses noted by Ker or Franzen.
4 Ker 178. Franzen 1991, pp. 53–54.
5 For other MSS containing glosses by the Worcester tremulous hand see Franzen 1991, Ker, p. lvii and the entry for Worcester Cathedral, Dean and Chapter Library F 174.
6 MS from Worcester. Ker *Med Lib*, p. 207.
7 Latin glosses in the Worcester tremulous hand.

1 **London, British Library, Cotton Otho B xiv.**
2 *C14.
3 [δ] Fragments of registers from Ramsey. English on fols. 263r–v.
4 Davis 795. Sawyer 1110 (K 904); 1109 (K 853).
5 For other versions of the same charters see PRO Ch R 8 Edw III, m 13; PRO E 164/28, fols. 52v–53r, 59v–60r, 165v–166v.
6 Ramsey Abbey, Hunts.
7 English in one hand.
8 Contains some interesting East Midland forms.

1 **London, British Library, Cotton Otho C i, vol. 2.**
2 C13a2 (tremulous hand: see Ker 'Date').
3 [γ] C11 MS containing OE translation of Gregory's *Dialogues* and *Vitas Patrum* glossed throughout by the Worcester tremulous hand. Almost all the glosses are in Latin.
4 Ker 182. Franzen 1991, pp. 64–65. MS also described Pope *Ælfric*, pp. 85–87. Variants from the homily on fols. 153r–155v printed: Pope *Ælfric*, pp. 641–75. Glosses also noted but only one (*inmeddre: uel imundre*) seems to be English (p. 647).
5 For other MSS containing glosses by the tremulous hand, see Franzen 1991, Ker, p. lvii and the entry for Worcester Cathedral, Dean and Chapter Library F 174.
6 MS probably at Worcester by the second half of C11. Ker *Med Lib*, p. 207.
7 Glosses in the Worcester tremulous hand.

1 **London, British Library, Cotton Otho C xiii.**
2 C13b1 (*ca.* 1250, D&W; *ca.* 1275, *OBMEV*).
3 [λ] Fols. 1r–146v Laʒamon's *Brut* (Laʒamon B).
4 Wells III.3 (and cf. Wells *Suppl* 9, p. 1805). Hartung 8 XXI.3. *IMEV* 295. *OBMEV* 1. Hall i XIV, ii 450–79. Edited: F. Madden, *Laʒamon's Brut*, 3 vols. (London, 1847); G.L. Brook and R.F. Leslie, *Laʒamon's Brut*, EETS OS 250 (1963 for 1961) and 277 (1978).
5 Cf. Laʒamon A, BL Cotton Caligula A ix.
8 W Somerset. *LALME* LP 5230.

1 **London, British Library, Cotton Otho C xvi.**
2 C16b.
3 [δ] [λ] Fols. 65–102, transcript from BL Add 61901, q.v., containing the Middle English rhyming charter of King Athelstan to Beverley Minster.
5 Cf. BL Harley 560, also derived from BL Add 61901.

1 London, British Library, Cotton Roll ii 11.
2 *C13b2 (a1300, *MED Plan & Bibl*, p. 36).
3 [δ] A roll containing 21 documents (some in English, some in Latin) all relating to Crediton, Devon. They include:
  (1) copy of a declaration (possibly spurious) by Egger (Ethelgar), Bishop of Crediton concerning indulgences obtained from Pope Leo [VII] in favour of Crediton Minster;
  (2) copy of a list of donations of days of indulgence by nine named bishops;
  (3) copy of a statement concerning the departure of Bishop Living (Luuig) from Crediton to Exeter;
  (4) copy of a mortgage of land by the river Creedy.
4 (1) Sawyer 1387. (2) Birch 732. An excerpt from (4) is cited in *MED* s.v. *outgang* n. The first five documents edited (with facsimile and translations): J.B. Davidson, 'On some ancient documents relating to Crediton Minster', *Transactions of the Devonshire Association* 10 (1878), 237–54 (239). See also L. Morsbach, 'Umschriften angelsächsischer Urkunden in einer Pergamentrolle des späten 13. Jahrhunderts', in *Britannica. Max Förster, zum sechsigsten Geburtstage* (Leipzig, 1929), pp. 106–38 (115–20) and cf. A.S. Napier and W.H. Stevenson, *The Crawford Collection of Early Charters and Documents* (Oxford, 1895).
6 Crediton, Devon.
8 Birch says: "written in the Devonshire dialect".

1 London, British Library, Cotton Tiberius A vi.
2 *C12b.
3 [δ] Ely Cartulary containing on fol. 99r seq. a collection of privileges.
  (1) Fols. 99v–100r English bounds to a charter in Latin.
  (2) Fols. 102v–3 the Confessor's Writ.
4 Davis 365. Sawyer 907, 1100. Ker, p. xiv fn. 2 and p. 137 fn. 1. (2) Edited (with commentary): Laing 'Anchor texts', esp. pp. 38–40.
5 For other Ely cartularies containing copies of the Confessor's Writ see the Index of Old English Texts.
6 Ely Abbey.
7 Probably both texts in the same hand.

1 London, British Library, Cotton Tiberius A xiii.
2 *C14.
3 [δ] Hemming's Cartulary. Mostly too early (C11) but C14 bounds on fol. 193v.
4 Davis 1068. Sawyer 1335. N.R. Ker, 'Hemming's Cartulary: a description of the two Worcester cartularies in Cotton Tiberius A.XIII', in R.W. Hunt, W.A. Pantin and R.W. Southern, eds., *Studies in Medieval History Presented to F.M. Powicke* (Oxford, 1948), pp. 49–75.
6 Written at Worcester. Cf. Ker 190.
7 Fol. 193v is in one hand but the folio is badly damaged so it is very hard to read.

1 London, British Library, Cotton Tiberius B i.
2 C12a2–b1 (?a1150, *MED Plan & Bibl*, p. 33).
3 [λ] Fol. 164 contains a late addition to *Anglo-Saxon Chronicle* MS C.
4 Ker 191. Wells III.1 and cf. Wells *Suppl* 9, p. 1804. Hartung 5 XIII.6 and 8 XXI.1. Edited: C. Plummer and J. Earle, *Two of the Saxon Chronicles Parallel*, 2 vols. (Oxford 1892–99) 1, p. 198, lines 26–34. Cf. Watson *BL*, 552. The eight lines on fol. 164 are printed separately by C.T. Onions, 'Some early Middle-English spellings', *MLR* 4 (1909), 505. See also B. Dickins, 'The late addition to ASC 1066 C', *Leeds Philosophical and Literary Society* (*Lit and Hist Section*) 5 (1938–43), 148–49 (this refers to BL Cotton Tiberius B i, not A i as cited by Dickins).
6 Contents associate the MS with Abingdon Abbey. Ker *Med Lib*, p. 3.

1 London, British Library, Cotton Tiberius B iv.
2 C12a2 (?1130, *MED Plan & Bibl*, p. 33).
3 [λ] Late addition to *Anglo-Saxon Chronicle* MS D. Fol. 86v has a four-line annal for 1130 at the head of the page. This is the last entry in D.
4 Ker 192. Wells III.1. Edited: C.T. Onions, 'Some early Middle-English spellings', *MLR* 4 (1909), 506. Also edited: C. Plummer and J. Earle, *Two of the Saxon Chronicles Parallel*, 2 vols. (Oxford 1892–99) 1, p. 214 lines 33–35. Cf. Watson *BL*, 555.
6 The Chronicle itself is probably from Worcester. Ker *Med Lib*, p. 207. Dorothy Whitelock has argued, however, for York as the provenance of the Chronicle. See *The Peterborough Chronicle*, Early English Manuscripts in Facsimile 4 (Copenhagen, 1954), p. 28; see also the review by F.E. Harmer in *RES* 8 (1957), 51–54.

1 London, British Library, Cotton Tiberius B xiii.
2 C13a1.
3 [λ] MS of Giraldus Cambrensis *Speculum Ecclesie* (Latin). In chapter 13 appears a rhyming toast and its response in English: *Loke nu frere / Hu strong ordre is here* and *Ihe, la ful iwis / Swide strong ordre is dhis*.
4 *IMEV Suppl* 1940.5. Edited: J.S. Brewer, *Giraldi Cambrensis Opera* 4, RS 21 (1893), p. 209. The MS is said by Brewer to have been corrected, possibly by Giraldus himself, soon after the work was written in 1220. Cf. Wilson *Lost Lit*, pp. 161–62.

1 London, British Library, Cotton Tiberius C ix.
2 *C13.
3 [δ] Fols. 48r –260 General Cartulary of Waltham Abbey. Fols. 48r–49r copy of a writ of King Edward to Waltham Abbey; English bounds.
4 Davis 990. Sawyer 1036 (K 813). This text considered by Harmer and others to be a post-Conquest fabrication. See Sawyer, p. 308 and Harmer, pp. 37, 59, 560.
5 For other C13 copies of this writ see BL Harley 391, fols. 33–35v, PRO, Cart. Ant. R. 12 no. 1.
6 Waltham Abbey, Essex.
7 English in one hand.

1 London, British Library, Cotton Titus A i.
2 *C12b.
3 [δ] *Historia Eliensis*, etc. Fol. 25r–v copies of two charters of Edgar to Ely Abbey said by Sawyer to have English bounds. Apparently no English however.
4 Davis 368. Sawyer 780, 781.
6 MS from Ely Abbey. Ker *Med Lib*, p. 78.

1 London, British Library, Cotton Titus D xviii.
2 C13a1 (*ca.* 1220, Hall).
3 [λ] (1) Fols 14r–105r *Ancrene Riwle*.
   (2) Fols. 105v–112v *Sawles Warde*.
   (3) Fols. 112v–127r *Hali Meiðhad*.
   (4) Fols. 127r–133r *þe Wohunge of Ure Lauerd*.
   (5) Fols. 133v–147v *St Katherine*.
4 For contents of MS see R.M. Wilson, *Sawles Warde*, Leeds School of English Language Texts and Monographs 3 (1938).
   (1) Wells VI.40. Severs 2 VI.1. *IPMEP* 559. Hall ii 355. Cf. CB Reg i 284. Edited: F.M. Mack, *The English Text of the Ancrene Riwle, British Museum MS. Cotton Titus D. xviii*, EETS OS 252 (1963 for 1962). See also Dahood *AW*. For a six-line verse inserted in *Ancrene Riwle*, fol. 61v, see Wells *Suppl* 1, p. 975 (VII.15) and *IMEV* 3568.
   (2) Wells V.2. *IPMEP* 594. Edited: Wilson, op. cit.

(3) Wells V.1. (cf. Wells *Suppl* 9, pp. 1814–15). *IPMEP* 95. Edited: O. Cockayne rev. F.J. Furnivall, *Hali Meidenhad*, EETS OS 18 (1922 for 1920, repr. 1973); A.F. Colborn, *Hali Meiðhad* (London, 1940); Millett *Hali Meiðhad*.

(4) Wells XIII.171. *IPMEP* 420. Edited: W. Meredith Thompson, *þe Wohunge of Ure Lauerd*, EETS OS 241 (1958 for 1955; repr. 1970).

(5) Wells V.50. *IPMEP* 138. Edited: d'Ardenne & Dobson.

Facsimile of fols. 16v–17r in *Pal Soc*, Second Series, vol. 1, plate 75.

5 For other EME texts of *Ancrene Riwle* see the Index of Middle English Texts A: Titles. Later ME versions are found in Cambridge, Magdalene College, Pepys 2498; BL Royal 8 C i; Bodley, Eng. poet. a. 1, the Vernon MS. *Sawles Warde* is also found in Bodley 34 and BL Royal 17 A xxvii. *þe Wohunge of Ure Lauerd* is unique to this MS.

7 All one hand.

8 The language differs between texts. AM considers that of *Sawles Warde*, *Hali Meiðhad* and *St Katherine* to be close to AB language. *Ancrene Riwle* and *þe Wohunge of Ure Lauerd* display more northerly characteristics, slightly differing from each other. *Ancrene Riwle* is probably S Cheshire but with a heavy AB ingredient. *þe Wohunge* has features of a more N Midland (central) kind.

1 London, British Library, Cotton Titus D xx.

2 C12a.

3 [γ] Fols. 1–16 contain a few English glosses (and some Anglo-Norman ones) in Alexander Neckham's *De Utensilibus*.

4 See C.B. Heiatt and S. Butler *Curye on Englysch*, EETS SS 8 (1985), p. 1. Printed (privately): Thomas Wright *A Volume of Vocabularies* (1857), but apparently not in Wright-Wülcker.

6 MS from Abingdon Abbey. Ker *Med Lib Suppl*, p. 1.

1 London, British Library, Cotton Titus D xxiv.

2 C12b.

3 [λ] MS contains a collection of Latin verse. On fol. 156r–v (last leaf) two formulae at the visitation of the sick appear, first in French (red ink) then in Latin (black ink) and finally in English (green ink).

4 Ker 201. Hunt *Teaching* 1, p. 48.

6 *Ex libris* inscriptions on fols. 5 and 6 indicate MS was from the Cistercian Abbey of Rufford, Notts. Ker *Med Lib*, p. 164.

8 In the English þ occurs seven times, *th* once, *p* twice and *w* once. The special insular letter forms are not used.

1 London, British Library, Cotton Vespasian A xxii.

2 C12b2–C13a1.

3 [λ] Composite MS. Homilies in English appear on fols. 54r–58v, 59v (new foliation 52r–56v, 57v). Fols. 60r–129 Register of Rochester Priory in Latin.

4 Wells V.16 (and cf. Wells *Suppl* 2, p. 1058). Ker, p. xix (not included in the main body of the *Catalogue*). Hall i V, ii 269–85. *IPMEP* 519. Edited: Morris *OEH* 1, pp. 217–45. On date see E.G. Stanley, 'The prenominal prefix *ge-* in Late Old English and Early Middle English', *TPS* (1982), 25–66, esp. p. 62 and also fn. 51. See also Mary P. Richards, 'MS Cotton Vespasian A.XXII: the Vespasian Homilies', *Manuscripta* 22 (1978), 97–103.

6 *Ex libris* inscription of C14 on the flyleaf indicates that the volume belonged to Rochester Cathedral library. Ker *Med Lib*, p. 161. Hall: "the other articles bound up with this MS before and after are historical and largely connected with Rochester monastery". Cf. Davis 821.

7 English in one hand.

8 Hall considers the language to be south-eastern but with signs of a W-S original. Note that it contains the Norse word *loft*, "sky" (see *MED*, s.v. loft n) on fol. 54r (*loftes leom*). Richards, op. cit., considers that "the morphology is Southern, but the phonology is predominantly Kentish". See also Cecily Clark, 'Spelling and grammaticality in the *Vespasian Homilies*: a reassessment', *Manuscripta* 31 (1987), 7–10.

1 London, British Library, Cotton Vespasian B xxiv.
2 *C12b2–C13a1 (AID, pers. comm.).
3 [δ] Evesham register in several hands. English bounds on fols. 18v–20v, 21r, 22r, 25r–26r, 29r, 32v, 33r–v, 36r, 37v–38v, 40r–v, 55v, 64r, 65v, 68r–v (English with Latin), 70r, 71r, 72v, 74v.
4 Davis 381. Sawyer as follows: S 495 (K 402 and iii 421–23); S 1662 (B 1024, K 1357); S 1663 (B 1025, K 475 and iii 453); S 977 (K 736); S 1565 (K 1356); S 1594 (K 1355); S 54 (B 116, K 56 and iii 375); S 873 (K 662); S 1590 (K 1358); S 1174; S 1664 (K 1299); S 78 (B 120, K 59 and iii 376); S 1058 (K 797); S 79 (B 124, K 60 and vi 226); S 1238 (K 963); S 1599 (K 1368); S 203 (B 482, K 274 and iii 394); S 1550 (K 1359); S 80 (B 125, K 61 and iii 376–77); S 1553 (K 1365); S 1026; S 550 (K 1360); S 115 (B 229, K 136 and iii 384–85).
5 There is a transcript in BL Lansdowne 411.
6 Evesham, Worcs.
7 English in various hands.
8 Language has a few interesting EME forms.

1 London, British Library, Cotton Vespasian D xiv.
2 (*)C12a2–b1.
3 [λ] Fols. 4–169 Homilies, mainly copied OE from Ælfric's *Sermones catholoci* but including:
  (1) fols. 151v–157v *Sermo in festis Sancti Marie uirginis* which is a translation of a Latin sermon by Ralph d'Escures bp. of Rochester 1108–14 and abp. of Canterbury 1114–22;
  (2) fols. 159–163v a translation of part of the *Elucidarius* attributed to Honorius of Autun.
  (1) is "usually classed as the earliest ME" see Cecily Clark, *The Peterborough Chronicle 1070 1154* (Oxford, 1970), p. lii fn. 1 and for further references p. xli fn. 9.
4 Ker 209. Edited: R.D.-N. Warner, *Early English Homilies from the Twelfth-Century MS. Vespasian D xiv*, EETS OS 152 (1917 for 1915; repr. 1971). See also Max Förster, 'Der Inhalt der altenglischen Handschrift Vespasianus d. xiv', *EStn* 54 (1920), 46 seq. and 'Abt Raoul d'Escures und der spätae. *Sermo in Festis S. Marie*', *Archiv* 162 (1932), 43–48; Karl Glaeser, *Lautlehre der Ælfricschen Homilien en der Handschrift Cotton Vespasianus D. xiv* (Leipzig, 1916), p. 111; Pope *Ælfric*, pp. 24–26. Rima Handley, 'British Museum MS. Cotton Vespasian D.xiv', *N&Q* 219 (1974), 243–50 demonstrates that it was used as a school text.
  (1) Wells *Suppl* 1, p. 958 (V.1a). Hartung 3 VI.72.
  (2) Wells IX.13.
For prognostic *emb punre* on fol. 103 see Wells X.36 and *IPMEP* 510.
For prose New Year's prophecies on fol. 75v see Wells *Suppl* 1, p. 982 (X.36b).
6 Ker, p. 277: "Probably from Canterbury or Rochester, in view of the [prickly] script and of art. 44, but perhaps in female ownership in s. xii ex.: cf. art. 54". Ker *Med Lib*, p. 39 rejects the MS as having belonged to Christ Church. Handley, however, thinks the volume most likely to have been put together there.
7 Three hands, according to Ker, the main hand being of the "prickly" kind used at Canterbury and Rochester. Hand A: fols. 4v–6v (may be the main hand), 67v, 165r lines 14–22, 166r line 11 – 169r. Hand B (main hand): fols. 6v–67r, 68r–163v line 10, 169v. Hand C: fols. 163v line 11 – 165r line 13, 165v–166r line 10.
8 Förster's analysis of the language (based on Glaeser's study) suggests an origin in the south-east. See also Mary P. Richards, 'On the date and provenance of MS Cotton Vespasian D.XIV ff. 4–169', *Manuscripta* 17 (1973), 31–35. Richards considers the language and orthography to belong to Rochester and to be of the second quarter of the twelfth century.

1 London, British Library, Cotton Vitellius A xii.
2 *C12b2.
3 [λ] Fol. 184v col. 2 *Pater Noster* in OE in a blank space at the end of a copy of the *Penitential* of Bartholomew of Exeter.
4 Ker 214. *IPMEP* 171 where ref. given as fol. 181v (cf. Wells VI.13). Edited: S.A. Morey, *Bartholomew of Exeter, Bishop and Canonist* (1937), p. 300 and in *Rel Ant* i 204.

1 London, British Library, Cotton Vitellius A xiii.
2 *C13.
3 [δ] Fols. 20r–82 Chertsey Cartulary. English on fols. 20v–23r, 35v–37r, 50r–51v, 53v.
4 Davis 222. Sawyer as follows: S 1165 (B 34, K 967); S 353 (B 563, K 318 and iii 401–402); S 1095 (K 849); S 1094 (K 850); S 1093 (Har 40, K 848); S 1096 (K 856); S 1477 (K 844). Pelteret 7.
6 Chertsey, Surrey.

1 London, British Library, Cotton Vitellius A xv.
2 *C12a2–b1 (s. xii med., Ker).
3 [λ] (1) Fols. 4r–59v Augustine *Soliloquies*.
(2) Fols. 60r–86v *Gospel of Nicodemus*.
(3) Fols. 86v–93v debate of Solomon and Saturn.
(4) Fol. 93v a few lines of a homily on St Quintin.
4 Ker 215.
(1) Edited: W. Endter, *König Alfreds des grossen Bearbeitung der Soliloquien des Augustinus*, Bibliothek der angelsächsischen Prosa 11 (1922).
(2) Edited: W.H. Hulme, 'The Old English version of the Gospel of Nicodemus', *PMLA* 13 (1898), 473.
(3) Hartung 3 VII.68(d). Edited: B. Thorpe, *Analecta Anglo-Saxonica* (1834), p. 95 (cf. J.M. Kemble, *The Dialogue of Salomon and Saturnus*, Ælfric Society (1848), p. 178).
(4) Edited: M. Förster, 'Zur altenglischen Quintinus-Legende', *Archiv* 106 (1901), 258.
5 Transcript by Junius in Bodley, Junius 70 (*SC* 5181).
6 Ker, p. 280: "Belonged to Southwick Priory, Hants: the late-thirteenth-century inscription of ownership is at the foot of f. 5, 'Hic liber est Ecclesie beate marie de Suwika ...'".
7 One hand, see Ker, p. 280.

1 London, British Library, Cotton Vitellius C xii.
2 C13.
3 [λ] Latin MS containing the lives of SS. Edmund, Edward and Thomas Becket. The *Life of St Edmund*, fols. 280v–290, in the "Anonymous A" version, is said to quote in English Edmund's last words.
4 See Lawrence *St Edmund*, p. 50.
5 For other C13 MSS containing the "Anonymous A" and different versions of this text see the Index of Texts in Latin.

1 London, British Library, Cotton Vitellius D iii.
2 C13b (D&W, p. 44).
3 [λ] MS largely destroyed by the fire of 1731. Fols. 6r–8v (only surviving English) *Floriz and Blauncheflur*. 451 lines survive, only 180 completely legible.
4 Wells I.99. Severs 1 I.96. *IMEV Suppl* *2288.8 (*olim IMEV* *45). Edited: J.R. Lumby, rev. G.H. McKnight, *King Horn, Floriz and Blauncheflur, The Assumption of our Lady*, EETS OS 14 (1901; repr. 1962), 74–8, 84–91, 98–105.

5 Another C13b MS containing *Floriz and Blauncheflur* is CUL Gg.IV.27(2). Later MSS containing the same text are Edinburgh, National Library of Scotland, Advocates' 19.2.1, the Auchinleck MS and BL Egerton 2862.
7 One hand.
8 MLS places in N Gloucs (*LALME* LP 7120).

1 London, British Library, Cotton Vitellius D ix.
2 C13a2 (after 1227, Davis).
3 [δ] Fols. 24–182 Exeter Cartulary. Fol. 29r copy of a notification of 1096 x 1102 by Osbern bishop of Exeter concerning bell-ringing. Apparently no English in this version.
4 Davis 392. Pelteret 101.
5 An earlier version is in Exeter Cathedral 3501, fol. 5r.
6 Exeter, Devon.

1 London, British Library, Cotton Vitellius D xx.
2 *C12.
3 [λ] 16 damaged leaves remain of a MS of 131 fols. burnt in the fire of 1731. Fol. "20", now missing, contained on the verso an OE poem entitled *De Situ Dunelmi*.
4 Ker 223. Hartung 5 XIII.9. *IMEV Suppl* 1608.5. Murakami, pp. 88–89, no. 19. Edited: G. Hickes, *Linguarum Veterum Septentrionalium Thesaurus* (1705), p. 178, thence E. van K. Dobbie, *The Anglo-Saxon Minor Poems*, The Anglo-Saxon Poetic Records 6 (1942), p. 27.
5 Cf. CUL Ff.I.27, fol. 202.
6 Ker, p. 298: "Probably from Durham, but not certainly identifiable in the medieval catalogues". Ker *Med Lib*, p. 73.

1 London, British Library, Cotton Vitellius E xv.
2 *C13a1.
3 [δ] Cartulary, *ca.* 1200, of Osney Abbey. English bounds (imperfect) on fol. 5v?
4 Davis 731. Sawyer 909 (Sawyer says K 709 — but K cites as Cott. Vitell. F. 16, fol. 4v). See also S.R. Wigram, *The Cartulary of St Frideswides at Oxford* 1, Oxford Historical Society 28 (1895), pp. 2–6.
6 MS from Osney Abbey, Oxford. Ker *Med Lib*, p. 140.

1 London, British Library, Egerton 613.
2 C13a (*ca.* 1250, *OBMEV*).
3 [λ] Miscellanies in prose and verse in English, Anglo-Norman, Continental French and Latin. English on fols. 1v–2v, 3r–6r, 7r–12v and 64r–70v.
   (1) Fol. 1v a song of the Passion beg. *Somer is comen & winter gon.*
   (2) Fol. 2r a macaronic verse in praise of the BV beg. *Of on þat is so fayr and briȝt.*
   (3) Fol. 2r–v orison to the BV beg. *[IB]lessed beo þu lauedi ful of houene Blisse.*
   (4) Fol. 2v *Love Song of Our Lady* beg. *Litel uotit eniman hu trewe loue bistodet.*
   (5) Fols. 3r–6r English phrases in macaronic (Anglo-Norman and Latin) prose.
   (6) Fols. 7r–12v and (7) fols. 64r–70v two copies (E and e) of the *Poema Morale* in different hands. E begins *Ic æm elder þænne ic þæs a pinter and a lore.* e begins *Ich æm elder þen ich pes a pintre and a lore.*
   Fols. 71r–74v contain recipes in English in a C15 hand.
4 CB Reg i 287. For a full description of the contents see, Betty Hill, 'British Library MS. Egerton 613 – I', *N&Q* 223 (1978), 394–409.
   (1) Wells XIII.164. *IMEV* 3221. CB13 54. *OBMEV* 12.
   (2) Wells XIII.189. *IMEV* 2645. CB13 17B. D&W XXXIII. BSD VIII T. *OBMEV* 13.
   (3) Wells XIII.191. *IMEV* 1407. CB13 55.
   (4) Wells XIII.203. *IMEV* 1923. CB13, p. 236 (note to no. 91).
   For (5) see Betty Hill, 'British Library MS. Egerton 613 – II', *N&Q* (1978), 493–501.

For (6) and (7) see Hill 1977, pp. 97, 109 and cf. Hall i VIII, ii 312–54; Wells VII.25 and *IMEV* 1272.

5 For item (2) cf. Cambridge, Trinity College 323 (B.14.39) item (5). Item (4) is an adaptation of an originally secular lyric. Cf. a different adaptation in praise of Christ in Cambridge, Gonville and Caius College 512/543 and the two versions, one religious, one secular in BL Harley 2253 items (49) and (50). *The Poema Morale* survives in seven copies for which see the Index of Middle English Texts A: Titles where MSS containing short quotations from the text are also listed.

7 The hands of both versions of the *Poema Morale* also copied French texts into the MS (see Hill 1977, p. 109). Hand A: fol. 1v. Hand B: fol. 2r. Hand C: fols. 2r–v. Hand D: fol. 2v. Hand E: fols. 3r–6r. Hand F: fols. 7r–12v. Hand G: fols. 64r–70.

8 MLS (pers. comm.): "I do not know on what evidence the language [of the *Poema Morale* texts] has been assigned so precisely to Wilts. Certainly it's east of Laȝamon B, but the so-called south-western features could go anywhere from Gloucs to W Kent. I give these extremes because they are the areas that later could entertain an *-e-* in *wes* 'was'. But one perhaps has to discount such *e*'s as 'Anglo-Norman attempts at *æ*'. The *ie* in e.g. *died* 'dead' looks like Kentish (*dyad* etc.), but could conceivably be the ancestor of the *dyd* (etc.) for 'dead' (etc.) that appears later in the Central South (Sussex, Hants, Wilts). Egerton cannot therefore provide an initial anchor; it will have to be compared carefully with the whole EME Southern evidence". For a preliminary study of the language of the seven surviving copies of the *Poema Morale* see Laing 'Versions'.

1 London, British Library, Egerton 2733.

2 *C13b1 (after 1253, Davis).
3 [δ] 'Liber Cartularium et Privilegiorum Johannis de Trikyngham Prioris'. Copies of two Peterborough charters with English bounds, fols. 38r–42v, 44v–47v.
4 Davis 755. Sawyer 592; 533.
5 Cf. London Society of Antiquaries 60.
6 Peterborough, Northants.
7 English in one hand.

1 London, British Library, Egerton 2891.

2 C14a1 (c.1310–20, Görlach *SEL*, p. 92).
3 [λ] *South English Legendary*, imperfect.
4 CB Reg i 298–302. Görlach *SEL*, pp. 92–93. For individual entries in *IMEV* see Hamer 'MS index'.
5 This MS, according to Görlach, is very similar orthographically and textually to Cambridge, Corpus Christi College 145 and Leicester Museum 18 D 59, q.v. For other MSS containing parts of the *South English Legendary* see the Index of Middle English Texts A: Titles.
7 MS in one hand.

1 London, British Library, Harley 2.

2 C13.
3 [λ] A collection of *Passiones* and *Vitae Sanctorum* in hands of C13 and C14. Includes on fols. 88r–97 the *Life of St Edmund* by Eustace of Faversham which quotes in English Edmund's last words: *Men seith gamen gamen goth in wombe, ac ich saie gamen gamen goth in hert.*
4 See Lawrence *St Edmund*, p. 218 fn. 1.
5 For other C13 MSS containing versions of the *Life of St Edmund* with these English words see the Index of Texts in Latin.
6 *Ex libris* inscription on fol. 1 indicates that the MS belonged to the Augustinian abbey of St Mary, Thornton-on-Humber, Lincs. Ker *Med Lib*, p. 189.

1 London, British Library, Harley 47.

2 C13a2 (after 1229).
3 [λ] Devotional Latin prose. Contains on fol. 6v four English proverbs.

(1) *Ofte he bið efter roð; þet nule beon biuore þar.*
(2) *þis is þt þar is.*
(3) *Ofte he bið bicherred; þet alle men ileueð.*
(4) *God is skile.*
4 *IPMEP* 505. See R. Dahood, 'Four thirteenth-century English proverbs in MS Harley 47', *N&Q* 224 NS 26 (1979), 5–6.
7 English in one hand.

1 London, British Library, Harley 55, fols. 1–4.
2 C13a2 (tremulous hand: see Ker 'Date').
3 [γ] OE of C11; but fols. 3v and 4r have three glosses in the Worcester tremulous hand. Only one (*wo : vnriht*) is in English.
4 Ker 225. Franzen 1991, p. 70.
5 For other MSS containing glosses in the tremulous hand see Franzen 1991, Ker, p. lvii and the entry for Worcester Cathedral, Dean and Chapter Library F 174.
6 MS was at Worcester by beginning of C13. Ker *Med Lib*, p. 207.
7 Glosses in the Worcester tremulous hand.

1 London, British Library, Harley 55, fols. 5–13.
2 C12a2–b1 (s. xii med., Ker).
3 [δ] Laws of Cnut.
4 Ker 226. Edited: F. Liebermann, *Die Gesetze der Angelsachsen*, 3 vols. (1903) 1, p. 278.

1 London, British Library, Harley 61.
2 *C15a1.
3 [δ] Late medieval register from Shaftesbury Abbey. English, mostly bounds only, between fols. 1r and 22v.
4 Davis 885. English bounds for the most part to be found in Kemble vol. iii as listed below. Sawyer as follows: S 899 (K 706); S 850 (K 641); S 534 (B 868, K 418 and iii 426); S 478 (B 769, K 390 and iii 416); S 656 (B 1033, K 474 and iii 453); S 570 (B 923, K 455 and iii 445); S 485 (B 775, K 392 and iii 417); S 955 (K 730); S 459 (B 754, K 386 and iii 415); S 490 (B 781, K 394 and iii 417–18); S 502 (B 793, K 397 and iii 420); S 419 (B 691, K 361 and iii 409–10); S 562 (B 898, K 432 and iii 431); S 573 (B 910, K 435 and iii 432); S 744 (B 1186, K 522 and iii 465); S 710 (B 1115, K 501 and iii 459); S 762 (B 1218, K 547); S 429 (B 708, K 366 and iii 410–11); S 445 (B 744, K 376 and iii 413); S 655 (B 1026, K 470 and iii 452); S 632 (K iii 433); S 329 (B 499, K 283 and iii 395); S 277 (B 410, K 232 and iii 390); 326 (B 500, K 284 and iii 395); S 334 (B 525, K 300 and iii 397); S 342 (B 526, K 302 and iii 398, Rob 12); S 630 (B 970, K 447 and iii 440–41); S 357 (B 531, K 310, Rob 13). Pelteret 143.
6 Shaftesbury, Dorset.

1 London, British Library, Harley 153.
2 C16a1.
3 [λ] Text of the Latin life of Godric by Reginald, monk of Durham containing, fol. 26r, the first stanza of Godric's Hymn A and fol. 31r, Hymn B.
4 Wells *Suppl* 1, p. 985 (XIII.27). *IMEV* 2988 and 598. Hall ii 241. See also Zupitza 'Godric' and D&H, pp. 105, 108.
5 For other MSS containing copies of one or more of Godric's Hymns see the Index of Middle English Texts A: Titles.
7 English in one hand.

1 London, British Library, Harley 230.
2 *C14.
3 [δ] Fols. 123r–124r. Latin and English versions of the Ely privilege: King Edgar to Ely Abbey.

4 Cf. Davis 95. Sawyer 779. See Thomson *Archives*, pp. 132–33, no. 1286.
5 For other medieval copies of the same see the Index of Old English Texts. Cf. also BL Add 5819 for a C18 copy by William Cole. The earliest surviving text is BL Stowe Charter 31, C11b2. The English version may have been written by Ælfric. See AM 'Wulfstan', p. 113 and n. 8 (pp. 128–29) (repr. 1989, pp. 115, 130–31) and Pope 'Ely Privilege'.
6 Ely Abbey.
7 English in one hand.
8 Unintelligently copied OE.

1 London, British Library, Harley 322.
2 C12b2.
3 [λ] Anonymous redaction of *Vita S. Godrici* by Reginald, monk of Durham. The only English is on fol. 74v: first stanza of Godric's Hymn A, with music.
4 CB Reg i 306. Wells XIII.27. *IMEV* 2988. Hall ii 241. Murakami, p. 104, no. 37. See also Zupitza 'Godric' and D&H, p. 105.
5 For other MSS containing copies of one or more of Godric's Hymns see the Index of Middle English Texts A: Titles.
7 English in one hand.

1 London, British Library, Harley 391.
2 *C13a1 (c.1220, Davis).
3 [δ] General Cartulary. Fols. 33r–35v copy of a writ of King Edward to Waltham Abbey, English bounds.
4 Davis 989. Sawyer 1036. This text considered by Harmer and others to be a post-Conquest fabrication. See Sawyer, p. 308.
5 For other C13 copies see Cotton Tiberius C ix, fols. 48r–49r; PRO, Cart. Ant. R. 12 no. 1.
6 Waltham Abbey, Essex.
7 English in one hand.

1 London, British Library, Harley 436.
2 *C14a2 (1330).
3 [δ] Wilton Register. English bounds to Latin charters on fols. 1r–28v, 29v–64v, 66v–80r, 81v, 83r–87v.
4 Davis 1035. Sawyer as follows: S 531 (B 870, K 422 and iii 428); S 666 (B 956, K 462 and iii 451); S 469 (B 757, K 379 and iii 414–15); S 685 (B 1053, K 482 and iii 454); S 368 (B 600, K 335 and iii 403–404); S 647 (B 988, K 467 and iii 454–55); S 368 (a second text); S 492 (B 782, K 395 and iii 418–19); S 766; S 348 (B 567, K 320 and iii 402); S 642 (B 992, K 468); S 609 (B 958, K 454 and iii 444–44); S 519 (B 818, K 412 and iii 425); S 881 (K 687); S 364 (B 588, K 331 and iii 403); S 586 (B 1030, K 479 and iii 453–54); S 631 (B 985, K 456 and iii 446); S 493 (B 795, K 401 and iii 420–21); S 1010 (K 778); S 870 (K 665); S 438 (B 714, K 1115); S 789 (B 1286, K 572); S 784 (B 1285, K 571); S 612 (B 934, K 446 and iii 439–40); S 468 (B 756, K 387 and iii 415–16); S 424 (B 699, K 1109); S 1811 (B 783, K 396 and iii 419–20); S 543 (B 879, K 428 and iii 431); S 767 (B 1216, K 543); S 582 (B 917, K 436 and iii 433–36). Printed in full by R.C. Hoare, *Registrum Wiltonense* (1827).
6 Wilton, Wilts.
8 The language is OE except in a few minor details, e.g. regular *his/hys* for "is"; *c/ch* spellings alternate in e.g. "church" and *cump* alternates with *cymp* for "comes". Information supplied by MB.

1 London, British Library, Harley 505.
2 C13b2–C14a1.
3 [λ] MS is in several parts, a miscellany containing sermons in which appear exempla in English.
(1) Fol. 13r a saying about love beg. *Loue is knotte of mannes hertes*.

(2) Fol. 15r recommendations in English in the Sermo *Hora est iam nos de somno surgere* beg. *Auake son þat slepest*.
(3) Fol. 83v couplet beg. *Waylaway wy dude ich so*.
4 (1) Wenzel 1986, p. 223.
(2) Wenzel 1986, p. 70. This is the only English quoted by Wenzel in the sermon but the description "macaronic" implies that there may be more.
(3) Wenzel 1986, p. 239. *IMEV Suppl* 3902.5.
6 Written for the most part by "Frater Johannes de Candeuere" (fol.1v). Perhaps Brown, Chiltern or Preston Candover in Hants.
7 Hand of Johannes de Candeuere.

1 London, British Library, Harley 560.
2 C17a.
3 [δ] [λ] (1) Fols. 21–22v text of the Middle English rhyming version of King Athelstan's grant of privileges to St. John's, Beverley. This is a transcript from BL Add 61901, q.v.
(2) Fol. 40r–v two writs of King Edward concerning St John's, Beverley.
4 For (1) see Sawyer 451 (cf. *IMEV* 3300).
(2) See S 1067 (where the references to the Latin and English versions have been transposed) and S 1160 (Har 119) now extant only in Latin not English as indicated in Sawyer. Cf. also Pelteret 14.
5 For other versions of the same text(s) see BL Add 61901, Cotton Charter iv 18 and Lansdowne 269 and cf. Cotton Otho C xvi, fols. 65–102, which also derives from BL Add 61901.
6 Beverley, ERY.

1 London, British Library, Harley 585.
2 C13a1 (s. xiii in., Ker).
3 [λ] Herbal and *Lacnunga* of C10–C11 containing EME interpretations of OE words on fols. 1r, 3r, 5r–v, 8r, 14r, 15r, 60r, 61r, 164v, 170v. A blank space on fol. 151v has the words *Wwrche man gardclife on mid* in a hand of C13.
4 Ker 231. Glosses and notes edited: J.H.G. Grattan and Charles Singer, *Anglo-Saxon Magic and Medicine: illustrated specially from the Semi-Pagan Text "Lacnunga"*, Publications of the Wellcome Historical Medical Museum, NS 3 (London, 1952), pp. 96–205 textual notes.

1 London, British Library, Harley 638.
2 *C14.
3 [δ] 'Werketone' Register of Bury St Edmunds. Contains copies of grants of privileges and writs of King Edward to St Edmund's Abbey. English on fols. 25r–26r, 30v–31r
4 Davis 106. Sawyer as follows: S 980; S 1045; S 1084; S 1075 (Har 15); S 1085 (K 875); S 1069 (Har 9); S 507 (English in bounds only). See also Thomson *Archives*, pp. 126–27, no. 1281.
5 Cf. CUL Ff.II.33 for references to other Bury material.
6 Bury St Edmunds, Suffolk.
8 The texts printed by Harmer have only small traces of ME.

1 London, British Library, Harley 683.
2 C13a–b2.
3 [γ] A grammatical school book including two C13 copies (fols, 12r–19r and 38r–54v) of Alexander Neckham's *De Nominibus Utensilium* heavily glossed in the vernacular both French and English. Other texts are of C14.
4 Contents listed Hunt *Teaching* 1, pp. 178–79, 325. Vernacular glosses edited: Hunt *Teaching* 1, p. 138 and *Teaching* 2, pp. 90–108.

1 London, British Library, Harley 743.
2 *C14b2 (1379–81, Thomson).

3 [δ] Register of John Lakenheath. English on fols. 56v–57r, 59r–60r.
4 Davis 97. Sawyer as follows: S 507 (English in bounds only); S 1069; S 1079 (Har 19); S 1045 (K 895). Pelteret 19. Cf. Thomson *Archives*, pp. 129–30, no. 1283. See also AM *Havelok*, 41 seq. and fn. 12.
5 Cf. other Bury St Edmunds cartularies and registers CUL Add 6006; Ee.III.60; Ff.II.33; Gg.IV.4; Mm.IV.19; BL Add 14847.
6 Bury St Edmunds, Suffolk.
7 One hand.

1 London, British Library, Harley 746.
2 *C14a1 (c1325, *MED*).
3 [δ] Laws and charters.
4 See *MED* s.v. *ouen-hine* n: quotation (from *Leges Edw. Conf.*, q.v., *Plan & Bibl*, p. 52a).

1 London, British Library, Harley 913.
2 C14a2 (*ca.* 1330).
3 [λ] MS compiled by a Franciscan, mostly in Latin but with some French and English. English appears as follows.
  (1) Fols. 3r–6v *Land of Cokaygne* beg. *Fur in see bi west Spayngne*.
  (2) Fol. 6v *Five Evil Things* or *The Abuses of the Age* beg. *Bissop lorles / kyng redeles*.
  (3) Fols. 7r–8v *Satire on the People of Kildare* beg. *Hail seint Michael wiþ þe lange sper*.
  (4) Fols. 9r–10r Hymn by Michael Kildare beg. *Swet iesu hend and fre*.
  (5) Fols. 16r–20r *A Sarmun* beg. *Þe grace of godde and holi chirche*.
  (6) Fols. 20r–21v *XV Signa ante Iudicium* beg. *Þe grace of iesu fulle of miȝte*.
  (Fol. 22r is a continuation of item (12), q.v.)
  (7) Fols. 28r–29r *Christ on the Cross*. English versions of various Latin verses on the Passion, including *Respice in Faciem*, *Pendens nudatum pectus*, etc. English begins *Behold to þi lord man whare he hangiþ on rode*.
  (8) Fols. 29v–31v *Fall and Passion* beg. *Þe grace of god ful of miȝt*.
  (9) Fol. 31v exposition on *The Ten Commandments* beg. *Nou iesu for þi derworþ blode*.
  (10) Fol. 32r–v A Lullaby beg. *Lollai .l.* [for *lollai*] *litil child whi wepistou so sore*.
  (11) Fols. 44v–47r and 52r–v *Tierfabel — On the Times* beg. *Whose þenchiþ vp þis carful lif*.
  (12) Fols. 48r–v and 22r *Seven Sins* beg. *Þe king of heuen mid vs be*.
  (13) Fols. 50r–51v *Pers of Bermingham* beg. *Sith Gabriel gan grete / vre leuedi mari swete*.
  (Fol. 52r–v see item (11).)
  (14) Fol. 54v and 62r *Elde* beg. *Elde makiþ me geld an growen al grai*.
  (15) Fol. 58r end fragment of a poem. Fragment begins *[L]oue hauiþ me broȝt in liþir þoȝt*.
  (16) Fol. 58v *Nego* beg. *Hit nis bot trewþ iwend an afte*.
  (Fol. 62r see item (14).)
  (17) Fols. 62r–63v expanded version of the original quatrain *Erthe upon Erthe* beg. *Whan erþ haþ erþ iwonne wiþ wow*.
4 CB Reg i 308–309. Hartung 5 XIII.33–40. See also, A. McIntosh and M.L. Samuels, 'Prolegomena to a study of mediaeval Anglo-Irish', *MÆ* 37 (1968), 1–11. Edited: W. Heuser, *Die Kildare-Gedichte*, Bonner Beiträge zur Anglistik 14 (Bonn, 1904: repr. Darmstadt: Wissenschaftliche Buchgesellschaft, 1965).
  (1) Wells IV.29. *IMEV* 762. BSD IX. Robbins *HP* 48.
  (2) Wells VII.12. *IMEV* 1820. *OBMEV* 283. Robbins *HP* 56.
  (3) Wells IV.37. *IMEV* 1078.
  (4) Wells XIII.140. *IMEV* 3234.
  (5) Wells V.4. *IMEV* 3365.

(6) Wells V.75. *IMEV* 3367.
(7) Wells XIII.114. *IMEV* 1943 and 2047.
(8) Wells V.68. Severs 2 IV.29. *IMEV* 3366.
(9) Wells VI.15. *IMEV* 2344.
(10) Wells VII.44. *IMEV* 2025. CB14 28.
(11) *IMEV* 4144.
(12) Wells VI.12. *IMEV* 3400.
(13) *IMEV* 3126. Wells IV.11 and in contrast see M. Benskin, 'The style and authorship of the Kildare poems – (I) *Pers of Bermingham*' in *In Other Words*, Festschrift for Hans Heinrich Meier, ed. J. Lachlan MacKenzie and Richard Todd (Dordrecht, 1989), pp. 57–75.
(14) Wells VII.35. *IMEV* 718.
(15) Wells XIII.48. *IMEV* 2003.
(16) Wells IV.36. *IMEV* 1638.
(17) Wells VII.26. *IMEV* 3939.

5 BL Lansdowne 418 is a C17 copy of Harley 913 containing some items now missing from Harley. For different versions of items (2), (6), (7) and (17) see the Index of Middle English Texts A: Titles.
6 Twelve of the poems are likely to be of original medieval Hiberno-English authorship (see MB, op. cit., p. 57). C15 and C16 marks of ownership associate the MS with Waterford.
7 All the English is in the hand of one main scribe, probably a literatim copyist.
8 According to MB, the language of the internal usage of the poems is of Waterford. The rhyming usage may be ascribed to Kildare.

1 London, British Library, Harley 957.
2 C14a1?
3 [λ] Fol. 27v poem of three quatrains against pride, envy and wrath in early NME.
4 Wells VI.12. Hartung 7 XX.126. *IMEV* 2772. Edited: *Rel Ant* i 260.
6 Inscription of ownership associates the MS with Holy Trinity, Norwich. Ker *Med Lib Suppl*, p. 51.
7 English in one hand.
8 NME

1 London, British Library, Harley 978.
2 C13a2–b1 (between 1230 and 1240, CB13; *ca*. 1260, *OBMEV*).
3 [λ] [γ] Musical tracts containing
    (1) fol. 11v *Svmer is icumen in . Lhude sing cuccu* and
    (2) fol. 24v a vocabulary of the names of plants.
4 (1) Wells XIII.6; Wells *Suppl* 1, p. 985 and Wells *Suppl* 9, p. 1845. *IMEV* 3223. CB13 6. *OBMEV* 10. D&W XXIV. BSD VIII A and p. 318. Edited: A.J. Ellis, *On Early English Pronunciation* 2, EETS ES 7 (1869), p. 426 seq.
    (2) Printed: Wright-Wülcker, 554–59. See Wells X.23; Wells *Suppl* 2, p. 1127 (X.16a) and *MED Plan & Bibl*, 46a. Facsimile in *Pal Soc*, Parts i–viii, plate 125.
6 The MS is said to be a monk's commonplace-book written at Reading Abbey. See *Oxford History of Music* (2nd edn., Oxford, 1929) 1, p. 179. See also Ker *Med Lib*, p. 156.

1 London, British Library, Harley 1005.
2 *C12b2–C13a1
3 [γ] [δ] [λ] White Book of Bury St Edmunds. The first 96 fols. are of C14.
    (1) Fol. 98v names of the winds. Eight out of the twelve names of the winds, attached to a rough diagram on the verso of fol. 98, are rendered in OE as well as in Latin. Four of them are repeated in English in another hand.
    (2) Fol. 195r bequest of land at Dickleburgh and Semer to St Edmunds Abbey.
    (3) A fragment of English quoting Abbot Samson in the Latin text of the *Cronica* by Jocelin of Brakelond (fols. 121 seq.): *Ride ride Rome, turne Cantwereberei*.
4 Davis 105.

(1) Ker 233.
(2) Sawyer 1608. Edited: C. Hart, *The Early Charters of Eastern England* (Leicester, 1966), pp. 86–87. Cf. Thomson *Archives*, pp. 142–45, no.1293.
For (3) see Wilson 1943, p. 48. Edited: Thomas Arnold, *Memorials of St Edmund's Abbey* 1, RS 96 (1890), p. 253.
5 For other Bury MSS see the entry for CUL Ff.II.33.
6 *Ex libris* inscription indicates that the MS belonged to the Abbey of Bury St Edmunds, Suffolk. Ker *Med Lib*, p. 20. (1) Ker, p. 307: "The leaf on which the diagram occurs looks as if it was a flyleaf, but is actually in the middle of a manuscript of s. xiii ex., coming from Bury St Edmunds".
8 Item (2) has *drinklen* inf. "drown". Cf. Laing *Thesis* 2, p. 317.

1 London, British Library, Harley 1620.
2 C14.
3 [λ] Matthew Paris, *Chronica maiora* containing on fol. 172r St Godric's Hymn A.
4 Wells *Suppl* 1, p. 985 (XIII.27). *IMEV* 2988. Hall ii 241. D&H, p. 105.
5 This text derives from that in Cambridge, Corpus Christi College 26. For other versions see Zupitza 'Godric' and the Index of Middle English Texts A: Titles.
6 *Ex libris* inscription indicates the MS belonged to Jervaulx Abbey, Yorks. Ker *Med Lib*, p. 105.

1 London, British Library, Harley 2115.
2 C15 or later.
3 [δ][λ] Fol. 143v copy of a verse text granting the keeping of the hundred of Chelmar, etc. by King Edward to Randolfe Peperkinge.
4 Kemble 889. Not in Sawyer.
6 There is a River Chelmer in Essex.

1 London, British Library, Harley 2253.
2 C14a2 (*ca.* 1340, Ker intro. to facs. edn., pp. xxi–xxii).
3 [λ] Prose and verse miscellany in French, English and Latin. English in the main hand is on fols. 55v–61v, 62v–67r, 70v–76r, 77v–92v, 106r–107r, 114v–115r, 119r–121r, 124v–128r. English recipes in a hand not much later than the main one appear on fol. 52v. English texts are as follows.
(1) Fols. 55v–56v *The Harrowing of Hell* beg. *Alle herkneþ to me nou.*
(2) Fols. 57r–58v *Debate between the Body and the Soul* beg. *In a þestri stude y stod.*
(3) Fol. 58v *A Song of Lewes* beg. *Sitteþ alle stille & herkneþ to me.*
(4) Fol. 59v *Erthe upon Erthe* beg. *Erþe toc of erþe erþe wyþ woh.*
(5) Fols. 59v–61v *The Execution of Sir Simon Fraser* beg. *Lystneþ Lordynges a newe song ichulle bigynne.*
(6) Fol. 61v *The Follies of Fashion* beg. *Lord þat lenest vs lyf.*
(7) Fol.62v *The Three Foes of Man* beg. *Middelerd for mon wes mad.*
(8) Fol. 63r–v *Annot and John* beg. *Ichot a burde in a bour ase beryl so bryht.*
(9) Fol. 63v *Alysoun* beg. *Bytuene mersh & aueril.*
(10) Fol. 63v *The Lover's Complaint* beg. *Wiþ longyng y am lad.*
(11) Fol. 64r *Song of the Husbandman* beg. *Ich herde men vpo mold.*
(12) Fols. 64v–65v *Marina* beg. *Herkeþ hideward & beoþ stille.*
(13) Fol. 66r *The Poet's Repentance* beg. *Weping haueþ myn wonges wet.*
(14) Fol. 66v *The Fair Maid of Ribblesdale* beg. *Mosti ryden by rybbesdale.*
(15) Fols. 66v–67r *The Meeting in the Wood* beg. *In a fryht as y con fare fremede.*
(16) Fol. 67r verse beg. *A wayle whyt ase whalles bon.*
(17) Col. 1 of fols. 70v–71v *Satire on the Consistory Courts* beg. *Ne mai no lewed lued libben in londe.*
(18) Col. 2 of fols. 70v–71r *The Labourers in the Vineyard* beg. *Of a mon Matheu þohte.*
(19) Fol. 71v *Spring* beg. *Lenten ys come wiþ loue to toune.*

(20) Fols. 71v–72r *Advice to Women* beg. *In may hit murgeþ when hit dawes.*
(21) Fol. 72r–v *An Old Man's Prayer* beg. *Heȝe louerd þou here my bone.*
(22) Fols. 72v–73r verse beg. *Blow northerne wynd ... Ichot a burde in boure bryht.*
(23) Fol. 73r–v *Elegy on the Death of Edward I* beg. *Alle þat beoþ of huerte trewe.*
(24) Fols. 73v–74v *The Flemish Insurrection* beg. *Lustneþ lordinges boþe ȝonge ant olde.*
(25) Fol. 75r–v a version of *Iesu Dulcis Memoria* beg. *Suete ihu king of blysse.*
(26) Fol. 75v verse beg. *Iesu crist heouene kyng.*
(27) Fol. 75v *A Winter Song* beg. *Wynter wakeneþ al my care.*
(28) Fol. 76r *A Spring Song on the Passion* beg. *When y se blosmes springe.*
(29) Fol. 76r two lines of English at the end of a Latin/French macaronic verse beg. *Dum ludis floribus.* English begins *may y sugge namore so wel me is.*
(30) Fols. 77v–78v a version of *Iesu Dulcis Memoria* beg. *Iesu suete is þe loue of þe.*
(31) Fol. 79r–v a version of *Stabat iuxta Christi crucem* beg. *Stond wel moder vnder rode.*
(32) Fol. 79v verse beg. *Iesu for þi muchele miht.*
(33) Fol. 80r verse beg. *I syke when y singe.*
(34) Fol. 80r *An Autumn Song* beg. *Nou shrnkeþ* [sic] *rose & lylie flour.*
(35) Fol. 80v *De clerico et puella* beg. *My deþ y loue my lyf ich hate.*
(36) Fols. 80v–81r verse beg. *When þe nyhtegale singes.*
(37) Fol. 81r–v verse beg. *Blessed be þou leuedy ful of heouene blisse.*
(38) Fol. 81v *The Five Joys of the Virgin* beg. *Ase y me rod þis ender day.*
(39) Fols. 82r–83r *Maximian* beg. *Herkne to my ron.*
(40) Fol. 83r macaronic English/French verse beg. *Mayden moder milde.*
(41) Fols. 83r–92v *King Horn* beg. *Alle heo ben blyþe.*
(42) Fol. 106r verse beg. *God þat al þis myhtes may.*
(43) Fols. 106r–107r *The Sayings of St Bernard* (missing the first stanza) beg. *Lustneþ alle a lutel þrowe.*
(44) Fols. 114v–115r *The Man in the Moon* beg. *Mon in þe mone stond & strit.*
(45) Fols. 119r–121r *A Metrical Treatise on Dreams* beg. *Her comenseȝ a bok of sweuenyng.*
(46) Fols. 124v–125r *Satire on the Retinues of the Great* beg. *Of rybaudȝ y ryme / ant rede o my rolle.*
(47) Fols. 125r–127r *The Proverbs of Hending* beg. *Mon þat wol of wisdam heren.*
(48) Fol. 127r–v English prose (introduced in French): *Prophecy of Thomas of Erceldoune* beg. *When man as mad a kyng of a capped man.*
(49) Fol. 128r *The Way of Christ's Love* beg. *Lvtel wot hit anymon; hou loue hym haueþ ybounde.*
(50) Fol. 128r–v *The Way of Women's Love* beg. *Lutel wot hit anymon; hou derne loue may stonde.*

4 CB Reg i 320–22. Facsimile edition of pieces by the main hand with an introduction by N.R. Ker, EETS OS 255 (1965 for 1964), referred to below as Ker *Facs.* For a full listing of the contents and a description of the MS see Ker's introduction, pp. ix–xxiii. Edited: K. Böddeker, *Altenglische Dichtungen des MS. Harl. 2253* (Berlin, 1878). See also CB13, pp. xxxv–xl and Brook *HL.* For a list in numerical order of the individual entries in *IMEV* see Hamer 'MS index'. For the recipes on fol. 52v see *IPMEP* 626.
(1) Wells V.74. Severs 2 V.313. *IMEV* 185. Ker *Facs* 21. Edited: W.H. Hulme, *The Middle-English Harrowing of Hell and Gospel of Nicodemus,* EETS ES 100 (1907).
(2) Wells IX.1. Hartung 3 VII.18(f). *IMEV* 1461. Ker *Facs* 22. Edited: T. Wright, *The Latin Poems commonly attributed to Walter Mapes,* Camden Society 16 (1841), p. 346.
(3) Wells IV.5. Hartung 5 XIII.25. *IMEV* 3155. Ker *Facs* 23. CB13 72. D&W IV. *OBMEV* 41.

(4) Wells VII.26. *IMEV* 3939. Ker *Facs* 24b. Brook *HL* 1. CB13 73. *OBMEV* 284.
(5) Wells IV.7. Hartung 5 XIII.28. *IMEV* 1889. Ker *Facs* 25. Robbins *HP* 4.
(6) Wells IV.31. Hartung 5 XIII.32. *IMEV* 1974. Ker *Facs* 25a. CB13 74. D&W XXXII. Edited: T. Wright, *The Political Songs of England*, Camden Society 6 (1839), p. 153.
(7) Wells XIII.33. *IMEV* 2166. Ker *Facs* 27. Brook *HL* 2. CB13 75. Wright *Spec Lyr* IV.
(8) Wells XIII.15. *IMEV* 1394. Ker *Facs* 28. Brook *HL* 3. CB13 76. *OBMEV* 42. Wright *Spec Lyr* V.
(9) Wells XIII.12. *IMEV* 515. Ker *Facs* 29. Brook *HL* 4. CB13 77. *OBMEV* 43. Wright *Spec Lyr* VI.
(10) Wells XIII.16. *IMEV* 4194. Ker *Facs* 30. Brook *HL* 5. CB13 78. BSD VIII D. *OBMEV* 44. Wright *Spec Lyr* VII.
(11) Wells IV.30. Hartung 5 XIII.26. *IMEV Suppl* 1320.5. Ker *Facs* 31. Robbins *HP* 2. *OBMEV* 45.
(12) Wells V.53. *IMEV* 1104. Ker *Facs* 32. Edited: C. Horstmann, *Sammlung altenglischer Legenden* (Heilbronn, 1878), pp. 171–73.
(13) Wells XIII.24. *IMEV* 3874. Ker *Facs* 33. Brook *HL* 6. CB13 79. Wright *Spec Lyr* VIII.
(14) Wells XIII.17. *IMEV* 2207. Ker *Facs* 34. Brook *HL* 7. BSD VIII E. Wright *Spec Lyr* IX.
(15) Wells XIII.18. Hartung 3 VII.53. *IMEV* 1449. Ker *Facs* 35. Brook *HL* 8. BSD VIII F. *OBMEV* 46. Wright *Spec Lyr* X.
(16) Wells XIII.21. *IMEV* 105. Ker *Facs* 36. Brook *HL* 9. BSD VIII G. *OBMEV* 47. Wright *Spec Lyr* XI. For a new edition and reordering of this lyric (*A wayle whyt as whalles bon*) see Thomas G. Duncan, 'Textual notes on two Early Middle English lyrics', *NM* 93 (1992), pp. 109–20.
(17) Wells IV.33. Hartung 5 XIII.30. *IMEV* 2287. Ker *Facs* 40. Robbins *HP* 6.
(18) Wells VIII.36. Severs 2 IV.45. *IMEV* 2604. Ker *Facs* 41. Brook *HL* 10. CB13 80. Wright *Spec Lyr* XII.
(19) Wells XIII.14. *IMEV* 1861. Ker *Facs* 43. Brook *HL* 11. CB13 81. *OBMEV* 48. Wright *Spec Lyr* XIII.
(20) Wells XIII.23. *IMEV* 1504. Ker *Facs* 44. Brook *HL* 12. CB13 82. BSD VIII H. Wright *Spec Lyr* XIV.
(21) Wells XIII.135. *IMEV* 1216. Ker *Facs* 45. Brook *HL* 13. CB14 6. Wright *Spec Lyr* XV.
(22) Wells XIII.13. Hartung 6 XIV.445. *IMEV* 1395. Ker *Facs* 46. Brook *HL* 14. CB13 83. BSD VIII K. D&W XXVIII. *OBMEV* 49. Wright *Spec Lyr* XVI.
(23) Wells IV.8. Hartung 5 XIII.29. *IMEV* 205. Ker *Facs* 47. Robbins *HP* 5.
(24) Wells IV.6. Hartung 5 XIII.27. *IMEV* 1894. Ker *Facs* 48. Robbins *HP* 3.
(25) Wells XIII.157. *IMEV* 3236. Ker *Facs* 50. Brook *HL* 15. CB14 7. Wright *Spec Lyr* XVIII.
(26) Wells XIII.137. *IMEV* 1678. Ker *Facs* 51. Brook *HL* 16. CB14 8. Wright *Spec Lyr* XIX.
(27) Wells XIII.165. *IMEV* 4177. Ker *Facs* 52. Brook *HL* 17. CB14 9. *OBMEV* 50. Wright *Spec Lyr* XX.
(28) Wells XIII.163. *IMEV* 3963. Ker *Facs* 53. Brook *HL* 18. Wright *Spec Lyr* XXI.
(29) Wells *Suppl* 6, p. 1465 (XIII.24a). *IMEV Suppl* 694.5. Ker *Facs* 55. Brook *HL* 19.
(30) Wells XIII.158. *IMEV* 1747. Ker *Facs* 58. Wright *Spec Lyr* XXV.
(31) Wells IX.3. Hartung 3 VII.1(r). *IMEV* 3211. Ker *Facs* 60. Brook *HL* 20. D&W XXXVI. Wright *Spec Lyr* XXVII.
(32) Wells XIII.138. *IMEV* 1705. Ker *Facs* 61. Brook *HL* 21. CB13 84. Wright *Spec Lyr* XXVIII.
(33) Wells XIII.125. *IMEV* 1365. Ker *Facs* 62. Brook *HL* 22. Wright *Spec Lyr* XXIX.
(34) Wells XIII.204. *IMEV* 2359. Ker *Facs* 63. Brook *HL* 23. CB14 10. *OBMEV* 51. Wright *Spec Lyr* XXX.

(35) Wells XIII.19. Hartung 3 VII.54. *IMEV* 2236. Ker *Facs* 64. Brook *HL* 24. CB13 85. BSD VIII L. D&W XXIX. *OBMEV* 52. Wright *Spec Lyr* XXXI.
(36) Wells XIII.20. *IMEV* 4037. Ker *Facs* 65. Brook *HL* 25. CB13 86. BSD VIII M. D&W XXX. *OBMEV* 53. Wright *Spec Lyr* XXXII.
(37) Wells XIII.191. *IMEV* 1407. Ker *Facs* 66. Brook *HL* 26. Wright *Spec Lyr* XXXIII.
(38) Wells XIII.209. *IMEV* 359. Ker *Facs* 67. Brook *HL* 27. CB14 11. Wright *Spec Lyr* XXXIV.
(39) Wells VII.41. *IMEV* 1115. Ker *Facs* 68. Rel Ant i 119.
(40) Wells XIII.197. *IMEV* 2039. Ker *Facs* 69. Brook *HL* 28. CB13 87. Wright *Spec Lyr* XXXV.
(41) Wells I.1. Severs 1 I.1. *IMEV* 166. Ker *Facs* 70. D&W VII. Edited: J. Hall, *King Horn. A Middle English Romance* (Oxford, 1901).
(42) Wells XIII.134. *IMEV* 968. Ker *Facs* 73. Brook *HL* 29. CB13 88. Wright *Spec Lyr* XXXVI.
(43) Wells VII.30. *IMEV* 3310. Ker *Facs* 74. Wright *Spec Lyr* XXXVII. Edited: F.J. Furnivall, The Minor Poems of the Vernon MS. 2, EETS OS 117 (1901, repr. 1973), p. 511.
(44) Wells XIII.3. *IMEV* 2066. Ker *Facs* 81. Brook *HL* 30. CB13 89. BSD VIII N. D&W XXXI. *OBMEV* 54. Wright *Spec Lyr* XXXIX.
(45) Wells X.45. *IMEV* 1196. Ker *Facs* 85. Rel Ant i 261.
(46) Wells IV.32. Hartung 5 XIII.31. *IMEV* 2649. Ker *Facs* 88. Robbins *HP* 7.
(47) Wells VII.6. *IMEV* 2078. Ker *Facs* 89. Rel Ant i 109–116. *OBMEV* 303 (in part).
(48) Wells IV.24. Hartung 5 XIII.288. *IMEV* 3989. Ker *Facs* 90. Robbins *HP* 8. Edited: J.A.H. Murray, *The Romance and Prophecies of Thomas of Erceldoune*, EETS OS 61 (1875, repr. 1973), pp. xviii–xix.
(49) Wells XIII.46. *IMEV* 1922. Ker *Facs* 92. Brook *HL* 31. CB13 90. Wright *Spec Lyr* XL.
(50) Wells XIII.22. *IMEV* 1921. Ker *Facs* 93. Brook *HL* 32. CB13 91. *OBMEV* 55. Wright *Spec Lyr* XLII.

5 Part of BL Royal 12 C xii is in the same hand as the main hand of this MS. The ME in Harley 2253 was written down at a later date than most of the material in this *Catalogue*, but the MS shares several pieces with Bodley, Digby 86 and with other MSS known to have been written before 1300; it has therefore been included for comparison. For shared pieces with Digby 86 see Harley items (1) (also in Cambridge, Trinity College 323 (B.14.39)), (25), (31), (39), (43) (also in Bodley, Add. E.6) and (47). Harley shares item (37) with BL Egerton 613; item (28) with BL Royal 2 F viii; item (33) with Bodley, Digby 2 and items (41) and (43) with Bodley, Laud Misc. 108. It also shares texts with the roughly contemporary MSS, CUL Add. 4407, art 19; CUL Gg.I.1 and Edinburgh, National Library of Scotland, Advocates' 19.2.1, (Auchinleck MS). To identify material appearing in these and other MSS as well as in Harley, see the Index of Middle English Texts.

6 Harley is a Herefordshire MS, containing material relating to Leominster and to Hereford. Binding leaves contain accounts made in Ardmulghan, co. Meath. The Irish connection is through Roger de Mortimer, see Ker *Facs*, p. xxii.

7 English in one main hand. Another hand writes the recipes on fol. 52v. The main scribe worked in Ludlow at least between 1314 and 1349; see C. Revard, 'Richard Hurd and MS Harley 2253', *N&Q* 224 (1979), 199–202. The scribe himself was almost certainly of Leominster; see M.L. Samuels, 'The dialect of the scribe of the Harley Lyrics', *Poetica* (Tokyo) (1984), 39–47, repr. *Middle English Dialectology*, ed. M. Laing (Aberdeen, 1989), pp. 256–63.

8 Language of Leominster, Herefords, though in some of the texts there is an underlying linguistic ingredient from further north. Cf. G.L. Brook, 'The original dialects of the Harley Lyrics', *LSE* 2 (1933), 38–61.

1 London, British Library, Harley 2277.

2 C13b2–C14a1 (c1300, *MED Plan & Bibl*, p. 12).

3 [λ] *South English Legendary*.
4 CB Reg i 324–29. Görlach *SEL*, pp. 84–85. Wells v.19 (p. 294) and cf. Wells *Suppl* 4, p. 1267. See also Wells v.44, 47, 50, 51, 52, 54, 59, 67 (p. 322), 78 (p. 331), 80; X.34, 37. Severs 2 V.1 and cf. Severs 2, pp. 561–635. For individual entries in *IMEV* see Hamer 'MS index'. Edited: C. d'Evelyn and A.J. Mill, *The South English Legendary*, EETS OS 235, 236 and 244 (1956 for 1951, 1956 for 1952 and 1959 for 1957; repr. 1967 and 1969); F.J. Furnivall, *Early English Poems and Lives of Saints* (Berlin, 1862), 34 seq. (This is part ii of *TPS* (1858).)
5 For other early MSS containing parts of the *South English Legendary* see the Index of Middle English Texts A: Titles.
7 One hand.
8 Placed by MLS in W Somerset (*LALME* LP 5130).

1 London, British Library, Harley 3013.

2 C12b2.
3 [γ] Six glosses to Aldhelm's *De laude virginitatis*.
4 Ker 238. Edited: A.S. Napier, *Old English Glosses* (Anecdota Oxoniensia, Medieval and Modern Series xi, 1900), p. 174, no. 10. Murakami, p. 86, no. 14.
6 *Ex libris* inscription on fol. 1v indicates the MS belonged to the Cistercian abbey of Newminster, near Morpeth in Northumberland. Ker *Med Lib*, p. 134.

1 London, British Library, Harley 3221.

2 C13b2.
3 [λ] Latin sermon collection containing on fol. 3v, a verse in English beg. *Hwo þe wel bithoste*.
4 See Wenzel 1986, p. 163 fn. 68.

1 London, British Library, Harley 3376.

2 C13.
3 [λ] [γ] On margins of fols. 16–17 of a Latin/OE glossary, etc. (C10–C11) is pencilled writing, partly legible, in English of C13. Ker (p. 313) cites as follows: "Beg. 'in on efnigge stille þer istod. swetest alre þingge gledede mi mod': f. 16v begins 'brihture þen þe daisei him þet me longgeð': f. 17 ends 'min heorte beginneð to colden [...]'". Fol. 49r margin contains an additional C13 gloss *forweret* opposite the words *decrepita. forweren*.
4 Ker 240. Also edited and described: Theo Stemmler, 'Über die Schwierigkeit englische Lyrik des Mittelalters zu edieren', *Mannheimer Berihte* 15 (1977), 409–13.
7 There is some possibility that this writing could be in the Worcester tremulous hand. See Franzen 1991, pp. 73–74.
8 Ker says the linguistic forms in the marginalia are Western, e.g. *sunful, mon, leornen, muchele*. Significantly, perhaps, a gloss of fol. 43 (*guohioc* to *corupeta*) is Welsh.

1 London, British Library, Harley 3602.

2 C13.
3 [λ] Contains the second part (1181–1201) of Roger of Hoveden's *Chronicle* including a prophecy in English verse.
4 MS described as MS G by Stubbs *Hoveden* 1, pp. lxxxiii–lxxxiv. The prophecy is printed Stubbs *Hoveden* 3, p. 68 from Bodley, Laud Misc. 582. Variants from this MS (G) are supplied. See also Wilson 1943, p. 46 and Richter 1979, p. 74.
5 For other MSS containing Roger of Hoveden's *Chronicle*, with the English prophecy, see the Index of Texts in Latin.

1 London, British Library, Harley 3724.

2 C14a1 (a1325, *MED Plan & Bibl*, p. 35).
3 [λ] Latin except for English as follows.

(1) Fol. 49r (44r) *Creed* distributed among the apostles, beg. *I bileue in god fadir almichty*.
(2) Fol. 49v (44v) *Pater Noster* in verse beg. *Vre fader in heuene riche*.
(3) Fol. 59v a couplet *Silly sicht i seich, unsembly forte se, A fwil ar hit was fetherid, fundid forte fle*.
4 CB Reg i 337.
(1) *IPMEP* 316. Hartung 7 XX.38 and 40.
(2) Wells VI.11. *IMEV* 2703.
(3) Wells VII.21. *IMEV* 3104. Edited: *Rel Ant* i 57. See also Robin Flower, 'Manuscripts of Irish interest in the British Museum', *Analecta Hibernica* 2 (1931), 292–340 (314–15): "written in uncial hand".
6 Script and decoration are of Irish aspect.
7 Couplet on fol. 59v is in a different hand from the other English.
8 Language is early C14 Hiberno-English (information from MB).

1 London, British Library, Harley 3763.

2 *C12b2. Note that Birch dates his no. 116 as C14 and Ker *Med Lib*, p. 81 gives C15. Both these datings are incorrect. According to AID (pers. comm.) the dating for the whole codex should be C12–C14, but the English noted below is all in hands of C12b2.
3 [δ] Fols. 58–94 Evesham Cartulary. Charters with bounds in English on fols. 64v, 65v, 66v, 67r–v, 70v–71. On fol. 81v foot is added (C13–C14) "Hee [for Hec?] sunt littere anglice" and the symbols for thorn, wen, eie (yogh), and, that, long r, s and f, and "diptong" (aesc). Information from AID.
4 Davis 382. Sawyer as follows: S 935 (K 723); S 1565; S 1174 (B 117, K 57 and iii 375); S 54 (B 116, K 56 and iii 375); S 1599 (K 1368).
6 MS from Evesham Abbey, Worcs. Ker *Med Lib*, p. 81.
7 AID (pers. comm.): "Fols. 62r–67v are in the same hand, Latin and English, which reminds me somewhat in style of the last hand of the Peterborough Chronicle". On fols. 70r–71r the English (though not the Latin) is probably also in the same hand though the distinction between *g* and *ȝ* is here observed while the English on fols. 64v–67v has only *ȝ*.

1 London, British Library, Harley 3776.

2 C13–C14 ("thirteenth-century", Utley in Hartung 3, p. 681; s.xiv, Ker *Med Lib*).
3 [λ] On fol. 39r are six long lines consisting of a dialogue between man and Christ on the Cross beg. *Swete ihu my swete leman*.
4 Hartung 3 VII.2(h). *IMEV* and *IMEV Suppl* 3237. Edited: W. Winters, 'Historical notes on ... MSS ... of Waltham Holy Cross', *Transactions of the Royal Historical Society* 6 (1877), 229.
6 Contents associate the MS with Waltham Abbey, Essex. Ker *Med Lib*, p. 193.

1 London, British Library, Harley 3823.

2 C13.
3 [λ] Latin sermons containing verse exempla in English.
(1) Fol. 129r one six-line stanza from the *Proverbs of Hending*.
(2) Fol. 182v couplet on Christ's love for mankind.
(3) Fol. 183r couplet adapting the Latin proverb 'Ubi amor ibi oculus'. Repeated in garbled form on fol. 265r.
(4) Fol. 354v two short couplets.
(5) Fol. 354v couplet lamenting a fallen woman.
4 Wenzel 1974 (in order of appearance in the MS), nos. 51 (cf. *IMEV* 2817), 53 (cf. *IMEV Suppl* 3167.3), 65, 87, 8.
5 Cf. the entries for Durham Cathedral B.I.18 and Berlin-Dahlem, Stiftung Preussischer Kulturbesitz, Staatsbibliothek, MS theol. lat., fol. 249 for some of the same verses.

1 London, British Library, Harley 4967.
2 C13a–b2 (Hunt dates the different texts variously as s.xiii[1] and s.xiii ex.).
3 [γ] MS of legal and school texts (Latin) heavily glossed including many vernacular glosses. Most of these are French but some are English.
4 Contents listed Hunt *Teaching* 1, pp. 75, 299–300. Vernacular glosses edited: Hunt *Teaching* 1, p. 155 and *Teaching* 2, pp. 9–10.
6 MS belonged to the Benedictine Cathedral Priory, Worcester. Ker *Med Lib*, p. 207.

1 London, British Library, Harley 6258 B.
2 *C12b–C13a1 ("after 1200", Ker; but cf. de Vriend, p. xxx).
3 [λ] (1) Fols. 1r–44r *Herbarium Apuleii*.
   (2) Fols. 44v–51r *Medicina de Quadrupedibus*.
   (3) Fol. 51r–v herb cures in OE.
   (4) Fols. 51v–66v *Peri didaxeon* (incomplete).
4 Ker, p. xix. Cf. also Ker *Suppl*, p. 126 fn. 1 where Ker considers the MS "a good deal later" than the second half of the twelfth century. MS described H.J. de Vriend, *The Old English Herbarium and Medicina de Quadrupedibus*, EETS OS 286 (1984), pp. xxviii–xxxviii, and see refs. there cited.
   (1) Wells X.15. *IPMEP* 849. Edited: H. Berberich, *Das Herbarium Apuleii nach einer frühmittelenglischen Fassung*, Anglistische Forschungen 5 (Heidelberg, 1901, repr. Amsterdam, 1966); H.J. de Vriend, op. cit., pp. 31–233.
   (2) Wells X.4. *IPMEP* 663. Edited: J. Delcourt, *Medicina de Quadrupedibus, an early ME Version*, Anglistische Forschungen 40 (Heidelberg, 1914); H.J. de Vriend, op. cit., pp. 235–73.
   (4) Wells X.3. *IPMEP* 289. Edited: M. Löweneck, *Peri Didaxeon*, Erlanger Beiträge 12 (Erlangen, 1896).
   See also O. Cockayne, *Leechdoms, Wortcunning and Starcraft of Early England*, 3 vols. (London, 1864–66; rev. edn. with new introduction by Ch. Singer, London, 1961).
7 Ker, p. xix: "written in small ill-formed script".
8 Language is described by de Vriend, op. cit., pp. lxxv–lxxix. *Peri didaxeon* is in the same hand as the rest of the MS but the language seems to be further removed from late W-S than the other texts (cf. J. Schliessl, *Laut- und Flexionsverhältnisse der frühmittelenglischen Rezeptensammlung Peri Didaxeon* (Erlangen, 1905)).

1 London, British Library, Harley 6968.
2 *C17.
3 [δ] Partial transcription of Wells, Dean and Chapter, Liber Albus I, q.v.
4 Sawyer, p. 56.

1 London, British Library, Harley Charter 43 D 29.
2 *C14.
3 [δ] Copy of a writ of King Edward granting privileges to his priests at Wolverhampton.
4 Sawyer 1155 (Har 114, p. 527).
5 The text survives in four other versions, see Sawyer.
6 Wolverhampton, Staffs.
8 Language contains some interesting forms.

1 London, British Library, Harley Charter 111 B 49.
2 C12b1 (1155).
3 [δ] Charter of Henry II in French and English. King Henry II confirms to Theobald, abp. of Canterbury, and the monks of Christ Church their lands and privileges of jurisdiction.
4 Hall i IV, ii 264–69. Pelteret 51. Cf. Wells *Suppl* 1, p. 983 (X.51a) and Wells *Suppl* 2, p. 1071. Facsimile in N. Denholm Young, *Handwriting in England and Wales*, 2nd edn. (Cardiff, 1964), plate 9.

5 See Pelteret for other copies of the same. Contemporary copies/?originals are to be found in Canterbury, D & C Library, Ch. Ant. C. 17, 18 and 20 and Ch. Ant. C. 1310 (3) (Roll) (damaged); London, Lambeth Palace, Cart. Misc. XI/3 and Lambeth 873. C13–C14 copies are to be found in Lambeth 1212, fols. 99r (p. 190) and 100 (pp. 192–93). See Hall ii 264 for the background to the charter which is based on those in Campbell Charters xxi 6 and xxix 5 and on Cotton Charter vii 1.
6 Given at York but probably prepared by a Canterbury scribe.
7 Hall ii 264: "The document is in a French record hand, and the writer was evidently little versed in the insular script. He uses both þ and th, ƿ and w".
8 Hall considers that the language shows a mixture of Kentish and the conservative influence of the older [West-Saxon] documents on which it is modelled.

1 London, British Library, Lansdowne 269.
2 C17.
3 [δ] [λ] Fol. 97r–v (Birch says fol. 213) transcript of the Middle English rhyming charter of King Athelstan to St John's Beverley.
4 *IMEV* 3300. Sawyer 451. Birch 644. Cf. Birch 645, Kemble 359, from *Mon Angl* ii 129. The text was probably concocted in the early fourteenth century. See J.R. Witty, 'The rhyming charter of Beverley', *TYDS* 22 (1921), 36–44.
5 C14 versions are in BL Cotton Charter iv 18, BL Add 61901 and Harley 560. Two further C17 versions are in Bodley, Dodsworth 9, fol. 22 (incomplete) and Dodsworth 10, fols. 43v–44v.

1 London, British Library, Lansdowne 417.
2 *C14b2–C15a1 (after 1393, Davis).
3 [δ] Malmesbury Cartulary. English bounds to charters on fols. 13r–15v (Latin with English); 21r–22v; 24r–v; 25r.
4 Davis 645. Sawyer as follows: S 322 (B 447, K 1048) 4 lines of English; S 305 (B 470, K 271); S 862 (2 texts — the first is K 654); S 1552; S 1578; S 1585.
6 Malmesbury, Wilts.

1 London, British Library, Lansdowne 442.
2 *C14b2.
3 [δ] Cartulary of Edington (Romsey), Wilts. English on fols. 35r–36v.
4 Davis 355. Sawyer as follows: 812 (B 1187); 727 (B 1127); 765 (B 1215).
6 Romsey and Steeple Aston, Wilts.

1 London, British Library, Loans MS 30 (Marquess of Anglesey).
2 *C13a2 (c.1230–41, Davis).
3 [δ] Fols. 8–73 Cartulary of Burton Abbey. Fols. 8–9, 10r–v, 10v–11 three charters with English bounds. Fols. 9r–v will of Wulfric in English.
4 Davis 91. Sawyer as follows: S 906 (*Mon Angl* iii, 39–40, K 710 from *Mon Angl*); S 920; S 930 and S 1536. See P.H. Sawyer, *Charters of Burton Abbey*, Anglo-Saxon Charters 2 (Oxford, 1979), nos. 28, 29, 31, 35.
5 Fols. 8–9 and 9r–v were copied from the same exemplar as Aberystwyth, NLW, Peniarth 390, fols. 179v–180v and 180v–181v. Cf. BL Cotton Vespasian E iii.
6 Burton-upon-Trent, Staffs.

1 London, British Library, Royal 1 A xiv.
2 *C12b.
3 [γ] West-Saxon Gospels. Corrections and glosses in a contemporary hand throughout.
4 Ker 245. Cf. Max Reimann, *Die Sprache der mittelkentischen Evangelien (Codd. Royal I A 14 und Hatton 38)*, Diss. Berlin (1883). For contemporary glosses on fol. 142r see Ker, p. 316. In margin of fol. 148 a C13 addition is marked for insertion after *man* John 7/22. It reads *gyf ymbsnyoenesse tache man on restdaige* and translates the first part of verse 23 which is omitted in all OE copies of the gospel.

Ker, p. 316: "Evidently the OE version was still the subject of careful study at this date".
5 Cf. Bodley, Hatton 38.
6 MS from Christ Church, Canterbury. Ker *Med Lib*, p. 36.
8 Linguistic forms are Kentish.

1 London, British Library, Royal 2 D vi.
2 C13.
3 [λ] Latin MS containing commentary on the Psalms, etc. and on fols. 151r–165v the *Life of St Edmund* by Eustace of Faversham. On fol. 162v Edmund's last words are quoted in English: *Me seid, game gath on wombe ac ich segge game goth on horte.*
4 Edited: Lawrence *St Edmund*, p. 218 where variants from other MSS are also given. Cf. Wilson 1943, p. 59.
5 For other C13 MSS containing this and the "Anonymous A" version of the *Life of St Edmund* see the Index of Texts in Latin. A Continental version known as the Pontigny Life is also said to contain the English words. This version survives in at least eight MSS in two different recensions. See the entry under Auxerre, Bibl. et Musée, MS 123.
6 *Ex libris* inscription indicates the MS belonged to Rochester Cathedral priory. Ker *Med Lib*, p. 161.

1 London, British Library, Royal 2 F viii.
2 C13b2 (*ca.* 1275–1300, *OBMEV*).
3 [λ] *Psalter* in Latin. On fol. 1v are two poems in English in honour of the Virgin and Our Lord.
  (1) An orison to the BV in five stanzas beg. *In hyre ys al my lyf ylong.*
  (2) *A Spring Song on the Passion* in six stanzas (but lacking the last three lines of stanza 4) beg. *Nv yh she blostme sprynge.*
4 CB Reg i 360.
  (1) Wells *Suppl* 1, p. 991 (XIII.201). *IMEV* 2687. CB13 32C. D&H, p. 131.
  (2) Wells *Suppl* 1, p. 990 (XIII.163). *IMEV* 3963. CB13 63. BSD VIII W. *OBMEV* 23.
5 Other texts of item (1) are in Cambridge, Trinity College 323 (B.14.39) item (43); BL Cotton Caligula A ix item (3) and (an incomplete copy from the same original as Cotton) Oxford, Jesus College 29 item (8). Another version of (2) omitting the second stanza and reversing the order of stanzas four and five is in BL Harley 2253 item (28).
6 *Ex libris* inscription indicates the MS belonged to St Albans Abbey, Herts. Ker *Med Lib*, p. 167.
7 Both poems are in the same hand.
8 Dobson says (D&H): "a poor and ill-spelt text, probably written by a North-West Midland scribe". The language is mixed and cannot be from very far north: *-vore* "for". But note *gyvvs* "give us" with *g-*; *hvnne* "hence" and (in rhyme) *henne.*

1 London, British Library, Royal 4 A xiv.
2 C12a2–b1 (s. xii med., Ker).
3 [λ] Commentary on the Psalms in Latin. On fol. 106v charm for a wen in English beg. *Wenne, wenne, wenchichenne.*
4 Wells X.42. *IMEV* and *IMEV Suppl* 3896. Ker 250. Edited: *OBMEV* 2 and E. van K. Dobbie, *The Anglo-Saxon Minor Poems*, The Anglo-Saxon Poetic Records 6 (1942), p. 128. See also G. Storms, *Anglo-Saxon Magic* (1948), p. 154 and Douglas Gray, 'Notes on some Middle English charms' in *Chaucer and Middle English Studies in Honour of Rossell Hope Robbins*, ed. Beryl Rowland (London, 1974), pp. 56–71 (68–69).
6 Ker, p. 320, says the MS was later in Worcester, perhaps already in the 12th century. See also Ker *Med Lib*, p. 207.
7 The charm is in a later hand than the rest of the MS.

1 London, British Library, Royal 5 F vii.
2 C13a1 (*ca.* 1200–1225, *OBMEV*).
3 [λ] St Godric's Hymns A, B and C. These are on an inserted leaf (fol. 85r) in the Latin life of Godric by Geoffrey, monk of Durham.
4 CB Reg i 360. Wells *Suppl* 1, p. 986 (XIII.27). *IMEV* 2988 (*OBMEV* 265), 598 and 3031. Hall i II, ii 241–45. Murakami, p. 106, no. 40. On the various MSS containing one or more of these three hymns see Hall ii 241 and Zupitza 'Godric'. See also D&H, pp. 103 seq. and 108–109.
5 This is the only MS containing Hymn C. Hymns A and B are also found in Harley 153, fols. 26r, 31r; Bodley, Laud Misc. 413, fols. 39v, 47r. Hymn A only is in Cambridge, Corpus Christi College 26, p. 259; CUL Mm.IV.28, fol. 149r; BL Cotton Nero D v, fol. 150v; BL Cotton Otho B v, fol. 32v; Harley 322, fol. 74v; Harley 1620, fol. 172r; London, Lambeth Palace 51; Bodley, Douce 207, fol. 125v and Bodley, Fairfax 6.
7 All three hymns are written in a single hand accompanied by musical notation and in the order B, A, C. B is preceded and followed by *Kyrie eleison*. A has a Latin translation under it in a C14 hand.
8 The hymns are interesting as examples of early compositions in NME.

1 London, British Library, Royal 7 C iv.
2 C12–C13.
3 [λ] In a MS of C11 appear scribbles in a hand of C12–C13 on fol. 106v, viz. two lines (partly erased) of the *Poema Morale*, (lines 17–18): *elde me is bestolen on er[...] Ne mæg ic geseo before me [...]*.
4 Ker 256.
5 The *Poema Morale* survives in seven main versions for which see the Index of Middle English Texts A: Titles where other MSS containing short quotations from the text are also listed.
6 *Ex libris* inscription associates MS with Christ Church, Canterbury. Ker *Med Lib*, p. 37.
7 Hand of C12–C13 uses the insular forms of *f*, *g* and *r*.

1 London, British Library, Royal 7 D ii.
2 C12a2–b1 (s. xii med., Ker).
3 [γ] Fols. 18v–19v fourteen English glosses, among others in Latin (and French), in an alphabetical glossary, A–C only.
4 Ker 258. Edited: H.D. Merritt, *Old English Glosses*, The Modern Language Association of America, General Series 16 (New York, London, 1945), no. 69. See also Hunt *Teaching* 1, p. 20.
6 MS from St Augustine's, Canterbury. Ker *Med Lib*, p. 44.

1 London, British Library, Royal 8 C i.
2 C15.
3 [λ] Theological tracts in Latin and English. Fols. 122v–143v contain a late adaptation of the *Ancrene Riwle* perhaps by William Lichfield, rector of Allhallows the Great (*ob.* 1447).
4 Joliffe *Checklist* F.2(n), G.4(d), M.15. Edited: A.C. Baugh, *The English Text of the Ancrene Riwle edited from British Museum MS. Royal 8 C i*, EETS OS 232 (1956 for 1949; repr. 1984). See also G.F. Warner and J.P. Gilson, *Catalogue of Western Manuscripts in the Old Royal and King's Collections* 1 (London, 1921), p. 228.
5 For EME texts of Ancrene Riwle see the Index of Middle English Texts A: Titles. Other later ME versions are to be found in Cambridge, Magdalene College, Pepys 2498 and Bodley, Eng. poet. a.1, the Vernon MS.
8 C15 language.

1 London, British Library, Royal 8 C iv.
2 C13b2.

3 [γ] Fols. 16r–23v contain the Latin text of John of Garland's *Stella Maris* with some interlinear vernacular glosses. These are mostly French but a few are in English.
4 Hunt *Teaching* 1, pp. 37–38.
6 MS from Bury St Edmunds. Ker *Med Lib*, p. 20.

1 London, British Library, Royal 8 D xiii.
2 C13a1.
3 [λ] On top margin of fol. 25r of a Latin MS of C12a are thirteen lines of an English lyric beg. *ic an* [or *am*] *witles fuli wis of worldles blisse nabbe ic nout for a lafdi*. On palaeographical and linguistic grounds Carleton Brown judges the lines were written soon after 1200.
4 CB 13 p. xii. Wells *Suppl* 5, pp. 1363–64 (XIII.2a). *IMEV* 3512 (where the MS is erroneously cited as Royal 18 D xiii). The verse is written in pencil and is very faint. The reading of the incipit above is taken from CB13 emended. Wells has a slightly differing reading. Emendations to Brown's text are given by Theo Stemmler, 'Textologische Probleme mittelenglischen Dichtung', *Mannheimer Berihte* 8 (1974), 245–48 (247). See also P. Dronke, *The Medieval Lyric*, 2nd edn. (London, 1978), p. 280.
6 *Ex libris* inscription indicates that the MS once belonged to Worcester Cathedral Priory. Ker *Med Lib*, p. 208.
7 For a suggestion that the hand of the lyric may be the Worcester tremulous hand see Franzen 1991, pp. 72–73. Franzen, however, thinks the attribution very unlikely.

1 London, British Library, Royal 8 E xvii.
2 C13b2–C14a1 (c1300, *MED Plan & Bibl*, p. 67).
3 [λ] MS containing theological tracts, tales and proverbs in Latin with some French verses and a few lines of English.
  (1) Fol. 83v four lines of verse in English (following a version in French): *Wyht suylc a betel be he smyten / That al the werld hyt mote wyten / That gyfht his sone al his thing / And goht hym self a beggyn.*
  (2) Fol. 107 (margins) two English proverbs: *Er þu do eny þing þenk one þe ending* and *Betere his red þan res.*
  (3) Fol. 109r a single stanza of the *Proverbs of Hending: Riche and pouere ʒong and eld / þere whiles þou hauest þi wil a weld / Sek þi sowle bote / Ofte wan man weneþ best / Lif and haleþe and rest / Deþ is at his fote.*
4 CB Reg i 362.
  (1) Wells *Suppl* 1, p. 976 (VII.21a). *IMEV* 4202. Edited: T. Wright, *Latin Stories*, Percy Society 8 (1843), no. xxvi.
  (3) *IMEV* 2817.
5 For other MSS containing all or part of *The Proverbs of Hending* see the Index of Middle English Texts A: Titles.
7 English in one hand.

1 London, British Library, Royal 8 F ii.
2 C13b2–C14a1 (*ca*. 1300, CB13).
3 [λ] A Latin sermon preserved on the fly leaves quotes (fol. 180r) the first stanza of *Stabat iuxta Christi crucem* beg. *Stonde wel moder*.
4 CB Reg i 362. Wells *Suppl* 1, p. 988 (XIII.129). (Cf. Wells *Suppl* 5, p. 1358 (IX.3)). Hartung 3, VII.1(r). *IMEV* 3211. CB13, p. 204 (notes to 49). Edited: Wenzel 1986, pp. 51–52.
5 For other versions of this lyric see the Indexes of Middle English Texts.

1 London, British Library, Royal 8 F xiv.
2 C13.
3 [λ] MS in various hands of C13 and C14 containing religious texts in Latin. Includes on fols. 198–201v the *Life of St Edmund* by Eustace of Faversham in which are

quoted Edmund's last words in English: *Men seid game goth on wombe ac ic segge game got on herte.*
4 See Lawrence *St Edmund*, p. 218 fn. 1.
5 For other C13 MSS containing this and the "Anonymous A" version of the *Life of St Edmund* see the Index of Texts in Latin.
6 MS from Bury St Edmunds. Ker *Med Lib*, p. 20.

1 London, British Library, Royal 10 A viii.
2 C12–C13.
3 [γ] MS containing works of Ivo of Chartres. On fol. 150v thirteen names of winds in Latin and English are added in a blank space on the verso of the last leaf of the MS.
4 Ker 261.
8 þ and p are used in the English names but no other special insular letters appear.

1 London, British Library, Royal 10 C v.
2 C12b2 (1193–94, Ker).
3 [γ] Fols. 18r and 74v notes in the lower margins of a copy of the commentary of Petrus Cantor on the Psalms. Added in Paris in 1193–94 by a somewhat conservative scribe.
4 Ker 262. Cf. Parkes *Orrm*, p. 124.
6 Possible C13 associations with St Paul's, see Ker, p. 331.

1 London, British Library, Royal 12 C xii.
2 C14a.
3 [λ] Miscellany in Latin, French and English containing 30 articles by the same hand as wrote BL Harley 2253. English appears as follows.
  (1) On fol. 7r are 36 lines of macaronic verses (Latin, French and English) on the evils of the times.
  (2) On fol. 27r, in the French text of Edmund Riche's *Speculum Ecclesie*, (not written by the Harley scribe) is the usual English quatrain *Nu goþ sunne under wode / me reweþ marie þi feire rode / nu goþ sunne under tre / me reweþ marie þi sune ant þe.*
  (3) Fols. 62r–68v *Chronicle of the Brut* in English.
  (4) Inserted on fol. 107v a charm in English (not written by the Harley scribe) beg. *Haske furst þe nome of þe seke body.*
4 CB Reg i 363 and 527. See N.R. Ker, intro. to *Facsimile of B.M. MS. Harley 2253*, EETS OS 255 (1965 for 1964), pp. xx–xxi.
  (1) Wells IV.34. *IMEV* 2787.
  (2) Wells *Suppl* 1, p. 988 (XIII.127a). *IMEV* 2320/A11.
  (3) Hartung 8 XXI.6. *IMEV* 1105.
5 Other MSS containing item (2) are listed in the Index of Texts in French. Cf. the Index of Middle English Texts B: Incipits.
6 West-Midlands. See the entry for Harley 2253.
7 Ker says, "The internal evidence is at one with the script in suggesting that Royal was being added to over a number of years [1312–1340]". The hand of item (2) is said by Ker to be a "contemporary professional textura".

1 London, British Library, Royal 12 E i.
2 C13b2–C14a1 (*ca.* 1300, *OBMEV*).
3 [λ] Lives of the saints and theological collections in Latin. English lyrics on the Passion appear as follows.
  (1) Fols. 193r–194v *Stabat iuxta Christi crucem* beg. *Stonde wel moder vnder rode.*
  (2) Fol. 194v a version of the lyric *My Leman on the Rood* beg. *Quanne hic se on rode Iesu mi leman.*
  (3) Fol. 194v *þenc man of min harde stundes.*
4 CB Reg i 363.

(1) Wells *Suppl* 1, p. 988 (XIII.129). (Cf. Wells *Suppl* 5, p. 1358 (IX.3)). Hartung 3 VII.1(r). *IMEV* 3211. CB13 49B. D&H, pp. 152–53. *OBMEV* 56.
(2) Wells *Suppl* 5, p. 1365 (XIII.107b). *IMEV* 3964. CB13 35B. *OBMEV* 57.
(3) Wells *Suppl* 3, p. 1179 (XIII.114a). *IMEV Suppl* 2079.5 (*olim IMEV* 3565). CB14 3.

5 For other versions of items (1) and (2) see the Index of Middle English Texts A: Titles. For item (2) cf. also CB13 36 and 37.

7 English all in one hand.

1 London, British Library, Royal 14 C ii.

2 C12b2–C13a1.

3 [λ] [γ] Roger of Hoveden's *Chronicle* (part I to 1180). The last part dealing with the Laws of England contains scraps of English and a Latin/English legal gloss.
(1) In the section on the King's peace, the proverb *Bige spere osside other bere*.
(2) In the section on receiving strangers, the phrase *cuth other uncuth* and the proverb *Tuain nichte gest, thridde nicht hawen man*.
(3) Fol. 225r legal gloss.

4 (1) and (2) edited: Stubbs *Hoveden* 2, pp. 224, 229–30.
(3) Wells X.20. See *MED Plan & Bibl*, p. 51b. Edited: Stubbs *Hoveden* 2, p. 242. See also Wilson 1943, p. 46 and Richter 1979, p. 74.

5 Cf. Bodley, Laud Misc. 582 which contains part II of the *Chronicle* and which Stubbs considers may be the second volume of this MS. See Stubbs *Hoveden* 1, pp. lxxx–lxxxiv for other MSS of the *Chronicle*.

7 The gloss is in the main hand of the chronicle, described in Stubbs *Hoveden* 1, pp. lxxiv–lxxvi.

1 London, British Library, Royal 14 C vii.

2 C13b1 (1250–1253, Madden).

3 [λ] A holograph MS of Matthew Paris *Historia Anglorum* and part III of *Chronica Maiora*. Scraps in English appear as follows.
(1) Fol. 12rA (*olim* fol. 3) in an entry for the year 1075 *Sort red god red. Slea we þe bissop*
(2) Fol. 47vB (*olim* 39, *olim* 72, *olim* 36) on the Battle of the Standard, 1138: *yry. yry Standard*.
(3) In a note in the right margin of fol. 49r (*olim* 41, *olim* 76, *olim* 38) is quoted a snatch of song said to have been sung by the followers of Geoffrey de Mandeville during their ravages in the Fen District and referring to the sacking of the monasteries at Ramsey and St Ives: *I ne mai a liue – for benoit ne for Iue*.
(4) Fol. 54vB (*olim* 46, *olim* 86, *olim* 43) in an account of a dream of Bartholomew Bishop of Exeter, *ca*. 1161, appears: *Riseth op alle cristes icorne . leuenoth ure / fader of þis wrold fundeth*.
(5) Fol. 64rB (*olim* 56, *olim* 106, *olim* 53) two lines of a song said to have been sung in 1173 by the Flemish mercenaries of the Earl of Leicester: *hoppe hoppe wilekin hoppe wilekin. Engelond is min ant tin*.

MB (pers. comm.) also notes on fol. 12vA foot (in figure) the word *domesdai* and on fol. 54v, in the gutter between the columns, a line running from the text *Eodem anno defuncto papa adriano ... Alexander papa tum optinuit*, with the letters *leuenothus* (?*leue noth us*). This addition is in brown ink in the hand of Matthew Paris.

4 Edited: F. Madden, *Matthaei Parisiensis Monachi Sancti Albani Historia Anglorum* 1, RS 44 (1866), pp. 22, 260, 271 fn. 3, 312, 381. See Hartung 5 XIII.10; but note that Robbins wrongly says, both in Hartung 5 and in *IMEV*, that there is no MS extant.
(1) Not listed in *IMEV*.
(2) *IMEV Suppl* 4284.8.
(3) *IMEV* 1335.
(4) *IMEV* 2830.
(5) *IMEV* 1252.

Cf. Wilson 1943, p. 54; Wilson *Lost Lit*, p. 201 and James F. Royster, 'English tags in Matthew of Paris', *MLR* 4 (1908–1909), 309–10.

6 MS given by Matthew Paris to St Albans Abbey, Herts. For the later history of the MS see Madden op. cit., pp. xxxviii–xliv. See also G.F. Warner and J.P. Gilson, *Catalogue of Western Manuscripts in the Old Royal and King's Collections* 2, (London, 1921), pp. 135–36. Cf. Ker *Med Lib*, p. 167.

7 The hand of Matthew Paris. See Vaughan 1953, p. 390.

1 London, British Library, Royal 15 A xxxi.

2 C13.

3 [γ] A school book containing didactic texts in Latin with glosses and marginal commentary. The various texts belonging to the 'Liber Catonianus' (fols. 9r–43v) have a handful of vernacular glosses. John of Garland's *Accentarium* (fols. 44r–73r) is heavily glossed with many of the glosses being in the vernacular, both French and English.

4 For the vernacular glosses see Hunt *Teaching* 1, pp. 74 and 147–48.

1 London, British Library, Royal 17 A xxvii.

2 C13a1 (*ca.* 1220–1230).

3 [λ] Fols. 1r–70v (the rest of the MS is C15) contains texts in English as follows.
  (1) Fols. 1r–10v *Sawles Warde*.
  (2) Fols. 11r–32r *St Katherine*.
  (3) Fols. 37r–56r *St Margaret*.
  (4) Fols. 56r–70r *St Juliana*.
  (5) Fol. 70r–v *Oreisun of Seinte Marie* (incomplete).

4 (1) *IPMEP* 594. Wells V.2. Hall i XVI, pp. 127–28, ii 492–524. For the verse introducing *Sawles Warde* see *IMEV* 4098. Edited: R.M. Wilson, *Sawles Warde*, Leeds School of English Texts and Monographs 3 (1938).
  (2) *IPMEP* 138. Wells V.50. Hall i XVII, ii 524–31. Edited: d'Ardenne & Dobson.
  (3) *IPMEP* 29. Wells V.52. For a moral warning inserted into the text of the *Life of St Margaret* on fol. 49r see *IMEV Suppl* 3570.5. Edited: F.M. Mack, *Seinte Marherete*, EETS OS 193 (1934 for 1933, repr. 1958).
  (4) *IPMEP* 359. Wells V.49. Hall i XIX, ii 543–53. Edited: d'Ardenne *Iulienne*.
  (5) *IPMEP* 617. Wells XIII.206. Edited: Morris *OEH* 1, p. 305 and W.M. Thompson, *þe Wohunge of ure Lauerd*, EETS OS 241 (1958 for 1955; repr. 1970), p. 19.

5 For other copies of *Sawles Warde* and *St Katherine* see Bodley 34 and BL Cotton Titus D xviii. The other saints' lives are in Bodley but not in Titus. This MS does not have *Hali Meiðhad*. For item (5) cf. BL Cotton Nero A xiv item (4).

7 There are three hands.
  Hand A: fols. 1r–8v, 11r – close of paragraph 1 on fol. 45v.
  Hand B: fols. 9r–10v, 58v–70v.
  Hand C: fols. 45v beg. of paragraph 2 – 58r (end).

8 All three hands write in West-Midland language similar to but not identical with AB language. George Jack considers the dialect to be for the most part self-consistent; see George Jack, 'The language of the Early Middle English texts in MS Royal 17 A.xxvii', *Studia Neophilologica* 63 (1991), 129–42. See also Janet Bately, 'On some aspects of the vocabulary of the West Midlands in the early Middle Ages: the language of the Katherine Group' in *Medieval English Studies presented to George Kane*, ed. E.D. Kennedy, R. Waldron and J.S. Wittig (Woodbridge, 1988), pp. 55–77.

1 London, British Library, Sloane 146.

2 C13b2.

3 [λ][γ] (1) Fols. 1r–68r a collection of medical recipes in Latin, French and English. English on fols. 33v, 37v–38r.

(2) Fols. 69v–72v botanical glossary with trilingual entries in Latin, French and English.
A few English entries also appear on fol. 73r. The rest of the MS is in French and Latin.
4 See Hunt *Pop Med*, pp. 264–96.
7 English in two hands of late C13.
Hand A (main hand): fols. 1r–68r.
Hand B: fols. 69v seq.
Other hands contribute to the later part of the MS.

1 London, British Library, Sloane 420.
2 C13b2–C14a1 (*ca.* 1300).
3 [γ] A collection of medical texts including on fols. 107r–109v a list of *synonyma* with English and French equivalents of Latin plant names. Two vernacular entries also appear on fol. 110r–v.
4 See Hunt *Plant Names*, p. xxi.
7 Hunt: "Written in a large, clumsy hand of c.1300".

1 London, British Library, Sloane 809.
2 C13b2.
3 [γ] A parchment roll containing *Le Tretiz* of Walter de Bibbesworth with ME glosses.
4 Variants from this MS are given in the edition by Annie Owen, *Le Traité de Walter de Bibbesworth sur la langue française* (Paris, 1929; repr. Geneva, 1977). Corrections to this edition may be found in W. Rothwell, 'A mis-judged author and a mis-used text: Walter de Bibbesworth and his "Tretiz"', *MLR* 77 (1982), 282–93.
5 For other early MSS containing this text with the ME glosses see the Index of Texts in French.

1 London, British Library, Sloane 3550.
2 C13b2–C14a1 (*ca.* 1300, Hunt).
3 [γ] A medical MS containing on fols. 33r–36r *nomina herbarum* with French and English equivalents of Latin plant names and on fols. 41r–76r a medical glossary with about two dozen vernacular entries.
4 See Hunt *Plant Names*, p. xxi and Hunt *Pop Med*, pp. 297–310.
7 One hand.

1 London, British Library, Sloane Charter xxxiv.1.
2 *C12.
3 [δ] Copy of a writ of King Edward declaring that he intends to have legal possession of the land at Ickworth, Suffolk.
4 Sawyer 1124 (Har 80). *BM Facs* iv 35.
5 Later (C13 and C14) copies are in BL Cotton Faustina A iii and London, Westminster Abbey Muniment Book 11, fol. 648.
6 Ickworth, Suffolk.

1 London, British Library, Stowe 34 (*olim* 240).
2 C13a1.
3 [λ] *Vices and Virtues* (beginning missing).
4 Wells IX.2. Hartung 3 VII.26. Hall i XIII, ii 438–49. D&W XVI. *IPMEP* 69. Edited: F. Holthausen, *Vices and Virtues*, vol. 1 Text and Translation, EETS OS 89 (1888, repr. 1967), vol. 2 Notes and Glossary, EETS OS 159 (1921, repr. 1967). Facsimile of fol. 51r in *Pal Soc*, Second Series, vol. 1, plate 94.
5 This is the only surviving copy of this text.
7 Hall ii 438: "by three scribes, with numerous corrections by at least three other hands". Hall i XIII A is by Scribe A; XIII B is by scribe C.
8 MLS (pers. comm.) considers Stowe 34 *Vices and Virtues* to be critical as evidence of the language of Essex. He believes that it belongs to Essex itself rather than the environs.

1 London, British Library, Stowe 57.
2 C12b2 (?c1200, *MED Plan & Bibl*, p. 77).
3 [γ] MS (Latin) is entitled (fol. 1) 'Scutum Bede Collectiuus. Gaufridi de Vfford' and is a world history ending with a short history of England to the accession of Henry II. English appears as follows.
  (1) Fol. 3v names of the letters of the alphabet.
  (2) Fols. 155v–165r trilingual glossary containing on fols. 156r–v, 158r–v, 160r Middle English glosses to names of animals, etc.
4 Ker 272. Wells X.19. R.M. Garret, 'Middle English and French glosses from MS Stowe 57', *Archiv* 121 (1908), 411–12. See also Hunt *Teaching* 1, pp. 22–23.
6 Ker, p. 337: "compiled in the reign of Henry II, perhaps by a native of Lincoln, and displays special interest in Peterborough, St Guthlac, and Thorney", etc; "seems to come from the Peterborough region and perhaps from Peterborough itself".

1 London, British Library, Stowe 104.
2 *C12a2–b1 (s. xii med., Ker).
3 [λ] Bede's *Historia ecclesiastica* followed by Cuthbert's *Epistola de obitu Bedae* containing on fol. 112v Bede's Death Song.
4 Ker 273. Edited: Dobbie 1937, p. 75.
5 For other MSS containing Bede's Death Song see the Index of Old English Texts.

1 London, British Library, Stowe 944.
2 C12b.
3 [δ] Winchester Register and Martyrology (Newminster and Hyde Abbey) ca. 1016–1020 with additions of 1031. Fol. 40r–v (an originally blank leaf) contains a C12 writ of the monk Edwin, child-master at New Minster, Winchester concerning an agreement between Old and New Minster.
4 Davis 1050. Ker 274. Sawyer 1428 (Har 113).
6 MS from Hyde Abbey, Winchester, Hants. Ker *Med Lib*, p. 104.
7 C12 English in one hand.

1 London, British Library, Stowe Charter 43.
2 C12a1 (February?, 1123).
3 [δ] One of three surviving originals of a writ of King Henry I granting rights and privileges to William of Corbeil and the monks of Christ Church, Canterbury.
4 Pelteret 48. *OS Facs* iii 44.
5 The other originals of this text are BL Campbell Charter xxi 6 and Lambeth Palace, Cart. Misc. X/109.
6 Canterbury, Kent.

1 London, British Library, Stowe Charter 44.
2 C12b1–2 (1154 x 1161/1172 x 1189).
3 [δ] Writ of King Henry II to his bishops, earls, sheriffs and thegns, etc. in Canterbury.
4 Pelteret 54. *OS Facs* iii 45.
5 Other manuscripts of the same are Canterbury, D & C Library, Ch. Ant. C. 14 and 18a and Lambeth Palace, Cart. Misc. XI/2.
6 Canterbury, Kent.

1 London, Corporation of London Records Office, 'Liber custumarum'.
2 *C14a2 (ca. 1324).
3 [δ] Part of a MS of over 370 fols. the rest of which is in BL Cotton Claudius D ii and Oxford, Oriel College 46. The Corporation of London MS has part of the original MS beginning from the old fol. 95 and containing almost entirely documents relating to the City of London. The leaves have been renumbered but the old foliaion is usually legible. Fols. 13r (English) and 187r (two versions in English, one in Latin), contain

copies of a writ of King William (1067) to the bishop, portreeve and burghers of London, declaring that the laws should stand as they did in King Edward's day.
4 For a description of the MS see Ker *Med MSS* 1, pp. 20–22. For the English texts see Pelteret 8 nos. 31 and 32. Edited: H.T. Riley, *Liber Custumarum* 2, RS 12 (1860), pp. 25–26 and 246–47.
6 London.

1 London, Corporation of London Records Office, 'Liber de antiquis Legibus'.
2 C13a2 (*ca.* 1225, D&H). Dobson says that these leaves are an insertion at the end of a volume which is itself a chronicle covering the years 1178–1274.
3 [λ] Fols. 160–162 are possibly fragments of a service book preserved by Arnald Thedmar, the main scribe of the MS. Fols. 160v–161v contain *A Prisoner's Prayer* in alternate French and English verses. The poem has 44 lines in each language.
4 Ker *Med MSS* 1, pp. 22–27 (esp. p. 27 art. 40). Wells XIII.30. Hartung 5 XIII.269. *IMEV* 322. CB13 5. *OBMEV* 9. D&H, pp. 111–12. Edited: A.J. Ellis, *On Early English Pronunciation* 2, EETS ES 7 (1869), p. 428 seq.
6 Dobson thinks the text had an origin "in London or nearby, north of the Thames".
7 English in one hand.
8 London. The English is said to be a translation of the French, reproducing the syllable pattern of the French version. It is, technically, a *contrafactum*.

1 London, Corporation of London Records Office, 'Liber Horn'.
2 *C14a1 (1311).
3 [δ] On each of fols. 205v and 362r, three versions (two English, one Latin) of a writ of King William (1067) to the bishop, portreeve and burghers of London, declaring that the laws should stand as they did in King Edward's day.
4 Pelteret 8 nos. 33 and 34.
6 London.

1 London, Corporation of London Records Office, 'Liber Memorandum'.
2 *C13b2 (1298).
3 [δ] On fols. 110v–111r, three versions (two English, one Latin) of a writ of King William (1067) to the bishop, portreeve and burghers of London, declaring that the laws should stand as they did in King Edward's day.
4 Pelteret 8 no. 35.
6 London.

1 London, Dulwich College XXII.
2 C13b2 (c1300, *MED Plan & Bibl*, p. 40; 1250–1300, Wells).
3 [λ] Fols. 81v–85v contain 519 lines of a Middle English poem in quatrains entitled *La Estorie del Euangelie*.
4 *IMEV* 3194. Wells V.69. Edited: Gertrude H. Campbell, 'The Middle English Evangelie', *PMLA* 30 (1915), 529–613 (851–53 contain additions and corrections). An edition of all the surviving MSS is in preparation by Celia Millward for Middle English Texts (General Editors Manfred Görlach and O.S. Pickering). See also Angus McIntosh, 'The Middle English *Estorie del Euangelie*: the dialect of the original version', *NM* 88 (1987), 186–91.
5 Later ME copies of the *Euangelie* are in Bodley, Add C 38, fols. 71v–82r (?Worcs C15a); Bodley, Eng. poet. a.1, the Vernon MS, fol. 105r seq. (C14b2); Bodley, Rawlinson C 655 (contains *Northern Passion* with bits of *Euangelie* incorporated, C14b Somerset); University of London SL.V.17 (C15 Worcs).
7 One hand.
8 Language is probably of S Lincs.

1 London, Guildhall Library 25272, 'Carte Libertatum Ecclesie Sci. Pauli' (*olim* London, St Paul's, 1/69).
2 *C13b.
3 [δ] Copies of writs are as follows.
 (1) Writ of King Edward (1042 x 1066) granting rights to St Paul's, London.
 (2) m. 2, no. 13 Bilingual writ of King William I (1072 x 1078) granting rights to St Paul's Church.
 (3) m. 1, no. 1 Writ of William I (1071 x 1087) concerning St Paul's Church.
 (4) m. 1, no. 2 similar to (3).
 (5) m. 1, no. 4 Writ of William I (1085–1087) to Osmund bp. of Salisbury.
 (6) m. 1, no. 3 Writ of Henry I (25 Dec, 1100) re the bishopric of London.
4 Davis 598. Sawyer 1104. Pelteret 27, 36, 37, 39, 43.
6 London.

1 London, Guildhall Library 25501, 'Liber A sive Pilosus' (*olim* London, St Paul's, WD 1).
2 *C13a2 (1241).
3 [δ] Copies of writs are as follows.
 (1) Fol. 1 Writ of King Edward (1042 x 1066) granting rights to St Paul's, London.
 (2) I, no. 3 Writ of William I (1071 x 1087) concerning St Paul's Church.
 (3) I, no. 2 similar to (2).
 (4) I, no. 5 Writ of William I (1085–1087) to Osmund bp. of Salisbury.
 (5) IIa no. 9 Writ of William I (1072 x 1078) concerning St Paul's Church.
 (6) IIb (=2r) no. 19 Writ of Henry I (25 Dec, 1100) re the bishopric of London.
4 Davis 597. Sawyer 1104. Pelteret 27, 36, 37, 39, 43. Cf. Marion Gibbs, *Early Charters of the Cathedral Church of St Paul, London*, Camden Society 3rd Series 58 (1939), pp. 9–13, 20.
6 London.

1 London, Guildhall Library 25504, 'Liber L' (*olim* London, St Paul's, WD 4).
2 *C13.
3 [δ] Fols. 16v–17r copy of a bilingual writ of King William I (1072 x 1078) granting rights to St Paul's Church.
4 Davis 596. Pelteret 27.
6 London.

1 London, Guildhall Library 25516, 'Liber I' (*olim* London, St Paul's, WD 16).
2 *C13b2 (?1299).
3 [δ] Fol. 40v (*olim* 36v) Record of dues rendered to the church at Lambourn, Berks.
4 Pelteret 141. Edited: Robertson 240, App. i, no. 5.
6 Lambourn, Berks.

1 London, Lambeth Palace, Cart. Misc. X/109.
2 C12a1 (February?, 1123).
3 [δ] One of three surviving originals of a writ of King Henry I granting rights and privileges to William of Corbeil and the monks of Christ Church, Canterbury. This version is damaged.
4 Pelteret 48.
5 The other originals of this text are BL Campbell Charter xxi 6 and BL Stowe Charter 43.
6 Canterbury, Kent.

1 London, Lambeth Palace, Cart. Misc. XI/1.
2 C12a1 (?1107).

3 [δ] One of three originals of the bilingual writ granted to St Anselm and Christ Church, Canterbury by Henry I, *ca.* 1107.
4 Pelteret 46.
5 The other originals of this text are BL Campbell Charter xxix 5 and BL Cotton Charter vii 1.
6 Canterbury, Kent.

1 London, Lambeth Palace, Cart. Misc. XI/2.
2 C12b1–2 (1154 x 1161/1172 x 1189).
3 [δ] Writ of King Henry II to his bishops, earls, sheriffs and thegns, etc. in Canterbury.
4 Pelteret 54.
5 Other manuscripts of the same are Canterbury, D & C Library, Ch. Ant. C. 14 and 18a and BL, Stowe Charter 44.
6 Canterbury, Kent.

1 London, Lambeth Palace, Cart. Misc. XI/3.
2 C12b1 (1155).
3 [δ] Charter of Henry II in French and English. King Henry II confirms to Theobald, abp. of Canterbury, and the monks of Christ Church their lands and privileges of jurisdiction.
4 Pelteret 51.
5 See Pelteret for other copies of the same. Contemporary copies/?originals are to be found in Canterbury, D & C Library, Ch. Ant. C. 17, 18 and 20 and Ch. Ant. C. 1310(3) (Roll) (damaged); BL Harley Charter 111 B 49 and Lambeth 873. C13–C14 copies are to be found in Lambeth 1212, fols. 99r (p. 190) and 100 (pp. 192–93). See Hall ii 264 for the background to the charter which is based on those in Campbell Charters xxi 6 and xxix 5 and on Cotton Charter vii 1.
6 Given at York but probably prepared by a Canterbury scribe.

1 London, Lambeth Palace Library 51.
2 C13a1.
3 [λ] Compilation of religious material by Peter, prior of Holy Trinity, Aldgate, 1197–1221. Contains a version of Godric's Hymn A in chapter cliiii of Reginald's *Vita S. Godrici.*
4 CB Reg i 427. Wells *Suppl* 1, p. 986 (XIII.27). *IMEV* 2988. Apparently not in D&H or Zupitza 'Godric'.
5 For other MSS of the same see see the Index of Middle English Texts A: Titles.
6 MS from the Priory of the Holy Trinity, Aldgate, London. Ker *Med Lib*, p. 123.

1 London, Lambeth Palace Library 135.
2 C13.
3 [λ] Lives of SS. Thomas and Edmund of Canterbury. The latter (fols. 118r–137v), in the "Anonymous A" version, is said to contain the last words of Edmund in English.
4 MS described James *Cat*, pp. 214–16. Cf. Wilson 1943, p. 59 and Lawrence *St Edmund*, p. 49.
5 For other C13 MSS containing this version of the *Life of St Edmund*, and that of Eustace of Faversham also containing Edmund's last words, see the Index of Texts in Latin.

1 London, Lambeth Palace Library 236.
2 C12b2–C13a1.
3 [λ] MS of Giraldus Cambrensis in Latin. Contains two quotations in English in chapters 43 and 48 of a text of the *Gemma Ecclesiastica: swete lamman dhin are*, and *Roriese þe rorie ne wrthe nan.*
4 Edited: J.S. Brewer, *Giraldi Cambrensis Opera* 2, RS 21 (1862), pp. 120 and 121. Cf. Wilson 1943, p. 51; Richter 1979, p. 72 and Wilson *Lost Lit*, pp. 161–62.

1 London, Lambeth Palace Library 342.
2 C13b2 (end of the thirteenth century, Hunt).
3 [γ] Composite MS containing on fols. 231v–233v a list of *nomina herbarum* with English and French glosses to Latin plant names.
4 See Hunt *Plant Names*, p. xx. James *Cat*, pp. 449–53.

1 London, Lambeth Palace Library 487.
2 C12b2 (*ca.* 1200).
3 [λ] (1) Fols. 1r–59v Lambeth Homilies including on fols. 21v–24v an exposition on the *Pater Noster* in verse beg. *Vre feder þat in heouene is.*
(2) Fols. 59v–65r *Poema Morale* beg. *ich em nu alder þene ich pes a pintre & a lare.*
(3) Fols. 65v–67r *On Ureison of Ure Loverde.*
4 Ker, p. xix: not treated in the body of the Catalogue.
(1) *IPMEP* 556. Wells V.12. Hall i X and XI, ii 407–427. For fols. 25v–27r, How the Apostles made the Creed, see Hartung 7 XX.40. For the verse *Pater Noster* see Wells VI.13; Hartung 7 XX.36 and *IMEV* 2709. Edited: Morris *OEH* 1, pp. 3–159 (odd pages).
(2) CB Reg i 440. Wells VII.25. *IMEV* 1272. Hall i VIII, ii 312–54. Edited: Morris *OEH* 1, pp. 159–83 (odd pages). See also Hill 1977, pp. 97, 107 seq.
(3) *IPMEP* 419. Wells XIII.169. Edited: Morris *OEH* 1, pp. 183–89 (odd pages) and cf. p. vii.
On the dual textual history of the homilies see Celia Sisam, 'The scribal tradition of the *Lambeth Homilies*', *RES* NS 6 (1951), 105–13. Cf. also Sarah O'Brien, 'An edition of seven homilies from Lambeth Palace Library MS 487', Diss. D.Phil., University of Oxford (1985), unpubl. The homilies edited are i, v, vi, ix, x, xvi and xvii.
5 Lambeth shares five sermons and the *Poema Morale* with Cambridge, Trinity College 335 (B.14.52), edited: Morris *OEH* 2. Compare in Morris the sermons Lambeth vii – Trinity iv; L xiii – T xxvi; L xv – T xxxii; L xvi – T xxx; L xvii – T xxv. The parallel texts reveal numerous interesting differences including some of a lexical kind. Morris prints (pp. 200–203) from BL Cotton Nero A xiv, fols. 123v–126v: "a somewhat later but unmutilated copy of the 'Orison' under the title of 'On Wel Swuðe God Ureisun of God Almihti'". *Poema Morale* survives in seven copies for which see the Index of Middle English Texts A: Titles, where MSS containing short quotations from the text are also listed.
6 Hill (1977, p. 109) says: "Professor Dobson has stated twice that Lambeth MS 487 possibly came from Lanthony near Gloucester, but he has given no reasons for his opinion". She cites EETS OS 267, p. lxxix (should be lxxxix) and *The Origins of Ancrene Wisse* (Oxford, 1976), p. 359. On provenance see R.M. Wilson, 'The provenance of the Lambeth Homilies with a new collation', *LSE* 4 (1935), 24–43. For MLS's views see his review of A.J. Bliss, *Sir Orfeo* (Oxford, 1954) in *MÆ* 24 (1955), 56–60 and Hill 1977, pp. 108–109.
7 Hand A: fols. 1r–65r.
Hand B (slightly later — C13a1): 65v–67r.
8 MLS places the language on the border of N Herefords and Salop. For a preliminary study of the language of the seven surviving copies of the *Poema Morale* see Laing 'Versions'.

1 London, Lambeth Palace Library 499.
2 C13b2.
3 [λ] Latin MS containing English as follows.
(1) On the lower margins of fols. 64v–68v a group of eight heavily alliterated secular English lyrics.
(2) Fol. 69r four lines of unrhymed English verse.
(3) Fol. 124r several macaronic phrases (English, French and Latin).
(4) Fol. 125v the ME verse *Three Sorrowful Things* beg. *Wenne I thenke on thingres* [sic] *thre.*

4 (1) Edited (with commentary): O.S. Pickering, 'Newly discovered secular lyrics from later thirteenth-century Cheshire', *RES* NS 43, no. 170 (1992), 157–180.
   (2) See O.S. Pickering, 'An Early Middle English verse inscription', *Anglia* 106 (1988), 411–14.
   (4) Cf. *IMEV* 3969 but not recorded there from this MS.
5 The alliterative lyrics are unique to this MS. For other texts of item (4) see the Index of Middle English Texts B: Incipits.
6 MS from Stanlaw Abbey, Cheshire.
7 English in one hand.
8 There is no doubt that the lyrics were written down in their present form at Stanlaw Abbey. The language, however, is very difficult to assess being in an elliptical poetic style using much specialised alliterative vocabulary. Moreover, they provide too little linguistic information to make possible a precise placing of the original language. Nevertheless, AM considers that such evidence as is available points to an origin either in the S of Cheshire or in N Salop or N Staffs. He sees a fairly close resemblance between the language of the lyrics and the NW Midland overlay in the BL Cotton Titus D xviii text of the *Ancrene Riwle*.

1 London, Lambeth Palace Library 502.

2 C13b.
3 [γ] Grammatical works (in Latin) by John of Garland heavily glossed and with marginal commentary. The glosses include some in the vernacular, French and English.
4 Vernacular glosses edited: Hunt *Teaching* 1, p. 150 and *Teaching* 2, pp. 171–73.

1 London, Lambeth Palace Library 557.

2 C13b2 (*ca.* 1275, *OBMEV*).
3 [λ] Sermons, etc. in Latin with two English verses.
   (1) Fol. 185v two six-line stanzas beg. *Allas, allas vel yuel y sped.*
   (2) Fol. 186r five couplets on Christ's wounds beg. *Alle þat gos and rydys loket op-on me.*
4 (1) Hartung 3 VII.2(a). *IMEV Suppl* 3825 (*olim IMEV* 143). *OBMEV* 20.
   (2) *IMEV* 207. Edited: James *Cat*, p. 760. See also R. Woolf, *RES* 13 (1962), 9 and *The English Religious Lyric in the Middle Ages* (Oxford, 1968), p. 51 n. 2.
5 The second stanza of item (1) begins *Vndo my lef my downe dere* and may be identified with the lyric beg. *Vndo þi dore my spuse dere* which appears in Edinburgh, National Library of Scotland, Advocates' 18.7.21 (Grimestone).
6 On fol. 310r is a Latin memorandum, dated 10 Jan 1487, recording debt bondage at Cashel (Co. Tipperary) in a contemporary hand.
7 Verses are in a charter hand of the late C13. In the same hand are Latin verses on the Council of Lyons 1274, fol. 183r.
8 In the opinion of MB (pers. comm.) the language of the verses is MHE of an early type.

1 London, Lambeth Palace Library 873.

2 C12.
3 [δ] Charter of Henry II in French and English. King Henry II confirms to Theobald, abp. of Canterbury, and the monks of Christ Church their lands and privileges of jurisdiction. Text on the verso of a loose parchment used as wrapping for a case containing an Almanack made at or for Croyland Abbey.
4 Pelteret 51.
5 See Pelteret for other copies of the same. Contemporary copies/?originals are to be found in Canterbury, D & C Library, Ch. Ant. C. 17, 18 and 20 and Ch. Ant. C. 1310(3) (Roll) (damaged); BL Harley Charter 111 B 49 and London, Lambeth Palace, Cart. Misc. XI/3. C13–C14 copies are to be found in Lambeth 1212, fols. 99r (p. 190) and 100 (pp. 192–93). See Hall ii 264 for the background to the charter

which is based on those in Campbell Charters xxi 6 and xxix 5 and on Cotton Charter vii 1.
6 Given at York but probably prepared by a Canterbury scribe. MS itself from Crowland Abbey, Lincs. Ker *Med Lib*, p. 56.

1 London, Lambeth Palace Library 1212.
2 *C13.
3 [δ] Composite Cartulary of Christ Church, Canterbury. English on pp. 189, 190–93, 382, 387–88, 391–92, 396–97, 399–400, 403, 406–408.
4 Davis 159. Pelteret 46, 51 (2 copies), 54. Sawyer as follows: S 50 (B 197); S 108 (B 208); S 175 (B 346); S 286 (B 419); S 546; S 497 (B 791); S 489 (B 784); S 168 (B 335); S 1188 (B 330); S 1202; S 981.
6 MS from Christ Church, Canterbury, Kent. Ker *Med Lib*, p. 37.
7 There are many different hands in the MS. English appears in at least three hands. Hand A copies the post-Conquest charters between pp. 189 and 193.
Hand B is responsible for the English bounds on p. 382 and
Hand C for the English between pages 387 and 408.
8 Described Birch 330 as "very corrupt and inaccurate" which suggests that the language may have interesting modifications.

1 London, Lincoln's Inn, Hale 135.
2 C13b2–C14a1 (*ca.* 1300).
3 [λ] MS of Bracton's *Summa de Legibus*. English only on flyleaf (badly faded), fol. 137v: a song in three stanzas beg. *No[u] spri[nke]s the sprai*.
4 Wells XIII.25. Hartung 3 VII.52 and 6 XIV.447. *IMEV* 360. CB13 62. *OBMEV* 38. Edited: R.L. Greene, *Early English Carols* (Oxford, 1935), no. 450 and K. Sisam, *Fourteenth Century Verse and Prose* (Oxford, 1921), no. xv A.
6 Ker: "Belonged apparently in 1297 and later to Alan de Thorneton, a Lincs landowner employed (as a lawyer?) by the abbot of Ramsey". For this and further evidence of associations with Lincs, see Ker *Med MSS* 1, pp. 132–33 and Laing *Thesis* 1, pp. 12–13. Notes in the MS refer to Ancholme, Blyborough and Cabourne, N Lincs.
7 English in one hand.
8 Important as a rare example of a northerly text of early date. Probably Lincs language, see AM *Havelok*, fn. 5.

1 London, Public Record Office, C 52, Cartae Antiquae, Roll 1, m. 1, no. 1.
2 *C13.
3 [δ] Copy of a writ of King William I (1072 x 1078) granting rights to St Paul's Church, London.
4 Pelteret 27. Edited: L. Landon, *The Cartae Antiquae Rolls 1–10*, Pipe Roll Society NS 17 (1939), p. 1.
6 London.

1 London, Public Record Office, C 52, Cartae Antiquae, Roll 4, nos. 7–9.
2 *C13.
3 [δ] Copies of three writs of King Edward (1053 x 1066) granting rights to Chertsey Abbey, Surrey.
4 Sawyer as follows: S 1094 (K 850, Har 41); S 1095 (Har 42); S 1096 (Har 43).
6 Chertsey, Surrey.

1 London, Public Record Office, C 52, Cartae Antiquae, Roll 6, m. 1, no. 2.
2 C13.
3 [δ] Copy of a writ of King Henry II (1155 x 1161) granting rights to Christ Church, Canterbury.

4 Pelteret 51.
6 Canterbury, Kent.

1 London, Public Record Office, C 52, Cartae Antiquae, Roll 9, no. 12.
2 *C13.
3 [δ] Copy of a writ of King Edward (1042 x 1050) granting rights to St Augustine's, Canterbury.
4 Sawyer 1091 (K 831).
6 Canterbury, Kent.

1 London, Public Record Office, C 52, Cartae Antiquae, Roll 9, m. 1, no. 13.
2 *C13.
3 [δ] Copy of a writ of King William I (*ca.* 1067) granting rights to St Augustine's, Canterbury.
4 Pelteret 6. Edited: L. Landon, *The Cartae Antiquae Rolls 1–10*, Pipe Roll Society NS 17 (1939), p. 131.
6 Canterbury, Kent.

1 London, Public Record Office, C 52, Cartae Antiquae, Roll 12, no. 1.
2 *C13.
3 [δ] Copy of a writ of King Edward (1062) granting rights to Waltham Abbey, Essex.
4 Sawyer 1036. Edited: J. Conway Davies, *The Chartae Antiquae Rolls 11–20*, Pipe Roll Society 71 NS 33 (1960 for 1957), pp. 35–38. This text is considered by Harmer and others to be a post-Conquest fabrication. See Sawyer, p. 308.
5 For other C13 copies see BL Cotton Tiberius C ix, fols. 48r–49r and Harley 391, fols. 33–35v.
6 Waltham Abbey, Essex.

1 London, Public Record Office, C 52, Cartae Antiquae, Roll 15, nos. 1–4.
2 *C13.
3 [δ] Copies of writs of King Edward (1042 x 1066) to Bury St Edmunds.
4 Sawyer as follows: S 1045; S 184; S 1075; S 1085. Edited: J. Conway Davies, *The Chartae Antiquae Rolls 11–20*, Pipe Roll Society 71 NS 33 (1960 for 1957), pp. 87–88.
5 Cf. BL Harley 638 and CUL Gg.IV.4.
6 Bury St Edmunds, Suffolk.

1 London, Public Record Office, C 52, Cartae Antiquae, Roll 15, m. 1, no. 6.
2 *C13.
3 [δ] Copy of a writ of King William I (1066 x 1070) to Bury St Edmunds.
4 Pelteret 19. Edited: J. Conway Davies, *The Chartae Antiquae Rolls 11–20*, Pipe Roll Society 71 NS 33 (1960 for 1957), p. 89.
6 Bury St Edmunds, Suffolk.

1 London, Public Record Office, C 52, Cartae Antiquae, Roll 19, m. 1, col. b, no. 4.
2 C13.
3 [δ] Copy of a writ of King Henry II (1155 x 1161) granting rights to Christ Church, Canterbury.
4 Pelteret 51.
6 Canterbury, Kent.

1 London, Public Record Office, C 52, Cartae Antiquae, Rolls 26, no. 9 and 27, no. 14.
2 *C13.

3 [δ] Copy of a writ of King William I (1072 x 1078) granting rights to St Paul's Church, London.
4 Pelteret 27.
6 London.

1 London, Public Record Office, C 52, Cartae Antiquae, Roll 29, no. 1.
2 *C13.
3 [δ] Copy of a writ of King Edward (1042 x 1046) to Fécamp Abbey granting land at Steyning, Sussex.
4 Sawyer 1054 (K 890).
6 Steyning, Sussex.

1 London, Public Record Office, C 53, Charter Rolls, 50 Henry III (damaged) (C 53/55), m. 1A (1).
2 *C13b1 (1265/6).
3 [δ] Copy of a grant of William II to the Church of St Andrew the Apostle, Rochester. Latin with English rights clause.
4 Pelteret 42.
6 Rochester, Kent.

1 London, Public Record Office, C 53, Charter Rolls, 3 Edward I (C 53/63), m. 2 (4), m. 2, no. 2 (7), m. 1 (4), m. 1 (5).
2 C13b2 (1274–75).
3 [δ] Copies of grants by William II, Henry I and Henry II to St Andrew's Church, Rochester. Latin with English rights clauses.
4 Pelteret 42, 49, 52, 55.
6 Rochester, Kent.

1 London, Public Record Office, C 53, Charter Rolls, 2 Edward II (C 53/95), m. 3, no. 4.
2 *C14a1 (1308/9).
3 [δ] Copy of a diploma of William I to St Martin's, London.
4 Pelteret 10.
6 London.

1 London, Public Record Office, C 53, Charter Rolls, 4 Edward II (C 53/97), m. 20, and m. 20, no. 52 (2).
2 *C14a1 (1310/11).
3 [δ] Copies of writs of King Edward and William I granting rights to St John's, Beverley.
4 Sawyer 1067 (Har 7); Pelteret 14 (Thorpe 438–39).
6 Beverley, ERY.

1 London, Public Record Office, C 53, Charter Rolls, 6 Edward II, no. 21.
2 *C14a1 (1312/3).
3 [δ] Copy of writ of King Æthelred to St Frideswide's Abbey, Oxford confirming land in Bucks and Oxon. Latin with English bounds.
4 Sawyer 909.
6 Oxford.

1 London, Public Record Office, C 53, Charter Rolls, 6 Edward II, no. 27.
2 *C14a1 (1312/3).
3 [δ] Copy of a writ of King Edward to his monk Ælfstan.
4 Sawyer 1157 (Har 116).
6 Worcester.

1 London, Public Record Office, C 53, Charter Rolls, 8 Edward II (C 53/101), m. 3, no. 5.
2 *C14a1 (1314/5).
3 [δ] Copies of two writs of King Edward and one of William I relating to Abbotsbury, Dorset.
4 Sawyer 1063 (Har 1, K 871); S 1064 (Har 2, K 841). Pelteret 26.
6 Abbotsbury, Dorset.

1 London, Public Record Office, C 53, Charter Rolls, 8 Edward II, no. 11.
2 *C14a1 (1314/5).
3 [δ] Copies of writs of King Edward to Bury St Edmunds.
4 Sawyer as follows: S 1045, S 1084, S 1075, S 1085, S 1069.
5 See the entry under CUL Ff.II.33 and other Bury St Edmunds cartularies cited there.
6 Bury St Edmunds, Suffolk.

1 London, Public Record Office, C 53, Charter Rolls, 9 Edward II (C 53/102), m. 12 and m. 12, no. 37 (2).
2 *C14a1 (1315/6).
3 [δ] Copies of writs of King Edward and William I granting rights to St Paul's, London.
4 Sawyer 1104 and Pelteret 27.
6 London.

1 London, Public Record Office, C 53, Charter Rolls, 10 Edward II, no. 7.
2 *C14a1 (1316/7).
3 [δ] Copies of writs of King Edward granting rights to the Old Minster, Winchester.
4 Sawyer 1153, 1152.
6 Winchester, Hants.

1 London, Public Record Office, C 53, Charter Rolls, 10 Edward II (C 53/103), m. 6, no. 7 (3).
2 *C14a1 (1316/7).
3 [δ] Copy of a writ of William I granting rights to Hyde Abbey, Winchester.
4 Pelteret 31.
6 Winchester, Hants.

1 London, Public Record Office, C 53, Charter Rolls, 12 Edward II, no. 48.
2 *C14a1 (1318/9).
3 [δ] Copy of a writ of King Æthelstan to Old Minster, Winchester. Latin with English bounds.
4 Sawyer 444.
6 Winchester, Hants.

1 London, Public Record Office, C 53, Charter Rolls, 20 Edward II, no. 6.
2 *C14a2 (1326/7).
3 [δ] Copies of writs of Kings Edmund, Æthelwulf and Edward concerning lands in Kent.
4 Sawyer as follows: S 501, S 300, S 1092.
5 Cf. BL Cotton Claudius D x.
6 Kent.

1 London, Public Record Office, C 66, Patent Rolls, 43 Henry III, m. 15.40.
2 C13b1 (1258).
3 [δ] Huntingdon redaction of the Proclamation of Henry III of 18 October 1258.
4 Edited: D&W III, pp. 7–9. Rolf Kaiser, *Mediaeval English*, 3rd edn. (Berlin, 1958), pp. 347–48 (with French version). A.J. Ellis, 'The only English proclamation of Henry III, etc.' *TPS* (1869), 1–135. Facsimile: W.W. Skeat, *English Dialects* (1912); *New Pal Soc*, First Series, vol. 1, plate 73.
5 For the Oxford redaction see Oxford City Archives, Town Hall, St Aldates, H 29.
6 Hunts.
7 One hand.

1 London, Public Record Office, C 66, Patent Rolls, 10 Edward 1, m. 10.
2 *C13b2 (1281/2).
3 [δ] Copy of a writ of King Edward to his monk Ælfstan.
4 Sawyer 1157.
6 Worcester.

1 London, Public Record Office, DL 41/6/1 (Duchy of Lancaster, Miscellanea, Bundle 6, roll 1).
2 C15a1.
3 [δ] [λ] Rhyming English version of writ of King Athelstan for Ripon Minster.
4 *IMEV* 4183. Sawyer 457 (B 859). Also B 647 and K 360 from *Mon Angl* ii 133. Edited (with other versions of the same): J.T. Fowler, *Memorials of the Church of SS. Peter and Wilfrid, Ripon* 1, Surtees Society 74 (1881), pp. 89–93. The charter was probably concocted in the fourteenth century. See Ian Doyle, Appendix 1 (pp. 20–21) of Richard Morris and Eric Cambridge, 'Beverley Minster before the early thirteenth century' in *Medieval Art and Architecture in the East Riding of Yorkshire*, (British Archaeological Association, 1989), pp. 9–32; and J.R. Witty, 'The rhyming charter of Beverley', *TYDS* 22 (1921), 39. Facsimile in Fowler, op. cit., facing p. 91.
5 Cf. the similar rhyming charter of King Athelstan for Beverley Minster, BL Add 61901 and Cotton Charter iv 18.
6 Ripon, WRY.
8 Hand of C15a1, but the language is of C14.

1 London, Public Record Office, E 132 (Exchequer, K.R., Transcripts of Deeds and Charters), Bundle 1, no. 2.
2 *C13.
3 [δ] Copy of a writ of King Edward granting rights to St Augustine's, Canterbury.
4 Sawyer 1091.
6 Canterbury, Kent.

1 London, Public Record Office, E 164/24 (Exchequer, K.R., Misc. Books i. 24).
2 *C13b2.
3 [δ] Malmesbury Cartulary.
  (1) Fols. 127r–128r contain some English in a grant of lands in Gloucs and Wilts.
  (2) Fol. 132r–v English bounds of Brokenburgh, Wilts.
  (3) Fol. 134r–v English bounds of land at Littleton on Severn, Gloucs.
4 Davis 644. Sawyer as follows: S 305, S 1577, S 862. Edited: J.S. Brewer, *Registrum Malmsburiense* 1, RS (1879), pp. 297–99, 313–15, 320–21.
6 Malmesbury, Wilts.

1 London, Public Record Office, E 164/28 (Exchequer, K.R., Misc. Books i. 28).
2 *C14.
3 [δ] Composite register of Ramsey Abbey.
  (1) Fols. 52v (*olim* 44v) and 229v Kingsdelf — boundary of Fen between Ramsey and Thorney.
  (2) Fols. 52v–53r and 169v–170r two copies of a writ of King Edward concerning exchange of land in Northants.
  (3) Fols. 59v–60r and 170r–v two copies of a writ of King Edward granting judicial and financial rights and shipwreck and what is cast up by the sea (cf. *MED, seupwerp*) at Brancaster and Ringstead, etc.
4 Davis 788.
  For (1) see C. Hart, *The Early Charters of Eastern England* (Leicester, 1966), no. 44.
  (2) Sawyer 1110.
  (3) Sawyer 1109.
  Most of this volume ed. W.H. Hunt and P.A. Lyons, *Cartularium Monasterii de Rameseia*, 3 vols., RS 79 (1884–93).
5 Another copy of item (1) is in CUL Add 3021, fol. 372.
6 MS from Ramsey Abbey, Hunts. Ker *Med Lib*, p. 154.
7 English probably all in one hand except fol. 229v.

1 London, Public Record Office, listed as being somewhere in K.R. Series, but lost.
2 *Post-Conquest.
3 [δ] Milton Abbey Cartulary.
4 See Davis 668 for C16 and C17 extracts. Sawyer 391. Edited: *Mon Angl* ii 349 and from this Kemble 1119 (a ME version of Kemble 375); B 738 and Rob 23.
6 Relates to Dorset and Hants.
8 Language is of some interest; suggests perhaps late C12.

1 London, Public Record Office, 31/5/12/18.
2 *C19.
3 [δ] Transcript of a grant by King Eadred to Glastonbury Abbey.
4 Sawyer 553 (B 887).
6 Glastonbury, Somerset.

1 London, St Paul's DC, A Box 69 dorse: now London, Guildhall Library 25272, q.v.

1 London, St Paul's DC, W.D. 1: now London, Guildhall Library 25501, q.v.

1 London, Society of Antiquaries 60.
2 *C12a2 (c.1125–28, Davis).
3 [δ] The Black Book of Peterborough. Fols. 6–74 a survey of the abbey's manors. English, some bounds only, on fols. 29r–31r, 32r–35v, 38r–40v, 46r–v, 47r, 50r–55r.
4 Davis 754. Sawyer as follows: S 592 (B 943, K 443 and iii 439); S 533 (B 871, K 423 and iii 428); S 1014 (K 784); S 681 (B 1052, K 480 and iii 454); S 834 (K 621); S 782 (B 1270, K 568); S 1448 (B 1128, Rob 39); S 1440 (B 464, K 267, Rob 7); S 1566 (B 1129); S 566 (B 909, K 433, Rob 30); S 1377 (B 1131, K 591, Rob 37). Fol. 47r (not in Sawyer) Birch 1130 (Rob 40): list of sureties for Peterborough estates. Fol. 50v (not in Sawyer) Kemble 953. Fols. 50v–51r Pelteret 68 (K 953, Whi 39); fols. 52r–54v Pelteret 142 (Rob App. 1 no. 3). Fol. 46r–v edited: Laing 'Anchor texts', p. 41.
5 Cf. BL Egerton 2733.
6 MS from Peterborough Abbey, Northants. Ker *Med Lib*, p. 151.

8 Note that charters in this MS which are only in Latin may well have interest because of the spelling of names. E.g. Kemble 575 (Sawyer 787).

1 London, Wellcome Historical Medical Library 801ᴬ.
2 C13.
3 [γ] Miscellany of texts in Latin including on fols. 104r–118v Alexander Neckham's *De Nominibus Utensilium* with vernacular glosses some of which are English.
4 Contents listed Hunt *Teaching* 1, pp. 179–80, 350. For a full description see S.A.J. Moorat, *Catalogue of Western MSS on Medicine and Science in the Wellcome Historical Medical Library* 2 (London, 1973), pp. 1464–67. Vernacular glosses edited: Hunt *Teaching* 1, pp. 49, 52.
6 One of the original books from the Library of Bury St Edmunds Abbey, listed Ker *Med Lib*, p. 16 as Bury St Edmunds, Cathedral 4.
7 According to Hunt, glosses to Neckham are in at least four C13 hands.

1 London, Westminster Abbey, W.A. Muniment Book 1.
2 *C15b2 (c.1474–85, Davis).
3 [δ] Liber Niger Quaternus. Fol. 12r–v copies of two writs of King Edward granting lands to Westminster Abbey.
4 Davis 1015. Sawyer 1141, 1142.
5 Cf. BL Cotton Faustina A iii.
6 London.

1 London, Westminster Abbey, W.A. Muniment Book 11, 'Westminster Domesday'.
2 *C14a1–C15a (post 1308–1445).
3 [δ] Copies of writs in English, some bounds only, on fols. 46r, 53r, 75v–76v. 77v–78r, 79v, 96r, 114v, 129v, 133r, 154v, 185v–186r, 204r–v, 226v–227r, 243r, 269r, 270r, 273r, 275r, 278r–v, 316, 465r–v, 505r, 506r–v, 594r, 647r–648r.
4 Davis 1013. Sawyer as follows: S 1126; S 1127 (Har 83); S 1125; S 670; S 1450; S 903; S 1149 (Har 105); S 1150 (Har 106); S 1121; S 1133 (Har 89); S 1141; S 1142; S 1130 (Har 86); S 1131 (Har 87); S 124; S 1122 (Har 78); S 1031; S 1135 (Har 91); S 1123 (Har 79); S 753; S 1118; S 1148 (Har 104); S 1147 (Har 103); S 1139 (Har 95); S 1146 (Har 102); S 1144 (Har 100); S 1145; S 1143 (Har 99); S 1551 (Finburg 1961, no. 187); S 1137; S 1136 (Har 92); S 1119 (Har 75); S 1138; S 1120; S 1134; S 1129 (Har 85); S 1124; S 1140. Pelteret 12, 13, 15, 21, 24, 38, 66.
5 Cf. BL Cotton Faustina A iii.
6 London.
8 The language is for the most part only slightly modernised.

1 London, Westminster Abbey, W.A.M., IV, XI, XIII, XIV, XVII.
2 *C12.
3 [δ] Copies of writs of King Eadwig and of King Edward relating to Westminster Abbey.
4 Sawyer as follows: S 645 (B 994); S 1120 (Har 76); S 1140; S 1138 (Har 94); S 1137 (Har 93).
6 London.

1 Longleat. See Private: Bath, Marquess of.

1 Lowther Castle, Westmorland, Gospatric's Writ. See Carlisle, Cumbria Record Office.

1 Macclesfield, Earl of. See Private: Macclesfield, Earl of, Shirburn Castle.

1 Maidstone, Kent County Archives Office, DRb/Ar 2 (*olim* DRc/R3), 'Registrum Temporalium'.
2 C14.
3 [δ] Register of the temporalities of Rochester Priory. Fols. 11v, 12v, 13r–14r, copies of diplomas of William II, Henry I and Henry II in Latin with English rights clauses.
4 Davis 820. Pelteret 42, 49, 52, 55.
6 Rochester, Kent.

1 Maidstone, Kent County Archives Office, DRc/T51.
2 C12a (1123 x 1135).
3 [δ] Diploma of Henry I to the monks of St Andrew's, Rochester; Latin with English rights clause — purported original.
4 Pelteret 49 (Thorpe 34).
6 Rochester, Kent.

1 Maidstone, Kent County Archives Office, DRc/T53 (*inspeximus* of Henry III).
2 C13b1 (*ca.* 1265).
3 [δ] Writ of Henry II confirming St Andrew's, Rochester in its rights and possessions; Latin with English rights clause.
4 Pelteret 52.
6 Rochester, Kent.

1 Maidstone, Kent County Archives Office, DRc/T58/1, 2 and 3.
2 C13b1 (*ca.* 1265).
3 [δ] Copies of writs of William I, Henry II and Diploma of Pope Alexander III in favour of St Andrew's, Rochester; Latin with English rights clauses.
4 Pelteret 40, 53, 60.
6 Rochester, Kent.

1 Maidstone, Kent County Archives Office, DRc/T60/1, 3, 5 and 6 (*inspeximus* of Henry III).
2 C13b1 (*ca.* 1265).
3 [δ] Copies of diplomas of William II, Henry I and Henry II in favour of St Andrew's, Rochester; Latin with English rights clauses.
4 Pelteret 42, 49, 52, 55.
6 Rochester, Kent.

1 Maidstone Museum A.13.
2 C13a.
3 [λ] MS has 252 leaves, contents are mostly Latin. English is as follows.
  (1) Fol. 93r a shortened version of *The Proverbs of Alfred* including two lines of *The Poema Morale*, beg. *Swines brede is Swiþe Swete* and close to the version in Lambeth 487. The couplet also appears on fols. 46v and 253r.
  (2) Fol. 93v a version of the poem *Long Life* beg. *Man mei longe him liues wene.*
  (3) Fol. 243v a few lines on *Three Sorrowful Tidings* written as prose in a Latin sermon and beg. *þru tidigge us cumet iche dei.*
For further scraps in English added at various times see Ker *Med MSS* 3, pp. 317–18 item 2 and p. 320 item 14. There are also two short pieces in Anglo-Norman: (a) An orison to the Blessed Virgin in five 14-line stanzas; (b) a fragment of 11 stanzas of *Les Vers de la Mort* by Hélinant, monk of Froidmont; and a longer poem (c) of 50 stanzas ed. F. Wulff and E. Walberg, 'Les Vers de la Mort par Hélinant', *Société des anciens textes français* 52 (1905).
4 Ker *Med MSS* 3, pp. 317–21.
  (1) Wells *Suppl* 3, p. 1173 (VII.5). *IMEV* 433 and for further information see Arngart *P of A*; esp. vol. 1, pp. 8, 133–135 and vol. 2, pp. 25–30. For the two lines of the *Poema Morale* see *IMEV* 3246.

(2) Wells *Suppl* 5, p. 1356 (VII.46). *IMEV* 2070. CB13 10A. D&H, p. 122 seq.
(3) Wells *Suppl* 3, p. 1173 (VII.37). *IMEV* 695. CB13 11.
For further refs. see Hill (1977), p. 114 and note 70.
5 This MS shares *The Proverbs of Alfred* and *Long Life* with Oxford, Jesus College 29 part II. For other copies of these two texts see the Index of Middle English Texts A: Titles. For item (3) cf. a different version shared by Cambridge, Emmanuel College 27 (I.2.6) item (17) and Jesus College 29 item (22).
6 The MS has been associated with the Cluniac Priory of St Andrew at Northampton. For evidence see C. Brown, 'A thirteenth-century manuscript at Maidstone', *MLR* 21 (1926), 1–12; text and further evidence 'The Maidstone text of the "Proverbs of Alfred"', ibid. 249–260. This ascription is rejected, however, by Ker *Med Lib*, p. 135. The manuscript does contain accounts of, and other material relating to, the hospital of St John the Baptist and St John the Evangelist, Northampton, where it was owned C13–C14. See Ker *Med MSS* 3, p. 321.
7 MS written by several C13 hands.
8 Dobson (D&H, p. 122) believes item (2) to be southern with "a few Midland linguistic forms". AM, however, thinks the language of the text of *The Proverbs of Alfred* is consistent with an origin in the Northampton area. Ker's rejection of the MS as part of the holdings of the Cluniac Priory does not preclude the possibility that it was nevertheless compiled in Northampton.

1 Manchester University, John Rylands Library 420.

2 *C12.
3 [δ] Fol. 33r (*olim* 78r) copy of Regulations of King William I concerning exculpation.
4 Pelteret 145.
5 Many versions of this are Latin only. Pelteret 145 no. 19 is from the *Textus Roffensis* Maidstone, Kent County Archives Office, DRc/R1 — not indexed here because it is too early (C12a1).

1 New York, Pierpont Morgan Library M.761.

2 C13b2.
3 [λ] MS of French texts but including on fol. 1v a poem on the vanity of human affairs in alternating lines of French and English. There are probably nine lines of English but half the leaf is torn away. Reference from AID.
4 See S. de Ricci and W.J. Wilson, *Census of Medieval and Renaissance Manuscripts in the United States and Canada* 2 (New York, 1937), p. 1498.
6 "Constat Kyrkby" appears in a hand of C15a.
8 AID (pers. comm.) says that the provisional catalogue suggests the language is northeastern, but that the first line he has noted runs *vel ne fayre. þar-fore is holi church* which does not confirm this description.

1 Nottingham University Library Mi Lm 7/1 (*olim* Wollaton Hall MS).

2 C14a1 (c1300, *MED Plan & Bibl*, p. 73; c1310–20, Görlach *SEL*, p. 117).
3 [λ] Two fragments (which had been used as patches on fol. 161 of a *Sarum Antiphonale*) containing, in a hand of *ca.* 1300, parts of the *Life of St Bridget* (vv. 5–24, 39–59) from the *South English Legendary*.
4 CB Reg i 496. *IMEV Suppl* 2872. Görlach *SEL*, p. 117. Edited: *Report on the Manuscripts of Lord Middleton etc.* (Historical Manuscripts Commission, 1911), pp. 622–25.
5 For other early MSS containing parts of the *South English Legendary* see the Index of Middle English Texts A: Titles.

1 Oxford, Balliol College 226.

2 C13b.
3 MS of *Vitae Sanctorum* in Latin. Fols. 47v–64r contain the *Life of St Edmund* (in the "Anonymous A" version) in which the archbishop's last words are quoted in English: *Men seyeth gamen god on wombe and i segge mi gamen godt on heorte.*

4 Edited: H.W.C. Davis, 'An unpublished life of Edmund Rich', *EHR* 22 (1907), 84–92 (90). Cf. Wilson 1943, p. 59 and Lawrence *St Edmund*, p. 50.
5 This text of the *Life of St Edmund* is a copy of that in CUL Mm.IV.6. See R.A.B. Mynors, *Catalogue of the Manuscripts of Balliol College Oxford* (Oxford, 1963), p. 225. For other MSS containing versions of the *Life of St Edmund* with the English words see the Index of Texts in Latin.

1 Oxford, Balliol College 227.
2 C13–C14.
3 [λ] Latin MS containing *Gesta Sanctorum*, etc. On fol. 258r is a Latin verse with English translation: *Men hem pleynit of mikel untrewthe / Ryt is det and yat is rewthe / Trecherye levit and is above / Nouthe is buryit trewe love.*
4 See *IMEV Suppl* 2145, and for variants *IMEV* 2146 and 3650. Wenzel 1986, p. 191.
5 Cf. other versions of the English text: Oxford, Merton College 248 item (36); Bodley, Hatton 107, fol. 1v; and Cambridge, Pembroke College 258 item (4).

1 Oxford, Balliol College 230.
2 C13
3 [λ] Miscellanea theologica in Latin. English scraps appear as follows.
  (1) Fol. 122v four lines translating 'Sol luna lucidior' beg. *þe sonne is brithere þane þe monne*.
  (2) Fol. 153v contains *Ha ha petipas ȝuot ich am þer ich was*.
Mynors' Catalogue indicates that there are also English phrases in *De Luxuria*, fols. 207r–230v.
4 (1) *IMEV Suppl* 3478.5.
  (2) Hartung 5 XIII.169. *IMEV Suppl* 0.3 where the reference is given erroneously as Balliol 320.
See R.A.B. Mynors, *Catalogue of the Manuscripts of Balliol College Oxford* (Oxford, 1963), pp. 241 and 242.
6 There is no indication as to the provenance of the MS. It is interesting, however, that the English phrase on fol. 153v is part of a question and answer formula in Latin of the type "How many miles to Babylon?", but that here Beverley is the place used rather than Babylon.
7 One hand of English.

1 Oxford, Bodleian Library, Add E.6 (*SC* 30314).
2 C13b.
3 [λ] Roll of four membranes containing three poems in English.
  (1) *The Sayings of St Bernard* (180 lines).
  (2) *The XV signs of Judgement* (212 lines partly on the verso of the roll).
  (3) An Exposition of *The Lord's Prayer* beg. *Lestnit nou and habbit lest* (128 lines on the verso).
4 CB Reg i 128.
  (1) Wells *Suppl* 1, p. 977 (VII.27). *IMEV* 3310.
  (2) Wells *Suppl* 1, p. 965 (VI.75). *IMEV* 796.
  (3) Wells *Suppl* 1, p. 968 (VI.13) and Wells *Suppl* 7, p. 1571 (V.8a). Hartung 7 XX.36. *IMEV* 1904.
5 For other copies of items (1) and (2) see the Index of Middle English Texts A: Titles.
7 Wells: "the first 82 verses [of (3)] in a thirteenth-century hand, the rest in a hand with fourteenth-century characteristics".

1 Oxford, Bodleian Library, Ashmole 43 (*SC* 6924).
2 C14a2 ("second quarter of the fourteenth century", D'Evelyn, p. 5 and n. 7).
3 [λ] Fols. 4r–169r *South English Legendary* imperfect at beginning and end.
4 CB Reg i 83. Wells V.19 (p. 295) and cf. Wells V.44, 51, 52, 59, 67 (p. 322), 78 (p. 331), 80. Severs 2 V.1 and cf. Severs 2, pp. 561–635. For individual entries in

IMEV see Hamer 'MS index'. Görlach *SEL*, pp. 73–75. MS also described by C. D'Evelyn, *The South English Legendary*, vol. 3 Introduction and Glossary, EETS OS 244 (1959 for 1957, repr. 1969), pp. 5–6. Edited: C. Horstmann, *Altenglische Legenden* (Paderborn, 1875) and cf. C. Horstmann, 'Die altenglische Legende von St Brendan', *Archiv* 53 (1874), 17–48 (17–37).
5 For other early MSS containing parts of the *South English Legendary* see the Index of Middle English Texts A: Titles.
7 One hand.
8 Placed by MLS in N Gloucs (*LALME* LP 7170).

1 Oxford, Bodleian Library, Ashmole 360, part VII (*SC* 6641).
2 C13b2.
3 [λ] (1) Fol. 145r a five-line poem translating 'Memoria passionis tue' beg. *þe minde of þi passiun suete ihu* and continuing *þe teres it tollid / þe heine it bolled*, etc.
  (2) Fol. 145v three six-line stanzas on the theme *My Leman on the Rood* beg. *Qvanne I zenke onne þe rode*.
4 (1) Wells *Suppl* 5, p. 1367 (XIII.136a). Cf. *IMEV* 1977 and 3433. CB13 56A.
  (2) CB Reg i 73. Wells *Suppl* 5, p. 1365 (XIII.107b). *IMEV* 3968. CB13 37.
5 For other versions of item (1) see under *teres tollet*, etc. in the Index of Middle English Texts B: Incipits. For various different realisations of item (2) see the Index of Middle English Texts A: Titles and cf. CB13 35 and 36.
7 English in one hand.
8 Language of Norfolk.

1 Oxford, Bodleian Library, Ashmole 1280 (*SC* 8216).
2 C13a2–b1.
3 [λ] Handbook for parish priests in Latin and French except for English as follows.
  (1) Fol. 48 a dozen words of early ME in a Latin text said to be Richard of St Victor's *Allegoriae in Novum Testamentum*: *over al ich finde tho be sori ouer al ich finde mi lef blodi*.
  (2) Fol. 192v contains in English a prayer to ease childbirth beg. *Hail be yow holie crowche blesfolle*.
4 (1) *IMEV* 2736. See C.A. Robson, *Maurice of Sully and the Medieval Vernacular Homily* (Oxford, 1952), p. 63 and *IMEP* for Ashmole MSS, ed. L.M. Eldridge, forthcoming. Reference from AID.
  (2) *IPMEP* 277. Edited (with some minor omissions): Mary P. Richards, 'A Middle English prayer to ease childbirth', *N&Q* 225, NS 27 (1980), 292.
6 MS said to have been in London *ca.* 1400.
7 Richards (re fol. 192v): "a thirteenth-century hand distinct from those of the main body of the manuscript". AID says that the two bits of English are in the same hand.

1 Oxford, Bodleian Library, Ashmole 1285 (*SC* 8221).
2 C13a2–b1.
3 [λ] Religious and medical MS, mainly in Latin but with one piece in French. On fol. 47r is a scribble of three lines in English: (*Sorhg*) *Soruhe and sey / Leth and beth / hold and haue*.
4 *IMEV* 3200. W.H. Black, *A Descriptive Analytical and Critical Catalogue of the Manuscripts bequeathed unto the University of Oxford by Elias Ashmole esq.* (Oxford, 1845), p. 1045. See also L. Eldredge, 'On reclaiming a fragment of prose from *The Index of Middle English Verse:* a brief lesson in textual criticism', *NM* 92 (1991), 29–30.
5 Cf. another version of the same in Cambridge, Trinity College 323, fol. 28v.
6 *Ex libris* inscription associates the MS with Southwark Priory, Surrey. Ker *Med Lib*, p. 180.
7 English in one hand.

1 Oxford, Bodleian Library, Ashmole 1431 (*SC* 7523).
2 C12.
3 [γ] Fols. 3–43 early C12 copy of the herbal of Apuleius Barbarus containing between fols. 5 and 42v glosses to 57 names of herbs and the diseases of which they are remedies.
4 Ker 289. Edited: R.T. Gunther, *The Herbal of Apuleius Barbarus* (Roxburghe Club, 1925); includes facsimiles of fols. 31 and 34 in pl. 2.
6 *Ex libris* inscription associates MS with St Augustine's, Canterbury. Ker *Med Lib*, p. 45.
8 Ker, p. 350: "Spellings are South-Eastern".

1 Oxford, Bodleian Library, Auct. F.6.8 (*SC* 8840).
2 C13b.
3 [γ] Latin texts with vernacular glosses including: fols. 1r–8v *Prepositiones Grece*; fols. 9r–12v (and Bodley, Digby 92, fols. 96r–98r) the *Exoticon* of Alexander of Hales; fols. 13r–61v the *Panormia* of Osbern of Gloucester. Most of the vernacular glosses are French but a few are English.
4 See Hunt *Teaching* 1, pp. 296, 299; and vernacular glosses edited: *Teaching* 1, pp. 297, 379–80.

1 Oxford, Bodleian Library, Bodley 34 (*SC* 1883).
2 C13a1 (*ca.* 1225, Dobson *Origins*, p. 163).
3 [λ] *The Katherine Group*.
   (1) Fols. 1r–18r *St Katherine*.
   (2) Fols. 18r–36v *St Margaret*, including on fol. 29v a moral warning in verse inserted into the text and beg. *þenchen hu spart þing & suti is þat sunne*.
   (3) Fols. 36v–52r *St Juliana*.
   (4) Fols. 52r–71v *Hali Meiðhad*.
   (5) Fols. 72r–80v *Sawles Warde*.
   On the top margin of fol. 75v appears a scrap of C14 verse: *ly þow me ner lemmon in þy narmus*.
4 Edited: S.R.T.O. d'Ardenne, *The Katherine Group Edited from MS Bodley 34* (Paris, 1977). See also *Facsimile of MS. Bodley 34* with an Introduction by N.R. Ker, EETS OS 247 (1960).
   (1) Wells V.50. *IPMEP* 138. Edited: d'Ardenne & Dobson.
   (2) Wells V.52. *IPMEP* 29. D&W XVIII. For the verse insertion see *IMEV Suppl* 3570.5. This MS is cited erroneously as *SC* 1898 in *IMEV Suppl*. Edited: F.M. Mack, *Seinte Marherete*, EETS OS 193 (1934 for 1933, repr. 1958).
   (3) Wells V.49. *IPMEP* 359. Hall i XIX, ii 543–53. Edited: d'Ardenne *Iulienne*.
   (4) Wells V.1 (cf. Wells *Suppl* 9, p. 1814). *IPMEP* 95. Edited: Millett *Hali Meiðhad*.
   (5) Wells V.2. *IPMEP* 594. Hall i XVI, ii 492–524. BSD XIX. Edited: R.M. Wilson, *Sawles Warde*, Leeds School of English Language Texts and Monographs 3 (Leeds, 1938) and Morris *OEH* 1, pp. 245–67 (odd pages).
   For the scrap of verse on fol. 75v see *IMEV Suppl* 1871.5.
5 The three saints' lives and *Sawles Warde* are found also in BL Royal 17 A xxvii. *St Katherine*, *Sawles Warde* and *Hali Meiðhad* are also in BL Cotton Titus D xviii.
6 Entries in C16 hands associate the MS with Ledbury, Godstow and Much Cowarne in Herefords. See Ker, EETS OS 247, pp. xiii–xiv.
7 One hand throughout, though there are corrections in a different hand between fols. 18r (beginning of *St Margaret*) and 21v.
8 Written in a form of the "AB language" (B) common to the precursor of this MS and *Ancrene Wisse* of Cambridge, Corpus Christi College 402 (A). On AB language as a literary standard see J.R.R. Tolkien, 'Ancrene Wisse and Hali Meiðhad', *Essays and Studies* 14 (1929), 104–126; J.R. Hulbert, 'A thirteenth-century English literary standard', *JEGP* 45 (1946), 411–14 (esp. p. 413); A.J. Bliss, 'A note on "Language AB"' *English and Germanic Studies* 5 (1952–53), 1–6; Millett *Hali Meiðhad*, pp. xiv–xvi and refs. there cited. For a more lengthy account see d'Ardenne *Iulienne*, pp.

177–250. The most generally accepted view of the language of this MS is that the scribe of Bodley was a literatim copyist who failed to write AB language where his exemplar failed to provide it. See Mack, *Seint Marherete*, pp. xiv–xv; d'Ardenne *Iulienne*, p. xxxv and Benskin & Laing, p. 105 n. 44. See also Janet Bately, 'On some aspects of the vocabulary of the West Midlands in the early Middle Ages: the language of the Katherine Group' in *Medieval English Studies presented to George Kane*, ed. E.D. Kennedy, R. Waldron and J.S. Wittig (Woodbridge, 1988), pp. 55–77.

1 Oxford, Bodleian Library, Bodley 42 (*SC* 1846).
2 C13b2–C14a1 (1300–1320, CB Reg).
3 [λ] Latin MS containing theologica. Fol. 250r two lyrics in English, versions of
  (1) *Candet Nudatum Pectus* beg. *Wit was his nakede brest* and
  (2) *Respice in Faciem* beg. *Loke man to iesucrist. hi neiled an þo rode.*
4 CB Reg i 21.
  (1) Wells XIII.116. *IMEV* 4088. CB14 1B. See also Thomson *Candet*.
  (2) Wells *Suppl* 1, p. 987 (XIII.114). *IMEV* 1940.
5 For other versions in English of *Candet Nudatum Pectus* and *Respice in Faciem* see the Index of Middle English Texts A: Titles..
6 On fol. 277 is a note "Regula & vita Fratrum Minorum" as confirmed in 1223. On fol. 283 is a letter from Pope Innocent IV recommending Fredericus de Lavania to a canonry at Lincoln, 1253 with Grosseteste's refusal. *Ex libris* inscription indicates that the MS belonged to Exeter College, Oxford. Ker *Med Lib*, p. 146.
7 English in one hand.

1 Oxford, Bodleian Library, Bodley 57 (*SC* 2004).
2 C13b2–C14a1 (*ca.* 1300, SC).
3 [λ] Miscellaneous theological and moral pieces in Latin "surrounded by numberless odd notes and memoranda" and including on fol. 102v a version of the lyric *My Leman on the Rood* beg. *Vven i .o. þe rode se / Faste nailed to þe tre.*
4 CB Reg i 23. Wells *Suppl* 5, p. 1365 (XIII.107b). *IMEV* 3961. CB13 36.
5 For other versions of this lyric see the Index of Middle English Texts A: Titles and cf. CB13 35 and 37.
6 The contents associate the MS with St Mary's Abbey, Leicester. Ker *Med Lib*, p. 113.

1 Oxford, Bodleian Library, Bodley 297 (*SC* 2468).
2 *C12a2–b1 (s. xii med., Ker; ?1131–1134, Watson).
3 [λ] [δ] Chronicle extending to the year 1131. On p. 281 Bede's Death Song appears in the text of Cuthbert's *Epistola de obitu Bedae*. Pp. 328–29 English boundary clauses at the foot of the main text (Latin) of a copy of a writ of King Edmund to Bury St Edmunds.
4 Ker 306. Sawyer 507. Watson *Ox Lib* 1, p. 14.
5 For other MSS containing Bede's Death Song see the Index of Old English Texts. For the bounds, cf. CUL Ff.II.33, fol. 20.
6 Ker, p. 360: "The manuscript was at Bury St Edmund's soon after it was written". *Ex libris* inscription of the Abbey of St Edmund, Bury St Edmunds, Suffolk. Ker *Med Lib*, p. 21.
7 Bede's Death Song is in the main hand. The English bounds are a contemporary addition to the text in a different hand.

1 Oxford, Bodleian Library, Bodley 343 (*SC* 2406).
2 *C12 (Part A), C12b2 (Part C) (c1175, *MED Plan & Bibl*, p. 28) and C13 (Part D).
3 [λ] Part A fols. vi–x: parts of four OE sermons.
Part B: 67 Latin sermons.
Part C fols. 1–164v: 74 sermons, chiefly from Ælfric's *Sermones Catholici*, four are from his *Saints' Lives* and six are by Wulfstan. Others are unattributed.

Part D fols. 165r–173r: Latin and OE sermons including on fol. 170r a fragment of an address by Soul to Body, beg. *ðe wes bold gebyld er þu iboren were*.
4 Wells V.11. Ker 310 for which see contents and further refs. Edited: A.O. Balfour, *Twelfth Century Homilies in MS Bodley 343* part 1, EETS OS 137 (1909, repr. 1962); Susan E. Irvine, 'A critical edition of some homilies in MS. Bodley 343', Diss. D.Phil., University of Oxford (1987), unpubl. For lives of SS. Peter, Edmund and Martin, see W.W. Skeat, *Ælfric's Lives of the Saints*, EETS OS 76 (1881), 82 (1885), 94 (1890), 114 (1900) (repr. as one vol. 1966). For Ælfric's English letters to Archbishop Wulfstan see B. Fehr, *Die Hirtenbriefe Ælfrics*, Grein: Bibliothek der angelsächsischen Prosa 9 (1914), pp. 69–143, 147–221. See also B. Assmann, *Angelsächsische Homilien und Heiligenleben*, Grein: Bibliothek der angelsächsischen Prosa 3 (1889), pp. 49–64 and 117–137. For a fragment of Ælfric's 'Libellus de veteri Testamento et Novo', fols. 129r–132r, see S.J. Crawford, *The Old English Version of the Heptateuch, Ælfric's Treatise on the Old and New Testament and his Preface to Genesis*, EETS OS 160 (1922), pp. 18–33, 39–51. For *History of the Holy Rood Tree*, fol. 14v, see A.S. Napier, EETS OS 103 (1894, repr. 1973), even pp. 2–34. He says the MS is *ca*. 1175 but that the text is probably of OE origin. This is a prose piece (see Wells V.58 and Severs 2 V.305). For the address by Soul to Body see CB Reg i 27. Wells IX.1. Hartung 3 VII.18(b). *IMEV* 3497. Edited: R. Buchholz, *Die Fragmente der Reden der Seele an den Leichnam*, Erlanger Beiträge 2.6 (Erlangen, 1890), p. 11. The MS is said by Buchholz to belong to the twelfth century but he notes that the last three lines are in a C13 hand. Cf. Pope *Ælfric*, pp. 14–18 and Malcolm Godden, *Ælfric's Catholic Homilies*, EETS SS 5 (1979), pp. xxxvii–xl.
5 For other versions of poems on the "Body and Soul" theme, see under *Debate between the Body and Soul* in the Index of Middle English Texts A: Titles.
6 Ker (p. 375) considers the MS to be from the West Midlands, largely because on fol. iii verso appears a rhymed antiphon commemorating St Wulfhad who was chiefly honoured at Stone in Staffs (*SC* 2406) and because on fol. 173 is a drawing of a bishop with an inscription including the name *þolstane* perhaps for Wulfstan II of Worcester.
8 Napier considers the language to be southern and to represent the Early Middle English descendant of W-S though of a more archaic nature than would be expected from its date because the scribe was copying from pre-Conquest exemplars. Pope, following Napier, believes that the MS was written in the south and then sent to some W Midland library (Pope *Ælfric*, p. 18).

1 Oxford, Bodleian Library, Bodley 652 (*SC* 2306).

2 C13b1.
3 [λ] Fols. 1r–10v *Iacob and Iosep*. The rest of the MS is in French.
4 CB Reg i 25. Wells VIII.2 (cf. Wells *Suppl* 1, p. 978). Severs 2 IV.3. *IMEV* 4172. D&W XXI. Edited: A.S. Napier (Oxford, 1916).
5 No other version of this text survives.
7 English in one hand.
8 Napier: "The dialect is that of the South-west". *LALME* LP 6930, Gloucs.

1 Oxford, Bodleian Library, Bodley 730 (*SC* 2709).

2 C12b2–C13a1 (*ca*. 1200).
3 [γ] A MS of C12 containing Cassian's *Institutes*. The last three leaves contain material of a slightly later date: fol. 144r–v Anglo-Norman and Middle English glosses; fol. 145r Latin glosses with a few English and Anglo-Norman entries; fol. 146r–v a list of the parts of the body; fol. 146v a set of OE vocabularies based on Ælfric's *Glossary*.
4 Ker 317. Hunt *Teaching* 1, p. 26. Edited: Tony Hunt, 'The Old English vocabularies in MS. Oxford, Bodley 730, *ES* 62 (1981), 201–209.
6 Ker, p. 380: "a Buildwas manuscript" — evidence from binding, bosses and MS layout. See also Ker *Med Lib*, p. 14.

8 Ker: "The orthography of the English glosses is throughout extremely confused".

1 Oxford, Bodleian Library, Dep. c. 392 (*olim* Northleach, Stowell Park, Lord Vestey, 'Registrum A').
2 *C13a2–b1 (after 1249, Davis).
3 [δ] Cirencester Cartulary. English on p. 26: writ of King Edward and two writs of William I.
4 Davis 255. Sawyer 1097 (Har 44). Pelteret 4 and 9. Edited: C.D. Ross, *The Cartulary of Cirencester Abbey, Gloucestershire*, 2 vols. (London, 1964).
6 Cirencester, Gloucs.

1 Oxford, Bodleian Library, Digby 2 (*SC* 1603).
2 C13b2 ("end XIII cent", CB Reg; *ca.* 1275, *OBMEV*).
3 [λ] MS of astronomica containing English as follows.
 (1) Fol. 6r a song of the Passion in six stanzas beg. *Hi sike al wan hi singe*.
 (2) Fol. 6v a prayer of penitence to the BV in five stanzas beg. *Hayl mari hic am sori*.
 (3) Fol. 15r three six-line stanzas beg. *No more ne willi wiked be*.
 (4) Fol. 111r an incantation against the flowing of blood beg. *vre louerd crist was on erthe iwondid*.
4 CB Reg i 17. Murakami, p. 111, no. 45.
 (1) Wells XIII.124. *IMEV* 1365. CB13 64. *OBMEV* 18.
 (2) Wells XIII.199. *IMEV* 1066. CB13 65. *OBMEV* 19.
 (3) Wells XIII.28. *IMEV* 2293. CB13 66. D&W XXXVII. BSD VIII X.
 (4) *IMEP* III, p. 1.
 Cf. F.J. Furnivall, *The Minor Poems of the Vernon MS.* 2, EETS OS 117 (1901, repr. 1973), p. 753 seq.
5 For item (1) cf. BL Harley 2253 item (33).
6 The MS was perhaps a production of the Oxford Franciscans. See Watson *Ox Lib* 1, p. 66.
7 Fols. 6r–v and 111r are probably in the same hand. Fol. 15r is in a different hand.
8 Item (2) is of special interest because it is in northern language but items (1) and (3) are not.

1 Oxford, Bodleian Library, Digby 4 (*SC* 1605).
2 C13a.
3 [λ] Tractatus super canonem misse, etc. Fols. 97r–110v *Poema Morale* beg. *Ic am elder þanne ic pes / a pintre & ec a lore*. It is written in half lines arranged as quatrains — 764 short lines the equivalent of 382 long lines.
4 CB Reg i 17. Wells VII.25. *IMEV* 1272. Hall ii 312–13. See also Hill 1977 and refs. there cited. Edited: Julius Zupitza, 'Zum Poema Morale', *Anglia* 1 (1878), 5–38.
5 N.R. Ker, 'MS. Cotton Galba A. XIX: The Proverbs of Alfred', *MÆ* 5 (1936), 115–120 indicates that BL Cotton Galba A xix, *Proverbs of Alfred*, was once part of Bodley, Digby 4. See also Ker *Med Lib*, pp. 36, 38. *Poema Morale* survives in seven copies for which see the Index of Middle English Texts A: Titles, where MSS containing short quotations from the text are also listed.
6 MS from Christ Church, Canterbury. Hall says MS probably copied there. Ker *Med Lib*, p. 38.
7 English in one hand. This is the only vernacular text in the MS and the hand is not elsewhere in it.
8 For MLS's views on the language see Hill 1977, p. 110. It displays Kentish features which may possibly be mixed with an ingredient from the London area. The language may, however, represent a linguistically homogeneous dialect from somewhere in between, such as NW Kent or NE Surrey. For a preliminary study of the language of the seven surviving copies of the *Poema Morale* see Laing 'Versions'.

1 Oxford, Bodleian Library, Digby 20 (*SC* 1621).
2 C13.

3 [λ] Fols. 62–168 Miscellanea theologica. On fol. 155r, in the French text of Edmund Riche's *Speculum Ecclesie*, is the usual English quatrain *Nou goth sonne vnder wode / Me rewes Marie yi faire Rode. / Nou goth sonne vnder tre / Me rewes Marie yi sone and ye.*
4 CB Reg i 17. Wells *Suppl* 1, p. 988 (XIII.127a). *IMEV* 2320/A1. See CB13 1.
5 For other MSS containing this text with the English quatrain see the Index of Texts in French.
6 Contents associate the MS with Tynemouth Priory, Northumberland. Ker *Med Lib Suppl*, p. 66.
7 English in one hand.

1 Oxford, Bodleian Library, Digby 45 (*SC* 1646).
2 ?C13.
3 [λ] Homilies in Latin containing a copy in English (fol. 25r) of *Candet Nudatum Pectus*: *Naked was hys wite brest red of blod hys side / bloc was hys faire neb hys wounde dep and wide / starke were hys armes yspred op hon þe rode / In vif stede on hys bodie stremes ourne of blode.*
4 This MS is not mentioned in Thomson *Candet* and is not listed in *IMEV*; but cf. the entry between *IMEV* 2282 and 2283 and also *IMEV* 461 and 4088.
5 For other versions in English of *Candet Nudatum Pectus* see the Index of Middle English Texts A: Titles.
7 English in one hand.

1 Oxford, Bodleian Library, Digby 53 (*SC* 1654).
2 C12b2.
3 [λ] [γ] Fol. 5v seq. the proverbs of Serlo of Wilton. The proverbs are written in French (two in English) and are followed by their Latin equivalents. The two English proverbs are:
(1) Fol. 9v *Selden gifis men dumb man land*;
(2) Fol. 10r *þar þe clild* [= child] *is kings and þe inerl* [? for churl] *is Alderman and þe pale* [i.e. foreigner] *biscop pa þene lede.*
The text of Serlo of Wilton's *Versus de Differenciis* on fols. 3r–5v contains a few vernacular glosses, mostly French.
4 Murakami, p. 87, no. 16. Ker 348 (pp. 426–27) indicates that fol. 53 of this MS contains another proverb — untraced. *IMEV Suppl* cites fol. 10r of this MS under the entries for 906 and 2668.5. However, item (2) is not *IMEV* 906 but a translation of an unrelated Latin poem 'Ve populo cuius puer rex' (see Wenzel 1986, p. 189 fn. 57) and the couplet listed under *IMEV* 2668.5 *Oft bryngeth on day*, etc. belongs not in this MS but in Bodley, Rawlinson C 641, fol. 13v, q.v. Proverbs edited: A.C. Friend, 'The proverbs of Serlo of Wilton', *Medieval Studies* 16 (1954), 179–218; Paul Meyer, *Documents manuscrits de l'ancienne littérature de la France conservés dans les Bibl. de la Grande-Bretagne* (Paris, 1871), pp. 168–82 (174–75). Vernacular glosses edited: Hunt *Teaching* 1, scattered between pp. 131 and 135.
6 *Ex libris* inscription indicates that the MS was probably from Bridlington, ERY. Ker *Med Lib*, p. 12.
7 English in one hand.
8 The text of the proverbs is early enough to use þ for w. Interesting as an early example of NME.

1 Oxford, Bodleian Library, Digby 55 (*SC* 1656).
2 C13b.
3 [λ] Commentary on Aristotle in Latin. Fol. 49r contains English as follows.
(1) A copy of *Candet Nudatum Pectus* in Latin and English. English begins *Wyt is yi nachede brest.*
(2) Five short couplets paraphrasing a 'Vox Christi in cruce' and a 'Responsio peccatoris' beg. *Suete leman y deye for yi loue* and *Wen ihc aue al don mine folie.*
4 (1) Wells *Suppl* 6, p. 1466 (XIII.116). *IMEV* 4087. See Thomson *Candet*.

(2) Wells *Suppl* 6, p. 1466 (XIII.114b). *IMEV* 3242.
5 For other versions in English of *Candet Nudatum Pectus* see the Index of Middle English Texts A: Titles.
7 English in one hand.
8 þ is y-shaped, but *th* and *z* are also often used as substitutes.

1 Oxford, Bodleian Library, Digby 69 (*SC* 1670).
2 C13.
3 [γ] Fols. 66r–84v a text of Macer's *De virtutibus herbarum* with a small number of thirteenth-century vernacular glosses beside the rubrics introducing each plant.
4 See Hunt *Plant Names*, p. xxii.

1 Oxford, Bodleian Library, Digby 86 (*SC* 1687).
2 C13b2 (1272–1282).
3 [λ] Commonplace-book of which about half is in French and a quarter in Latin and which contains after fol. 119 twenty-two pieces in English as follows.
   (1) Fols. 119r–120r *Harrowing of Hell* beg. *Hou ihu crist herowede helle ... Leue frend nou beþ stille.*
   (2) Fols. 120v–122v *The XV Signs before Judgement* beg. *Fiftene toknen ich tellen of.*
   (3) Fols. 122v–125v *The Life of St Eustace* beg. *Alle þat louieþ godes lere.*
   (4) Fols. 125v–126v *The Sayings of St Bernard* beg. *Þe blessinge of heuene king.*
   (5) Fols. 126v–127r 'Ubi sunt' beg. *Uuere beþ þey bifore vs weren.*
   (6) Fol. 127r–v *Stabat iuxta Christi crucem* beg. *Stond wel moder ounder rode.*
   (7) Fol. 127v–130r *The Sayings of St Bede* or *Sinners Beware* beg. *Holi gost þi miȝtte.*
   (8) Fols. 130r–132r *Our Lady's Psalter* beg. *Leuedi swete and milde.*
   (9) Fols. 132r–134v *The XI Pains of Hell* beg. *Hounseli gost wat dest þou here.*
   (10) Fols. 134v a version of *Iesu dulcis memoria* beg. *Swete ihu king of blisse.*
   (11) Fols. 134v–136v *Le Regret de Maximian* beg. *Herkneþ to mi ron.*
   (12) Fols. 136v–138r *The Thrush and the Nightingale* beg. *Somer is comen wiþ loue to toune.*
   (13) Fols. 138r–140r *The Fox and the Wolf* beg. *A vox gon out of þe wode go.*
   (14) Fols. 140v–143r *The Proverbs of Hending* incorporating four lines from *The Proverbs of Alfred* on fol. 143r. Begins *Ihu crist al þis worldes red.*
   (15) Fols. 163v–164r lyric on the vanity of this world beg. *Worldes blisse ne last non þrowe.*
   (16) Fols. 165r–168r *Dame Siriz* beg. *As I com bi an waie.*
   (17) Fol. 168r–v *The Names of the Hare in English* beg. *þe mon þat þe hare I-met.*
   (18) Fols. 195v–197v *Debate between the Body and Soul* beg. *Hon an þester stude I stod.*
   (19) Fols. 197v–198r *Doomsday* beg. *Uuen I þenke on domes-dai.*
   (20) Fols. 198r–200r *The Latemest Day* beg. *Þench of þe latemeste dai hou we shulen fare.*
   (21) Fol. 200r lyric beg. *Loue is sofft loue is swet loue is goed sware.*
   (22) Fol. 206r *In Manus Tuas* beg. *In þine honden louerd mine.*
4 CB Reg i 17–18. Watson *Ox Lib* 1, p. 68 and 2, pl. 125.
   (1) Wells V.74. Severs 2 V.313. *IMEV Suppl* 1850.5 (*olim IMEV* 1258). Edited (all versions): W.H. Hulme, *The Middle English Harrowing of Hell and Gospel of Nicodemus*, EETS ES 100 (1908 for 1907; repr. 1976).
   (2) Wells V.75. *IMEV* 796.
   (3) Wells V.42. *IMEV* 211. Edited: C. Horstmann, *Altenglische Legenden*, Neue Folge (Heilbronn, 1881), pp. 211–19.
   (4) Wells VII.30. *IMEV* 3310.
   (5) *IMEV* 3310. CB13 48. D&W XXXV. *OBMEV* 14.

(6) Wells IX.3. Hartung 3 VII.1(r). *IMEV* 3211. CB13 49. Edited: H. Varnhagen, 'Zu mittelenglischen Gedichten', *Anglia* 2 (1879), 225–55 (253–54).
(7) Wells VII.31. Hartung 3 VII.18(c). *IMEV* 1229.
(8) Wells II.4. *IMEV* 1840.
(9) Wells V.79. Severs 2 V.320. *IMEV* 3828. Edited: C. Horstmann, 'Nachträge zu den Legenden', *Archiv* 62 (1879), 403–15.
(10) Wells XIII.157. *IMEV* 3236. CB13 50. BSD VIII U. *OBMEV* 15.
(11) Wells VII.41. *IMEV* 1115. CB13 51. Edited: H. Varnhagen, 'Zu mittelenglischen Gedichten', *Anglia* 3 (1880), 275–92 (278–82).
(12) Wells IX.9. Hartung 3 VII.46. *IMEV* 3222. CB13 52. D&W XIII.
(13) Wells II.25. *IMEV* 35. BSD V. D&W XII. *OBMEV* 16.
(14) Wells VII.6 (and cf. Wells *Suppl* 6, p. 1456 (VII.5)). *IMEV* 1669, 2093. Edited: H. Varnhagen, 'Zu mittelenglischen Gedichten', *Anglia* 4 (1881), 191–200 and G. Schleich, 'Die Sprichwörter Hendings und die Prouerbis of Wysdom', *Anglia* 51 (1927), 247–77.
(15) Wells XIII.31. *IMEV* 4223. Cf. CB13 46.
(16) Wells II.20. *IMEV* 342. BSD VI.
(17) Wells X.43. *IMEV* 3421. Edited: A.S.C. Ross, 'The Middle English poem on the names of a hare', *Proceedings of the Leeds Philosophical and Literary Society* 3. 6 (1935), 350–51.
(18) Wells IX.1. Hartung 3 VII.18(f). *IMEV* 1461.
(19) Wells VII.32. Hartung 3 VII.18(g). *IMEV* 3967. Cf. CB13 28.
(20) Wells *Suppl* 5, p. 1356 (VII.36). Hartung 3 VII.18(h). *IMEV* and *IMEV Suppl* 3517. Cf. CB13 29.
(21) Wells XIII.7. *IMEV* 2009. CB13 53. *OBMEV* 17.
(22) Wells *Suppl* 6, p. 1454 (VI.11). *IMEV* 1571.
Items (4)–(8) edited: F.J. Furnivall, *The Minor Poems of the Vernon MS* 2, EETS OS 117 (1901, repr. 1973), pp. 757–85.
Items (13) and (16) edited: G.H. McKnight, *Middle English Humorous Tales in Verse* (Boston, 1913).
See also, E. Stengel, *Cod. MS. Digby 86* (Halle, 1871).
5 This MS shares texts with several others. Cf. especially Cambridge, Trinity College 323 (B.14.39); BL Cotton Caligula A ix; Oxford, Jesus College 29. It also shares material with the rather later MSS, CUL Gg.I.1; Edinburgh, National Library of Scotland, Advocates' 19.2.1 (Auchinleck MS) and BL Harley 2253. For information on other shared pieces see CB13, p. xxxiii and see further cross references to titles and incipits in the Indexes of Middle English Texts.
6 Marginalia refer to three families, Grimhill, Pendock and Underhill, of which the Pendocks are most prominent. Places mentioned are Ridmerley, SW Worcs (viz. Redmarley D'Abitot, now in Gloucs), and Pendock, SW Worcs (6.5 miles W of Tewkesbury). See CB13, pp. xxviii–xxxii; the review of CB13 by B.J. Whiting, *Speculum* 9 (1934), 219–25 (221–25); M.L. Samuels, 'Langland's dialect', *MÆ* 54 (1985), 232–47. A detailed survey of the evidence concerning the origin of the MS is given by B.D.H. Miller, 'The early history of Bodleian MS. Digby 86', *Annuale Medievale* 4 (1963), 23–56. Miller argues against CB's suggestion that the MS was written in Worcester Priory on the grounds that the kalendar of saints, on fols. 68v–74r, is devotional not liturgical. Miller suggests that the most that can be said is that the MS was copied for, and probably by, a layman, between 1272 and 1282, in the diocese of Worcester which then occupied most of Worcs and the modern diocese of Gloucester and most of the modern diocese of Bristol.
7 English in one hand, the main hand of the MS.
8 The language is congruent with the later S Worcs/Gloucs material in *LALME*.

1 Oxford, Bodleian Library, Digby 92 (*SC* 1693).

2 C13b.
3 [γ] Astrologica, etc. Fols. 96r–98r contain a fragment of the *Exoticon* of Alexander of Hales the first part of which is in Bodley, Auct. F.6.8, q.v. The text is in Latin with some Anglo-Norman glosses but apparently no glosses in English in this text.

4 See Hunt *Teaching* 1, p. 299.

1 Oxford, Bodleian Library, Digby 172 (*SC* 1773).
2 C12b2–C13a1.
3 [λ] Theologica in Latin with English appearing as follows.
   (1) On the upper margin of fol. 55r five long lines of macaronic verse beg. *God send vs þe dew of heuene.*
   (2) Fols. 143r–150v glosses on the letters of Sidonius Apollinaris in Latin, French and Middle English. There are only fifteen ME words represented.
4 CB Reg i 20. (1) *IMEV* 963. (2) Wells X.17. *IMEP* III, p. 75. Hunt *Teaching* 1, pp. 26–27. Edited: Tony Hunt, 'The vernacular entries in the *Glossae in Sidonium* (MS Oxford Digby 172)', *Zeitschrift für französische Sprache und Literatur* 89 (1979), 130–50; R. Ellis, 'Glosses in Sidonivm', *Anecdota Oxoniensia*, Classical Series 1, v (Oxford, 1885), pp. 27–62. See also M. Förster, 'Fruhmittelenglische und anglofranzösische Glossen aus Digby 172', *Archiv* 109 (1902), 314–37.

1 Oxford, Bodleian Library, Digby 211 (*SC* 1812).
2 *C12–C13.
3 [λ] Bede's *Historia ecclesiastica* followed by Cuthbert's *Epistola de obitu Bedae* containing on fol. 108r Bede's Death Song.
4 Ker 321. Edited: Dobbie 1937, p.76.
5 For other MSS containing Bede's Death Song see the Index of Old English Texts.
6 Ker, p. 383: "The Waltham Abbey *ex libris* inscription, 'Liber sancte crucis de waltham,' is contemporary with the text". See also Ker *Med Lib*, p. 193.
7 The Death Song is in the main hand.

1 Oxford, Bodleian Library, Douce 139 (*SC* 21713).
2 C13a2–b1 (*ca.* 1250, *OBMEV*; *ca.* 1270, E.W.B Nicholson).
3 [λ] *Statuta Angliae*, etc. in Latin. English appears as follows.
   (1) Fol. 5r one five-line stanza beg. *Foweles in þe frith.*
   (2) Fol. 157r four mono-rhyming lines beg. *Loue is a selkud wodenesse.*
4 (1) Wells XIII.5. *IMEV* 864. CB13 8. *OBMEV* 266. D&W XXVI. BSD VIII C. D&H, p. 142.
   (2) Wells *Suppl* 3, p. 1176 (XIII.5a). *IMEV* 2005. CB13 9.
6 MS is from Coventry. It contains legal and miscellaneous pieces some of which, especially added documents, relate to Coventry. Lists of the bps. of Coventry and Lichfield also appear in the MS. See also Ker *Med Lib*, p. 54.
7 The two poems are in different hands.

1 Oxford, Bodleian Library, Douce 207 (*SC* 21781).
2 C13b2.
3 [λ] Roger of Wendover's *Flores Historiarum* containing on fol. 125v Godric's Hymn A.
4 CB Reg i 113. Wells XIII.27. *IMEV* 2988. Edited: H.G. Hewlett, *The Flowers of History by Roger de Wendover* 1, RS 84 (1886), p. 73. See also Hall ii 241; Zupitza 'Godric'; D&H, p. 103 seq. and 108–109.
5 For other MSS containing one or more of Godric's Hymns see the Index of Middle English Texts A: Titles.
7 English in one hand.

1 Oxford, Bodleian Library, Douce 210 (*SC* 21784).
2 C13b2–C14a1 (*ca.* 1300).
3 [λ] On fol. 44r in the French text of Edmund Riche's *Speculum Ecclesie* appears the usual English quatrain beg. *Nou goth sunne vnder wode / me rueȝ Marie þi faire rude.*
4 CB Reg i 113. *IMEV* 2320/A5.

5 For other MSS containing this text and the English quatrain see the Index of Texts in French.

1 Oxford, Bodleian Library, Eng. hist. a. 2, no. II b (*SC* 31346).
2 *C15.
3 [δ] English bounds to a copy of a grant by Æthelheard of land at Crediton, Devon.
4 Sawyer 255 (B 1333). Edited: A.S. Napier and W.H. Stevenson, *The Crawford Collection of Early Charters and Documents*, Anecdota Oxoniensa (Oxford, 1895), pp. 4–5.
6 Creedy (Crediton), Devon.
8 Language contains some interesting forms.

1 Oxford, Bodleian Library, Eng. th. c. 70.
2 C14a (1330–1340, Napier).
3 [λ] The Lanhydrock Fragment. A single leaf of parchment containing a fragment of the *Ancrene Riwle*.
4 Severs 2 VI.1. Edited: A.S. Napier, 'A fragment of the Ancrene Riwle', *Journal of Germanic Philology* 2 (1898), 199–202 and A. Zettersten, *The Lanhydrock Fragment*, EETS OS 252 (1963), pp. 163–71.
7 One hand.

1 Oxford, Bodleian Library, Fairfax 6 (*SC* 3886).
2 C14b.
3 [λ] Chronicles and Lives of Saints in Latin compiled at Durham Priory. Contains the *Life of St Godric* by Reginald, monk of Durham (fols. 185–199) including a text of Godric's Hymn A.
4 *IMEV* 2988. See also Hall ii 241; Zupitza 'Godric'; D&H, p. 103 seq. and 108–109.
5 For other MSS containing texts of one or more of Godric's Hymns see the Index of Middle English Texts A: Titles.
6 MS from Durham. Ker *Med Lib*, p. 74.

1 Oxford, Bodleian Library, Gough Cambridge 22 (*SC* 17772).
2 *C14b2 (after 1386, Thomson).
3 [δ] Fols. 1r–2r. Latin and English versions of the Ely privilege: King Edgar to Ely Abbey. English also on fols. 13r–v, 15v.
4 Sawyer as follows: S 779, S 980, S 1045, S 1084, S 1075, S 1085, S 1069, S 507 (bounds only). Cf. Thomson *Archives*, p. 162, no. 1317.
5 For other medieval copies of the Ely privilege see the Index of Old English Texts. Cf. also BL Add 5819 for a C18 copy by William Cole. The earliest surviving text is BL Stowe Charter 31, C11b2. The English version may have been written by Ælfric. See AM 'Wulfstan', p. 113 and n. 8 (pp. 128–29) (repr. 1989, pp. 115, 130-31) and Pope 'Ely Privilege'.
6 The other English material in the MS also concerns Bury St Edmunds for which cf. CUL Ff.II.33.
8 The language of the Ely privilege is garbled OE. The other English is considerably modified and late looking.

1 Oxford, Bodleian Library, Hatton 20 (*SC* 4113).
2 C13a2 (tremulous hand: see Ker 'Date').
3 [γ] Gregory's *Pastoral Care* in OE with glosses (almost all in Latin) on fols. 1–41v, 43r line 1, 93r and 95r in the Worcester tremulous hand.
4 Ker 324. Franzen 1991, pp. 59–60. MS described in the facsimile edition by N.R. Ker, *The Pastoral Care*, Early English Manuscripts in Facsimile 6 (Copenhagen, 1956), pp. 17–26. Crawford 1928, p. 19 prints only two ME glosses. For some earlier (C12) annotations on fols. 53v and 55r see K. Sisam, *Studies in the History of Old English Literature* (Oxford, 1953), pp. 110–11 and, for a description of the MS, pp. 140–47. See also Angus Cameron, 'Middle English in Old English

manuscripts' in *Chaucer and Middle English Studies in Honour of Rossell Hope Robbins*, ed. Beryl Rowland (London, 1974), pp. 218–29 (221).
5 For other MSS containing glosses in the tremulous hand see Franzen 1991, Ker, p. lvii and the entry for Worcester Cathedral, Dean and Chapter Library F 174.
6 Sent to Worcester by order of King Alfred. Annotated at Worcester in C11 by Wulfstan and others. Ker *Med Lib*, p. 209.
7 Glosses in the Worcester tremulous hand.

1 **Oxford, Bodleian Library, Hatton 26 (*SC* 4061).**
2 C13a (*ca.* 1234).
3 [λ] Part D, fols. 205r–231v, theological pieces and notes in Latin. On fol. 211r appears a note in English on *The Ten Commandments* in eight couplets beg. *Leue men þis beoþ þe ten heste*. There is also some prose in English on the gifts of the Holy Ghost.
4 Hartung 7 XX.43 and 127. *IMEV Suppl* 1856.5. See also Watson *Ox Lib* 1, p. 84 and 2, pl. 102.
6 *Ex libris* inscription indicates that the MS belonged to the Augustinian priory at Stafford. Ker *Med Lib*, p. 182.
7 The hand of the English note is said to be only slightly later than the hand of the rest of Part D which writes a Latin chronological note in 1234.

1 **Oxford, Bodleian Library, Hatton 38 (*SC* 4090).**
2 *C12b2.
3 [λ] *West-Saxon Gospels*.
4 Ker 325. Edited: W.W. Skeat, *The Four Gospels in Anglo-Saxon, Northumbrian, and Old Mercian Versions* (Cambridge, 1871–1887; repr. Darmstadt, 1970). Cf. Max Reimann, *Die Sprache der mittelkentischen Evangelien (codd. Royal I A 14 und Hatton 38)*, Diss. Berlin (1883).
5 This text is probably a copy of BL Royal 1 A xiv (a Christ Church, Canterbury book, C12b), which is a copy in its turn of Bodley 441 (C11).
6 Canterbury, Kent.
8 Ker, p. 387: "The linguistic forms are Kentish".

1 **Oxford, Bodleian Library, Hatton 76 (*SC* 4125).**
2 C13a2 (tremulous hand: see Ker 'Date').
3 [γ] A. Fragments of an OE translation of Gregory's *Dialogues*; fragment of St Basil, *Monita*. B. OE versions of the *Herbarium* and the *Medicina de quadrupedibus* in hands of C11. MS glossed by the Worcester tremulous hand, mainly in Latin. ME versions of OE herb names appear fols. 75v–118v.
4 Ker 328. Franzen 1991, pp. 65–69. For ME herb names in the tremulous hand see Crawford 1928, pp. 19–21.
5 For other MSS containing glosses in the tremulous hand see Franzen 1991, Ker, p. lvii and the entry for Worcester Cathedral, Dean and Chapter Library F 174.
6 MS was at Worcester by the beginning of C13. Ker *Med Lib*, p. 209.
7 Glosses in the Worcester tremulous hand.

1 **Oxford, Bodleian Library, Hatton 107 (*SC* 4031).**
2 C13b2–14a1.
3 [λ] Sermons in Latin containing on fol. 1v Latin, English and French verses in a hand of *ca.* 1300. English (imperfect) as follows: *Me[n þam com]pleynes of vntrewyth / la[we e]s dede and þat es Rewth / trechery es al oboue / and grauen he as trewlouf.*
4 CB Reg i 71. Wells *Suppl* 1, p. 975 (VII.14a). *IMEV* 2146, and for variants see *IMEV* 2145 and 3650. See also Wenzel 1986, p. 191.
5 Cf. other versions of the English text: Oxford, Merton College 248 item (36); Oxford, Balliol College 227, fol. 258; and Cambridge, Pembroke College 258 item (4).

1 Oxford, Bodleian Library, Hatton 113 (*SC* **5210,** *olim* **Junius 99).**
(Once formed one collection of homilies with Bodley, Junius 121 and Hatton 114.)

2 C13a2 (tremulous hand: see Ker 'Date').

3 [γ] Homilies, mainly by Wulfstan but some by Ælfric, in a hand of C11b1. Contains very early glosses in English and also glosses and annotations throughout in the Worcester tremulous hand. ME glosses by what Franzen calls the D state of the tremulous hand appear mainly on fols. 1–8 and 80v–81, but almost all have been erased. M state glosses in Latin and English appear throughout and also some B state glosses.

4 Ker 331. For a description of the complex layers of glossing in this MS by the tremulous hand see Franzen 1991, pp. 30–34, 155–66 and cf. Franzen *Thesis*. See also Crawford 1928. The MS is described in Pope *Ælfric*, pp. 70–71. Cf. N.R. Ker, 'Old English notes signed "Coleman"', *MÆ* 18 (1949), 29. For a note on a ME gloss by the tremulous hand on fol. 143r see N.R. Ker, 'Old English *hrohian*', *MÆ* 1 (1932), 208 and see also fn. 2 for a gloss not in Crawford.

5 For other MSS containing glosses in the tremulous hand see Franzen 1991, Ker, p. lvii and the entry for Worcester Cathedral, Dean and Chapter Library F 174.

6 Ker, p. 399: "Written [with Hatton 114] at Worcester as companion volumes to Junius 121". See also Ker *Med Lib*, p. 209.

7 Glosses in the Worcester tremulous hand.

1 Oxford, Bodleian Library, Hatton 114 (*SC* **5134,** *olim* **Junius 22).**
(Once formed one collection of homilies with Bodley, Junius 121 and Hatton 113.)

2 C13a2 (tremulous hand: see Ker 'Date').

3 [γ] Continuation of the homily collection in Hatton 113 containing mainly works by Ælfric. There are a few early or contemporary glosses and also many by the Worcester tremulous hand, though these are mostly in Latin. In the margin of fols. 9v–10r appear Latin–English word pairs in the tremulous hand.

4 Ker 331. Franzen 1991, pp. 34–37, 155–66 and cf. Franzen *Thesis*. See also Crawford 1928. The MS is described in Pope *Ælfric*, pp. 70–71. It was a marginal (Latin) gloss on fol. 10r of this MS that enabled Neil Ker to date the tremulous hand as late as 1225–50; see Ker 'Date'.

5 For other MSS containing glosses in the tremulous hand see Franzen 1991, Ker, p. lvii and the entry for Worcester Cathedral, Dean and Chapter Library F 174.

6 Ker, p. 399: "Written [with Hatton 113] at Worcester as companion volumes to Junius 121". See also Ker *Med Lib*, p. 209.

7 Glosses in the Worcester tremulous hand.

1 Oxford, Bodleian Library, Hatton 115 (*SC* **5135,** *olim* **Junius 23).**

2 C12b2 and C13a2 (tremulous hand: see Ker 'Date').

3 [γ] [λ] (1) Fols. 1r–139r homilies and shorter pieces of instruction and admonition, mainly by Ælfric, in a hand of C11b and containing nearly 700 ME glosses by the Worcester tremulous hand.

(2) Fols. 140r–147r sermon in an earlier hand than the main one with Latin glosses by the tremulous hand.

(3) Fols. 148r–155r prognostications in a C12 hand with, on fol. 154v, three lines in the tremulous hand on what it means to pray in the name of Jesus.

(4) Fol. 155r contains a few words in a hand of the end of the twelfth century.

4 Ker 332. For a description of the MS and the tremulous glosses including corrections to Crawford's (1928) attributions see Franzen 1991, pp. 38–44, 95–102. For the tremulous hand see also Max Förster, 'Die altenglische Traumlunare', *EStn* 60 (1925–1926), 89. For EME glosses to the Book of Judges see S.J. Crawford, *The Heptateuch*, EETS OS 160 (1922), p. 422 and cf. Crawford 1928 (corrected in Franzen 1991). MS also described in Pope *Ælfric*, pp. 53–59.

5 Most of the English glosses are by the tremulous scribe in what Franzen calls the D state of his work. For other MSS containing glosses in the tremulous hand see Franzen 1991, Ker, p. lvii and the entry for Worcester Cathedral, Dean and Chapter

Library F 174. A lost leaf after fol. 82 is now Kansas University Library Y 104 (see Ker *Suppl* 73 and B. Colgrave and A. Hyde, 'Two recently discovered leaves from Old English manuscripts', *Speculum* 37 (1962), 60–78).

6 The MS was at Worcester by early C13 but Pope (*Ælfric*, p. 58) thinks the texts were originally written elsewhere. See also Ker *Med Lib*, p. 209.

7 Glosses and other additions in the Worcester tremulous hand. C12b2 hand (Ker 332 item 37) is a caroline script with the extra letters þ, ð and p.

1 Oxford, Bodleian Library, Hatton 116 (*SC* 5136, *olim* Junius 24).

2 C13a2 (tremulous hand: see Ker 'Date').

3 [γ] [λ] MS of C12a, containing homilies; all but the first and last items are by Ælfric. Note that item 1, pp. 1–18, *Life of St Chad*, is unique to this MS. There are glosses throughout in Latin and English in the Worcester tremulous hand. On p. 396 the tremulous hand writes two lines of music. On pp. 397–98 he scribbles a few Latin-English word pairs and on p. 398 he quotes a scrap from an English lyric: *ic am nout for þisse þinge þo*.

4 Ker 333. Franzen 1991, pp. 44–48, 155–66 and cf. Franzen *Thesis*. MS also described in Pope *Ælfric*, pp. 67–70. English glosses listed in Crawford 1928 (corrected Franzen 1991, p. 46 fn. 30). *Life of St Chad* edited: A.S. Napier, 'Ein altenglisches Leben des heiligen Chad', *Anglia* 10 (1881), 131 seq., and R. Vleeskruyer, *The Life of St Chad: an Old English Homily* (Amsterdam, 1953). For the snatch of English verse see *IMEV Suppl* 1276.5.

5 For other MSS containing glosses in the tremulous hand see Franzen 1991, Ker, p. lvii and the entry for Worcester Cathedral, Dean and Chapter Library F 174.

6 The MS was in Worcester by early C13. Ker *Med Lib*, p. 209.

7 Glosses and other additions in the Worcester tremulous hand. There are no glosses or annotations in earlier hands. The C12a hand of the OE text is "A handsome, round hand of a type found commonly in West of England manuscripts of s. xii": Ker, p. 406.

8 The language of the *Life of St Chad* is not late W-S but a late OE more reminiscent of the language of the Katherine Group.

1 Oxford, Bodleian Library, Junius 1 (*SC* 5113).

2 C12b2 (early in last quarter of C12, Parkes *Orrm*).

3 [λ] *The Ormulum*.

4 Ker, p. xix. CB Reg i 73. Wells v.14. *IMEV* 2305. Hall ii 479–92. Parkes *Orrm*. Edited: R.M. White (Oxford, 1852), rev. R. Holt, 2 vols. (Oxford, 1878) and in part BSD XIII, Hall i XV and D&W XV. For early literature (up to 1920) see Hall ii 479–80. See also: A.S. Napier, 'Notes on the orthography of the Ormulum' appended to *History of the Holy Rood Tree*, EETS OS 103 (1894); W. Zenke, 'Synthesis und Analysis im Orrmulum', *Studien zur englishe Philologie* 40 (1910), 1–4, incl. bibliog. E. Björkmann, 'Orrms Doppelkonsonanten', *Anglia* 37 (1913), 351 seq., incl. bibliog.; B. Laeseke, *Ein Beitrag zur Stellung des Verbums im Orrmulum*, Diss. Kiel (1917), incl. bibliog.; Sigurd Holm, *Corrections and Additions in the Ormulum Manuscript* (Uppsala, 1922), incl. bibliog.; H. Flasdieck, 'Die sprachliche Einheitlichkeit des "Orrmulums"', *Anglia* 47 (1923), 289–331; H.C. Matthes, *Die Einheitlichkeit des Orrmulum: Studien zur Textkritik, zu den Quellen und zur sprachlichen Form von Orrmins Evangelienbuch* (Heidelberg, 1933); N.R. Ker, 'Unpublished parts of the *Ormulum* printed from MS Lambeth 783', *MÆ* 9 (1940), 1–21; Joan E. Turville-Petre, 'Studies on the *Ormulum* MS', *JEGP* 46 (1947), 1–27; H.C. Matthes, 'Die Orrmulum-Korrekturen', *JEGP* 50 (1951), 183–99; R.W. Burchfield, 'Two misreadings of the *Ormulum* manuscript', *MÆ* 21 (1952), 37–39 and 'A source of scribal error in Early Middle English manuscripts', *MÆ* 22 (1953), 10–17; Martin Lehnert, *Sprachform und Sprachfunktion im Orrmulum* (um 1200), Zeitschrift für Anglistik und Amerikanistik, Beiheft I (Berlin, 1953); R.W. Burchfield, 'The language and orthography of the Ormulum MS', *TPS* (1956), 56–87 and '*Ormulum*: words copied by Jan van Vliet from parts now lost', in *English* *and Medieval Studies presented to J.R.R. Tolkien on the Occasion of his Seventieth Birthday*, ed. N. Davis and C.L. Wrenn (London, 1962), 94–111; A. McIntosh, 'A new approach to Middle English dialectology' *ES* 44 (1963), 11; R.A. Palmatier, *A Descriptive Syntax of the "Ormulum"*, Janua Linguarum, Series Pratica 74 (The Hague, 1969); Laing *Thesis* 1, pp. 20–23.

Facsimile of fol. 51r in *Pal Soc*, Second Series, vol. 2, plate 133.

5 London, Lambeth Palace 783 is a C17 transcript containing portions now missing from this MS.
6 Parkes has convincingly argued that Orm came from the Arroaisian House of SS. Peter and Paul in Bourne, S Lincs. See also Ker *Med Lib Suppl*, p. 4.
7 One hand.
8 Language of SW Lincs.

1 Oxford, Bodleian Library, Junius 121 (*SC* 5232). (Once formed one collection of homilies with Hatton 113 and 114.)

2 C13a2 (tremulous hand: see Ker 'Date').
3 [λ] [γ] MS of C11b1 containing ecclesiastical institutes and homilies, etc. contains on a flyleaf, fol. vi, a version of the *Nicene Creed* in EME written in the Worcester tremulous hand. Also contains ME glosses in what Franzen labels the D state of the tremulous hand, most of which have been erased. They occur mainly on fols. 9r–24r and 82v–83r.
4 Ker 338, item 41. Franzen 1991, pp. 54–58. MS also described in Pope *Ælfric*, pp. 70–77. For *Creed* see Hartung 7 XX.38 and *IPMEP* 317. Edited: J. Zupitza, 'Das Symbolium in englischer Aufzeichnung des 12. Jhds', *Anglia* 1 (1878), 286; and Crawford 1928 (facsimile p. 5). For the English glosses see Crawford 1928, pp. 24–25 and Franzen 1991, p. 55 and fn. 44.
5 For other MSS containing glosses in the tremulous hand see Franzen 1991, Ker, p. lvii and the entry for Worcester Cathedral, Dean and Chapter Library F 174.
6 Written at Worcester. Ker *Med Lib*, p. 209.
7 Worcester tremulous hand.

1 Oxford, Bodleian Library, Laud Misc. 108 (*SC* 1486).

2 C13b2–14a1 (c1300, *MED Plan & Bibl*, pp. 73–74).
3 [λ] Part I.
   (1) Fols. 1r–198r *South English Legendary*, preceded by (fols. 1r–10v) *The Life of Christ* beg. (imperfectly) *And spatte a luyte on is fingur* (ends imperfectly) and by fols. 11r–22r *The Infancy of Christ*.
   (2) Fol. 198r–v *The Sayings of St Bernard*.
   (3) Fols. 199r–200r *The Vision of St Paul*.
   (4) Fol. 200v *Debate between the Body and the Soul*.
Part II.
   (5) Fols. 204r–219v *Havelok*.
   (6) Fols. 219v–228r *King Horn*.
Part III, fols. 228v–end, is in hands of late C14 and C15.
4 CB Reg i 6–10. For contents see C. Horstmann, 'Die Legenden des Ms. Laud 108', *Archiv* 49 (1872), 395–414 and *Altenglische Legenden* (Paderborn, 1875), p. x seq.
   (1) Görlach *SEL*, pp. 88–90. Wells V.19 (p. 294) and cf. Wells V.31, 44, 50, 51, 54, 59, 67 (p. 322), 79, 80; X.34. See also Severs 2 IV.67 and 68; 2 V.1 (and cf. Severs 2, pp. 561–635); 2 V.321. *IMEV* 3452 and for *The Life of Christ* and *The Infancy of Christ*, *IMEV* *15 and 1550 (Severs 2 V.311). For other individual entries in *IMEV* see Hamer 'MS index'. Edited: C. Horstmann, *The Early South-English Legendary*, EETS OS 87 (1887, repr. 1973), see esp. p. xiii. Extract, *St Kenelm*, in BSD VII.
   (2) Wells VII.30. *IMEV* 3310.
   (3) Severs 2 V.320. *IMEV* 3089.

(4) Wells IX.1. Hartung 3 VII.18(e). *IMEV* 351. Edited: W. Linow, *þe Desputisoun bitwen þe Bodi and þe Soule*, Erlanger Beiträge zur Englische Philologie 1 (Erlangen and Leipzig, 1889), pp. 25–65 (odd pages).
(5) Wells I.5. Severs 1 I.5. *IMEV* 1114. D&W VIII. BSD IV. *OBMEV* 34. Edited: G.V. Smithers, *Havelok* (Oxford, 1987). See also AM *Havelok* and W.W. Skeat, *The Lay of Havelok the Dane*, 2nd edn. rev. K. Sisam (Oxford, 1915).
(6) Wells I.1. Severs 1 I.1. *IMEV* 166. Edited: J. Hall, *King Horn. A Middle English Romance* (Oxford, 1901). See also Rosamund Allen, 'The date and provenance of *King Horn*: some interim reassessments' in *Medieval English Studies presented to George Kane*, ed. E.D. Kennedy, R. Waldron and J.S. Wittig (Woodbridge, 1988), pp. 99–125.

For contents of part III, see CB Reg i 10.

5 Fragments of *Havelok* are in CUL Add 4407, art. 19. Other MSS containing *King Horn* are CUL Gg.IV.27(2) and BL Harley 2253. For other early MSS containing parts of the *South English Legendary* and for further versions of items (2) and (4) see the Index of Middle English Texts A: Titles.

7 Hand A: fols. 1r–200r.
Hand B: fols. 200v–203v.
Hand C: fols. 204r–228r which Smithers describes as "a compact 'textura' hand of the early fourteenth century".

8 The language of the *Havelok* text is probably from W Norfolk. The language of *King Horn*, which is in the same hand as *Havelok*, has a non-Norfolk substratum which MLS considers to have characteristics pointing to an origin in SE Surrey, SW Kent or N Suffolk. *SEL* is placed by MLS in W Oxon.

1 Oxford, Bodleian Library, Laud Misc. 413 (*SC* 970).

2 C12b.

3 [λ] Text of the Latin *Vita S. Godrici* by Reginald, monk of Durham. Fol. 39v St Godric's Hymn A; fol. 47r St Godric's Hymn B.

4 Ker 342. CB Reg i 3. Wells *Suppl* 1, p. 986 (XIII.27). *IMEV* 2988 and 598. Murakami, p. 105, no. 39. Edited: W.H. Stevenson, *De Vita S. Godrici Heremitae*, Surtees Society 20 (1845), see especially, pp. 119, 144.

5 On the various MSS containing one or more of these three hymns see Hall ii 241 and Zupitza 'Godric'. See also D&H, pp. 103 seq. and 108–109 and the Index of Middle English Texts A: Titles.

6 *Ex libris* inscription indicates that the MS is from Durham. Ker *Med Lib*, p. 74; Ker *Med Lib Suppl*, p. 32.

7 The two poems are in different hands.

1 Oxford, Bodleian Library, Laud Misc. 471 (*SC* 1053).

2 C13b2.

3 [λ] Two MSS bound together.
Part I is mostly Latin but has on fol. 65r the poem *Memento Mori* or *Long Life* beg. *Man may longe liwes wenen*.
Part II (fol. 92 seq.) has French works including sermons by Maurice de Sully on fols. 128r and 138v seq. Fols. 128v–133v contain the Kentish Sermons.

4 *Memento Mori*: CB Reg i 3. Wells VII.46. *IMEV* 2070. CB13 10B. D&H, pp. 122–30. Cf. Hall ii 308. The first two lines of this same poem are cited in part II of the MS in a sermon, fol. 133. Cf. Hall, p. 222 lines 274–275.
Kentish Sermons: *IPMEP* 140. Wells V.15. BSD XVII. D&W XIX. Hall i XXIII and ii 657–75. Hall says (ii 657) that the sermons are translations from French, but that the original French versions of these particular sermons are not in the MS. Edited: Morris *OE Misc*, pp. 26–36 and F. Kluge, *Mittelenglisches Lesebuch* (Halle, 1904), pp. 19–25. See also J. Zupitza, 'Zu R. Morris, An Old English Miscellany pp. 156–159', *Anglia* 1 (1878), 410–14.

5 For other versions of this lyric see the Indexes of Middle English Texts.

8 The language of the Sermons is Kentish in character. Dobson (D&H, p. 122) says that the scribe of *Memento Mori* "was probably a North Midlander" but that he "preserves a number of South-Eastern forms".

1 Oxford, Bodleian Library, Laud Misc. 482 (*SC* 1054).
2 C13a2 (tremulous hand: see Ker 'Date').
3 [γ] Fols. 9v–20v contain glosses and marks by the Worcester tremulous hand in a C11 MS containing an OE *Penitential*. All the glosses are in Latin.
4 Ker 343. Franzen 1991, pp. 58–59.
5 For other MSS containing glosses in the tremulous hand see Ker, p. lvii, Franzen 1991 and the entry for Worcester Cathedral, Dean and Chapter Library F 174.
6 MS in Worcester by early C13. Ker *Med Lib*, p. 209.
7 Latin glosses in the Worcester tremulous hand.

1 Oxford, Bodleian Library, Laud Misc. 511 (*SC* 969).
2 C13.
3 [λ] Latin sermons. Two short quotations from ME lyrics are as follows.
   (1) Fol. 110v *Maiden stod at welle and wep Weilawei / Late cemet* [sic] *þe lith of dai*.
   (2) Fol. 123v *Wan Ics on rode se / Iesu mi lemon*, etc.
4 Wenzel 1986, pp. 226 and 236.
5 Item (2) is a quotation from a lyric of the type *My Leman on the Rood* for which see the Index of Middle English Texts A: Titles and CB13 35–37.

1 Oxford, Bodleian Library, Laud Misc. 567 (*SC* 1507).
2 C12.
3 [γ] MS containing medical texts in Latin. On fols. 68–73 are about 250 OE glosses of herb names.
4 Ker 345. Murakami, p. 87, no. 17. Edited: J. Richard Stracke, *The Laud Herbal Glossary* (Amsterdam, 1974).
7 The glossary is in the same hand as the rest of the MS.

1 Oxford, Bodleian Library, Laud Misc. 582 (*SC* 1582).
2 C13a1.
3 [λ] MS contains part 2 of Roger of Hoveden's *Chronicle* (1181–end) including a prophecy in English beg. *þan þu seches in Here hert yreret*.
4 Edited: Stubbs *Hoveden* 3, p. 68. Cf. also Wilson 1943, p. 46 and Richter 1979, p. 74.
5 Cf. BL Royal 14 C ii which contains the first part of the *Chronicle* and which Stubbs considers may once have formed part of the same copy as this MS. For other copies of this text containing the English prophecy see the Index of Texts in Latin.

1 Oxford, Bodleian Library, Laud Misc. 636 (*SC* 1003).
2 C12a1–b1.
3 [λ] *The Peterborough Chronicle*, MS E of the *Anglo-Saxon Chronicle*. Fols. 88v–91v Second Continuation, 1132–1154.
4 Ker 346. Dorothy Whitelock, *The Peterborough Chronicle*, Early English Manuscripts in Facsimile 4 (Copenhagen, 1954). Wells III.1 and cf. Hartung 5 XIII.6 and 8 XXI.1. *IPMEP* 752. Hall ii 246–64. Edited: Cecily Clark, *The Peterborough Chronicle 1070–1154*, 2nd edn. (Oxford, 1970) and in part BSD XVI, D&W II and Hall i III. Cf. N.R. Ker, 'Some notes on the Peterborough Chronicle', *MÆ* 3 (1934), 136–38 and Cecily Clark, 'Notes on MS. Laud Misc. 636', *MÆ* 23 (1954), 71–75. See also Watson *Ox Lib* 2, pl. 62.
6 Written at Peterborough, Northants. Ker *Med Lib*, p. 151.
7 A neat round hand, very like that of BL Cotton Tiberius C i, wrote the entries up to the annal for 1121 at one time. It continued adding entries at intervals up to the end of the entry for 1131 (The First Continuation), as is evident from the changes in the colour of the ink. A second scribe wrote, all at one time, the annals for 1132–1154

(The Second Continuation, fols. 88v–91v), in a more compressed and later type of script. See Ker, pp. 425–26.
8 The language of the Second Continuation may be taken to represent Peterborough language. The language of the main scribe, especially as interpolater and continuer of the copied text, is also of some local interest.

1 Oxford, Bodleian Library, Laud Misc. 647 (*SC* 1595).
2 *C12.
3 [λ] [δ] *Historia Eliensis* containing English as follows.
  (1) Fol. 45v a four-line lyric beg. *Merie sungen ðe muneches binnen ely.*
  (2) Fol. 47v the Confessor's Writ.
4 (1) Hartung 5 VII.8. *IMEV Suppl* 2164.
  (2) Sawyer 1100. Edited (with commentary): Laing 'Anchor texts', esp. pp. 38–40.
5 For other Ely cartularies containing copies of the Confessor's Writ see the Index of Old English Texts.
6 MS from Ely. Ker *Med Lib*, p. 78.
7 English in one hand.
8 OE not much modified.

1 Oxford, Bodleian Library, Rawlinson B 329 (*SC* 11668).
2 *C15.
3 [δ] Hereford Cartulary. Fol. 104r copy of a writ of King Edward granting rights to St Æthelbert's, Hereford.
4 Davis 482. Sawyer 1101 (Har 49).
6 Hereford.
7 English in one hand.

1 Oxford, Bodleian Library, Rawlinson C 22 (*SC* 15408).
2 C13a.
3 [λ] MS in Latin containing on p. 298 a four-line monorhyming poem in English: *Eueriche freman hach to ben hende / for to be Large of þat him crist sende / þan it es al ydon that cume to þe nende / na huues numan of þis werld bot gnedeliche his Lenge.*
4 CB Reg i 108. Wells *Suppl* 1, p. 975 (VII.13a). *IMEV* 740. CB13 57.
7 English in one hand.

1 Oxford, Bodleian Library, Rawlinson C 317 (*SC* 12173).
2 C13a1.
3 [λ] Theological pieces in Latin containing on fol. 89v an English version of *Candet Nudatum Pectus: With was is nakede brest. Ant red his blodi side. / Blake weren is lires his wondes depe ant wyde. / Stratthe wern is armmes sprad op on þe rode. / In fife studes on his bodi stremes urner* [sic] *on blode.*
4 Cf. *IMEV* 4088 though this MS is not listed there; nor is it mentioned in Thomson *Candet.*
5 For other versions in English of *Candet Nudatum Pectus* see the Index of Middle English Texts A: Titles..
6 MS has associations with Cockersand Abbey, Lancs. Ker *Med Lib*, p. 52.
7 English in one hand.

1 Oxford, Bodleian Library, Rawlinson C 510 (*SC* 12357).
2 C13b1 (*ca.* 1270).
3 [λ] Theological collection in Latin. Fol. 3r contains a fragment in English: *so hend and so god he is / he aues broct us into blis; /superni. / and i dit þe fule pit inferni.*
4 See Laing *Thesis* 1, p. 12.
5 This is a quotation from the lyric beg. *For on þat is so feir ant brist,* versions of which are to be found in Cambridge, Trinity College 323 (B.14.39), fol. 24v and BL Egerton 613, fol. 2r. Cf. CB13 17A and 17B lines 41–45.

6 MS associated with Bardney Abbey, Lincs. Ker *Med Lib*, p. 6.
7 English in one hand.

1 Oxford, Bodleian Library, Rawlinson C 534 (*SC* 12381).
2 C13.
3 [λ] English verses in Latin sermons.
   (1) Fol. 6r four rhyming lines beg. *þe vnseli man seyde of God þat hym ne rouhte*.
   (2) Fol. 73v couplet on the wretchedness of a fallen girl: *Nu hur is goo wroth and hyre frendes loth*.
   The MS also contains several English and French proverbs.
4 Wenzel 1974, nos. 64 and 46.

1 Oxford, Bodleian Library, Rawlinson C 641 (*SC* 12487).
2 C12b–13.
3 [λ] [γ] (1) Fol. 13v contains two proverbs in English: *Si stille suge fret þere grunniende mete* and *On dai bringd þet al ier ne mai* in an anonymous collection which occupies fols. 13v–18r.
   (2) Fols. 32r, 33r, 34v, 40v six interlinear glosses to *Instituta Cnuti*.
4 Ker 348. Proverbs edited: E. Stengel, 'Die beiden Sammlungen altfranzösischer Sprichwörter in der Oxforder Handschrift Rawlinson C 641', *Zeitschrift für französische Sprache und Literatur* 21 (1899), 1–21. Thence Max Förster, 'Frühmittelenglische Sprichwörter' *EStn* 31 (1902), 1–20 (16). For the second proverb see *IMEV Suppl* 2668.5 where it is wrongly attributed to Bodley, Digby 53.
5 Ker (pp. 426–27) indicates that the first proverb also appears in Bodley, Digby 53, fol. 53 — untraced.
6 Ker (p. 427) says that the "prickly" script of fols. 7v–10 and the close relationship of the texts (including *Instituta Cnuti*) to those in the *Textus Roffensis* suggest Kentish provenance.
7 The hands of the proverbs and glosses are different from each other but in each case are identical with the hand of the surrounding script.

1 Oxford, Bodleian Library, Rawlinson G 18 (*SC* 14751).
2 C13b.
3 [λ] Latin Psalter, etc. On fol. 102 is a French poem and on fols. 105v–106r a ten-line poem in English beg. *Worldes blis ne last no prowe*.
4 CB Reg i 107. Wells XIII.31 (cf. Wells *Suppl* 1, p. 986). *IMEV* 4223. CB 13 46B.
5 This poem also appears in Bodley, Digby 86 item (15) and BL Arundel 248 item (3).
6 Ker *Med Lib*, p. 15 rejects the MS as having belonged to the Abbey of Burnham, Bucks.
7 English in one hand.
8 Language looks to be western.

1 Oxford, Bodleian Library, Rawlinson G 22 (*SC* 14755).
2 C13a2 (*ca.* 1225, *OBMEV* and CB13; 1230–1240, D&H).
3 [λ] Latin Psalter written *ca.* 1200. A flyleaf (fol. 1v) of the first half of C13 contains parts of two French songs and seven lines of an English lyric, with music, beg. *[M]irie it is while sumer ilast*.
4 Wells XIII.4. *IMEV* 2163. CB13 7. *OBMEV* 3. D&W XXV. BSD VIII B. D&H, p. 121.
6 In D&H, E.W.B. Nicholson is stated to have suggested that the main MS may have belonged to Thorney Abbey, N Cambs; but this ascription is rejected by Ker *Med Lib*, p. 189.
7 English in one hand.
8 The poem has *p* beside *w* for /w/. Its forms suggest a NE Midland provenance. The word *oc* "but" appears in line 3. Cf. E.G. Stanley, 'Early Middle English "Oc" = "but, and"' in *Five Hundred Years of Words and Sounds: a Festschrift for Eric Dobson*, ed. E.G. Stanley and Douglas Gray (Woodbridge, 1983), pp. 144–50.

1 Oxford, Bodleian Library, Rawlinson G 57 and G 111 (*SC* 14788 and 14836).
2 C12a2–b1.
3 [γ] The two MSS originally constituted a single codex. There are OE glosses to the following texts:
  (1) G 57, fols. 1r–5v *Disticha Catonis*;
  (2) G 57, fols. 6r–27r *Ilias Latina*;
  (3) G 111, fols. 1r–16r *Fabulae* of Avianus.
4 Wells X.18. Hunt *Teaching* 1, p. 67. Edited: M. Förster and A.S. Napier, 'Englische Cato und Ilias-glossen des 12. Jahrhunderts', *Archiv* 117 (1906), 17–28 and A.S. Napier, *Old English Glosses* (Oxford, 1900), no. 28.

1 Oxford, Bodleian Library, Rawlinson G 96 (*SC* 15567).
2 C13b.
3 [γ] Vernacular glosses (mainly French but some English) in the following Latin works:
  (1) pp. 1–90 John of Garland's *Unum Omnium*;
  (2) pp. 91–130 John of Garland's revision of the *Doctrinale* of Alexander of Villa Dei;
  (3) pp. 154–76 John of Garland's *Morale Scolarium*;
  (4) p. 201 seq. Horace's *Epistolae*.
4 Vernacular glosses edited:
  (1) Tony Hunt, 'Les gloses en langue vulgaire dans les mss de l'*Unum omnium* de Jean de Garlande', *Revue de linguistique romane* 43 (1979), 162–78;
  (2) Tony Hunt, 'Vernacular glosses in medieval manuscripts', *Cultura Neo-Latina* 39 (1979), 9–37 (31);
  (3) and (4) Hunt *Teaching* 1, pp. 63 and 151.

1 Oxford, Bodleian Library, Rawlinson G 99 (*SC* 15462).
2 C13.
3 [γ] Grammatical texts in Latin including:
  (1) fols. 138r–149v Alexander Neckham's *De Nominibus Utensilium*;
  (2) fols. 150r–155v Adam of Petit Pont's *De Utensilibus;*
  (3) fols. 156r–162v John of Garland's *Dictionarius*.
All three texts contain vernacular glosses, mostly French but some English.
4 Contents listed Hunt *Teaching* 1, p. 167. Vernacular glosses edited:
  (1) Tony Hunt, 'Les gloses en langue vulgaire dans les mss du *De Nominibus Utensilium* d'Alexandre Nequam', *Revue de linguistique romane* 43 (1979), 235–62 (239–56) (Hunt's MS R);
  (2) Hunt *Teaching* 2, pp. 37–52 (Hunt's MS O);
  (3) Tony Hunt, 'Vernacular glosses in medieval manuscripts', *Cultura Neo-Latina* 39 (1979), 9–37 (16–20).

1 Oxford, Bodleian Library, Rawlinson G 111. See Rawlinson G 57 above.

1 Oxford, Bodleian Library, Rawlinson poet. 241 (*SC* 14732).
2 C13b.
3 [λ] MS contains French religious poems and sermons and Latin sermons. On p. 184, in the French version of Edmund Riche's *Speculum Ecclesie*, appears the usual English quatrain *Nou goth sonne vnder wode / me rewez marie þi faire rode. / Nou goth sonne vder tre / me rewez þi sone and ike þe.*
4 CB Reg i 107. Wells *Suppl* 1, p. 988 (XIII.127a). *IMEV* 2320/A4. Cf. CB13 1 printed from Bodley, Selden Supra 74.
5 For other versions of this text with the English quatrain see the Index of Texts in French.
7 English in one hand.

1 Oxford, Bodleian Library, Selden Supra 74 (3462).
2 C13b2–14a1 (*ca.* 1275–1300, *OBMEV*).
3 [γ] MS contains French and Latin texts; English appears as follows.
  (1) Fol. 1 a fragment (the latter part) of *Le Tretiz* of Walter of Bibbesworth with ME glosses.
  (2) Fols. 44r–59v the French version of Edmund Riche's *Speculum Ecclesie* containing on fol. 55v, the usual English quatrain *Nou goth sonne vnder wod / me reweth marie þi faire Rode / Nou goþ sonne vnder tre / me reweþ marie þi sone and þe.*
4 (1) For variants from this MS see Annie Owen, *Le Traité de Walter de Bibbesworth sur la langue française* (Paris, 1929; repr. Geneva, 1977). Corrections to this edition may be found in W. Rothwell, 'A mis-judged author and a mis-used text: Walter de Bibbesworth and his "Tretiz"', *MLR* 77 (1982), 282–93.
  (2) CB Reg i 45. Wells *Suppl* 1, p. 988 (XIII.127a). *IMEV* 2320/A3. CB13 1. *OBMEV* 269. BSD VIII S.
5 For other versions of both these texts, including the English content, see the Index of Texts in French.
7 English in one hand.

1 Oxford, Bodleian Library, Tanner 169* (*SC* 9995).
2 C13b1.
3 [λ] Psalterium, etc. On p. 175 is a version (with music) of *Stabat iuxta Christi crucem* beg. imperfectly *stod ho þere neh / þat leueli leor wid spald ischent.*
4 CB Reg i 96. Wells XIII.129. *IMEV Suppl* *3216.5 (*olim IMEV* *52). CB13 4. D&H, pp. 146–52. Murakami, pp. 109–110, no. 43. Watson *Ox Lib* 1, pp. 116–17 dates the main part of the MS 1192–1193.
5 For other MSS containing this verse see the Index of Middle English Texts A: Titles.
6 The text occupies an originally separate single leaf written at St Werburgh's Abbey, Chester. Ker *Med Lib*, p. 50.
7 English in one hand. CB13, p. 167 says that the hand is of the third quarter of C13. Napier thought the language not later than 1250.
8 *þ* and *w* are both used. According to Napier the original poem was probably written in a northern dialect; but the text as we have it is probably NW Midland and so consonant with a Chester origin.

1 Oxford, Bodleian Library, Wood empt 1 (*SC* 8589).
2 *C14a2 (1340–1344, Watson *Ox Lib* 1, p. 117).
3 [δ] Glastonbury Cartulary 'Secretum Abbatis'. English bounds to charters on fols. 67v, 149v, 169r, 171r, 177r, 178v–179r, 181v, 182v–183v, 185r, 190v–191v, 201r–v, 206v–207r, 208r–v, 212r–v, 218r–v, 223v, 224r, 228r–229r, 234r–235r, 238r, 239r–v, 240v–241r, 242r, 245r–v.
4 Davis 435. Sawyer as follows: S 626 (B 920, K 438 and vi 236); S 270a (B 300, K 178 and vi 227); S 247 (2 copies see below) (B 112, K 49); S 509 (B 816, K 406 and vi 232); S 247 (second copy, see above); S 481 (B 776, K 393 and vi 231–32); S 462 (B 749, K 383 and vi 229–30); S 292 (B 438, K 253 and vi 227); S 236 (K 20 and vi 225); S 743 (B 1188, K 525 and vi 242); S 791 (B 1294, K 577); S 251 (B 143, K 74 and vi 226); S 721 (B 1104, K 505 and vi 236); S 498 (B 799); S 793 (B 1291); S 371 (B 606, K338 without bounds); S 431 (B 709); S 442 (B 728, K 372); S 764 (B 1214, K 545); S 474 (B 768, K 389 and vi 230–31); S 555 (B 889); S 347 (B 564, K 319 and vi 227–28); S 513 (B 817); S 747 (B 1196, K 537); S 541 (B 867, K 419 and vi 233); S 504 (B 800, K 398 and vi 232); S 472 (B 750, K 381 and vi 228–29); S 473 (B 751, K 382 and vi 229); S 466 (B 752, K 384 and vi 230); S 399 (B 664); S 341 (B 886); S 568 (B 904, K 434 and vi 235–36); S 524 (B 828, K 415 and vi 232–33). AM also notes bounds in B 472, K 1050 (which Sawyer 303 says is Latin).
5 Fols. 20–263 are said by Davis to be a copy of Longleat 39 (see Private: Marquess of Bath).

6 *Ex libris* inscription associates the MS with Glastonbury Abbey, Somerset. Ker *Med Lib*, p. 91.
8 Language is strongly ME.

1 Oxford, Bodleian Library, Wood empt 5 (*SC* 8593).
2 *C13.
3 [δ] Malmesbury Cartulary. Five lines of English on fol. 27r.
4 Davis 641. Sawyer 322, but these five lines of English not recorded by Sawyer. Sawyer 862 (fols. 47v–49r) claims to have English bounds but this MS in fact lacks the bounds.
6 MS from Malmesbury, Wilts. Ker *Med Lib*, p. 128.
7 English in one hand.

1 Oxford, Christ Church, Chapter Library, Eynsham Cartulary; Kitchin's Catalogue, no. 341.
2 *C12b2 (1196 or 1197, Watson).
3 [δ] Copies of charters relating to Eynsham; English on fols. 7r–10v, 17v.
4 Davis 399. Sawyer 911 and 1478 (Rob 115). Pelteret 41. Edited: H.E. Salter, *The Cartulary of the Abbey of Eynsham*, 2 vols. Oxford Historical Society 49, 51 (1907, 1908). Facsimile of two openings in Watson *Ox Lib* 2, pl. 92.
6 Eynsham, Oxon.

1 Oxford, Christ Church, Chapter Library, 'St Frideswide's Cartulary'.
2 *C15.
3 [δ] P. 7 copy of a writ of King Æthelred to St Frideswide's Abbey, Oxford; confirmation of land in Bucks and Oxon. Latin with English bounds.
4 Davis 740. Sawyer 909. Edited: S.R. Wigram, *The Cartulary of the Monastery of St Frideswide at Oxford*, Oxford Historical Society 28 (1895) and J. Parker, *The Early History of Oxford*, Oxford Historical Society (1885), pp. 320–22.
6 Oxford.

1 Oxford City Archives, Town Hall, St Aldates, H 29.
2 C13b1 (1258).
3 [δ] The Oxford redaction of the Proclamation of Henry III of 18 October 1258.
4 Edited: W.W. Skeat, 'The Oxford MS. of the only English proclamation of Henry III, etc.' *TPS* (1880–1881) Appendix vi, 171–77; O. Ogle, *Royal Letters Addressed to Oxford* (1892), p. 12.
5 Cf. PRO Patent Rolls 43 Henry III, m. 15.40 for the Huntingdon redaction.
6 Oxford.
7 One hand.

1 Oxford, Corpus Christi College 59.
2 C13b2.
3 [λ] MS of Alanus de Insulis, etc. contains three poems in English, unique to this MS.
  (1) Fol. 66r–v a prayer based on the *Pater Noster* beg. *Hit bilimpeȝ forte speke*.
  (2) Fol. 113v a hymn to the BV beg. *Edi beo þu heuene quene*.
  (3) Fol. 116v a prayer to the BV beg. *Moder milde flur of alle*.
  On fol. 3r appears a five-line rhymed macaronic inscription beg. *Rex regum riche kink*.
4 CB Reg i 139.
  (1) Wells VI.13 (wrongly cited as Cambridge, Corpus Christi 54, D, 5; corrected in Wells *Suppl* 1). *IMEV* 1617. CB13 59. Probably composed after 1265 (CB13, p. 213). The text of this poem is written in ink over an original written with a plummet. Some of the underlay is still visible. The ink text and the underlying variants are printed by Morris *OEH* 2, pp. 258–59. (This MS is labelled by Morris as Corpus Christi College MS 54, D.5.14.)

(2) Wells XIII.193. *IMEV* 708. CB13 60. *OBMEV* 22. Morris *OEH* 2, pp. 255–57. See also D&H, p. 166, where Dobson suggests it was originally NE Midland. Dobson prints the last three stanzas (lines 41–64) separately on p. 172.
(3) Wells XIII.194. *IMEV* 2220. CB13 61. Morris *OEH* 2, pp. 257–58.
For the inscription on fol. 3r see Wells *Suppl* 4, p. 1280 (XIII.25b). *IMEV* 2815.
6 C. Brown, 'A thirteenth-century manuscript from Llanthony Priory', *Speculum* 3 (1928), 587–95 presents evidence that the volume was compiled at Lanthony Priory, Gloucs, perhaps by the master of the grammar school there. See also Ker *Med Lib*, p. 112. The inscription on fol. 3r links the book with the family of Walding of the Forest of Dean, Herefords.
7 English almost certainly all in one hand, though variable.

1 Oxford, Corpus Christi College 62.
2 C13b2.
3 [γ] Fols. 1r–90v the *Graecismus* of Eberhard of Bethune containing marginal commentary (up to fol. 42v) and interlinear glosses (up to fol. 61v) many of which are in the vernacular, some English.
4 Vernacular glosses edited: Hunt *Teaching* 2, pp. 26–33 (Hunt's MS C). This is a corrected and expanded version of Tony Hunt, 'Vernacular glosses in medieval manuscripts', *Cultura Neo-Latina* 39 (1979), 9–37 (21–27). See Hunt *Teaching* 1, p. 97 fn. 55; unfortunately this MS has been omitted from the index of MSS in Hunt *Teaching* 2.
7 According to Hunt the vernacular entries are in a hand of late C13.

1 Oxford, Corpus Christi College 121.
2 C13.
3 [γ] MS of grammatical texts in Latin including:
   (1) fols. 1r–45r the *Doctrinale* of Alexander of Villa Dei in John of Garland's revision;
   (2) fols. 48r–83v the *Graecismus* of Eberhard of Bethune;
   (3) fols. 84r–125v John of Garland's *Unum Omnium*.
All three texts contain vernacular glosses, French and English.
4 Vernacular glosses edited:
   (1) and (2) Tony Hunt, 'Vernacular glosses in medieval manuscripts', *Cultura Neo-Latina* 39 (1979), 9–37 (27–30);
   (3) Tony Hunt, 'Les gloses en langue vulgaire dans les mss de l'*Unum Omnium* de Jean de Garlande', *Revue de linguistique romane* 43 (1979), 162–78 (174–78).

1 Oxford, Corpus Christi College 135.
2 C13.
3 [γ] A volume of medicinal and herbal recipes mostly of C15 but containing on fols. 28r–52v a C13 copy of a medical treatise in Latin with vernacular glosses both French and English. Also, fols. 53v–54r and 54v–55r, recipes with vernacular glosses.
4 See Hunt *Teaching* 1, pp. 50–51 where the vernacular glosses are printed. For the C15 material see *IMEP* VIII, pp. 20 and 128.
6 The recipes contain the names Will. de Deyncourt and Robert de Leham (Hunt *Teaching* 1, p. 51).
7 According to Hunt, one C13 hand is responsible for the glosses on fols. 28r–52v and two others of C13b write fols. 53v–54r and 54v–55r.

1 Oxford, Corpus Christi College 154.
2 C13a2–b1.
3 [λ] Latin MS containing on fols. 375v–385v the *Quadrilogus* of depositions concerning the life of St Edmund by four members of his *familia*. On fol. 384v the archbishop's last words are quoted in English: *Men seith game god en wombe; ac ich segge game gos en herte.*

4 Edited: Lawrence *St Edmund*, p. 201. See also Wilfrid Wallace, *St Edmund of Canterbury* (London, 1893), p. 2.
5 The material in this text, of which this MS is the only surviving version, were used in various different accounts of the *Life of St Edmund*. See Lawrence *St Edmund*, p. 9 and cf. the MSS of the different versions listed in the Index of Texts in Latin.
6 Fragments of charters and manorial accounts on the end papers show that the MS was owned by the Augustinian priory of Lanthony by Goucester. Ker *Med Lib*, p. 112.

1 Oxford, Jesus College 26.

2 C12a2–b1 (s. xii med., Ker).
3 [γ] Copy of the *Panormia* of Ivo of Chartres. Fol. 170v contains a table in Latin (with French and English annotations) of the degrees of consanguinity within which marriage is forbidden. English is as follows: *Vader And moder / Suster And broder / Braða cild / hiberna bearn / Isibba child / Maglingas / Siblingas*.
4 Ker 355. Hunt *Teaching* 1, p. 46. Cf. Watson *Ox Lib* 1, p. 132.
6 MS probably from Cirencester, Gloucs. Ker *Med Lib*, p. 52.
7 English in one hand.

1 Oxford, Jesus College 29, part II.

2 C13b2 (See Anna C. Paues, 'A newly discovered manuscript of the *Poema Morale*', *Anglia* 30 (1907), 217–37 (222)).
3 [λ] Two MSS have been bound together to form one. The first is C15 paper and vellum containing a Latin chronicle of the Kings of England 900–1445. The second (part II) has 114 fols. Fols. 144r–195r, 198r–200v contain 27 pieces in ME mostly in verse.
(1) Fols. 144r–155r (*olim* 217r–228r) *The Passion of Our Lord Jesus Christ* beg. *Iherep nv one lutele tale*.
(2) Fols. 156r–168v (229r–241v) *The Owl and the Nightingale* beg *Ich wes in one sumere dale*.
(3) Fols. 169r–174v (242r–247v) *Poema Morale* beg. *ICh am eldre þan ich wes a winter and ek on lore*.
(4) Fols. 175r–178v (248r–251v) *Sinners Beware* or *The Sayings of St Bede* beg. *Þeos holy gostes myhte*.
(5) Fols. 178v–179v (251v–252v) *The Woman of Samaria* beg. *Þo ihu crist an eorþe was*.
(6) Fol. 179v (252v) lyric on the curse of wealth beg. *Weole þu art a waried þing*.
(7) Fols. 179v–180v (252v–253v) *Death's Wither-Clench* or *Long Life* beg. *Mon may longe lyues wene*.
(8) Fol. 180v (253v) *An Orison to Our Lady* beg. *ON hire is al my lif ilong* (ends imperfectly).
(9) Fol. 181r (254r) the end of item (19) below — *A Song of the Annunciaton*.
(10) Fol. 181r–v (254r–v) *The Five Blisses* beg. *Leuedy for þare blisse*.
(11) Fols. 181v–182r (254v–255r) lyric against simony beg. *Hwon holy chireche is vnder uote*.
(12) Fol. 182r–v (255r–v) *Doomsday* beg. *Hwenne ich þenche of domes-day*.
(13) Fols. 182v–184v (255v–257v) *The Latemest Day* beg. *Iherep of one þinge*.
(14) Fol. 184v (257v) *The Ten Abuses* beg. *Hwan þu sixst vnleode king*.
(15) Fol. 185r–v (258r–v) *A lutel soth sermun* beg. *Herkneþ alle gode men*.
(16) Fol. 185v (258v) *Antiphon* of St Thomas the Martyr beg. *Haly thomas of heoueriche*.
(17) Fols. 185v–187r (258v–260r) lyric beg. *Hwi ne serue we Crist*.
(18) Fols. 187r–188v (260r–261v) Friar Thomas de Hales *Love Ron* beg. *A Mayde cristes me bit yorne*.
(19) Fol. 188v (261v) *Song of the Annunciation* beg. *FRom heouene in to eorþe* (ends fol. 181r).

(20) Fol. 189r (262r) a fragment on Doomsday beg. (imperfectly) *Nauep my saule bute fur and ys.*
(21) Fol. 189r (262r) *Signs of Death* beg. *[H]wenne þin heou blokeþ.*
(22) Fol. 189r (262r) *Three Sorrowful Tidings* beg. *yche day me cumeþ tydinges þreo.*
(23) Fols. 189r–192r (262r–) *The Proverbs of Alfred* beg. *At seuorde sete þeynes monie.*
(24) Fols. 192r–193r *An Orison of Our Lord* beg. *Louerd crist iche þe grete.*
(25) Fols. 193r–194r Homily on *Soþe Luue* beg. *Þeo soþe luue among vs beo.*
(26) Fols. 194r–195r Prose on the shires and hundreds of England beg. *ANgle lond is eyhte hundred myle long.*
(Fols. 195v–198r French — *de Tobye.*)
(27) Fols. 198r–200v *The XI Pains of Hell* beg. *VNsely gost hwat dostu here.*
(Fols. 201r–257v (end) French — *The Seven Sleepers, St Josaphat, Le Petit Plet.*)

4 CB Reg i 144–45. All English pieces apart from *The Owl and the Nightingale* edited Morris *OE Misc*, pp. 37–191.
(1) Wells VIII.37. Severs 2 IV.33. *IMEV* 1441.
(2) Wells IX.8. Hartung 3 VII.45. *IMEV* and *IMEV Suppl* 1384. Hall i XX, ii 553–79. *OBMEV* 5 and 277. Edited (all under the title *The Owl and the Nightingale*): J.E. Wells (Boston and London, 1907); J.W.H. Atkins (Cambridge, 1922); J.H.G. Grattan and G.F.H. Sykes, EETS ES 119 (1935).
(3) Wells VII.25. *IMEV* 1272. See also Hill 1977, pp. 97 and 110.
(4) Wells VII.31. Hartung 3 VII.18(i). *IMEV* 3607.
(5) Wells VIII.35. Severs 2 IV.44. *IMEV* 3704.
(6) Wells VII.45. *IMEV* 3873. CB13 40.
(7) Wells VII.46. *IMEV* 2070. Hall i VII, ii 308–12. D&H, p. 122 seq.
(8) Wells XIII.201. *IMEV* 2687. D&H, p. 130 seq.
(9) see item (19) below.
(10) Wells XIII.211. *IMEV* 1833. CB13 41.
(11) Wells IV.28. Hartung 5 XIII.96. *IMEV* 4085.
(12) Wells VII.32. Hartung 3 VII.18(g). *IMEV* 3967.
(13) Wells VII.36. Hartung 3 VII.18(h). See *IMEV* 3517 and CB13 29 (notes).
(14) Wells VII.12. *IMEV* 4051.
(15) Wells V.3. *IMEV* 1091. *OBMEV* 7.
(16) Wells XIII.29. *IMEV* 1233. CB13 42.
(17) Wells VII.33. *IMEV* 4162.
(18) Wells XIII.173. *IMEV* 66. CB13 43. D&W XX. *OBMEV* 8 (two stanzas only).
(19) Wells XIII.43. *IMEV* 877.
(20) Wells XIII.160. *IMEV Suppl* *2284.5 (*olim IMEV* *44).
(21) Wells VII.27. *IMEV* 4047. CB13 71 (notes).
(22) Wells VII.37. *IMEV* 695. CB13 11B.
(23) Wells VII.5. *IMEV* 433. Hall i VI, ii 285–308. D&W XIV. *OBMEV* 6 (extract). Edited: Arngart *P of A*; see especially vol. 1, pp. 7 seq. and 127–130; vol. 2, pp. 35–38. For contents in general see p. 35. Separate text of J printed vol. 2, pp. 135–150. Cf. also AM, '*The Proverbs of Alfred*: notes on the possible dialectal value of the four versions' (1986) unpubl.
(24) Wells XIII.141. *IMEV* 1948.
(25) Wells XIII.51. *IMEV* 3474.
(26) Wells X.27. Hartung 7 XIX.1. *IPMEP* 163. *IMEP* VIII, p. 38.
(27) Wells V.79. Severs 2 V.320. *IMEV* 3828.
Facsimile of *The Owl and the Nightingale*, ed. N.R. Ker, EETS OS 251 (1963 for 1962), contents listed pp. ix–x.

5 Much of the contents, including *The Owl and the Nightingale*, are also found in BL Cotton Caligula A ix (see CB13, p. xxiii seq.). *Poema Morale* (item (3)) survives in seven copies for which see the Index of Middle English Texts A: Titles, where MSS containing short quotations from the text are also listed. *The Proverbs of Alfred* (item

(23)) survives in four main versions (including the fragments in BL Cotton Galba A xix). These and other shared texts are also to be found in the Indexes.
6 For associations with John of Guildford, see C. Sisam, 'The broken leaf in MS. Jesus College, Oxford 29', *RES* NS 5 (1954), 337–43. Cf. *IMEV Suppl* 2128.5.
7 One hand throughout, for which see Ker, EETS OS 251, pp. xvi–xvii.
8 The language is placed in *LALME* as LP 7440 in SE Herefords. It would fit equally well in NW Gloucs. For a preliminary study of the language of the seven surviving copies of the *Poema Morale* see Laing 'Versions'.

1 Oxford, Lincoln College, Lat. 31.

2 *C12a2–b1 (s. xii med., Ker).
3 [λ] Cædmon's Hymn and Bede's Death Song on the lower margins of fols. 83r and 112v of Bede's *Historia ecclesiastica* and Cuthbert's *Epistola de obitu Bedae*.
4 Ker 356. Edited: Dobbie 1937, pp. 39 and 89.
5 For other MSS containing Bede's Death Song see the Index of Old English Texts.
7 The two pieces are in two different hands.

1 Oxford, Magdalen College, Lat. 105.

2 *C12a2–b1 (s. xii med., Ker).
3 [λ] Cædmon's Hymn in the margin of fol. 99r of a copy of Bede's *Historia ecclesiastica*.
4 Ker 357. Edited: Dobbie 1937, p. 39
7 Written in the main hand of the MS.

1 Oxford, Merton College 120.

2 C13.
3 [λ] Latin except for a quatrain in English (*The Sinner's Lament*) on fol. 1v: *Ye ioye of vr hert es withen to wo / ye floures of vr gerland erne fallen yar fro / ye gamen of vr carollyng es turned to sorowe / wo es vs for synne may no man vs b[orowe]*.
4 CB Reg i 146. See Wells *Suppl* 1, p. 986 (XIII.52a). *IMEV* 3398. For similar lines cf. *IMEV* 221, 3311, 3351 and 3397.
7 English in one hand.
8 Possibly Lincs language.

1 Oxford, Merton College 248.

2 C14a.
3 [λ] Sermons collected by Bishop John Sheppey during his time at Oxford University (master in 1332). Lyrics, verse divisions and tags in English appear as follows.
  (1) Fol. 65v refrain and three couplets on repentance beg. *Turn þe to vre louerd*.
  (2) Fol. 66r quatrain beg. *þat ich haue ben longe about*.
  (3) Fol. 66r six couplets on the terror of Judgement beg. *streit shul be þe waies*.
  (4) Fol. 66v a prayer to Jesus beg. *Iesu þat al þis world haþ wroʒt*.
  (5) Fol. 74r three lines on 'Tres mira' beg. *þer was kast a ston*.
  (6) Fol. 74r four rhyming lines translating 'Vexilla regis' beg. *þe kinges baner bigan to sprede*.
  (7) Fol. 78v couplet beg. *Stones beþ harde*.
  (8) Fol. 120r six lines on *The Abuses of the Age* beg. *Wis man wranglere / Richeman robbere*.
  (9) Fol. 131r rhyming headings in a sermon on the failings of women beg. *Swynes halle / fendes falle*.
  (10) Fol. 131r three lines on true love beg. *Trewe loue is a lawe*.
  (11) Fol. 131v three rhyming lines in a Latin/English sermon beg. *A war wys lokere*.
  (12) Fol. 132r debate between the heart and the eye beg. *þou vs ast shend þoru þi fol loking*.
  (13) Fol. 132v seven hindrances to love beg. *þe fol uise kakalere*.
  (14) Fol. 132v two short couplets beg. *þe loren is founden*.
  (15) Fol. 133r two long lines on 'voluptas carnis' beg. *þi lust þat lasteþ but a wile*.

(16) Fol. 134v couplet beg. *Who so is stef aʒens is fo.*
(17) Fol. 135r division in Latin followed by English beg. *Falsehede of the world.*
(18) Fol. 139v eight long lines on how Christ shall come beg. *I sayh hym wiþ fless al bi-sprad.*
(19) Fol. 139v four long lines in a Latin homily beg. *I come vram þe wedlok.*
(20) Fol. 139v sixteen lines on a Latin sermon based on the vision of the Four Horses of the Apocalypse and beg. *He rod vpon a whit hors.*
(21) Fol. 141v four couplets on the Harrowing of Hell beg. *An ernemorwe þe dayliʒt spryngeþ.*
(22) Fol. 146v four lines on the evils of the times beg. *Riʒtful dom is ouer cast.*
(23) Fol. 146v a couplet in a Latin sermon: *Ne bee þe day neuere so longe / euere comeþe euensong.*
(24) Fol. 146v three lines beg. *A gurdel of gile.*
(25) Fol. 148v twelve lines paraphrasing 'O gloriosa domina excelsa' beg. *Lefdy blisful of muchel miʒt.*
(26) Fol. 148v quotation in a Latin sermon *Ianekyn of Londone / Is loue is al myn etc.*
(27) Fol. 149r four monorhyming lines on the defilement of sin beg. *Now is my Robe y-ssape.*
(28) Fol. 166r Satan's reply to Adam and Eve beg. *In thys tre es alle hys myth.*
(29) Fol. 166r four lines in a Latin homily beg. *He sent me fro aboue.*
(30) Fol. 166r a four-line tag beg. *Wan we wor vnmyti.*
(31) Fol. 166v two quatrains on falsity beg. *Falsenesse and couetys er feris.*
(32) Fol. 166v two couplets on falsity beg. *falsenes I vnderstande.*
(33) Fol. 166v four monorhyming lines on cupidity beg. *I þinge al day.*
(34) Fol. 166v macaronic lines on the evils of the times beg. *lex lyis done ofuer.*
(35) Fol. 166v eight lines on the pains of hell beg. *Fyre & colde & teʒeghatyng.*
(36) Fol. 166v two couplets on the degeneracy of the times beg. *hallas men planys of litel trwthe.*
(37) Fol. 167r one quatrain on three sorrowful things beg. *Thre woys mosthe wyt thowth.*
(38) Fol. 167r three three-line stanzas beg. *My flesse þat wrothe was in mari blode.*
(39) Fol. 167r *Ave Maris Stella* beg. *Ayl be þow ster of se.*
(40) Fol. 167r one quatrain translating two Latin hexameters and beg. *If yow wise worʒe wille.*
(41) Fol. 167r six-line stanza paraphrasing 'Crux fidelis' and beg. *Steddefast crosse inmong alle oþer.*

4 CB Reg i 147–48. Wells *Suppl* 1, p. 975 (VII.21a).
(1) Wenzel 1974, no. 77.
(2) Wenzel 1974, no. 56.
(3) *IMEV* 3218.
(4) Wells *Suppl* 3, p. 1181 (XIII.222). *IMEV* 1749. CB14 35. Wenzel 1986, p. 98.
(5) *IMEV* 3549.
(6) *IMEV* 3403.
(7) *IMEV* 3216. Wenzel 1978, p.80.
(8) *IMEV* 4180. Wenzel 1986, pp. 179, 189 fn. 57.
(9) *IMEV Suppl* 3246.5.
(10) *IMEV* 3803.
(11) *IMEV Suppl* 103.5.
(12) Hartung 3 VII.28. *IMEV* 3699.
(13) *IMEV* 3355.
(14) Wenzel 1978, p. 77.
(15) Wenzel 1974, no. 73.
(16) *IMEV* 4130.
(17) Wenzel 1978, p. 78.
(18) Wells *Suppl* 3, p. 1182 (XIII.223). *IMEV* 1353. CB14 36.

(19) *IMEV* 1289. CB14 36.
(20) Wells *Suppl* 3, p. 1182 (XIII.224). *IMEV* 1143. CB14, p. 258.
(21) Wells *Suppl* 3, p. 1182 (XIII.225). *IMEV* 2684. CB14 37.
(22) *IMEV* 2829. Wenzel 1986, p. 175.
(23) *IMEV Suppl* 2284.8.
(24) BSD VIII O. Wenzel 1986, p. 224.
(25) Wells *Suppl* 3, p. 1182 (XIII.226). *IMEV* 1832. CB14 38.
(26) BSD VIII P. Wenzel 1986, p. 225.
(27) *IMEV* 2337.
(28) *IMEV* 1577.
(29) *IMEV* 1145.
(30) *IMEV* 4054.
(31) Wells *Suppl* 3, p. 1182 (XIII.227). *IMEV* 759. CB14 39.
(32) *IMEV* 760. CB14 39.
(33) *IMEV* 1373. CB14 39.
(34) *IMEV* 2787. CB14, p. 259.
(35) *IMEV* 797. Wenzel 1978, p. 70.
(36) Wells *Suppl* 2, p. 1064 (VII.14a). *IMEV* 2145. CB14 39. Wenzel 1986, p. 191.
(37) *IMEV* 3713.
(38) *IMEV* 2239.
(39) Wells *Suppl* 1, p. 991 (XIII.192) and Wells *Suppl* 3, p. 1182 (XIII.229). *IMEV Suppl* 1034.5 (*olim IMEV* 3887). CB14 41.
(40) Wenzel 1974, no. 28.
(41) Wells *Suppl* 3, p. 1182 (XIII.228). *IMEV* 3212. CB14 40.
The MS is discussed by H.G. Pfander, *The Popular Sermon of the Medieval Friar in England* (New York, 1937), pp. 49–51. Cf. AM *Havelok*, p. 39 and Laing *Thesis* 1, pp. 16–20. For a marginal jotting on fol. 150r beg. *þer was kast a ston þat no man myȝt lefte* see *IMEP* VIII, p. 52.
5 The ME in this MS is later in date than most of the other material listed here. The MS has been included because the northerly (S Lincs) language of the verses on fols. 166r–167r is of an earlier kind than appears for that area in *LALME*.
6 Bishop Sheppey was bp. of Rochester, Kent. Wenzel 1978: "A number of the sermons bear the names of Oxford preachers including several Dominicans and Franciscans".
7 CB Reg notes two hands, the second contributing material on fol 166r.
8 MLS places the language in Kent (*LALME* LP 5950). Despite the *LALME* entry, this does not refer to fols. 166r–167r, the language of which is different and probably belongs in S Lincs.

1 Oxford, New College 88.
2 C13b2 (*ca.* 1275–1300, *OBMEV*).
3 [λ] MS of Latin sermons containing four lyrics in English.
(1) Fol. 31r (32r) *Three Sorrowful Things* beg. *Wanne ich þenche þenges þre*.
(2) Fol. 179r (181r) appeal of Christ from the Cross based on *Respice in Faciem* and beg. *Man and wyman loket to me*.
(3) Fol. 179v (181v) a prayer of contrition beg. *Louerd þu clepedest me*.
(4) Fol. 488v (490v) *The Ten Commandments*.
Short quotations from ME lyrics appear on fols. 321r, 402v and 403v.
4 CB Reg i 148.
(1) Wells *Suppl* 1, p. 977 (VII.37). *IMEV* 3969. CB13 12A.
(2) Wells XIII.115. *IMEV* 2042. CB14 4.
(3) Wells *Suppl* 3, p. 1179 (XIII.137a). *IMEV* 1978. CB14 5. *OBMEV* 21.
(4) Wells *Suppl* 1, p. 969 (VI.15). Hartung 7 XX.42. *IMEV* 1129. CB13, pp. 181–82.
For the three short quotations see Wenzel 1986, pp. 178, 225 and 227.
5 Other versions of item (1) are found in BL Arundel 292 item (5) and London, Lambeth Palace Library 499 item (4). Items (2) and (3) are unique to this MS. For

numerous different adaptations of *The Ten Commandments* see the Index of Middle English Texts A: Titles and cf. Edinburgh, National Library of Scotland, Advocates' 18.7.21 (Grimestone's Commonplace Book), fol. 128v for which see Wilson *Grimestone*, p. 56, no. 217.
7 English in one hand.

1 Oxford, St John's College 190.
2 C13.
3 [λ] Theological miscellany in Latin and French. There are two English verses on fol. 232r.
   (1) Three couplets on remembering Christ's Passion beg. *þe munde of Cristes passion* and continuing *teres hit tollez / eches hit bollez*.
   (2) Quatrain on the separation at death beg. *Wanne frend schal fram frende go*.
4 Wenzel 1974, nos. 62 and 84. For variants of the first verse see *IMEV* 1977 and 3433.
5 For item (1) cf. Bodley, Ashmole 360, part VII item (1) and see under *teres tollet*, etc. in the Index of Middle English Texts B: Incipits.
6 *Ex libris* inscription associates MS with Abbey of St Peter, Westminster, Middx. Ker *Med Lib*, p. 197.

1 Oxford, St John's College 194.
2 *C13.
3 [δ] Gospel Book of C11 containing on a flyleaf (fol. 2v) copies of two writs of King Æthelred to Christ Church, Canterbury in Latin and English: grants of land in Kent.
4 Davis 180. Sawyer 1636.
6 MS from Christ Church, Canterbury, Kent. Ker *Med Lib*, p. 39.

1 Oxford, David Rogers Esq, c/o Bodleian Library: see Athelney Cartulary.

1 Paris, Archives nationales, LL 1156.
2 *C13.
3 [δ] Cartulary of St Denis, Paris. English bounds and writ on fols. 83–84, concerning land in Oxon.
4 Sawyer 1028 and 1105 (cf. Har 55).
6 Oxon.

1 Paris, Bibliothèque nationale, lat. 8846.
2 C12b.
3 [γ] Glosses in English to a Roman version of the Psalter.
4 Ker *Suppl* 419. Edited: H. Hargreaves and C. Clark, 'An unpublished Old English psalter-gloss fragment', *N&Q* 210 (1966), 443–46.
5 The text was copied directly or indirectly from Eadwine's Psalter: Cambridge, Trinity College 987 (R.17.1).

1 Pavia Biblioteca Universitaria 69.
2 C13b1 (*ca.* 1250).
3 [λ] Latin except for
   (1) fol. 41v (lower margin) *Pater Noster* in English beg. *Fader þat hart in heuene*;
   (2) fol. 64v (foot) some English words in a Latin *De Virtutibus et Viciis* ascribed to Grosseteste and concerning degrees of consanguinity.
4 (1) Wells *Suppl* 6, p. 1454 (VI.13). (Wells refers to Pavia Bibl. Univ. 68 rather than 69.) Hartung 7 XX.32. *IMEV* 2704. *IPMEP* 171. Edited: S. Harrison Thomson, 'A XIII century *Oure Fader* in a Pavia MS', *MLN* 49 (1934), 235–37.
   (2) Wells *Suppl* 6, p. 1459 (IX.2).
6 Contents connect the MS with Leicester and Lincoln.

7 Thomson: "Lord's Prayer, written in a neat small chancery hand probably closely contemporary with the text ... Two hands have been at work on its composition, the second certainly contemporary, to add a phrase or complete a line".

1 Private: Bath, Marquess of, Longleat 39.
2 *C14a2 (c.1338–40, Davis).
3 [δ] Glastonbury Cartulary. English, mostly bounds only, in writs on fols. 60v–61r, 134r–v, 153r, 155r, 160v–161v, 167r, 168r–v, 169v, 174r–v, 181r, 185r–186v, 188v–189r, 192v, 196r, 199r–v, 202r–203r, 204v–207r, 209r–v.
4 Davis 434. Sawyer as follows: S 783; S 626; S 270a; S 247; S 509; S 247; S 481; S 462; S 292; S 236; S 743; S 791; S 251; S 721; S 498; S 793; S 371 (B 606); S 431; S 442; S 764; S 474; S 555; S 347; S 513; S 747; S 541; S 504; S 472; S 473; S 466; S 399; S 341; S 568; S 524. Edited: Dom Aelred Watkin, *The Great Cartulary of Glastonbury*, Somerset Record Society 59, 63, 64 (1944–1956).
5 Sawyer (p. 64) says all these texts are copied in Bodley, Wood empt 1 from Longleat 39.
6 Glastonbury, Somerset.

1 Private: Blickling Hall, Norfolk 6864.
2 C13a1 (not before 1200, Ker *Suppl*).
3 [λ] *The Creed* (said by Ker to be *The Lord's Prayer*) in prose written in a blank space at the end of the last quire of a Latin MS containing Gregory's *Dialogues* (fol. 35r).
4 Ker *Suppl* 414. Ker *Med MSS* 2, p. 135. *IPMEP* 316. Wells VI.14. Hartung 7 XX.38. Edited: A.S. Napier, 'Odds and ends', *MLN* 4 (1889), p. 138 (col. 276).
6 Ker *Suppl*, p. 127: "The prominence of Osyth, Erkenwald and Mellitus in the litanies suggests an origin in the SE of England".
8 Napier: "Kentish dialect".

1 Private: Cardigan, Earl of, Sturmy House, Severnake Forest, Muchelney Cartulary.
2 *C13b.
3 [δ] English bounds following Latin charters relating to Muchelney Abbey and land in Somerset on fols. 1r–v, 6v, 63r–v.
4 Davis 685. Sawyer as follows: S 249, S 455, S 740, S 244, S 1570. Edited: E.H. Bates, *Two Cartularies of the Benedictine Abbeys of Muchelney and Athelney in the County of Somerset*, Somersetshire Record Society 14 (1899), pp. 35–36, 38, 48, 95–96, 99.
6 Muchelney Abbey, Somerset.

1 Private: Macclesfield, Earl of, Shirburn Castle (Watlington, Oxon), MS 24.9.9.
2 *C14b1 (after 1354).
3 [δ] Liber Abbatiae (= Liber de Hyda), chronicle of the New Minster, Winchester from 435–1023. Contains copies of 31 pre-Conquest charters, including nine written throughout in the vernacular, followed by translations into C14 English and into Latin. See fols. 8v–11r, 13v–17r, 18v–21r, 22r–25r, 29r–v, 31r–36v.
4 Davis 1051. Cf. Wells *Suppl* 1, p. 983 (X.65). Sawyer as follows: S 1507 (B 554, OE B 553, K 314); S 360 (B 596); S 365 (B 597); S 374 (B 604); S 379 (B 635); S 366 (B 598); S 418 (B 692); S 1509 (B 650, OE B 649, Rob 27); S 1491 (B 653, OE B 652, Whi 4); S 470 (B 748); S 1418 (B 805, OE B 804, Rob 28); S 1515 (B 913, OE B 912); S 526 (B 824); S 1419 (B 826, OE B 825, Rob 29); S 648 (B 1000); S 641 (B 988); S 1496 (B 990, OE B 989, Whi 6); S 660 (B 1045); S 1589 (B 1193, OE B 1192); S 842; S 845; S 865; S 1505 (OE Whi 12); S 869; S 877 (OE (part) Rob 63); S 1498 (OE Whi 10); S 1420 (OE Rob 70). Edited in its entirety: E. Edwards, *Liber Monasterii de Hyda*, RS 45 (1866). For a study of the language of the wills in this MS see Lowe *Thesis*, esp. pp. 144–56 and Lowe 'OE wills'. See also Matti Rissanen, 'Middle English translations of Old English charters in the *Liber Monasterii de Hyda*: a case of historical error analysis', in *Linguistics Across*

Historical and Geographical Boundaries, ed. D. Kastovsky and A. Szwedek, Trends in Linguistics: Studies and Monographs 32, 2 vols. (Berlin, 1986) 1, pp. 591–603. Microfilm in Bodley, MS. Film 184.
6 MS from Hyde Abbey, Winchester, Hants. Ker *Med Lib*, p. 104.
8 The C14 translations of the OE copied wills have been shown by Kathryn Lowe, ('OE wills') to be very inaccurate displaying the scribe's lack of familiarity with OE vocabulary. Their language appears in *LALME* as LP 550, Hants. The language of the OE wills is, Lowe argues, very little modified and is likely to be the result of accurate, though (judging by the ME translations) incompetent, transcription.

1 Rochester, Diocesan Registry, Liber Temporalium.
2 C14.
3 [δ] Later copies of documents in the *Textus Roffensis* (C12a); English bounds to documents on fols. 3v, 4v–6r, 7v–10v.
4 Davis 820. Sawyer as follows: S 1, S 327, S 321, S 35, S 514, S 864, S 1562, S 893, S 671, S 349, S 1456 (charter in English). Cf. A. Campbell, *The Charters of Rochester* (London, 1973).
6 Rochester, Kent.

1 Rouen, Bibliothèque d'Etude, Y 44 (1193).
2 *C13.
3 [δ] Fol. 26r–v English bounds to grant of Edward (1061) of Ottery St Mary, Devon to St Mary's, Rouen.
4 Sawyer 1033.
6 Devon.

1 Salisbury Cathedral Library 82.
2 C13b.
3 [λ] The Gospels of SS. Matthew, Luke and John in Latin with commentary and gloss. On a fly leaf, fol. 271v, is a copy of *The Lord's Prayer* in English beg. *Hure wader þat is in euene þyn oli name beyn olid.*
4 CB Reg i 449. Wells VI.13. Hartung 7 XX.32. *IMEV* 2710. *IPMEP* 171 (incipit p. 179). See E. Maunde Thompson, *Catalogue of the Manuscripts in the Cathedral Library of Salisbury* (London, 1880). Edited: E. Maunde Thompson, 'Scraps from Middle-English manuscripts', *EStn* 1 (1877), 215.
6 *Ex libris* inscription indicates that the MS is from Salisbury Cathedral, Wilts. Ker *Med Lib*, p. 174. On fol. 272 is a note of obligation, 'Tenebar Simoni Carnifici per omnia die Dominica ante Septuagesima in iij. s. ij. d.'
7 *LALME* LP 5390 but the form *good-* should be excluded since it belongs to a different Salisbury text. The source for this LP was E.M. Thompson's transcript which is incomplete and in places inaccurate. See M. Benskin, 'In reply to Dr Burton', *LSE* NS 22 (1991), 243–46.
8 Wells: "peculiar spelling due perhaps to an Anglo-Norman scribe". Notwithstanding, the language probably represents native Salisbury usage. It shares some otherwise unusual forms with Cambridge, Emmanuel College 27, q.v., which also has Salisbury connections.

1 Salisbury Cathedral Library 150.
2 C13 (probably of s. xiii, Ker).
3 [λ] MS contains continuous OE interlinear gloss (C11–C12) to the Psalms and Canticles. Fol. iv, an early flyleaf, contains on the verso two lines of English in a C13 hand: *mabbe þe d[.]uel þe habbe & bere to his owene neste & [.....] & [.]usse & [...]ppe & frete.*
4 Ker 379.
6 MS perhaps from Sherborne.
7 Ker, p. 450: "a large crude hand".

1 Shirburn Castle. See Private: Macclesfield, Earl of.

1 **Stratford-upon-Avon, Shakespeare Birthplace Library, Gregory Leiger-Book** (deposited by Major A.M.H. Gregory-Hood).
2 *C14.
3 [δ] Copy of a writ of King Edward in English (1043 x 1053) relating to Coventry.
4 Davis 275. Sawyer 1099. Edited: F.E. Harmer, 'A Bromfield and a Coventry writ of King Edward the Confessor' in *The Anglo-Saxons*, ed. P. Clemoes (1959), pp. 89–103.
6 Coventry, Warwicks.

1 **Troyes, Bibliothèque municipale 1380.**
2 C12–13.
3 [λ] In the Books of Solomon appear English versions of two proverbs.
 (1) Fol. 18r *Betere is æi mid uste þan oxæ mid ætire þan fliche mid chæste*, "Better an egg with charity than an ox with malice or a flitch with strife".
 (2) Fol. 93v *tunge breocþ boæn: þæoȝ / hæo nabbe suelf noan*, "Tongue breaks bones though she herself has none".
4 Edited: C.F.R. de Hamel, *Glossed Books of the late Bible and the Origin of the Paris Book Trade* (Woodbridge, 1984), p. 76 n. 72.

1 **Vienna, Nationalbibliothek 336.**
2 *C13.
3 [λ] A MS of *The Austrian Legendary* containing on fol. 235v Bede's Death Song in the text of Cuthbert's *Epistola de obitu Bedae*.
4 Murakami, pp. 101–102, no. 33. Edited: Dobbie 1937, p. 61.
5 For other MSS containing Bede's Death Song see the Index of Old English Texts.

1 **Wells, Dean and Chapter Muniments, Liber Albus I (*olim* Registrum I).**
2 *C13a2 (*ca.* 1240).
3 [δ] Fols. 2–64 General Cartulary with material of C11–C13. English on fols. 14r, 17v–18r.
4 Davis 1003. Sawyer as follows: S 1112 (Har 65, K 838); S 1116 (Har 69, K 839); S 1111 (Har 64, K 835); S 1163 (Har 71, K 976); S 1115 (Har 68, K 837); S 1241 (Har 72, K 918); S 1113 (Har 66, K 836); S 1240 (Har 70, K 917). Pelteret 57 (Har 72, K 918); and 29.
5 This MS is partly transcribed in BL Harley 6968 (C17).
6 Wells, Somerset.

1 **Wells, Dean and Chapter Muniments, Liber Albus II (*olim* Registrum III).**
2 *C14–C15.
3 [δ] General Cartulary containing copies of deeds and other material, C8–C15. English on fols. 21v–22r, 246v, 254r, 288v–90v.
4 Davis 1006. Sawyer as follows: S 1114 (cf. K 834, Har 67 from Lib. Fusc.); S 527 (B 821); S 709 (B 1116); S 579 (B 1023); S 380 (B 610). Pelteret 11 (edited: F.H. Dickinson, 'The Banwell Charters', *Proceedings of the Somersetshire Archaeological and Natural History Society* 23 (NS 3), part II (1877), 49–64) and Pelteret 56 (edited: Dickinson, 'The Sale of Combe', *Proceedings of the Somersetshire Archaeological and Natural History Society* 22 (NS 2), part II (1876), 106–13).
5 Fols. 1–87v are a direct copy of Liber Fuscus (Davis 1005), fols. 1–77.
6 Wells, Somerset.

1 **Wells, Dean and Chapter Muniments, Liber Fuscus (*olim* Registrum IV).**
2 *C14.
3 [δ] Fol. 14 copy of a writ of King Edward concerning the obligations of Bishop Giso.

4 Davis 1005. Sawyer 1114 (Har 67).
6 Wells, Somerset.

1 Winchester Cathedral, Dean and Chapter, 'St Swithun's Cartulary'.
2 *C13b–C14.
3 [δ] English relating to Winchester on fols. 6v no. 31, 136v no. 546, 138v no. 553.
4 Davis 1044. Sawyer 1153 (C13) and 804 (English only in bounds) (C14). Edited: A.W. Goodman, *Chartulary of Winchester Cathedral* (Winchester, 1923), pp. 14 and 235.
6 Winchester, Hants.

1 Winchester College 4.
2 C13b.
3 [λ] William of Canterbury's *Vita, Passio et Miracula S. Thomae Cantuariensis.* In book 1, chapter 11 of the *Miracula* appears in English *An Antiphon of St Thomas of Canterbury* beg. *Hali Thomas of hevenriche.*
4 CB13, p. 197. *IMEV* 1233. Wilson 1943, p. 51. Richter 1979, p. 65. Edited: J.C. Robertson, *Materials for the History of Thomas Becket* 1, RS 67 (1875), p. 151; MS described pp. xxx–xxxi.
5 Cf. Oxford, Jesus College 29 item (16).
6 A Winchester College book. Ker *Med Lib*, p. 202.

1 Wolfenbüttel, Herzog August Bibliothek, Helmstedt 1029.
2 C13b2–C14a1.
3 [λ] AID (pers. comm.) mentions short pieces of English on fols. 8r, 10r, 15r, 27v, 34r, 41r.
6 AID also notes: "On fol. 19v (after a reference to Robert Mayre myles of [?]) appears *iuxta Karlele* [= Carlisle, Cumbria]. On fol. 26r is a Latin exemplum about king Edward [I], and on 29r, added, a copy of a writ from Walter de Edny commissarius of the Bishop of St Andrews to Willian de Crale, capellanus of the same church, to cite William of Meldrom that he should appear before the commissary, in the parish church of the Trinity in St Andrews, on Friday next after the feast of St Valentine, to answer the prior and convent of St Andrews. No subject of suit mentioned. Given at St Andrews 12 Feb. 1368". The implication is that the MS had migrated from Cumbria to Fife by mid-C14.

1 Worcester Cathedral, Dean and Chapter Library B 1600a.
2 *C14.
3 [δ] Copy of a writ of King Edward in favour of the monk Ælfstan.
4 Sawyer 1157.
5 Cf. another version of the same: PRO Charter Rolls, 6 Edward II, no. 27 from which Harmer prints her no. 116.
6 Worcester.
7 One hand.

1 Worcester Cathedral, Dean and Chapter Library F 64.
2 C13b2 (*ca.* 1275–1300, *OBMEV*).
3 [λ] Latin MS containing on fol. 8r the English lines *Ne may cume to mi lef bute bi þe water / Wanne me lust slepen yanne moti wakie / Wnder is þat hi liuie.*
4 Wells *Suppl* 7, p. 1584 (XIII.7b). *IMEV* 1142. *OBMEV* 273. BSD VIII Q. Edited: B. Dickins, 'Two Worcester fragments of Middle English secular lyric', *LSE* 4 (1935), 44–46; repr. *LSE* 5 (1936), 36.
6 MS is from Worcester. Ker *Med Lib*, p. 211.
7 English in one hand. There is some confusion about the first word of this fragment. *Ne* has been misread as *He*. BSD corrects "MS He" to *I ne* and *OBMEV* corrects to *I*. The first letter is however quite clearly *N*, of the *H*-shaped kind usual at this date.

This can be verified by its reappearance (in the same hand) further down the folio in the Latin word *Nome*n. No emendation is therefore required.

1 Worcester Cathedral, Dean and Chapter Library F 174.
2 *C13a2 (Ker considers the date of at least some of the work of the tremulous hand to be within the second quarter of the thirteenth century. See Ker 'Date').
3 [λ] MS composed of sheets of different sizes most of which are incomplete having been cut up in C15 and pasted together for use as bindings. The MS was reconstituted in C19 but fol. 10 belongs between fols. 1 and 2.
  (1) Fols. 1r–63r Ælfric's *Grammar* and *Glossary*.
  (2) Fol. 63r, lines 14–28 short rhythmic prose text beg. [*S*]*anctus beda was iboren*.
  (3) Fols. 63v–66v fragments of an alliterative poem (Ker says rhythmic prose) on the "Body and Soul" theme, 349 lines in all.
4 Ker 398. Franzen 1991, pp. 70–71, 84–85 and 88–94.
  (1) Edited: Marilyn Sandidge Butler, 'An edition of the Early Middle English copy of Aelfric's "Grammar" and "Glossary" in Worcester Cathedral MS. F.174', Diss. Ph.D., Pennsylvania State University (1981), unpubl. Collated as W in Julius Zupitza, *Ælfrics Grammatik und Glossar, Sammlung englischer Denkmaler* 1 (Berlin, 1880; repr. with foreword by H. Gneuss, 1966). See also Franzen 1991, pp. 111–19, 128. Glossary printed: Wright-Wülcker, 538–52.
  (2) Wells IV.48. Hartung 5 XIII.79. *IMEV Suppl* 3074.3. Hall i IA, ii 223–28. D&W I.
  (3) CB Reg i 451. Wells IX.1. Hartung 3 VII.18(c). *IMEV Suppl* *2684.5 (*olim IMEV* *47). Hall i IB and IC; ii 228–40. Also edited: R. Buchholz, *Die Fragmente der Reden der Seele an dem Leichnam*, Erlanger Beiträge zur englischen Philologie vi (Erlangen, 1890). (This is an enlargement of an earlier edn. (Erlangen, 1889), by him); Douglas Moffat, *The Soul's Address to the Body: the Worcester Fragments* (East Lansing, 1987). See also Douglas Moffat, 'The recovery of Worcester Cathedral MS F.174', *N&Q* NS 32 (1985), 300–302.
5 For other MSS containing text in the same hand see Franzen 1991, Crawford 1928 and Ker *Med Lib*, p. 206 n. 3. Glosses in the Worcester tremulous hand appear in Ker nos. 23, 30, 41, 48, 67, 73, 178, 182, 225, 324, 328, 331, 332, 333, 338, 343. MSS containing a substantial number of EME glosses as well as Latin ones are: Cambridge, Corpus Christi College 198 and 391; Oxford, Bodleian Library, Hatton 76, 113, 114, 115, 116; Junius 121. On the tremulous hand see also Pope *Ælfric*, pp. 185–88; D. Bethurum, *The Homilies of Wulfstan* (Oxford, 1957), pp. 104–106 and W. Keller, *Die litterarischen Bestrebungen von Worcester in angelsächsischer Zeit*, Quellen und Forschungen 84 (1900). For other poems on the "Body and Soul" theme see under *Debate between the Body and Soul* in the Index of Middle English Texts A: Titles.
6 Written at Worcester. Ker *Med Lib*, p. 213.
7 MS all "in the backward-sloping 'tremulous' hand of the well-known Worcester glossator" (Ker, p. 467). This is the only extant MS in which the tremulous hand is the primary script and it here shows considerable variability. The state of the tremulous writing in all but fols. 1 and 10 of this MS is labelled "T" by Franzen.
8 Of item (1), Ker says, "The linguistic forms are consistently EME". Moffat, in his edition, considers the language of item (3) to represent neither literatim copying nor wholesale translating from the exemplar.

1 Worcester Cathedral, Dean and Chapter Library Q 29.
2 C12b2 (Atkins and Ker).
3 [λ] Theological miscellany in Latin. Fols. 130v–131v sermon in English on the Nativity which includes on fol. 130v a verse text in two couplets beg. *ȝare hit was isuteled*.
4 *MED Plan & Bibl Suppl*, p. 29. See E.G. Stanley, 'An inedited nativity sermon from Worcester', *English and Germanic Studies* 7 (1961), 53–79 (61–65). See also, Patrick Young's *Catalogus Librorum Manuscriptorum Bibliothecae Wigorniensis*, ed.

Sir Ivor Atkins and Neil R. Ker (1944), p. 59. For the couplet see *IMEV Suppl* 4273.3.
6 MS is from Worcester. Ker *Med Lib*, p. 213.

1 Worcester Cathedral, Dean and Chapter Library Q 46.
2 C13b2.
3 [λ] Latin MS containing two English lyrics on fol. 238r:
   (1) six triplets beg. *þeʒ þou habbe casteles & toures*;
   (2) ten lines beg. *Worldes blisse haue god day*.
4 Wenzel 1974, nos. 72 and 96 and Wenzel 1986, p. 181. Not listed in *IMEV* but cf. *IMEV* 3707 and *IMEV* 4220, 4221.
5 Note that Cambridge, Corpus Christi College 8, p. 547 has a song in three eight-line stanzas also beg. *Worldes blisce haue god day*. The two lyrics are, however, quite different, the Cambridge text being concerned with Christ's passion while that in this MS deals with the vanity of worldly possessions.
6 MS is from Worcester. Ker *Med Lib*, p. 214.

1 Worcester Cathedral, Dean and Chapter Library Q 50.
2 C13b2 (*ca.* 1275–1300, *OBMEV*).
3 [λ] [γ] On fol. 46r are ten lines of English verse beg. *Ne saltou neuer leuedi*. The first part of the MS, also C13, contains grammatical works by Adam de Petit Pont, Alexander Neckham and John of Garland. This part of the MS may once have formed a larger grammatical work with Worcester Cathedral Q 6. The texts contain some vernacular glosses but these are almost all French.
4 For a description of the MS see J.K. Foyer, rev. S.G. Hamilton, *Catalogue of Manuscripts preserved in the Chapter Library of Worcester Cathedral* (Oxford, 1906), pp. 132–34. Wells *Suppl* 7, p. 1584 (XIII.7c). *IMEV* and *IMEV Suppl* 2288. *OBMEV* 273. BSD VIII R. Edited: B. Dickins, 'Two Worcester fragments of Middle English secular lyric', *LSE* 4 (1935), 44–46; repr. *LSE* 5 (1936), 36–37. Also edited (more accurately) by C. Sisam, 'Ne saltou neuer leuedi', *N&Q* 210 (1965), 245–46 where she suggests that the verse represents snatches of three different ME lyrics. For vernacular glosses see Hunt *Teaching* 2, pp. 62, 119–22, 153–54.
6 MS is from Worcester. Ker *Med Lib*, p. 214. At the end of the verse is written in the same hand: "dixit Rob*ertu*s seynte Mary clericus".
7 English in one hand.

1 Worcester, Herefordshire and Worcestershire Record Office, BA 3814 (ref. 821), Liber Ruber (*olim* Liber Albus).
2 *C12b2–13a1 (*ca.* 1300).
3 [δ] Fol. 38v copy of a writ of King Edward in favour of bp. Wulfstan and St Mary's Minster.
4 Sawyer 1158 (Har 117). On this MS see Harmer, pp. 528–29.
6 Worcester.
7 English in one hand.
8 The language is strongly ME and contains some interesting forms.

1 York, Borthwick Institute, Magnum Registrum Album.
2 *C14.
3 [δ] Copies made in the time of Edward III of charters from the time of King Edgar to King William I. English is as follows.
   (1) Fol. 61r powers and laws of Thomas I, abp. of York.
   (2) Fol. 61v two writs of King Edward.
   (3) Fol. 62r–v two copies of a writ of William I.
Also English bounds to charters concerning lands in Yorks and Notts on fols. 56v–61v, 78r–v.
4 Davis 1087. Sawyer as follows: S 712 (B 1112, 1352, K 500 without bounds); S 716 (B 1113, 1353, K 504 without bounds); S 679 (B 1044, 1349); S 659 (B 1029, 1348); S 968 (K 749 without bounds); S 1159 (Har 118, K 893); S 1161 (Har 120);

S 968. Pelteret 16, 148. Edited: W. Farrer, *Early Yorkshire Charters*, 2 vols. (Edinburgh, 1914, 1915), nos. 6, 5, 3, 2, 8, 10, 12. Powers and laws of Thomas, edited: F. Liebermann, 'Drei nordhumbrische Urkunden um 1100', *Archiv* 111 (1903), 279–81.
6 York.

1 York Minster Library XVI.I.12.
2 C14a2–b1 (*ca.* 1350, *OBMEV*).
3 [λ] In an account of a lawsuit in 1331 as reported by Robert of Greystanes, a fourteenth-century historian of Durham, there appears on fol. 219v a quotation of four lines from a lament on the death of Lord Neville. The original song was probably composed *ca.* 1282, the year of the death of Robert de Neville.
4 Wells *Suppl* 7, p. 1568 (IV.29a). Hartung 5 XIII.14. Cf. *IMEV Suppl* 3857.5 (this MS not listed there). D&W XXII. *OBMEV* 276. Murakami, pp. 90–91, no. 22. Edited: James Raine, *Roberti de Greystanes Historia de Statu Ecclesiae Dunelmensis*, Surtees Society 9 (1839), p. 112.
5 BL Lansdowne 207 (fol. 434r) is a C17 transcript from the lost original in Durham Cathedral.
6 *Ex libris* inscription indicates the MS belonged to Durham Cathedral. Ker *Med Lib*, p. 76; Ker *Med Lib Suppl*, p. 34.
8 NME.

1 Zwettle (Lower Austria) MS 24.
2 *C13a.
3 [λ] A MS of *The Austrian Legendary* containing on fol. 183r Bede's Death Song in the text of Cuthbert's *Epistola de obitu Bedae*.
4 Murakami, pp. 101–102, no. 33. Edited: Dobbie 1937, p. 61.
5 For other MSS containing Bede's Death Song see the Index of Old English Texts.

INDEX OF MIDDLE ENGLISH TEXTS
A: TITLES

Texts are indexed by author, if cited; cross-references to titles have been given where they seemed desirable. Otherwise indexing is by text. Leading (in)definite articles are ignored. Under each entry are listed the manuscripts for which the particular text is cited in the *Catalogue*. When there is more than one item in Middle English listed for a given MS, the relevant item number is also supplied. Where a Middle English text is a translation from an original in Latin, the title is usually cited in Latin. This need not imply that a Latin version of the text is also present in the manuscript. Note that shared titles do not always indicate that the texts are the same; there are, for instance, several different realisations of the *Creed*, the *Pater Noster* and translations of Latin texts.

Abuses of the Age
    Cambridge, Trinity College 108 (B.3.29); BL Cotton Cleopatra C vi item (2); BL Harley 913 item (2); Oxford, Merton College 248 item (8)

Advice to Women
    BL Harley 2253 item (20)

Alfred. See (a) *Abuses of the Age*; (b) *Proverbs of Alfred*

Alysoun
    BL Harley 2253 item (9)

Ancrene Riwle
    Cambridge, Corpus Christi College 402; Cambridge, Gonville and Caius College 234/120; BL Cotton Cleopatra C vi; BL Cotton Nero A xiv item (1); BL Cotton Titus D xviii item (1); BL Royal 8 C i; Bodley, Eng. hist. a. 2, no II b (fragment)

Ancrene Wisse. See *Ancrene Riwle*

Angelus ad Virginem. (See also Index of Texts in Latin)
    BL Arundel 248 item (1)

Annot and John
    BL Harley 2253 item (8)

Antiphon of St Thomas of Canterbury. See St Thomas the Martyr, *Antiphon*

Assumpcion de nostre dame
    Cambridge University Library Gg.IV.27(2) item (3)

Autumn Song
    BL Harley 2253 item (34)

Ave Maria
    Cambridge, Emmanuel College 27 (I.2.6) item (5); Cambridge, Gonville and Caius College 52/29; Cambridge University Library Hh.VI.11 item (3); BL Arundel 57 items (3), (6), (7); BL Arundel 292 item (3); BL Cotton Cleopatra B vi item (3)

Ave Maris Stella
    Oxford, Merton College 248 item (39)

Ayenbite of Inwit. See Dan Michel of the Northgate

Bargain of Judas
    Cambridge, Trinity College 323 (B.14.39) item (29)

Benedictine Rule. See *Rule of St Benedict*

Bernard, sermon beg. *Quamdiu fuero*
    Cambridge, Trinity College 43 (B.1.45) (1); BL Cotton Cleopatra C vi item (4)

Bestiary
    BL Arundel 292 item (7)

Book of Penance, Prologue
    Göttingen University Library, MS Theol. 107r item (7)

Brut. See Laȝamon

Cambridge Prologue
    Cambridge University Library Mm.I.18

Candet Nudatum Pectus
   Cambridge, St John's College 15 (A.15) item (3);   Durham Cathedral, Dean and Chapter Library A.III.12;   BL Additional 11579 item (6);   Bodley 42 item (1);   Bodley, Digby 45;   Bodley, Digby 55 item (1);   Bodley, Rawlinson C 317

Christ on the Cross
   BL Harley 913 item (7)

Chronicle of the Brut
   BL Royal 12 C xii item (3)

Confiteor
   Cambridge, Emmanuel College 27 (I.2.6) item (7)

Creed. See also (a) *Lesse Crede*; (b) *Nicene Creed*
   Cambridge, Emmanuel College 27 (I.2.6) item (6);   Cambridge, Gonville and Caius College 52/29;   Göttingen University Library, MS Theol. 107r item (2);   BL Arundel 57 item (3);   BL Arundel 292 item (1);   BL Cotton Cleopatra B vi item (5);   BL Harley 3724 item (1);   Private, Blickling Hall, Norfolk 6864

Cursor Mundi
   Cambridge University Library Gg.IV.27(2) item (3) (part only);   Edinburgh, Royal College of Physicians MS of *Cursor Mundi* item (1);   Göttingen University Library, MS Theol. 107r item (1)

Dame Siriz
   Bodley, Digby 86 item (16)

Dan Michel of the Northgate, *Ayenbite of Inwit*
   BL Arundel 57 items (1), (2)

De clerico et puella
   BL Harley 2253 item (35)

Death's Wither-Clench. See *Long Life*

Debate between the Body and Soul
   Cambridge, Trinity College 323 (B.14.39) items (11), (26);   BL Harley 2253 item (2);   Bodley, Digby 86 item (18);   Bodley, Laud Misc. 108 item (4);   Cf. Bodley 343 (fragment) and Worcester Cathedral, Dean and Chapter Library F 174 item (3) (fragments)

Doomsday
   Cambridge, Trinity College 323 (B.14.39) item (35);   BL Cotton Caligula A ix, part II item (5);   Bodley, Digby 86 item (19);   Oxford, Jesus College 29, part II item (12)

Elde
   BL Harley 913 item (14)

Elegy on the Death of Edward I
   Cambridge University Library, Additional 4407, art. 19 item (1);   BL Harley 2253 item (23)

XI Pains of Hell
   Bodley, Digby 86 item (9);   Oxford, Jesus College 29, part II item (27)

Erthe upon Erthe
   BL Harley 913 item (17);   BL Harley 2253 item (4)

Estorie del Euangelie
   London, Dulwich College XXII

Execution of Sir Simon Fraser
   BL Harley 2253 item (5)

Fair Maid of Ribblesdale
   BL Harley 2253 item (14)

Fall and Passion
   BL Harley 913 item (8)

XV Signa ante Iudicium
   BL Harley 913 item (6);   Bodley, Add E.6 item (2);   Bodley, Digby 86 item (2)

XV Signs before Judgement. See *XV Signa ante Iudicium*

Five Blisses
   Oxford, Jesus College 29, part II item (10)

Five Evil Things. See *Abuses of the Age*

Five Joys of Our Lady, Song of. See *Five Joys of the Virgin*

Five Joys of the Virgin
   Göttingen University Library, MS Theol. 107r item (6);   BL Harley 2253 item (38)

Flemish Insurrection
   BL Harley 2253 item (24)

Floriz and Blauncheflur
   Cambridge University Library Gg.IV.27(2) item (1);   BL Cotton Vitellius D iii (fragments)

Follies of Fashion
  BL Harley 2253 item (6)

Fox and the Wolf
  Bodley, Digby 86 item (13)

Genesis and Exodus
  Cambridge, Corpus Christi College 444

Godric. See St Godric

God Ureison of Ure Lefdi
  BL Cotton Nero A xiv item (2)

Guy of Warwick
  Aberystwyth, National Library of Wales 572; BL Additional 14408

Harrowing of Hell
  BL Harley 2253 item (1); Bodley, Digby 86 item (1)

Havelok
  Cambridge University Library, Additional 4407, art. 19 item (2); Bodley, Laud Misc. 108 item (5)

Hending. See *Proverbs of Hending*

Hali Meiðhad
  BL Cotton Titus D xviii item (3); Bodley 34 item (4)

Homily for the anniversary of St Nicholas. See St Nicholas

Homily on *Soþe Luue*. See *Soþe Luue*

Honorius of Autun, *Elucidarius*, translation of
  BL Cotton Vespasian D xiv

Iacob and Iosep
  Bodley 652

Iesu Dulcis Memoria
  BL Harley 2253 items (25), (30); Bodley, Digby 86 item (10)

In Manus Tuas
  Cambridge, Emmanuel College 27 (I.2.6) item (11); Cambridge, Gonville and Caius College 52/29; BL Arundel 292 item (4); Bodley, Digby 86 item (22)

Infancy of Christ
  Bodley, Laud Misc. 108 item (1)

Interludium de Clerico et Puella
  BL Additional 23986

Katherine Group. See under separate entries, viz.: *Life of St Katherine, Life of St Margaret, Life of St Juliana, Hali Meiðhad, Sawles Warde*

Kildare, Michael, Hymn
  BL Harley 913 item (4)

King Athelstan, Middle English rhyming version of charter to Ripon Minster
  London, Public Record Office, DL 41/6/1

King Athelstan, Middle English rhyming version of charter to St John's, Beverley
  BL Additional 61901 item (1); BL Cotton Charter iv 18; BL Harley 560; BL Lansdowne 269

King Horn
  Cambridge University Library Gg.IV.27(2) item (2); BL Harley 2253 item (41); Bodley, Laud Misc. 108 item (6)

Labourers in the Vineyard
  BL Harley 2253 item (18)

Lambeth Homilies
  London, Lambeth Palace Library 487 item (1)

Land of Cokaygne
  BL Harley 913 item (1)

Langtoft, Pierre, *Chronicle*. English verses in
  Cambridge University Library Gg.I.1 item (2); BL Cotton Julius A v

Latemest Day
  Cambridge, Trinity College 323 (B.14.39) item (36); BL Cotton Caligula A ix, part II item (6); Bodley, Digby 86 item (20); Oxford, Jesus College 29, part II item (13)

Laȝamon's *Brut*
  BL Cotton Caligula A ix, part I; BL Cotton Otho C xiii

Lesse Crede
  BL Cotton Nero A xiv item (6)

Life of Christ
  Bodley, Laud Misc. 108 item (1)

160

Life of St Bridget
Nottingham University Library Mi Lm 7/1 (fragments)

Life of St Eustace
Bodley, Digby 86 item (3)

Life of St Juliana
BL Royal 17 A xxvii item (4); Bodley 34 item (3)

Life of St Katherine
BL Cotton Titus D xviii item (5); BL Royal 17 A xxvii item (2); Bodley 34 item (1)

Life of St Margaret
Cambridge, Trinity College 323 (B.14.39) item (2); BL Royal 17 A xxvii item (3); Bodley 34 item (2)

Litel Soth Sermun
BL Cotton Caligula A ix, part II item (8); Oxford, Jesus College 29, part II item (15)

Lofsong of Ure Lefdi. See *Oreisun of Seinte Marie*

Lofsong of Ure Louerde
BL Cotton Nero A xiv item (5)

Long Life
BL Additional 11579 item (8) (first stanza only); BL Arundel 57 item (2) (first stanza only); BL Cotton Caligula A ix, part II item (2); Maidstone Museum A.13 item (2); Bodley, Laud Misc. 471, part I (and part II quotation only); Oxford, Jesus College 29, part II item (7)

Lord Neville, lament on the death of
York Minster Library XVI.I.12

Lord's Prayer. See *Pater Noster*

Love Song of Our Lady
BL Egerton 613 item (4)

Lover's Complaint
BL Harley 2253 item (10)

Lullaby
BL Harley 913 item (10)

Magi and Herod, story of
Cambridge, Trinity College 323 (B.14.39) item (30)

Man in the Moon
BL Harley 2253 item (44)

Marina
BL Harley 2253 item (12)

Maximian
BL Harley 2253 item (39); Bodley, Digby 86 item (11)

Meeting in the Wood
BL Harley 2253 item (15)

Memento Mori. See *Long Life*

Metrical Treatise on Dreams
BL Harley 2253 item (45)

My Leman on the Rood
Cambridge, St John's College 15 (A.15) item (1); Dublin, Trinity College 432 (D.4.18); BL Royal 12 E i item (2); Bodley 57; Bodley, Ashmole 360, part VII item (2)

Names of the Hare in English
Bodley, Digby 86 item (17)

Nego
BL Harley 913 item (16)

Nicene Creed
Bodley, Junius 121

Northern Homily Collection
Edinburgh, Royal College of Physicians MS of *Cursor Mundi* item (2) (part only)

Northern Passion
Cambridge University Library Gg.I.1 item (1)

Old Man's Prayer
BL Harley 2253 item (21)

Old Textament History
Cambridge, Trinity College 323 (B.14.39) item (31)

Orison of Our Lord
Oxford, Jesus College 29, part II item (24)

Oreisun of Seinte Marie
BL Cotton Nero A xiv item (4); BL Royal 17 A xxvii item (5) (incomplete)

Orison to Our Lady
Cambridge, Trinity College 323 (B.14.39) item (43); BL Cotton Caligula A ix, part II item (3); Oxford, Jesus College 29, part II item (8)

Ormulum
   Bodley, Junius 1

Our Lady's Psalter
   Bodley, Digby 86 item (8)

Owl and the Nightingale
   BL Cotton Caligula A ix, part II item (1); Oxford, Jesus College 29, part II item (2)

Passion of Our Lord Jesus Christ
   Oxford, Jesus College 29, part II item (1)

Pater Noster
   Cambridge, Emmanuel College 27 (I.2.6) item (4); Cambridge, Gonville and Caius College 52/29; Cambridge University Library Hh.VI.11 item (2); Göttingen University Library, MS Theol. 107r item (3); BL Arundel 57 item (3); BL Arundel 292 item (2); BL Cotton Cleopatra B vi item (2); BL Cotton Vitellius A xii; BL Harley 3724 item (2); London, Lambeth Palace Library 487 item (1); Bodley, Add E.6 item (3); Oxford, Corpus Christi College 59 item (1); Pavia Biblioteca Universitaria 69 item (1); Salisbury Cathedral Library 82

Pendens Nudatum Pectus. See*Christ on the Cross* and cf. *Candet Nudatum Pectus*

Pers of Bermingham
   BL Harley 913 item (13)

Peterborough Chronicle
   Bodley, Laud Misc. 636

Poema Morale
   Cambridge, Fitzwilliam Museum, McClean 123; Cambridge, Trinity College 335 (B.14.52) item (1); Durham University Library, Cosin V.III.2 (two lines only); BL Egerton 613 items (6), (7); BL Royal 7 C iv (fragments of two lines); London, Lambeth Palace Library 487 item (2); Maidstone Museum A.13 item (1) (two lines only); Bodley, Digby 4; Oxford, Jesus College 29, part II item (3)

Poet's Repentance
   BL Harley 2253 item (13)

Prayer for the Hours of the Passion
   Göttingen University Library, MS Theol. 107r item (5)

Prayer to the Trinity
   Göttingen University Library, MS Theol. 107r item (4)

Prisoner's Prayer
   London, Corporation of London Records Office, 'Liber de antiquis Legibus'

Proclamation of Henry III of 18 October 1258
   London, Public Record Office, C 66, Patent Rolls, 43 Henry III, m. 15.40; Oxford, City Archives, Town Hall, St Aldates, H 29

Prophecy of Thomas of Erceldoune
   BL Arundel 57, fol. 8v; BL Cotton Julius A v; BL Harley 2253 item (48)

Proverbs of Alfred
   Cambridge, Trinity College 323 (B.14.39) item (48); BL Additional 11579 item (8) (quotation only); BL Cotton Galba A xix (fragments); Maidstone Museum A.13 item (1); Bodley, Digby 86 item (14) (four lines only); Oxford, Jesus College 29, part II item (23)

Proverbs of Hending
   Cambridge, Gonville and Caius College 351/568 item (3) (one stanza only); Cambridge, Pembroke College 100 item (2) (one couplet only); Cambridge, St John's College 145 (fragments); Cambridge University Library, Additional 4407, art. 19 item (4) (fragments); Cambridge University Library Gg.I.1 item (3); Durham Cathdral, Dean and Chapter Library B.I.18 item (1) (one stanza only); BL Harley 2253 item (47); BL Harley 3823 item (1); BL Royal 8 E xvii item (3) (one stanza only); Bodley, Digby 86 item (14)

Pseudo-Anselm, translation of
   BL Arundel 57 item (4)

Regret de Maximian. See *Maximian*

Respice in Faciem (cf. *Christ on the Cross*)
   Cambridge, St John's College 15 (A.15) item (2); BL Additional 11579 item (7); Bodley 42 item (2); Oxford, New College 88 item (2)

Rhyming Charter of Beverley. See King Athelstan

Rhyming Charter of Ripon. See King Athelstan

Rule of St Benedict. (See also Index of Texts in Latin)
    BL Cotton Claudius D iii

St Bridget. See *Life of St Bridget*

St Edmund, last words of, quoted in English in *Life of St Edmund* (Latin)
    BL Cotton Vitellius C xii;   BL Cotton Cleopatra B i; BL Harley 2; BL Royal 2 D vi; BL Royal 8 F xiv

St Godric, Hymn A
    Cambridge, Corpus Christi College 26; Cambridge University Library Mm.IV.28; BL Cotton Nero D v; BL Cotton Otho B v, part II; BL Harley 153; BL Harley 322; BL Harley 1620; BL Royal 5 F vii; London, Lambeth Palace Library 51; Bodley, Douce 207; Bodley, Fairfax 6

St Godric, Hymn B
    BL Harley 153; BL Royal 5 F vii

St Godric, Hymn C
    BL Royal 5 F vii

St Juliana. See *Life of St Juliana*

St Katherine. See *Life of St Katherine*

St Margaret. See *Life of St Margaret*

St Nicholas, Homily for the anniversary of
    Cambridge, Trinity College 323 (B.14.39) item (10)

St Thomas the Martyr, *Antiphon*
    Oxford, Jesus College 29, part II item (16); Winchester College 4

Sarmun
    BL Harley 913 item (5)

Satire on the Consistory Courts
    BL Harley 2253 item (17)

Satire on the People of Kildare
    BL Harley 913 item (3)

Satire on the Retinues of the Great
    BL Harley 2253 item (46)

Sayings of St Bede
    Bodley, Digby 86 item (7); Oxford, Jesus College 29, part II item (4)

Sayings of St Bernard
    BL Harley 2253 item (43); Bodley, Add E.6 item (1); Bodley, Digby 86 item (4); Bodley, Laud Misc. 108 item (2)

Sentence of Cursing
    BL Additional 11579 item (11)

Septem Cogitanda
    Cambridge, Emmanuel College 27 (I.2.6) item (15)

Serlo of Wilton, Proverbs. (See also Indexes of Texts in Latin and French)
    Bodley, Digby 53

Sermon on Isaiah
    Cambridge, Trinity College 335 (B.14.52) item (3)

Sermon on the Nativity
    Worcester Cathderal, Dean and Chapter Library Q 29

Seven Works of Mercy
    Cambridge, Emmanuel College 27 (I.2.6) item (16)

Sermo in festis Sancti Marie uirginis
    BL Cotton Vespasian D xiv

Seven Sins
    BL Harley 913 item (12)

Shires and hundreds of England
    Oxford, Jesus College 29, part II item (26)

Signs of Death
    Oxford, Jesus College 29, part II item (21)

Sinners Beware. See *Sayings of St Bede*

Sinner's Lament
    Oxford, Merton College 120

Song of Lewes
    BL Harley 2253 item (3)

Song of the Annunciation
    Oxford, Jesus College 29, part II items (9), (19)

Song of the Husbandman
    BL Harley 2253 item (11)

Soþe Luue, Homily on
    Oxford, Jesus College 29, part II item (25)

Sawles Warde
BL Cotton Titus D xviii item (2); BL Royal 17 A xxvii item (1); Bodley 34 item (5)

South English Legendary
Cambridge, Corpus Christi College 145; Kilkenny Corporation Archives, *Liber Primus Kilkenniensis* (Prologue only); Leicester Museum 18 D 59 (fragments); BL Egerton 2891 (imperfect); BL Harley 2277; Nottingham University Library Mi Lm 7/1 (fragments); Bodley, Ashmole 43; Bodley, Laud Misc. 108 item (1)

Spring
BL Harley 2253 item (19)

Spring Song on the Passion
BL Harley 2253 item (28); BL Royal 2 F viii item (2)

Stabat iuxta Christi crucem
Cambridge, St John's College 111 (E.8); Dublin, Trinity College 301 (C.3.19); BL Arundel 248 item (4); BL Harley 2253 item (31); BL Royal 8 F ii (first stanza only); BL Royal 12 E i item (1); Bodley, Digby 86 item (6); Bodley, Tanner 169* (begins imperfectly)

Ten Abuses
BL Cotton Caligula A ix, part II item (7); Oxford, Jesus College 29, part II item (14)

Ten Commandments
Cambridge, Emmanuel College 27 (I.2.6) items (2), (8); Cambridge, Trinity College 43 (B.1.45) item (3); Cambridge, Trinity College 323 (B.14.39) item (25); Cambridge University Library Ff.VI.15; BL Additional 25031; BL Harley 913 item (9); Bodley, Hatton 26; Oxford, New College 88 item (4)

Thomas de Hales, *Love Ron*
Oxford, Jesus College 29, part II item (18)

Three Foes of Man
BL Harley 2253 item (7)

Three Sorrowful Things
BL Arundel 292 item (5); London, Lambeth Palace Library 499 item (4); Oxford, New College 88 item (1)

Three Sorrowful Tidings
Cambridge, Emmanuel College 27 (I.2.6) item (17); Maidstone Museum A.13 item (3); Oxford, Jesus College 29, part II item (22)

Thrush and the Nightingale
Bodley, Digby 86 item (12)

Tierfabel — On the Times
BL Harley 913 item (11)

Treatise on the difference between men and beasts
BL Arundel 57 item (5)

Trinity Homilies
Cambridge, Trinity College 335 (B.14.52) item (2)

Ureison of Ure Loverde. See *Wel swuþe god Ureison of God Almihti*

Vespasian Homilies
BL Cotton Vespasian A xxii

Vices and Virtues
BL Stowe 34

Vision of St Paul
Bodley, Laud Misc. 108 item (3)

Way of Christ's Love
BL Harley 2253 item (49)

Way of Women's Love
BL Harley 2253 item (50)

Wel swuþe god Ureison of God Almihti
BL Cotton Nero A xiv item (3); London, Lambeth Palace Library 487 item (3)

Will and Wit
BL Cotton Caligula A ix, part II item (4)

Winter Song
BL Harley 2253 item (27)

Woman of Samaria
Oxford, Jesus College 29, part II item (5)

Wohunge of Ure Lauerd
BL Cotton Titus D xviii item (4)

INDEX OF MIDDLE ENGLISH TEXTS
B: INCIPITS

Incipits are given in the form they appear in the *Catalogue*. Under each entry are listed the manuscripts for which the particular incipit is cited. When there is more than one item in Middle English listed for a given manuscript, the relevant item number is also supplied. Wherever possible, the incipits have been alphabetised according to the modern spelling of the first word(s). Cross-references have been provided where they seemed desirable for clarity. When incipits are very similar the relevant manuscripts are listed under a single heading and variants are not usually given. No distinction has been made in the Index between verse and prose texts.

A vox gon out of þe wode go
    Bodley, Digby 86 item (13)

A gurdel of gile
    Oxford, Merton College 248 item (24)

A Mayde cristes me bit yorne
    Oxford, Jesus College 29, part II item (18)

A þeif of is treunesse to widnesse drou
    Cambridge, Trinity College 323 (B.14.39) item (17)

A war wys lokere
    Oxford, Merton College 248 item (11)

A wayle whyt ase whalles bon
    BL Harley 2253 item (16)

A vidue pouere was & freo
    Cambridge, Trinity College 323 (B.14.39) item (18)

Abel was looset in treunesse
    Cambridge, Trinity College 323 (B.14.39) item (47)

Allas, allas vel yuel y sped. See also *Vndo my lef my downe dere*
    London, Lambeth Palace Library 557 item (1)

hallas men planys of litel trwthe
    Oxford, Merton College 248 item (36)

Al fram [eh] vuele þinge / me schulde iesus þat may
    Cambridge, Emmanuel College 27 (I.2.6.) item (13)

Alle herkneþ to me nou
    BL Harley 2253 item (1)

Alle þat beoþ of huerte trewe
    BL Harley 2253 item (23)

Alle þat gos and rydys loket op-on me
    London, Lambeth Palace Library 557 item (2)

Al þat ys shal com to was
    Cambridge, St John's College 255 (S.19)

Alle þat louieþ godes lere
    Bodley, Digby 86 item (3)

Alle heo ben blyþe
    BL Harley 2253 item (41)

All vnder sunne is wyt swynk her yvonne
    Cambridge, Corpus Christi College 405

And spatte a luyte on is fingur
    Bodley, Laud Misc. 108 item (1)

As I com bi an waie
    Bodley, Digby 86 item (16)

Ase y me rod þis ender day
    BL Harley 2253 item (38)

Haske furst þe nome of þe seke body
    BL Royal 12 C xii item (4)

Ate feste of seint benedist
    Cambridge, Trinity College 323 (B.14.39) item (32)

At siforde setin kinhis monie. Cf. next entry
   Cambridge, Trinity College 323 (B.14.39) item (48)

At seuorde sete þeynes monye. Cf. previous entry
   Oxford, Jesus College, part II item (23)

Atte wrastling mi lemman iches
   Cambridge, Trinity College 43 (B.1.45) item (2)

Auake son þat slepest
   BL Harley 505 item (2)

Barred girdel wo þe be.
   Durham Cathedral, Dean and Chapter Library B.I.18 item (5)

Behold to þi lord man whare he hangiþ on rode
   BL Harley 913 item (7)

Bi þench þe wat þe wole bitiden yf þou so dest
   Cambridge, Trinity College 323 (B.14.39) item (12)

Betere is æi mid uste þan oxæ mid ætire þan fliche mid chæste
   Troyes, Bibliothèque municipale 1380 item (1)

Betere is red thene rap and liste thene lither streingthe
   BL Cotton Domitian i

Betere his red þan res
   BL Royal 8 E xvii item (2)

Bytuene mersh & aueril
   BL Harley 2253 item (9)

Boe war soe ih boe
   Cambridge, Emmanuel College 27 (I.2.6.) item (17)

[B]Idde huue with milde steuene
   BL Cotton Cleopatra B vi item (1)

Bige spere osside other bere
   BL Royal 14 C ii item (1)

Bryd one brere brid brid one brere
   Cambridge, King's College, Muniment Roll 2 W. 32 verso

bisete þine ponevis sire eode
   Cambridge, Trinity College 323 (B.14.39) item (7)

Bissop lorles / kyng redeles
   BL Harley 913 item (2)

[IB]lessed beo þu lauedi ful of houene Blisse (and variants)
   BL Egerton 613 item (3);   BL Harley 2253 item (37)

Blind and dyaf and alsuo domb
   BL Arundel 57 item (1)

Blow northerne wynd. See also *Ichot a burde in boure bryht*
   BL Harley 2253 item (22)

brihture þen þe daisei him þet me longgeð
   BL Harley 3376

Bi þis tokninge of þare rode
   Cambridge, Emmanuel College 27 (I.2.6.) item (14)

Cum þu man ne dred þe nast
   Edinburgh University Library 107

Cuth other uncuth
   BL Royal 14 C ii item (2)

[D]rightin dere wid blisful beildes
   Göttingen University Library, MS Theol. 107r item (7)

yche day me cumeþ tydinges þreo. See *Eueri day me comeʒ tiþinge þre*

Erþe toc of erþe erþe wyþ woh. Cf. *Whan erþ haþ erþ iwonne wiþ wo*
   BL Harley 2253 item (4)

Edi beo þu heuene quene
   Oxford, Corpus Christi College 59 item (2)

Elde makiþ me geld an growen al grai
   BL Harley 913 item (14)

ANgle lond is eyhte hundred myle long
   Oxford, Jesus College 29, part II item (26)

Er þu do eny þing þenk one þe ending
   BL Royal 8 E xvii item (2)

Eueir asse mon liuit lengore
    Cambridge, Trinity College 323 (B.14.39) item (38)

Eueri day me comeȝ tiþinge þre (and variants)
    Cambridge, Pembroke College 258 item (2); Oxford, Jesus College 29, part II item (22)

Eueriche freman hach to ben hende
    Bodley, Rawlinson C 22

vuele men goid þe siechen
    Cambridge, Trinity College 323 (B.14.39) item (28)

Falsehede of the world
    Oxford, Merton College 248 item (17)

Falsenesse and couetys er feris
    Oxford, Merton College 248 item (31)

falsenes I vnderstande
    Oxford, Merton College 248 item (32)

Fur in see bi west Spayngne
    BL Harley 913 item (1)

Vader And moder / Suster And broder
    Oxford, Jesus College 26

[F]adir and sune and hali gast
    Göttingen University Library, MS Theol. 107r item (4)

Fader ure ðatt art in heuene blisse
    BL Arundel 292 item (2)

Vader our þet art ine heuenes
    BL Arundel 57 item (3)

[F]Adir vr þᵗ es in heuen
    Göttingen University Library, MS Theol. 107r item (3)

Fader þat hart in heuene
    Pavia Biblioteca Universitaria 69 item (1)

Fiftene toknen ich tellen of
    Bodley, Digby 86 item (2)

Fyre & colde & teȝeghatyng
    Oxford, Merton College 248 item (35)

For on þat is so feir ant brist. Cf. *Of on þat is so fayr and briȝt*
    Cambridge, Trinity College 323 (B.14.39) item (5)

Uor to sseawy þe lokynge of man wyþ-inne
    BL Arundel 57 item (4)

Foweles in þe frith
    Bodley, Douce 139 item (1)

FRom heouene in to eorþe
    Oxford, Jesus College 29, part II item 19)

Ful feir flour is þe lilie
    Cambridge, Trinity College 323 (B.14.39) item (9)

Gabriel fram evene-king
    BL Arundel 248 item (1)

Glade us maiden moder milde
    Cambridge, Trinity College 323 (B.14.39) item (24)

God is skile
    BL Harley 47 item (4)

Godes to gedere gamen and wisdom
    BL Cotton Domitian i

God send vs þe dew of heuene
    Bodley, Digby 172 item (1)

God þat al þis myhtes may
    BL Harley 2253 item (42)

Godis wreche late arecheit
    Cambridge, Trinity College 323 (B.14.39) item (37)

Godefrey þe guede
    Cambridge, Trinity College 323 (B.14.39) item (16)

Ha ha petipas ȝuot ich am þer ich was
    Oxford, Balliol College 230 item (2)

Hail be yow holie crowche blesfolle
    Bodley, Ashmole 1280 item (2)

Heyl boe þov Marie; ful of godes grace
    Cambridge, Emmanuel College 27 (I.2.6.) item (5)

[H]Aile be þu mari maiden bright
    Göttingen University Library, MS Theol. 107r item (6)

Ayl be þow ster of se
    Oxford, Merton College 248 item (39)

Heyl god ye schilde
  Cambridge, Corpus Christi College 405 item (2)

Hayl godes moder Marie / Mayde uol of þonke
  BL Arundel 57 item (6)

[H]eil marie. ful of grace
  BL Cotton Cleopatra B vi item (3)

Hayl mari hic am sori
  Bodley, Digby 2 item (2)

Hayl Marie / of þonke uol
  BL Arundel 57 item (3)

Hail seint Michael wiþ þe lange sper
  BL Harley 913 item (3)

Herknied alle gode men (and variants)
  BL Cotton Caligula A ix part II item (8); Oxford, Jesus College 29, part II item (15)

Herkeþ hideward & beoþ stille
  BL Harley 2253 item (12)

Herkne to my ron (and variants)
  BL Harley 2253 item (39); Bodley, Digby 86 item (11)

Hawe on god in wrchipe
  Cambridge, Trinity College 323 (B.14.39) item (25)

He rod vpon a whit hors
  Oxford, Merton College 248 item (20)

He sent me fro aboue
  Oxford, Merton College 248 item (29)

Ihereþ nv one lutele tale
  Oxford, Jesus College 29, part II item (1)

Ihereð of one þinge (and variants)
  BL Cotton Caligula A ix part II item (6); Oxford, Jesus College 29, part II item (13)

Her comenseʒ a bok of sweuenyng
  BL Harley 2253 item (45)

Her lith Odo the gode
  Cambridge, Corpus Christi College 438

Heʒe louerd þou here my bone
  BL Harley 2253 item (21)

Ynguar. and Ubbe. Beorn wæs þe þridde
  Cambridge, Pembroke College 82 item (1)

Holy archan[g]le Michael
  BL Arundel 57 item (1)

Holi gost þi miʒtte
  Bodley, Digby 86 item (7)

Haly thomas of heoueriche (and variants)
  Oxford, Jesus College 29, part II item (16); Winchester College 4

hoppe hoppe wilekin hoppe wilekin
  BL Royal 14 C vii item (5)

Hou ihu crist herowede helle
  Bodley, Digby 86 item (1)

Ic æm elder þænne ic pæs a pinter and a lore (and variants). See *Ich am nu elder* etc.

hic am michel of airas
  Cambridge, Trinity College 323 (B.14.39) item (20)

ic am nout for þisse þinge þo
  Bodley, Hatton 116

Ich am nu elder þan ich pas a pintre & a lore (and variants)
  Cambridge, Fitzwilliam Museum, McClean 123; Cambridge, Trinity College 335 (B.14.52) item (1); BL Egerton 613 items (6), (7); London, Lambeth Palace Library 487 item (2); Bodley, Digby 4; Oxford, Jesus College 29, part II item (3)

I am Rose wo is me
  Cambridge University Library Hh.VI.11 item (1)

Ic an [or *am*] *witles fuli wis*
  BL Royal 8 D xiii

Ih bi-leue in god, fader almiʒti (and variants)
  Cambridge, Emmanuel College 27 (I.2.6.) item (6); BL Harley 3724 item (1)

I come vram þe wedlok
  Oxford, Merton College 248 item (19)

Ih cristin þe, N, In þe name of þe fader
    Cambridge, Emmanuel College 27 (I.2.6.) item (18)

Ich herde men vpo mold
    BL Harley 2253 item (11)

Ih knovlechy to god and to vre / Leuedi seynte Marie
    Cambridge, Emmanuel College 27 (I.2.6.) item (7)

I leue in godd almicten fader
    BL Arundel 292 item (1)

Ich leue ine god / uader almiȝti
    BL Arundel 57 item (3)

I ne mai a liue – for benoit ne for Iue
    BL Royal 14 C vii item (3)

I sayh hym wiþ fless al bi-sprad
    Oxford, Merton College 248 item (18)

Hi sike al wan hi singe. See next entry

I syke when y singe (and variants)
    BL Harley 2253 item (33); Bodley, Digby 2 item (1)

I senege ilch dai
    BL Additional 11579 item (10)

I þinge al day
    Oxford, Merton College 248 item (33)

[H]I true in god fader hal-michttende
    BL Cotton Cleopatra B vi item (5)

Ich pas in one sumere dale (and variants)
    BL Cotton Caligula A ix part II item (1); Oxford, Jesus College 29, part II item (2)

Ic chule bere to wasscen doun iþe toun
    Cambridge, Trinity College 323 (B.14.39) item (13)

Ichot a burde in a bour ase beryl so bryht
    BL Harley 2253 item (8)

Ichot a burde in boure bryht
    BL Harley 2253 item (22)

Yc ou rede ye sitten stille
    Cambridge, Trinity College 323 (B.14.39) item (10)

If man him biðocte
    BL Arundel 292 item (6)

If yow wise worȝe wille
    Oxford, Merton College 248 item (40)

Ihe, la ful iwis / Swide strong ordre is dhis
    BL Cotton Tiberius B xiii

in on efnigge stille þer istod
    BL Harley 3376

In a fryht as y con fare fremede
    BL Harley 2253 item (15)

In an þestrei stude ic stod (and variants)
    Cambridge, Trinity College 323 (B.14.39) item (26); BL Harley 2253 item (2); Bodley, Digby 86 item (18)

In clench qu becche under ane þorne
    Cambridge, Pembroke College 82 item (2)

In hyre ys al my lyf ylong. See *On hire is al mi lif ylong*

In may hit murgeþ when hit dawes
    BL Harley 2253 item (20)

In þe daye of seynte Svythone; vane ginneþ rinigge
    Cambridge, Emmanuel College 27 (I.2.6.) item (20)

In þine honden louerd mine
    Bodley, Digby 86 item (22)

In thys tre es alle hys myth
    Oxford, Merton College 248 item (28)

In toe þine honden. louerd
    Cambridge, Emmanuel College 27 (I.2.6.) item (11)

Hit bilimpeȝ forte speke
    Oxford, Corpus Christi College 59 item (1)

Hit nis bot trewþ iwend an afte
    BL Harley 913 item (16)

Hit wes up-on a screþorsday
    Cambridge, Trinity College 323 (B.14.39) item (29)

Ianekyn of Londone / Is loue is al myn
    Oxford, Merton College 248 item (26)

Ihu crist al þis worldes red
Bodley, Digby 86 item (14)

Iesu crist heouene kyng
BL Harley 2253 item (26)

Iesu cristes milde moder
BL Arundel 248 item (4)

Iesu for þi muchele miht
BL Harley 2253 item (32)

Iesu suete is þe loue of þe
BL Harley 2253 item (30)

Iesu þat al þis world haþ wroȝt
Oxford, Merton College 248 item (4)

Iesu þᵗ wald efter midnight
Göttingen University Library, MS Theol. 107r item (5)

King conseilles / Bissop lore les
BL Cotton Cleopatra C vi item (2)

Kyng Edward wanne þu havest Berwic, pike þe
BL Cotton Claudius D vi

kyneriche wel idist
Cambridge, Gonville and Caius College 221/236 item (3)

Lefdy blisful of muchel miȝt
Oxford, Merton College 248 item (25)

Leuedy for þare blisse
Oxford, Jesus College 29, part II item (10)

Leuedie ic þonke þe wid herte suiþe milde
Cambridge, Trinity College 323 (B.14.39) item (34)

Leuedi sainte marie moder and meide
BL Additional 27909

Leuedi swete and milde
Bodley, Digby 86 item (8)

Leue frend nou beþ stille
Bodley, Digby 86 item (1)

Leue men þis beoþ þe ten heste
Bodley, Hatton 26

Lenten ys come wiþ loue to toune
BL Harley 2253 item (19)

Let for þy senne
BL Additional 11579 item (4)

Lete þe cukewald syte at hom
Dublin, Trinity College 347 (C.5.8)

lex lyis done ofuer
Oxford, Merton College 248 item (34)

ly þow me ner lemmon in þy narmus
Bodley 34

Lustneþ alle a lutel þrowe
BL Harley 2253 item (43)

Lystneþ Lordynges a newe song ichulle bigynne
BL Harley 2253 item (5)

Lustneþ lordinges boþe ȝonge ant olde
BL Harley 2253 item (24)

Lestnit nou and habbit lest
Bodley, Add E.6 item (3)

Liþer lok and tuingling (and variants)
Cambridge, Trinity College 43 (B.1.45) item (1); BL Cotton Cleopatra C vi item (1)

Lutel wot hit anymon; hou derne loue may stonde
BL Harley 2253 item (50)

Lytel wotyt onyman hu derne loue was fnde
Cambridge, Gonville and Caius College 512/543

Lvtel wot hit anymon; hou loue hym haueþ ybounde
BL Harley 2253 item (49)

Litel uotit eniman hu trewe loue bistodet
BL Egerton 613 item (4)

liuis firist & licames hele
Cambridge, Trinity College 323 (B.14.39) item (33)

longe scleparis ouerleparis
Cambridge, Trinity College 323 (B.14.39) item (21)

Loke man to iesucrist. hi neiled an þo rode
Bodley 42 item (2)

Loke nu frere / Hu strong ordre is here
   BL Cotton Tiberius B xiii

Loke to þi louerd man þar hanget he arode
   Cambridge, St John's College 15 (A.15) item (2)

Louerd asse þu ard on god
   Cambridge, Trinity College 323 (B.14.39) item (31)

Louerd crist iche þe grete
   Oxford, Jesus College, part II item (24)

Louerd crist þou hauest us boust.
   Cambridge, Trinity College 323 (B.14.39) item (3)

Louerd godd in hondes tine
   BL Arundel 292 item (4)

Lord ihu almiȝti kyng
   BL Arundel 57 item (1)

Louerd ihesu crist ich ȝe bid for ȝe vif wunde
   Cambridge, Trinity College 1149 (O.2.45) item (1)

Lord þat lenest vs lyf
   BL Harley 2253 item (6)

Loverd þi passion. Who þe þenchet arist þar on
   Cambridge, St John's College 62 (C.12)

Louerd þu clepedest me
   Oxford, New College 88 item (3)

Luue bendes me bindet
   Durham University Library, Cosin V.III.2

[L]oue hauiþ me broȝt in liþir þoȝt
   BL Harley 913 item (15)

Loue is a selkud wodenesse
   Bodley, Douce 139 item (2)

Loue is knotte of mannes hertes
   BL Harley 505 item (1)

Loue is sofft loue is swet loue is goed sware
   Bodley, Digby 86 item (21)

Lollai .l[ollai] litil child whi wepistou so sore
   BL Harley 913 item (10)

mabbe þe d[.]uel þe habbe & bere to his owene neste
   Salisbury Cathedral Library 150

Mayde and moder mylde, uor loue of þine childe
   BL Arundel 57 item (7)

[M]aidin and moder þat bar þe heuene kinge
   BL Cotton Cleopatra B vi item (4)

Mayden moder milde
   BL Harley 2253 item (40)

Maiden stod at welle and wep Weilawei
   Bodley, Laud Misc. 511 item (1)

Man and wyman loket to me
   Oxford, New College 88 item (2)

Man folwe sentt Bernardes trace
   BL Additional 11579 item (7)

Mon in þe mone stond & strit
   BL Harley 2253 item (44)

Man may longe liues wene (and variants)
   BL Additional 11579 item (8) (first stanza only); BL Arundel 57 item (2); BL Cotton Caligula A ix part II item (2); Maidstone Museum A.13 item (2); Bodley, Laud Misc. 471, part I; Oxford, Jesus College 29, part II item (7)

Man seid gamen god an uombe . See *Men seith gamen goth in wombe*

Mon þat wol of wisdam heren
   BL Harley 2253 item (47)

Meni man syngat / wan he hom bringat
   Cambridge, Gonville and Caius College 351/568 item (3)

Marie ful off grace weel de be
   BL Arundel 292 item (3)

may y sugge namore so wel me is
   BL Harley 2253 item (29)

Me ydrechez þroe yfoon. mid þroe kunne rute
Cambridge, Emmanuel College 27 (I.2.6.) item (12)

Me[n þam com]pleynes of vntrewyth. Cf. next entry
Bodley, Hatton 107

Men hem pleynit of mikel untrewthe. Cf. previous entry
Oxford, Balliol College 227

Men seith gamen goth in wombe (and variants)
BL Cotton Cleopatra B i; BL Harley 2; BL Royal 2 D vi; BL Royal 8 F xiv; Oxford, Balliol College 226; Oxford, Corpus Christi College 154

Men ða leffostan us lareowhum gedafenað
Cambridge, Corpus Christi College 302

Murie a tyme I telle in may
Cambridge, Pembroke College 258 item (5)

[M]irie it is while sumer ilast
Bodley, Rawlinson G 22

Merie sungen ðe muneches binnen ely
Cambridge, Trinity College 1105 (O.2.1) item (2); Cambridge University Library EDC 1 item (1); Bodley, Laud Misc. 647 item (1)

Middelerd for mon wes mad
BL Harley 2253 item (7)

Myn oȝen deþ; and cristes
Cambridge, Emmanuel College 27 (I.2.6.) item (15)

Mosti ryden by rybbesdale
BL Harley 2253 item (14)

Moder milde flur of alle
Oxford, Corpus Christi College 59 item (3)

My deþ y loue my lyf ich hate
BL Harley 2253 item (35)

My flesse þat wrothe was in mari blode
Oxford, Merton College 248 item (38)

Naked was hys wite brest red of blod hys side. Cf. *Hwyt was hys nakede brest*
Bodley, Digby 45

Naueþ my saule bute fur and ys
Oxford, Jesus College 29, part II item (20)

Ne bee þe day neuere so longe / euere comeþe euensong
Oxford, Merton College 248 item (23)

Ne be þi winpil [for *wimpil*] *neuere so Ielu*
Cambridge, Trinity College 43 (B.1.45) item (1); BL Cotton Cleopatra C vi item (3)

Ne haue þou no god botin on
Cambridge, Trinity College 43 (B.1.45) item (3)

Ne halt nocht alsor isaid ne al sorghe atwite
BL Cotton Domitian i

Ne leue leuedi ne be þi wimpil neuere so Ielu. See *Ne be þi winpil neuere so Ielu*

Ne may cume to mi lef bute bi þe water
Worcester Cathedral, Dean and Chapter Library F 64

Ne mai no lewed lued libben in londe
BL Harley 2253 item (17)

Ne saltou neuer leuedi
Worcester Cathedral, Dean and Chapter Library Q 50

No god ne haue þov; boten on
Cambridge, Emmanuel College 27 (I.2.6.) item (8)

Nammore ne is be-tuene ane manne / and ane beste
BL Arundel 57 item (5)

No more ne willi wiked be
Bodley, Digby 2 item (3)

NON [for *Mon*] *mai longe liues þene.* See *Man may longe liues wene*

Nou goth sonne vnder wode (and variants)
    Cambridge, Pembroke College 258 item (1); Durham University Library, Cosin V.V.15; BL Arundel 288; BL Royal 12 C xii item (2); Bodley, Digby 20; Bodley, Douce 210; Bodley, Rawlinson poet. 241; Bodley, Selden Supra 74 item (2)

Nu hur is goo wroth and hyre frendes loth.
    Bodley, Rawlinson C 534 item (2)

Nw ych habbe þat y nolde.
    BL Additional 11579 item (1)

Nv yh she blostme sprynge. Cf. *When y se blosmes springe*
    BL Royal 2 F viii item (2)

Nou ich wille. þet ye ywyte hou hit is y-went
    BL Arundel 57 item (2)

Nou is mon hol & soint
    Cambridge, Trinity College 323 (B.14.39) item (11)

Now is my Robe y-ssape
    Oxford, Merton College 248 item (27)

Nou iesu for þi derworþ blode
    BL Harley 913 item (9)

Nou shrnkeþ rose & lylie flour
    BL Harley 2253 item (34)

No[u] spri[nke]s the sprai
    London, Lincoln's Inn, Hale 135

Nu þis fules singet
    Cambridge, Trinity College 323 (B.14.39) item (42)

Nu þu vnseli bodi
    Cambridge, Trinity College 323 (B.14.39) item (46)

Of a mon Matheu þohte
    BL Harley 2253 item (18)

Of aye ich the brouste of athele ich ne miste
    BL Additional 11579 item (9)

Of is lif of foly & of synn þorw lawe
    Cambridge, Gonville and Caius College 221/236 item (2)

Of my husband giu I noht
    Dublin, Trinity College 347 (C.5.8)

Of noman liche makeʒ hao in a stound many riche
    Cambridge, Corpus Christi College 405 item (1)

Of one stable was is halle
    Cambridge, Trinity College 323 (B.14.39) item (41)

Of on þat is so fayr and briʒt. Cf. *For on þat is so feir ant brist*
    BL Egerton 613 item (2)

Of rybaudʒ y ryme / ant rede o my rolle
    BL Harley 2253 item (46)

Ofte he bið bicherred; þet alle men ileueð
    BL Harley 47 item (3)

Ofte he bið efter roð; þet nule beon biuore þar
    BL Harley 47 item (1)

Olde ant yonge i preit ou
    Cambridge, Trinity College 323 (B.14.39) item (2)

[Ald man] witles / yung man recheles
    Cambridge, Trinity College 108 (B.3.29)

Hon an þester stude I stod. See *In an þestrei stude ic stod*

An ernemorwe þe dayliʒt spryngeþ
    Oxford, Merton College 248 item (21)

On folie.was myn silwyr leyd
    Cambridge University Library, Additional 4407, art. 19 item (3)

On hire is al mi lif ylong (and variants)
    Cambridge, Trinity College 323 (B.14.39) item (43); BL Cotton Caligula A ix part II item (3); BL Royal 2 F viii item (1); Oxford, Jesus College 29, part II item (8)

On dai bringd þet al ier ne mai
    Bodley, Rawlinson C 641 item (1)

Ane god þov schalt wrschupe
    Cambridge, Emmanuel College 27 (I.2.6.) item (2)

On leome is in þis world ilist
    Cambridge, Trinity College 323 (B.14.39) item (27)

Vre fader in heuene; yhalȝed bo þy name
    Cambridge, Emmanuel College 27 (I.2.6.) item (4)

Vre fader in heuene riche
    BL Harley 3724 item (2)

[V]Re fadir þat hart in heuene
    BL Cotton Cleopatra B vi item (2)

Vre feder þat in heouene is
    London, Lambeth Palace Library 487 item (1)

Hure wader þat is in euene
    Salisbury Cathedral Library 82

vre louerd crist was on erthe iwondid
    Bodley, Digby 2 item (4)

over al ich finde tho be sori
    Bodley, Ashmole 1280 item (1)

Penaunce is in herte reusinge
    Cambridge, Trinity College 323 (B.14.39) item (14)

Prute coueitise, slevþe, wreþe and Onde
    Cambridge, Emmanuel College 27 (I.2.6.) items (3), (9)

Prute. ȝisscinge. slevþe. wrethe, and Onde. See previous entry

Rex regum riche kink
Oxford, Corpus Christi College 59

Riche and pouer yunge and halde (and variants)
    Durham Cathedral, Dean and Chapter Library B.I.18 item (1); BL Royal 8 E xvii item (3)

Ride ride Rome, turne Cantwereberei
    BL Harley 1005 item (3)

Riȝtful dom is ouer cast
    Oxford, Merton College 248 item (22)

Riseth op alle cristes icorne
    BL Royal 14 C vii item (4)

Roriese þe rorie ne wrthe nan
    London, Lambeth Palace Library 236

Seinte marie leuedi brist
    Cambridge, Trinity College 323 (B.14.39) item (6)

\Seinte mari moder milde
    Cambridge, Trinity College 323 (B.14.39) item (4)

[S]anctus beda was iboren
    Worcester Cathedral, Dean and Chapter Library F 174 item (2)

Say me viit in þe brom. Cf. next entry
    Cambridge, Trinity College 323 (B.14.39) item (15)

Sey wist y þe brom. Cf. previous entry
    BL Additional 11579 item (5)

Selde comet the lattere the betere
    BL Additional 11579 item (9)

Selden gifis men dumb man land
    Bodley, Digby 53 item (1)

Sort red god red. Slea we þe bissop
    BL Royal 14 C vii item (1)

Schrude and fede and drenche
    Cambridge, Emmanuel College 27 (I.2.6.) item (16)

Si stille suge fret þere grunniende mete
    Bodley, Rawlinson C 641 item (1)

Silly sicht i seich, unsembly forte se
    BL Harley 3724 item (3)

Sith Gabriel gan grete / vre leuedi mari swete
    BL Harley 913 item (13)

Sitteþ alle stille & herkneþ to me
    BL Harley 2253 item (3)

so hend and so god he is / he aues broct us into blis
    Bodley, Rawlinson C 510

So lange ik aue lefman stonden at þe yathe.
    Durham Cathedral, Dean and Chapter Library B.I.18 item (2)

Son [?] *so he hauet coperun and te hod*
    Cambridge, Gonville and Caius College 408/414

Serue & sai leit & beit (and variants)
    Cambridge, Trinity College 323 (B.14.39) item (23); Bodley, Ashmole 1285

Stand wel moder vnder rode (and variants)
    Cambridge, St John's College 111 (E.8); Dublin Trinity College 301 (C.3.19); BL Harley 2253 item (31); BL Royal 8 F ii (first stanza only); BL Royal 12 E i item (1); Bodley, Digby 86 item (6)

Steddefast crosse inmong alle oþer
    Oxford, Merton College 248 item (41)

Stones beþ harde
    Oxford, Merton College 248 item (7)

stod ho þere neh / þat leueli leor wid spald ischent
    Bodley, Tanner 169*

streit shul be þe waies
    Oxford, Merton College 248 item (3)

Somer is comen & winter gon
    BL Egerton 613 item (1)

Svmer is icumen in. Lhude sing cuccu
    BL Harley 978 item (1)

Somer is comen wiþ loue to toune
    Bodley, Digby 86 item (12)

Swarte smeked smithes smatered with smoke
    BL Arundel 292

suete bet swines brede ant of wilde dere
    Durham University Library, Cosin V.III.2

Swet iesu hend and fre
    BL Harley 913 item (4)

Suete ihu king of blysse (and variants)
    BL Harley 2253 item (25); Bodley, Digby 86 item (10)

Swete ihu my swete leman
    BL Harley 3776

Zuete iesu þin holy blod
    BL Arundel 57 item (1)

Suete leman y deye for yi loue
    Bodley, Digby 55 item (2)

swete lamman dhin are
    London, Lambeth Palace Library 236

Swines brede is Swiþe Swete
    Maidstone Museum A.13 item (1)

Swynes halle / fendes falle
    Oxford, Merton College 248 item (9)

teres tollet eyne bollet (and variants)
    Cambridge, Gonville and Caius College 408/414. Cf. Cambridge, St John's College 62 (C.12); Bodley, Ashmole 360 item (1); Oxford, St John's College 190 item (1)

þat ful uneþe eny more me miȝt þer on bringe
    Kilkenny Corporation Archives, *Liber Primus Kilkenniensis*

þat ich et þat ich hadde
    Cambridge, Pembroke College 32

þat ich haue ben longe about
    Oxford, Merton College 248 item (2)

That mi lef askes with sare weping
    Durham University Library, Cosin V.II.8

þe blessinge of heuene king
    Bodley, Digby 86 item (4)

þe fol uise kakalere
    Oxford, Merton College 248 item (13)

þe grace of godde and holi chirche
    BL Harley 913 item (5)

þe grace of god ful of miȝt
    BL Harley 913 item (8)

þe grace of iesu fulle of miȝte
    BL Harley 913 item (6)

[þ]e holi gostes miȝte us all helpe & diȝte.
    Cambridge, Fitzwilliam Museum, McClean 123

Ye ioye of vr hert es withen to wo
    Oxford, Merton College 120

þe king of heuen mid vs be
    BL Harley 913 item (12)

þe kinges baner bigan to sprede
   Oxford, Merton College 248 item (6)

þe loren is founden
   Oxford, Merton College 248 item (14)

þe mon þat þe hare I-met
   Bodley, Digby 86 item (17)

þe milde Lomb isprad o rode
   BL Arundel 248 item (2)

þe munde of Cristes passion
   Oxford, St John's College 190 item (1)

þe minde of þi passiun suete ihu
   Bodley, Ashmole 360, part VII item (1)

Þeo soþe luue among vs beo
   Oxford, Jesus College 29, part II item (25)

þe sonne is brithere þane þe monne
   Oxford, Balliol College 230 item (1)

þe vnseli man seyde of God þat hym ne rouhte
   Bodley, Rawlinson C 534 item (1)

þe whyle þᵗ ich wore gold on mi gloue
   Cambridge, Emmanuel College 27 (I.2.6.) item (1)

Zanne is to late Zanne the wlf etc.
   Cambridge, Pembroke College 100 item (2)

Þene latemeste dai wenne we sulen farren. Cf. þench of þe latemeste dai hou we shulen fare
   Cambridge, Trinity College 323 (B.14.39) item (36)

þan þu seches in here hert yreret.
   Cambridge, Trinity College 1435 (O.9.23); Bodley, Laud Misc. 582

þer I luuie þer leik i noth
   Durham Cathedral, Dean and Chapter Library B.I.18 items (3), (4)

þar þe clild [= child] is kings and þe inerl [? for churl] is Alderman
   Bodley, Digby 53 item (2)

þer was kast a ston
   Oxford, Merton College 248 item (5)

þeys bet ȝe þre þat god for les
   Cambridge, Gonville and Caius College 365/728

They thou the vulf hore hod to preste
   BL Additional 11579 item (9)

þine mot ihc gon mayde
   Cambridge, Corpus Christi College 188

þenchen hu spart þing & suti is þat sunne
   Bodley 34 item (2)

þenc man of min harde stundes
   BL Royal 12 E i item (3)

Þench of þe latemeste dai hou we shulen fare. Cf. Þene latemeste dai wenne we sulen farren
   Bodley, Digby 86 item (20)

þis boc is ywrite uor englisse men þet hi wyte
   BL Arundel 57 item (2)

Þeos holy gostes myhte
   Oxford, Jesus College 29, part II item (4)

þyf [? þys] yc loue in þe
   BL Additional 11579 item (3)

Yis world hymn pleynez of mikel ontrewe
   Cambridge, Pembroke College 258 item (4)

Þo ihu crist an eorþe was
   Oxford, Jesus College 29, part II item (5)

þu deþis ezechiel / Biþenc þe nu suiþe wel
   Cambridge, Trinity College 323 (B.14.39) item (1b)

þu salt hauen na god buten An
   Cambridge University Library Ff.VI.15

þu schald o god louien and heren
   London, British Library Additional 25031

þu þad madist alle þinc
   Cambridge, Trinity College 323 (B.14.39) item (44)

þou vs ast shend þoru þi fol loking
   Oxford, Merton College 248 item (12)

þw wreche gost wid mud y det
   BL Additional 11579 item (2)

þeʒ þou habbe casteles & toures
   Worcester Cathedral, Dean and Chapter Library Q 46 item (1)

þreo dawes beoð on tweolf moneþ
   Cambridge, Corpus Christi College 391

þre þinges it ben þat I hold pris
   Cambridge, Pembroke College 258 item (3)

þru tidigge us cumet iche dei. Cf. *Eueri day me comeʒ tiþinge þre*
   Maidstone Museum A.13 item (3)

Thre woys mosthe wyt thowth
   Oxford, Merton College 248 item (37)

þi lust þat lasteþ but a wile
   Oxford, Merton College 248 item (15)

tunge breocþ boæn: þæoʒ / hæo nabbe suelf noan
   Troyes, Bibliothèque municipale 1380 item (2)

Trou in godd fadir all-mighti
   Göttingen University Library, MS Theol. 107r item (2)

Trewe loue is a lawe
   Oxford, Merton College 248 item (10)

Turn þe to vre louerd
   Oxford, Merton College 248 item (1)

Tuain nichte gest, thridde nicht hawen man
   BL Royal 14 C ii item (2)

Uncomly in cloistre I cowre ful of care
   BL Arundel 292

understond wel gris wat ʒou were and wat þu ert
   Cambridge, Gonville and Caius College 351/568 item (1)

Vndo my lef my downe dere. See also *Allas, allas vel yuel y sped*
   London, Lambeth Palace Library 557 item (1)

Hounseli gost wat dest þou here (and variants)
   Bodley, Digby 86 item (9); Oxford, Jesus College 29, part II item (27)

Weole þu art a waried þing
   Oxford, Jesus College 29, part II item (6)

Weping haueþ myn wonges wet
   BL Harley 2253 item (13)

Wolcome louerd; in likninge of bred
   Cambridge, Emmanuel College 27 (I.2.6.) item (10)

Wenne, wenne, wenchichenne
   BL Royal 4 A xiv

Were þat his don / for to done
   Durham Cathedral, Dean and Chapter Library B.I.18 item (7)

Wayloway so dere boht / þat it sal þus ben
   Cambridge, Gonville and Caius College 221/236 item (1)

Welawey swych wenet wel to lede god lyf
   Cambridge, Pembroke College 32

Waylaway wy dude ich so
   BL Harley 505 item (3)

Whan erþ haþ erþ iwonne wiþ wow. Cf. *Erþe toc of erþe erþe wyþ woh*
   BL Harley 913 item (17)

Wanne frend schal fram frende go
   Oxford, St John's College 190 item (2)

Hwon holy chireche is vnder uote
   Oxford, Jesus College 29, part II item (11)

Wen ihc aue al don mine folie
   Bodley, Digby 55 item (2)

Wan Ics on rode se / Iesu mi lemon
   Bodley, Laud Misc. 511 item (2) (quotation only)

Vven i .o. þe rode se / Faste nailed to þe tre
   Bodley 57

When y se blosmes springe. Cf. *Nv yh she blostme sprynge*
   BL Harley 2253 item (28)

Wenne hic soe on rode idon
    Cambridge, St John's College 15 (A.15) item (1)

Quanne hic se on rode Iesu mi leman
    BL Royal 12 E i item (2)

Whanne i þe o rode i-se / ihu mi leman
    Dublin, Trinity College 432 (D.4.18), part I

Wenne Hi þenche on domes dai (and variants)
    Cambridge, Trinity College 323 (B.14.39) item (35); BL Cotton Caligula A ix part II item (5); Bodley, Digby 86 item (19); Oxford, Jesus College 29, part II item (12)

Qvanne I zenke onne þe rode
    Bodley, Ashmole 360, part VII item (2)

Wanne ich þenche þenges þre (and variants)
    BL Arundel 292 item (5); London, Lambeth Palace Library 499 item (4); Oxford, New College 88 item (1)

When man as mad a kyng of a capped man
    BL Harley 2253 item (48)

Wanne mine eyhnen misten
    Cambridge, Trinity College 43 (B.1.45) item (4)

Hpenne-so wil þit ofer-stieð
    BL Cotton Caligula A ix part II item (4)

When þe nyhtegale singes
    BL Harley 2253 item (36)

wen þe rede is god
    Cambridge, Trinity College 323 (B.14.39) item (22)

Wen þe turuf is þi tuur
    Cambridge, Trinity College 323 (B.14.39) item (40)

wenne þin eþen beit ihut
    Cambridge, Trinity College 323 (B.14.39) item (19)

[H]wenne þin heou blokeþ
    Oxford, Jesus College 29, part II item (21)

H pan þu sixst onleoð king (and variants)
    BL Cotton Caligula A ix part II item (7); Oxford, Jesus College 29, part II item (14)

Wan we wor vnmyti
    Oxford, Merton College 248 item (30)

Uuere beþ þey bifore vs weren
    Bodley, Digby 86 item (5)

Wyt is yi nachede brest. Cf. next entry
    Oxford, Digby 55 item (1)

Hwyt was hys nakede brest (and variants)
    Cambridge, St. John's College 15 (A.15); Durham Cathedral, Dean and Chapter Library A.III.12; BL Additional 11579 item (6); Bodley 42 item (1); Bodley, Rawlinson C 317

þho haues hornes als ha ram
    Cambridge, Gonville and Caius College 408/414

Wose wartt wid pritte abeit amadde
    Cambridge, Trinity College 323 (B.14.39) item (39)

[W]ho þat wol nyde clippe and kisse aboute mydnyth
    Cambridge, Gonville and Caius College 351/568 item (2)

Ho þat wol nyde hore be
    Cambridge, Gonville and Caius College 351/568 item (4)

Hwo þe wel bithoste
    BL Harley 3221

Quo sabet long ligge in sinne
    Cambridge, Pembroke College 100 item (1)

Wose is ene firsuoren; he is ever firt
    Cambridge, Trinity College 323 (B.14.39) item (8)

Who so is stef aȝens is fo
    Oxford, Merton College 248 item (16)

Wose seþe on rode
    Cambridge, Trinity College 323 (B.14.39) item (45)

Whose þenchiþ vp þis carful lif
    BL Harley 913 item (11)

Hwi ne serue we Crist
    Oxford, Jesus College 29, part II item (17)

Wolle ye iheren of twelte day
    Cambridge, Trinity College 323 (B.14.39) item (30)

Wille Gris Wille Gris, Thinche twat you was and qwat you es
    BL Cotton Claudius D vii

Wynter wakeneþ al my care
    BL Harley 2253 item (27)

þis is þt þar is
    BL Harley 47 item (2)

Wis man wranglere / Richeman robbere
    Oxford, Merton College 248 item (8)

Wiþ longyng y am lad
    BL Harley 2253 item (10)

Wyht suylc a betel be he smyten
    BL Royal 8 E xvii item (1)

vid word & wrid ic warne þe sire ode
    Cambridge, Trinity College 323 (B.14.39) item (1)

Worldes blisce haue god day (and variants)
    Cambridge, Corpus Christi College 8; Worcester Cathedral, Dean and Chapter Library Q 46 item (2)

Worldes blisse ne last non þrowe (and variants)
    BL Arundel 248 item (3); Bodley, Digby 86 item (15); Bodley, Rawlinson G 18

Worldlih eʒte is ywonne
    Cambridge, Emmanuel College 27 (I.2.6.) item (19)

Wwrche man gardclife on mid
    BL Harley 585

ʒare hit was isuteled
    Worcester Cathedral, Dean and Chapter Library Q 29

yry. yry Standard
    BL Royal 14 C vii item (2)

INDEX OF OLD ENGLISH TEXTS

Texts are indexed by author, if cited; cross-references to titles have been given where they seemed desirable. Otherwise indexing is by text. Under each entry are listed the manuscripts for which the particular text is cited in the *Catalogue*.

Adrian and Ritheus, dialogue between
   BL Cotton Julius A ii, fols. 136–144 item (2)

Ælfric, *Grammar* and *Glossary*
   BL Cotton Faustina A x;   Worcester Cathedral, Dean and Chapter Library F 174 item (1)

Ælfric, Homilies
   Cambridge, Corpus Christi College 188;   Cambridge, Corpus Christi College 303;   Cambridge University Library Ii.I.33;   Bodley, Hatton 113, 114, 115 item (1), 116

Ælfric, *Lives of the Saints*
   Cambridge University Library Ii.I.33;   Bodley 343

Ælfric, *Sermones catholoci*
   BL Cotton Vespasian D xiv;   Bodley 343

Ælfric, translation of Bede, *De temporibus*
   Cambridge, Corpus Christi College 367, part II

Anglo-Saxon Chronicle
   BL Cotton Tiberius B i;   BL Cotton Tiberius B iv;   Bodley, Laud Misc. 636

Augustine, *Soliloquies*
   BL Cotton Vitellius A xv item (1)

Basil, *Monita*
   Bodley, Hatton 76

Bede, *De temporibus*. See Ælfric, translation of

Bede's Death Song
   Admont (Styria, Austria), Stiftsbibliothek 24;   Cambridge, Trinity College 770 (R.7.28);   Dublin, Trinity College 492 (E.2.23);   Exeter Cathedral, Dean and Chapter Library 3514;   Heiligenkreuz, Stiftsbibliothek 12;   Klosterneuburg (Lower Austria), Stiftsbibliothek 708;   Klosterneuburg (Lower Austria), Stiftsbibliothek 787;   BL Stowe 104;   Bodley 297;   Bodley, Digby 211;   Oxford, Lincoln College, Lat. 31;   Zwettle (Lower Austria) MS 24

Benedictine Rule. See *Rule of St Benedict*

Cædmon's Hymn
   Oxford, Lincoln College, Lat. 31;   Oxford, Magdalen College, Lat. 105

Cato, Distichs of
   BL Cotton Julius A ii, fols. 136–144 item (4)

Confessor's Writ
   Cambridge, Trinity College 1105 (O.2.1);   Cambridge, Trinity College 1145 (O.2.41);   Cambridge University Library EDC 1 item (2);   BL Cotton Tiberius A vi item (2);   Bodley, Laud Misc. 647 item (2)

De Situ Dunelmi beg. *Is ðeos burch breome geond Breotenrice*
   Cambridge University Library Ff.I.27;   BL Cotton Vitellius D xx (no longer extant)

Ely Privilege. (See also Index of Texts in Latin)
   BL Additional 5819;   BL Additional 9822;   BL Cotton Augustus ii 13;   BL Cotton Domitian xv;   BL Harley 230;   Bodley, Gough Cambridge 22

Genesis
   Cambridge University Library Ii.I.33

Gospatric's Writ
   Carlisle, Cumbria Record Office: D/Lons/L Medieval deeds C1

Gospel of Nicodemus
   BL Cotton Vitellius A xv

180

Gregory, *Dialogues*
   BL Cotton Otho C i, vol. 2; Bodley, Hatton 76

Gregory, *Pastoral Care*
   Cambridge, Corpus Christi College 12

Hemming's Cartulary
   BL Cotton Tiberius A xiii

Herbal
   BL Harley 585

Herbarium Apuleii
   BL Harley 6258 B item (1); Bodley, Hatton 76

Hexateuch
   BL Cotton Claudius B iv

History of the Holy Rood Tree. See *Legend of the Cross*

Homilies, unattributed
   Cambridge, Corpus Christi College 178 + 162, pp. 139–160; Cambridge, Corpus Christi College 198; Cambridge, Corpus Christi College 302; Cambridge, Corpus Christi College 367, Part II item (2)

Judith and Holofernes
   BL Cotton Otho B x

Lacnunga
   BL Harley 585

Laws of Cnut
   BL Harley 55, fols. 5–13

Legend of the Cross
   Cambridge, Corpus Christi College 557; Kansas University Library Y 103; Bodley 343, fol. 14v

Life of St Chad
   Bodley, Hatton 116

Malchus
   BL Cotton Otho B x

Medicina de Quadrupedibus
   BL Harley 6258 B item (2); Bodley, Hatton 76

Metrical prayer beg. *Æla drihten leof. æla dema god*
   BL Cotton Julius A ii, fols. 136–144 item (1)

Pastoral Care. See Gregory

Penitential
   Bodley, Laud Misc. 482

Peri didaxeon
   BL Harley 6258 B item (4)

Rule of St Benedict (See also Index of Texts in Latin)
   Cambridge, Corpus Christi College 178 + 162, pp. 139–160; BL Cotton Faustina A x

St Quintin, homily on
   BL Cotton Vitellius A xv item (4)

Solomon and Saturn, debate of
   BL Cotton Vitellius A xv item (3)

Soul to Body, address by
   Bodley 343

Vitas Patrum
   BL Cotton Otho C i, vol. 2

West-Saxon Gospels
   BL Royal 1 A xiv; Bodley, Hatton 38

Wulfstan, Homilies
   Bodley 343; Bodley, Hatton 113

INDEX OF TEXTS IN LATIN

Texts are indexed by author, if cited; cross-references to titles have been given where they seemed desirable. Otherwise indexing is by text. Where an author is designated by place with no surname, see under the personal name (e.g. Roger of Hoveden, see under Roger). Under each entry are listed the manuscripts for which the particular text is cited in the *Catalogue*.

Adam of Petit Pont
 Cambridge, Gonville and Caius College 136/76; Dublin, Trinity College 270 (D.4.9); Worcester Cathedral, Dean and Chapter Library Q 50

Adam of Petit Pont, *De Utensilibus*
 BL Additional 8092; Bodley, Rawlinson G 99 item (2)

Alanus de Insulis
 Oxford, Corpus Christi College 59

Aldhelm, *De laude virginitatis*
 Hereford Cathedral Library P.i.17; BL Harley 3013

Alexander of Hales, *Exoticon*
 Bodley, Auct. F.6.8; Bodley, Digby 92

Alexander of Villa Dei, *Doctrinale*. See also John of Garland, revision of
 Cambridge, Peterhouse 215

Angelus ad Virginem. (See also Index of Middle English Texts A: Titles)
 BL Arundel 248

Annales Asserii. See *Chronicon Fani Sancti Neoti*

Apuleius Barbarus, Herbal. (See also Index of Old English Texts *Herbarium Apuleii*)
 Bodley, Ashmole 1431

Aristotle, commentary on
 Bodley, Digby 55

Aristotle, *Prior and Posterior Analytics*
 Glasgow University Library, Hunterian 292 (U.6.10)

Austrian Legendary
 Admont (Styria, Austria), Stiftsbibliothek 24; Heiligenkreuz, Stiftsbibliothek 12; Vienna, Nationalbibliothek 336; Zwettle (Lower Austria) MS 24

Avianus, *Fabulae*
 Bodley, Rawlinson G 57 and G 111 item (2)

Bartholomew of Exeter, *Penitential*
 BL Cotton Vitellius A xii

Bede, *De temporibus*
 Cambridge, Corpus Christi College 367, Part II

Bede, *Historia ecclesiastica*
 Cambridge, Pembroke College 82; Cambridge University Library Kk.III.18; Dublin, Trinity College 492 (E.2.23); BL Stowe 104; Bodley, Digby 211; Oxford, Lincoln College, Lat. 31; Oxford, Magdalen College, Lat. 105

Benedictine Rule. See *Rule of St Benedict*

Bracton, *Summa de Legibus*
 London, Lincoln's Inn, Hale 135

Candet Nudatum Pectus. (See also Index of Middle English Texts A: Titles)
 Durham Cathedral, Dean and Chapter Library A.III.12; BL Additional 11579 item (6); Bodley, Digby 55 item (1); Bodley, Rawlinson C 317

Cassian, *Institutes*
 Bodley 730

Cato, *Disticha*
 Bodley, Rawlinson G 57 and G 111 item (1)

Chronicon Fani Sancti Neoti
Cambridge, Trinity College 770 (R.7.28)

Cornutus antiquus. See *Distigium*

Cuthbert, *Epistola de obitu Bedae*
Admont (Styria, Austria), Stiftsbibliothek 24; Cambridge, Trinity College 770 (R.7.28); Dublin, Trinity College 492 (E.2.23); Exeter Cathedral, Dean and Chapter Library 3514; Heiligenkreuz, Stiftsbibliothek 12; Klosterneuburg (Lower Austria), Stiftsbibliothek 708; Klosterneuburg (Lower Austria), Stiftsbibliothek 787; BL Stowe 104; Bodley 297; Bodley, Digby 211; Oxford, Lincoln College, Lat. 31; Vienna, Nationalbibliothek 336; Zwettle (Lower Austria) MS 24

De Luxuria
Oxford, Balliol College 230

De Virtutibus et Viciis. See Grosseteste

Disticha Catonis. See Cato

Distigium
Cambridge, Gonville and Caius College 136/76

Eadwine's Psalter
Cambridge, Trinity College 987 (R.17.1)

Eberhard of Bethune, *Graecismus.*
BL Arundel 394; Oxford, Corpus Christi College 62; Oxford, Corpus Christi College 121

Ely Privilege. (See also Index of Old English Texts)
BL Additional 5819; BL Additional 9822; BL Cotton Augustus ii 13; BL Cotton Domitian xv; BL Harley 230; Bodley, Gough Cambridge 22

Epistola de obitu Bedae. See Cuthbert

Eustace of Faversham, *Life of St Edmund*
BL Cotton Cleopatra B i; BL Harley 2; BL Royal 2 D vi; BL Royal 8 F xiv

Gervase of Canterbury, *Actus Pontificum Cantuarensium*
Cambridge, Corpus Christi College 438

Gesta Sanctorum
Oxford, Balliol College 227

Giraldus Cambrensis, *Descriptio Kambriae*
BL Cotton Domitian i

Giraldus Cambrensis, *Gemma Ecclesiastica*
London, Lambeth Palace Library 236

Giraldus Cambrensis, *Speculum Ecclesie*
BL Cotton Tiberius B xiii

Gilbertus Anglicus, *Compendium medicinae*
Cambridge, Pembroke College 169

Gospels of SS. Matthew, Luke and John
Salisbury Cathedral Library 82

Gregory, *Dialogues*
Private: Blickling Hall, Norfolk 6864

Grosseteste, *De Virtutibus et Viciis*
Pavia Biblioteca Universitaria 69 item (2)

Historia Eliensis Insulae
Cambridge, Trinity College 1105 (O.2.1); Cambridge University Library EDC 1; BL Cotton Titus A i; Bodley, Laud Misc. 647

Horace, *Epistolae*
Bodley, Rawlinson G 96 item (4)

Ilias Latina
Bodley, Rawlinson G 57 and G 111 item (2)

Instituta Cnuti
Bodley, Rawlinson C 641 item (2)

Ivo of Chartres
BL Royal 10 A viii

Ivo of Chartres, *Panormia*
Oxford, Jesus College 26

Jocelin of Brakelond, *Cronica*
BL Harley 1005 item (3)

John of Garland
Cambridge, Gonville and Caius College 136/76; Cambridge, Gonville and Caius College 385/605; Dublin, Trinity College 270 (D.4.9); Durham Cathedral, Dean and Chapter Library C.IV.26; London, Lambeth Palace Library 502; Worcester Cathedral, Dean and Chapter Library Q 50

John of Garland, *Accentarium*
BL Additional 41476; BL Royal 15 A xxxi

John of Garland, *Compendium Grammaticae*
Cambridge, Gonville and Caius College 593/453

John of Garland, *Dictionarius*
Bodley, Rawlinson G 99 item (3)

John of Garland, *Morale Scolarium*
Brugge, Stadsbibliotheek 546 item (1); Bodley, Rawlinson G 96 item (3)

John of Garland, *Parisiana Poetria*
Brugge, Stadsbibliotheek 546 item (2)

John of Garland, revision of Alexander of Villa Dei, *Doctrinale*
BL Arundel 394; Bodley, Rawlinson G 96; Oxford, Corpus Christi College 121 item (1)

John of Garland, *Stella Maris*
BL Royal 8 C iv

John of Garland, *Unum Omnium*
Bodley, Rawlinson G 96 item (1); Oxford, Corpus Christi College 121 item (3)

Juvenal
Cambridge, Pembroke College 113

Liber Catonianus
BL Royal 15 A xxxi

Liber Hymnorum
Cambridge, Gonville and Caius College 136/76

Liber Sancti Edmundi. See *Life of St Edmund*

Life of St Edmund. See also
(a) Eustace of Faversham;
(b) *Quadrilogus*

Life of St Edmund "Anonymous A" recension
Cambridge University Library Mm.IV.6; BL Cotton Vitellius C xii; London, Lambeth Palace Library 135; Oxford, Balliol College 226

Life of St Edmund Pontigny version
Auxerre, Bibl. et Musée, MS 123 (ancien 110)

Life of St Edward
BL Cotton Vitellius C xii

Life of St Godric. See Reginald, monk of Durham

Life of St Thomas (Becket) of Canterbury. See also William of Canterbury
BL Cotton Vitellius C xii; London, Lambeth Palace Library 135

Macer, *De virtutibus herbarum*
Bodley, Digby 69

Merarium
Cambridge, Gonville and Caius College 136/76

Neckham, Alexander
Cambridge, Gonville and Caius College 136/76; Dublin, Trinity College 270 (D.4.9); Worcester Cathedral, Dean and Chapter Library Q 50

Neckham, Alexander, *De Nominibus Utensilium*
BL Cotton Titus D xx; BL Harley 683; London, Wellcome Historical Medical Library 801[A]; Bodley, Rawlinson G 99 item (1)

Nutzard, Adam, *Neutrale*
Cambridge, Gonville and Caius College 136/76

Odo of Cheriton, Fables
BL Additional 11579 item (9)

Osbern of Gloucester, *Panormia* or *Liber derivationem*
Hereford Cathedral Library P.v.5; Bodley, Auct. F.6.8

Panormia. See (a) Ivo of Chartres; (b) Osbern of Gloucester

Paris, Matthew
BL Cotton Claudius D vi

Paris, Matthew, *Chronica maiora*
Cambridge, Corpus Christi College 26; BL Cotton Nero D v; BL Harley 1620; BL Royal 14 C vii

Paris, Matthew, *Historia Anglorum*
BL Royal 14 C vii

Passiones
BL Harley 2

Pendens nudatum pectus. Cf. *Candet nudatum pectus*
BL Harley 913 item (7)

Peraldus, *Summa de Vitiis*
Dublin, Trinity College 347 (C.5.8)

Persius, *Satyrae*
Cambridge, Trinity College 598 (R.3.18); BL Additional 41476

Petrus Cantor, commentary on the Psalms
BL Royal 10 C v

Prepositiones Grece
Bodley, Auct. F.6.8

Psalms, commentary on. See also Petrus Cantor
BL Royal 4 A xiv

Psalter
BL Royal 2 F viii; Bodley, Rawlinson G 22

Pseudo-Boethius, *De disciplina scolarium*
Cambridge, Trinity College 598 (R.3.18)

Quadrilogus concerning the life of St Edmund
Oxford, Corpus Christi College 154

Reginald, monk of Durham, *Life of St Godric*
BL Harley 153; BL Harley 322; London, Lambeth Palace Library 51; Bodley, Fairfax 6; Bodley, Laud Misc. 413

Respice in Faciem. (See also Index of Middle English Texts A: Titles)
BL Additional 11579 item (7); BL Harley 913 item (7)

Richard of St Victor, *Allegoriae in Novum Testamentum*
Bodley, Ashmole 1280 item (1)

Rishanger, William, *Annales Angliae et Scotiae*
BL Cotton Claudius D vi

Robert of Greystanes, account of a lawsuit
York Minster Library XVI.I.12

Roger of Hoveden, *Chronicle*
Cambridge, Trinity College 1435 (O.9.23); BL Arundel 69; BL Harley 3602; BL Royal 14 C ii; Bodley, Laud Misc. 582

Roger of Wendover, *Flores Historiarum*
BL Cotton Otho B v part II; Bodley, Douce 207

Rule of St Benedict. (See also Indexes of Old and Middle English Texts)
Cambridge, Corpus Christi College 178 + 162, pp. 139–160; BL Cotton Claudius D iii

St Edmund. See *Life of St Edmund*

Serlo of Wilton, proverbs
Bodley, Digby 53

Serlo of Wilton, *Versus de Differenciis*
Bodley, Digby 53

Sidonius Apollinaris, letters
Bodley, Digby 172 item (2)

Stabat iuxta Christi crucem. (See also Index of Middle English Texts A: Titles)
Cambridge, St John's College 111 (E.8)

Statuta Angliae
Liverpool, Athenaeum, Gladstone 27; Bodley, Douce 139

Thomas of Elmham, *Historia Abbatiae S. Augustine*
Cambridge, Trinity Hall MS 1

Vita S. Alexis
Cambridge, Pembroke College 82

Vita S. Godrici. See *Life of St Godric*

Vitae Sanctorum
BL Harley 2

Vitas patrum
Cambridge University Library Mm.IV.28

William of Canterbury, *Vita, Passio et Miracula S. Thomae Cantuariensis*
Winchester College 4

INDEX OF TEXTS IN FRENCH

Texts are indexed by author, if cited; cross-references to titles have been given where they seemed desirable. Otherwise indexing is by text. Where an author is designated by place with no surname, see under the personal name (e.g. Walter de Bibbesworth, see under Walter). Under each entry are listed the manuscripts for which the particular text is cited in the *Catalogue*.

Cambridge Prologue. (See also Index of Middle English Texts A: Titles)
Cambridge University Library Mm.I.18

Day of Judgement, poem on
Cambridge, St John's College 111 (E.8)

de Tobye. See *Tobye*

Hélinant, monk of Froidmont, *Les Vers de la Mort*
Maidstone Museum A.13

Langtoft, Pierre, *Chronicle*
Cambridge University Library Gg.I.1; BL Cotton Julius A v

Orison to the Blessed Virgin
Maidstone Museum A.13

Petit Plet
BL Cotton Caligula A ix; Oxford, Jesus College 29, part II

Prisoner's Prayer. (See also Index of Middle English Texts A: Titles)
London, Corporation of London Records Office, 'Liber de antiquis Legibus'

Prose chronicle
BL Cotton Caligula A ix

Respice in faciem. (See also Index of Texts in Latin and Index of Middle English Texts A: Titles)
BL Additional 11579 item (7)

Riche, Edmund, *Speculum Ecclesie*.
Cambridge, Pembroke College 258 item (1); Durham University Library, Cosin V.V.15; BL Arundel 288; BL Royal 12 C xii item (2); Bodley, Digby 20; Bodley, Douce 210; Bodley, Rawlinson poet. 241; Bodley, Selden Supra 74 item (2)

St Josaphat
BL Cotton Caligula A ix; Oxford, Jesus College 29, part II

Serlo of Wilton, proverbs
Bodley, Digby 53

Seven Sleepers
BL Cotton Caligula A ix; Oxford, Jesus College 29, part II

Statuta Angliae
Liverpool, Athenaeum, Gladstone 27

Tobye
Oxford, Jesus College 29, part II

Walter de Bibbesworth, *Le Tretiz*
Cambridge University Library Gg.I.1; BL Sloane 809; Bodley, Selden Supra 74

Walter de Henley, *Hosbondria*
Cambridge, Gonville and Caius College 365/728